The Tudor and Stuart Town
1530–1688

Readers in Urban History
General Editors:
Peter Clark and David Reeder
The Centre for Urban History, Leicester University

THE MEDIEVAL TOWN
A Reader in English Urban History, 1200–1540
Edited by Richard Holt and Gervase Rosser

THE TUDOR AND STUART TOWN
A Reader in English Urban History, 1530–1688
Edited by Jonathan Barry

THE EIGHTEENTH-CENTURY TOWN
A Reader in English Urban History, 1688–1820
Edited by Peter Borsay

THE VICTORIAN CITY
A Reader in British Urban History, 1820–1914
Edited by R. J. Morris and R. Rodger

The Tudor and Stuart Town
A Reader in English Urban History
1530–1688

Edited by
Jonathan Barry

LONGMAN
London and New York

12/98

Longman Group UK Limited,
Longman House, Burnt Mill, Harlow,
Essex CM20 2JE, England
and Associated Companies throughout the world.

*Published in the United States of America
by Longman Inc., New York*

First published 1990

BRITISH LIBRARY CATALOGUING IN PUBLICATION DATA
Barry, Jonathan
    The Tudor and Stuart town 1530–1688: a reader in
    English urban history. – (Readers in urban history).
    1. Great Britain. Towns, history
    I. Title II. Series
    941.009732

ISBN 0-582-05131-2 CSD
ISBN 0-582-05130-4 PPR

Library of Congress Cataloging-in-Publication Data

The Tudor and Stuart town: a reader in English urban history,
    1530–1688 / edited by Jonathan Barry.
        p. cm. — (Readers in urban history)
    Includes bibliographical references.
    ISBN 0-582-05131-2. — ISBN 0-582-05130-4 (pbk.)
    1. Cities and towns — England — History — 16th century. 2. Cities and
towns — England — History — 17th century. I. Barry, Jonathan, 1956– .
II. Series. HT133.T83 1990
307.76'0942 — dc20

89-13807

Produced by Longman Singapore Publishers (Pte) Ltd.
Printed in Singapore

CONTENTS

Preface   vii
Acknowledgements   viii

1   Introduction   1
    Jonathan Barry

2   Urban development in England and Wales in the
    sixteenth and seventeenth centuries   35
    Penelope Corfield

3   English pre-industrial urban economies   63
    Nigel Goose

4   Household size and structure in early-Stuart
    Cambridge   74
    Nigel Goose

5   Social problems in Elizabethan London   121
    A. L. Beier

6   Change and stability in seventeenth-century London   139
    Valerie Pearl

7   Residential patterns in pre-industrial cities: Some
    case studies from seventeenth-century Britain   166
    John Langton

8   Civic mentality and the environment in Tudor York   206
    D. M. Palliser

9   'The Ramoth-Gilead of the Good': Urban change
    and political radicalism at Gloucester 1540–1640   244
    Peter Clark

Contents

10 Newcastle and the nation: The seventeenth-century
    experience   274
    Roger Howell, Jr.

11 The corporate town and the English State: Bristol's
    'little businesses' 1625–1641   297
    David Harris Sacks

Index   334

PREFACE

The articles reprinted here offer the student or general reader convenient access to some of the best writing on Tudor and Stuart towns published since 1975. Many of the articles come from journals or collected volumes which are not readily accessible to the student of urban history. Collectively they cover the main themes currently being explored in what remains one of the liveliest periods of urban history, indeed of historical study in general. Unlike other volumes in this series of readers, work before 1975 has not been included, because the best of the earlier articles are easily accessible in *The Early Modern Town: A Reader*, edited by Peter Clark. A number of excellent volumes of essays on urban history have been published since then, but I have avoided choosing essays from these, or, with one exception, from the *Urban History Yearbook*. A full bibliography of such recent work will be found in the footnotes to Chapter 1, Introduction, which surveys the changes that have occurred in the study of towns, offering a guide to the current state of knowledge, but also some suggestions about likely areas for future study. Brief editorial introductions to each chapter suggest the importance of each article, as well as indicating some of the criticisms and revisions of its ideas that have emerged subsequently.

It has been a great pleasure to collaborate with the rest of the editorial team in this series of Readers in Urban History. I am particularly grateful to Peter Clark, Peter Borsay and Gervase Rosser for their help. Ideas in the Introduction were aired and shaped at seminars organized by the Centre for South-Western Historical Studies, Exeter and the Wellcome Unit for the History of Medicine, Oxford. Special thanks are due to Harriet Barry, Colin Jones, Margaret Pelling and John Triffitt.

ACKNOWLEDGEMENTS

We are grateful to the following for permission to reproduce
copyright material: Council of the Society of Antiquaries of Newcastle Upon Tyne and the author, Roger Howell, Jr, for the article
'Newcastle and the nation: The seventeenth-century experience' in
Archaeologia Aeliana, VIII (1980); Institute of British Geographers
for the article 'Residential patterns in pre-industrial cities: Some
case studies from seventeenth-century Britain' by J. Langton in
Transactions of the Institute of British Geographers, 65 (1975); the
Editors of *The Journal of Interdisciplinary History* and MIT Press
for the article 'Social problems in Elizabethan London' by A. L.
Beier in *The Journal of Interdisciplinary History*, IX (1978), © 1978
by The Massachusetts Institute of Technology; London Journal
Trust and the author, Valerie Pearl, for the article 'Change and
stability in seventeenth-century London' in *London Journal*, 5
(1979); the Editor of *Northern History* on behalf of the University
of Leeds and the author, D. M. Palliser, for the article 'Civic
mentality and the environment in Tudor York' in *Northern History*,
XVIII (1982); The Past and Present Society and the author, David
Harris Sacks, for the article 'The corporate town and the English
State: Bristol's little businesses', 1625–1641' in *Past and Present*,
110 (Feb 1986), copyright The Past and Present Society; Pinter
Publishers Ltd for the extract 'The Ramoth-Gilead of the Good':
Gloucester 1540–1640' by P. Clark in *The English Commonwealth
1547–1640* edited by P. Clark *et al.* (Leicester University Press,
1979) and the extract 'English pre-industrial urban economies' by N.
Goose in *Urban History Yearbook* (Leicester University Press,
1982); the Editors of *Social History* and the author, N. R. Goose,
for the article 'Household size and structure in early-Stuart Cambridge'
in *Social History*, 5 (1980); George Weidenfeld & Niclson Ltd for
the extract 'Urban development in England and Wales' by P. Corfield in *Trade, Government and Economy in Pre-Industial England*
edited by D. Coleman and A. John (1976).

Chapter 1

INTRODUCTION

Jonathan Barry

If one had to pick a date when early modern urban history in England came of age, it would be 1976. The creation of an Open University course (A322) in English urban history 1500–1780 stimulated the publication that year of *The Early Modern Town: A Reader*, edited by Peter Clark, and the textbook, *English Towns in Transition 1500–1700*, written by Peter Clark and Paul Slack, complementing the excellent course materials available the following year. It was also in 1976 that Penelope Corfield published her stimulating essay on urban developments (reprinted below, Ch. 2). In 1978 John Patten, a historical geographer, provided an alternative synthesis, concentrating on the spatial issues of migration and the regional context of urban systems. Taken collectively, these works made public the fruits of two decades of postgraduate research, much of it associated with the influence of W. G. Hoskins, both at Oxford and at Leicester. At the latter, Alan Everitt maintained the distinctive alliance of early modern local and urban history, now reflected in Leicester's Centre for Urban History. Although much of this research was not published independently until later, its findings were fully incorporated into the accounts of English towns that emerged in those heady years.[1]

The aim of this Introduction is to chart what has happened to the study of sixteenth- and seventeenth-century English towns since 1976, and thus to set the context for the essays that follow. Superficially, the developments have been much less dramatic, as consolidation and refinement have replaced path-breaking synthesis.

1. P. Clark (ed.), *The Early Modern Town: A Reader* (1976); P. Clark and P. Slack, *English Towns in Transition 1500–1700* (1976); P. Clark *et al.* (eds), *English Urban History 1500–1780* (Open University, 1977); J. Patten, *English Towns 1500–1700* (Folkestone, 1978). See also J. Langton, 'Industry and towns 1500–1800', in R. A. Dodgshon and R. A. Butlin (eds), *An Historical Geography of England and Wales* (1978), pp. 173–198 and references in n. 10.

No alternative general interpretation has yet emerged to challenge that established before 1976; indeed most subsequent work has operated within the paradigms of that period, rarely even questioning the basic mapping of the urban system and its character established then, and summarized most ably by Corfield.[2] Inevitably, however, their findings have been modified, not least by the emergence of new ways of analysing urban society; this Introduction seeks to explore these developments and, it is hoped, suggest further lines of enquiry. After reviewing the general characteristics of the English urban scene, it will consider in turn the economic, social, political and cultural dimensions of urban life.

What had been learned about English urban history by 1976? In establishing the main features of the urban map of England, an admirable effort was made to overcome the problems and paradoxes of both identifying and classifying the towns of early modern England, and doing justice to their changing character over two centuries. Paradoxically, given the quantity and quality of historical attention devoted to the subject, the most obvious conclusion was that, compared to other countries or later periods, English towns were small fry. Even London was not a great city until it began its phenomenal growth in the mid-sixteenth century, and its rise to become one of Europe's largest cities (with over half a million inhabitants by 1688) only served to underlined the relative insignificance of other English towns compared to the major provincial cities of continental Europe. We may question the urban standing of a country whose handful of regional capitals, like York, Norwich and Exeter, ranged in population from 5000 to 15 000 in the mid-sixteenth century, rising to 10 000 to 30 000 by the late seventeenth century. How urban were the hundred or so other towns with populations of several thousand, including county towns, like Gloucester and Salisbury, and the larger ports and manufacturing centres? Most problematic are the 600 or so other market centres, usually considered as towns then and now, whose populations might be only 400 or 500, and rarely more than 1000 or so. Although the countryside was thickly dotted with small towns and their populations were growing, it seems likely that until the mid-seventeenth century the urban population outside London grew no faster than the population as a whole, so that while London's share of total

2. More recent surveys include: A. MacInnes, *The English Town 1660–1760* (1980); D. Palliser, 'London and the towns' in his *The Age of Elizabeth* (1983), pp. 202–36; C. G. A. Clay, 'The towns' in his *Economic Expansion and Social Change* (2 vols, Cambridge, 1984), vol. 1, pp. 165–213; ; R. Tittler, 'The end of the Middle Ages in the English country town', *Sixteenth Century Journal*, 18 (1987), pp. 471–87; P. N. Borsay, 'Urban development in the age of Defoe' in C. Jones (ed.), *Britain in the First Age of Party* (1987), pp. 195–219.

population quintupled to over 10 per cent, that of all other towns combined may not have exceeded that figure.

Of course population is not the only consideration; historians have developed a sophisticated array of other tests of urban status, including density of settlement, economic functions, political and social institutions and, more tentatively, cultural distinctions. These helped contemporaries to identify Tudor and Stuart towns as distinctive centres within rural society. But many towns lacked one or more of these urban features: market towns might have scattered buildings and a sizeable group involved in agriculture, while towns of varying size lacked borough status or other urban institutions. The economic distinctiveness of towns did not yet depend on a manufacturing sector clearly differentiated from rural agriculture. Through the putting-out system many of the simpler forms of industry were being dispersed through the countryside at the expense of urban employment, and although the towns tended to retain the more skilled and expensive finishing operations, these were generally still performed by a family or a few men in an artisan's workshop. The manufacturing sector was dominated by the cloth and leather trades and these, together with food and drink processing, ensured that most urban employment depended on the products of the countryside, whose richer inhabitants also formed the main customers. Distribution, not production, brought the greatest profits, so that it was merchants, retailers and professional men who dominated town life. Although trade between towns was growing, especially as London grew, most towns still responded to the cycles of rural life, waxing and waning with the seasons, as well as market days and fairs. The nature of urban identity varied with rural setting, taking on a different meaning, for example, in pastoral areas where the rural population lived in scattered hamlets, compared to arable areas with nucleated villages.

Equally, attempts to generalize about towns must be tempered with a sense of their great diversity. A variety of different types of town has been identified, reflecting the presence and balance of various urban features. The archetypal county town can be distinguished from the mere market town by its possession of the full range of urban features, including a relatively complex political and social structure reflected in its buildings and cultural life. None the less, county towns were heavily influenced by rural demands, especially those of the gentry class, whose quarter sessions and other meetings would add a further cycle to the urban calendar. This differentiates them from another group of towns, often of similar size, which had escaped from a simple marketing role by specializing in some economic function. The late seventeenth century saw the rapid growth of such towns, many of them ports, like Hull or Liverpool, but including some manufacturing centres, like Birmingham, and a few centres of leisure, like Bath.[3] These towns were less dependent on their immediate hinterland than the county towns; the same can be said of the regional capitals. They controlled important sectors of national or even international trade, and thus were able to support a complex social, political and cultural life which, although it often attracted gentry visitors, never depended too heavily on their patronage. Unlike their European counterparts, however, these regional capitals rarely exercised political or tax-gathering power over their areas. Not only was English government highly centralized in London, and becoming more so, but the governing classes of the provinces rarely resided in the towns, preferring their country houses or the capital.

It was the growth of the capital which most struck contemporaries. During this period London achieved an unprecedented dominance in every sphere of English life that was likely to stimulate urban growth. It controlled the lion's share of international trade and thus of the internal trade in the collection and distribution of imports and exports. It was still by far the largest manufacturing centre, stimulated by the needs of trade and maritime activity, but also by the presence of the largest and richest consumer market for finished goods. This market was swelled by the growing tendency of the upper classes to spend considerable time in London, attracted by its political, legal and cultural facilities. The employment generated by all these factors attracted migrants from all over the country, resulting in the unprecedented physical expansion of London far beyond its medieval limits, with distinct areas of commercial, industrial and upper-class activity emerging. Despite these divisions, however, the key to London's fortunes was the interdependence of these factors.[4]

Many contemporaries believed that London's growth was at the expense of the other towns, especially those above market-town level. Among historians too there has been a general consensus that rural change and the threat of London were bringing about major changes in the character of urban life. Whereas the late medieval town can be portrayed, if only in caricature, as a closed and inward-looking community, the late seventeenth-century town is seen as of necessity open to wider influences, looking to compete in wider markets. Towns specialized either in serving the prosperous of the countryside or in performing specific roles in the national economy.

---

3. For 'leisure towns' see: S. McIntyre, 'Bath: the rise of a resort town, 1660–1800', in P. Clark (ed.), *Country Towns in Pre-Industrial England* (Leicester, 1981), pp. 197–249; A. Rosen, 'Winchester in transition, 1580–1700' in ibid., pp. 143–95; A. MacInnes, 'The emergence of a leisure town: Shrewsbury 1660–1760', *Past and Present*, 120 (1988), pp. 53–87.
4. A. L. Beier and R. Finlay (eds), *London 1500–1700* (1986).

Initially, at least, this led to great competition between towns, with great fluctuations in the fortunes of individual towns. It also led to an increase in social divisions within the town, reinforcing the dominance of a wealthy minority and eroding the traditional sense of community. Economic pressures were intensified by the effects of the Reformation and subsequent cultural changes and by the problems of poverty caused by economic dislocation and the immigration of the rural poor.

No wonder, then, that Clark and Slack entitled their book *Towns in Transition*. Significantly, though, despite their emphasis on the challenges caused by change, their final stress is on both the resilience and capacity for change that towns displayed. Furthermore, like many others, they see the late seventeenth century as a time when the more substantial provincial towns began to reap the benefits of change, not merely in population growth, but in an increase of wealth and influence relative both to London and to rural society. The stage was set for the simultaneous growth of both the capital and provincial towns after 1688 which was to make England the world's first modern urban society.

As we can see, a great deal had been achieved in understanding the general character of *English* urbanization by 1976. By contrast it is only in the last decade or so that basic features of the urban network in the rest of the British Isles have been charted and debated, often drawing on models from the earlier English synthesis.[5] The different position of urban history in the rest of Britain is one reason why no such work is included in this volume, quite apart from the problem of space. The time is now ripe for a proper study of the *British* urban network, which will undoubtedly throw much light on the fortunes of English towns, particularly northern and western towns. Many of these, notably ports such as Chester and Bristol, had strong connections or rivalries with other British towns. Others, such as those of Cumbria, the Welsh borders and Cornwall shared with Scottish, Welsh and Irish towns their position in a largely pastoral/extractive economy. Historians of London, seeking to unravel the contributions of port and capital to its growth,

5. I. H. Adams, *The Making of Urban Scotland* (1978); G. Gordon and B. Dicks (eds), *Scottish Urban History* (Aberdeen, 1983); G. Gordon (ed.), *Perspectives on the Scottish City* (Aberdeen, 1985); M. Lynch (ed.), *The Early Modern Town in Scotland* (1987); F. Soulsby, *The Towns of Wales* (Chichester, 1983); R. A. Butlin (ed.), *The Development of the Irish Town* (1977); D. Harkness and M. O'Dowd (eds), *The Town in Ireland* (1981); R. Gillespie, 'The origins and development of the Ulster urban network', *Irish Historical Studies*, 26 (1984), pp. 15–29. A valuable sourcebook for British towns is R. C. Richardson and T. B. James (eds), *The Urban Experience: A Sourcebook. English, Scottish and Welsh Towns 1450–1700* (Manchester, 1983).

need to consider the cases of Edinburgh and, in particular, Dublin, whose growth in the second half of the seventeenth century was phenomenal.

Equally, Jan de Vries's comparative study of *European Urbaniz-ation 1500–1800* (1984) offers a fresh challenge to consider anew how far English urban patterns can appropriately be explained by factors specific to England (as Tony Wrigley has already suggested).[6] The rise of the capital and the unsettling demographic growth of the rest of the urban sector before 1650 can now be seen as common European phenomena, although their English manifestation was shaped by the low level of urbanization in England in the early six-teenth century. London's growth to match other European capitals was all the more intense, while the absence of major provincial rivals benefited both London and the many small market towns. Their suc-cess in turn helped to ensure that the growth of the major provincial towns was no better than that of their continental counterparts. After 1650, however, the pattern was very different. English his-torians had already identified the strong performance of many major and rising provincial towns in that period as a key development; the trend takes on new significance when it is realized that this pattern is quite unlike that occurring elsewhere in Europe. England's 'urban renaissance', if late, was to be uniquely significant, although its ef-fects fall outside the timespan of this volume.[7]

For the most part, however, recent work has eschewed these wider comparisons. One symptom of this is the silence that fell, about 1980, on the great debate about decay and crisis in English towns. In the late 1970s a prolonged controversy seemed likely be-tween two different theories of crisis/decay, and those sceptical of both. Charles Phythian-Adams and David Palliser, using tax returns and population figures, argued that the period *before* 1570 saw an intensification of the economic and demographic difficulties which had plagued many late medieval towns. By contrast Clark and Slack, with many others, stressed the strains brought about by population growth, especially *after* 1570, since this was not accompanied by suf-ficient stable economic improvement to prevent an increase in urban poverty and social polarization. Both these theories were criticized sharply by Alan Dyer, who maintained that, if certain towns un-doubtedly faced problems, other towns were always prospering, often at the expense of the decaying towns, and that there was no

6. J. De Vries, *European Urbanization 1500–1800* (1984); E. A. Wrigley, 'Urban growth and agricultural change', *Journal of Interdisciplinary History*, 15 (1985), pp. 683–728, reprinted in his *People, Cities and Wealth* (Oxford, 1987).

7. P. N. Borsay, 'The English urban renaissance c. 1680–1760', *Social History*, 5 (1977), pp. 581–603; *idem, The English Urban Renaissance: Culture and Society in the Provincial Town 1660–1770* (Oxford, 1989); P. Corfield, *The Impact of English Towns* (Oxford, 1982).

trustworthy evidence of an overall crisis facing towns as such. Dyer also offered a sceptical note about the otherwise universal assumption that the general improvement in the fortunes of most large and middle-sized towns after 1650 was at the expense of the smaller market towns. Neither of his contentions has commanded general assent, but his sceptical position has in some senses triumphed by default in the absence of recent reformulations.[8]

Why was the controversy abandoned? The debate itself served to educate historians in the pitfalls inherent in using such imprecise terms as crisis and decay. For example, it highlighted the problems of using population as a test of urban success, except in the very long term. Significantly, recent discussions of decay and crisis have restricted themselves to specific places and periods – notably the impact within England of the European-wide difficulties of the 1590s, and even here the terms have been used with extreme caution.[9] The rival critiques also drew attention to the problems associated with using many of the sources which had been deployed to establish national comparisons over time and space. Taxation figures and population returns now tend to be examined much more in local context, using local knowledge to test their validity and drawing local rather than national conclusions from them. None the less, the debate would surely have continued, as its late medieval counterpart has, had historians not become more interested in other questions, ones which did not, at least immediately, concern the overall fortunes of the urban system, nor indeed of individual towns as single entities.

The recent historiography has concentrated on the examination of particular issues and particular sub-groups within towns. There has been a shift away, not just from overall synthesis, but from the urban monograph, which offered a rounded picture of a single urban community. Initially such studies dominated both research and publication, but although the results of earlier work have continued to

8. C. Phythian-Adams, 'Urban decay in late medieval England' in P. Abrams and E. A. Wrigley (eds), *Towns in Societies* (Cambridge, 1978), pp. 159–85; D. Palliser, 'A crisis in English towns? The case of York 1480–1640', *Northern History*, 14 (1978), pp. 108–25; A. Dyer, 'Growth and decay in English towns 1500–1700', *Urban History Yearbook* (1979), pp. 60–76 (with response by Phythian-Adams); *idem*, 'Market towns of Southern England 1500–1700', *Southern History*, 1 (1979), pp. 123–34.

9. N. Goose, 'Decay and regeneration in seventeenth-century Reading: A study in a changing economy', *Southern History*, 6 (1984), pp. 53–74; P. Clark, 'A crisis contained: The condition of English towns in the 1590s' in his (ed.), *The European Crisis of the 1590s* (1985), pp. 44–66; M. Power, 'London and the control of the crisis of the 1590s', *History*, 70 (1985), pp. 371–85; *idem*, 'A "crisis" reconsidered: Social and demographic dislocation in London in the 1590s' *London Journal*, 12 (1986), pp. 134–45; M. Reed (ed.), *English Towns in Decline 1350–1800* (Leicester, 1986).

appear in print, the only scholarly urban monograph based wholly on work within the last decade is Graham Mayhew's excellent study of Tudor Rye.[10]

The changing approaches to the subject are perhaps clearest in the economic field. Those who compare this volume with *The Early Modern Town* will be struck by the much smaller number of pieces devoted to the urban economy, reflecting current trends in the literature. Arguments about urban economic fortunes have generated scepticism about the traditional data-sources, such as tax returns and records of freedom and apprenticeship. Recent work has explored the political and social assumptions and biases which render such data problematic, certainly for comparative purposes. How reliable are occupational sources such as freedom and apprenticeship rolls, when many people followed several occupations, at once or over their life, while political factors such as the electoral rights of freemen or guild membership often ensured that their occupational 'title' remained frozen? Many others participated in the same occupations without appearing in formal records. Women and those in the service sectors, two growing and overlapping categories, are generally under-recorded, and their role can only be reconstructed through the use of other records, such as inventories, accounts and parish registers, which do not lend themselves easily to systematic comparison between towns, or even over time within one town.[11]

10. G. Mayhew, *Tudor Rye* (Falmer, 1987). The most important publications based on earlier work are: A. Crossley (ed.), *The City of Oxford* (*Victoria History of the County of Oxford*, vol. 4, 1979); D. Palliser, *Tudor York* (Oxford, 1979); C. Phythian-Adams, *Desolation of a City: Coventry and the Urban Crisis of the Late Middle Ages* (Cambridge, 1979); T. S. Willan, *Elizabethan Manchester* (Chetham Society, 3rd Ser., 27, 1980); D. Sacks, *Trade, Society and Politics in Bristol 1500–1640* (1985); J. F. Pound, *Tudor and Stuart Norwich* (Chichester, 1988); P. Clark, 'Early Modern Gloucester', in N. Herbert (ed.), *The City of Gloucester* (*Victoria History of the County of Gloucester*, vol. 4, 1988), pp. 73–123. Clark has also edited two important collections of research papers: *Country Towns* and *The Transformation of English Provincial Towns* (1984).
11. J. Patten, 'Urban occupations in pre-industrial England', *Transactions of the Institute of British Geographers*, 3 (1977), pp. 296–313; G. Ramsay, 'The recruitment and fortunes of some London Freemen in the mid-sixteenth century', *Economic History Review*, 31 (1978), pp. 526–40; T. R. Forbes, 'Weaver and cordwainer: occupations in the parish of St Giles without Cripplegate London 1654–93 and 1729–43', *Guildhall Studies in Urban History*, 4(3) (1980), pp. 119–32; M. C. Burrage and D. Curry, 'At sixes and sevens: Occupation and status in the City of London from the fourteenth to the seventeenth centuries', *American Sociological Review*, 46 (1981), pp. 375–93; J. F. Pound, 'The validity of the Freemen's lists: Some Norwich evidence', *Economic History Review*, 34 (1981), pp. 48–59; M. Pelling, 'Occupational diversity: Barber-Surgeons and the trades of Norwich 1550–1640', *Bulletin of the History of Medicine*, 56 (1982), pp. 484–511; H. Swanson, 'The illusion of economic structure: Craft guilds in late medieval English towns', *Past and Present*, 121 (1988), pp. 29–48.

The growing conviction that the distinctiveness of Tudor and Stuart towns lay in their service and marketing roles, rather than their functions as centres of industrial production, has heightened dissatisfaction with the traditional forms of analysis. Although both Penelope Corfield and Nigel Goose (in his brief article reprinted as Ch. 3) rightly remind us not to neglect the evidence of industrial specialization in certain towns, the relative strengths of a fairly limited group of urban crafts may not be the best guide to the urban economy.[12] We need to reconstruct the whole gamut of urban activity; as indicated, valuable work is being done on the place of women and of service groups, including the professions.[13] Mounting evidence has corroborated the intuition that the range and specialization of occupations, more than their character, offers the best sign of urban growth. The larger and more successful the town, the greater the number of separate occupational labels that can be found in urban records of every kind. Clearly this rule has its exceptions, such as the dockyard towns of the late seventeenth century, but the unusual characteristics of such places emerge with greater clarity when set against the general trend.

One advantage of this approach has been that it throws light on 600 or so small towns which rarely kept records of freedom or apprenticeship, but can be studied through inventories, property records and other sources of random occupational material. Proper study of small towns is still in its infancy (hence its absence from this collection), and most of the work so far has been on the late seventeenth and eighteenth centuries, but things should soon change under the stimulus of the Small Towns project at Leicester Univer-

12. See also: A. L. Beier, 'Engine of manufacture: the trades of London', in Beier and Finlay (eds), *London*, pp. 141–67; S. M. Jack, *Trade and Industry in Tudor and Stuart England* (1977).
13. M. Prior, 'Women and the urban economy: Oxford 1500–1800' in her (ed.), *Women in English Society 1500–1800* (1985), pp. 93–117; S. Wright, '"Churmaids, huswyfes and hucksters": The employment of women in Tudor and Stuart Salisbury', in L. Charles and L. Duffin (eds), *Women and Work in Pre-Industrial England* (1985), pp. 100–21; M. Roberts, '"Words they are Women and Deeds they are Men": Images of work and gender in Early Modern England', in ibid., pp. 122–80; R. Grassby, 'Social mobility and business enterprise in 17C England', in D. Pennington and K. Thomas (eds), *Puritans and Revolutionaries* (Oxford, 1978), pp. 355–81; P. Earle, *The Making of the English Middle Class: Business, Society and Family Life in London 1660–1730* (1989); M. Pelling and C. Webster, 'Medical practitioners', in C. Webster (ed.), *Health, Medicine and Mortality in the Sixteenth Century* (Cambridge, 1979), pp. 165–235; G. S. Holmes, *Augustan England: Professions, State and Society 1680–1730* (1982); W. Prest (ed.), *The Professions in Early Modern England* (1987). For the new emphasis on consumption rather than production see also: J. Thirsk, *Economic Policy and Projects* (Oxford, 1978); L. Weatherill, *Consumer Behaviour and Material Culture in Britain 1660–1760* (1988).

sity.[14] Closely tied to interest in market towns, as such small towns generally were, is a growing concern to analyse urban economies in their rural context, as nodal points of England's diversifying regional economies. The work of Alan Everitt and Joan Thirsk on agricultural specialization and the forging of a national market is of fundamental importance in understanding all aspects of the urban system. Such changes were a necessary condition for London's massive expansion, and in turn owed much to London's financial and political ability to ensure that goods in ever more distant parts of the country would be produced and transported to meet London's needs. In the longer run, other provincial towns began to benefit from this process and even to rival or replace London as regional centres for the exchange and export of products.[15]

If the steady growth of the urban sector in general, and of most inland towns in particular, depended on the fortunes of the home market, we should not forget that many towns took their chances on the much riskier course of participation in international trade or related activities such as shipbuilding.[16] If things went well, such towns could expand much faster than any others, but decline could be equally precipitate, as Mayhew's book on Rye reveals. In this

14. A. Dyer, 'Warwickshire towns under the Tudors and Stuarts', *Warwickshire History*, 3 (1976–7), pp. 122–35; D. E. Smith, 'Otley: A study of a market town during the later seventeenth and eighteenth centuries', *Yorkshire Archaeological Journal*, 52 (1980), pp. 143–56; R. Unwin, 'Tradition and transition: Market towns in the Vale of York 1660–1830', *Northern History*, 17 (1981), pp. 72–116; J. M. Martin, 'A Worcestershire market-town in adversity: Stratford-upon-Avon in the sixteenth and seventeenth centuries', *Midland History*, 7 (1982), pp. 26–41; J. D. Marshall, 'The rise and transformation of the Cumbrian market towns 1660–1900', *Northern History*, 19 (1983), pp. 128–209.

15. A. Everitt, 'Country, county and town', *Transactions of the Royal Historical Society*, 5th ser., 29 (1979), pp. 79–108, reprinted in his *Landscape and Community in England* (1985); J. Thirsk, *England's Agricultural Regions* (1987); J. Chartres, *Internal Trade in England 1500–1700* (1977); idem, 'The marketing of agricultural produce' in J. Thirsk (ed.), *Agrarian History of England and Wales: Volume V, 1640–1750*, Part 2, *Agrarian Change* (Cambridge, 1985), pp. 406–502; idem, 'Food consumption and internal trade', in Beier and Finlay (eds), *London*, pp. 168–96; C. Phillips, 'Town and country: Economic change in Kendal c. 1550–1700', in Clark (ed.), *Transformation*, pp. 99–132; P. Large, 'Urban growth and agricultural change in the West Midlands during the seventeenth and eighteenth centuries', in ibid., pp. 169–89; P. Ripley, 'Village and town; Occupation and wealth in the hinterland of Gloucester 1660–1700', *Agricultural History Review*, 32 (1984), pp. 170–8.

16. In addition to studies already cited see: B. Dietz, 'Overseas trade and metropolitan growth', in Beier and Finlay (eds), *London*, pp. 115–40; A. R. Myers, 'Tudor Chester', *Journal of Chester Archaeological Society*, 63 (1980), pp. 43–57; S. and J. H. Farrant, 'Brighton 1580–1820', *Sussex Archaeological Collections*, 118 (1980), pp. 331–50; P. Ripley, 'The economy of the city of Gloucester 1660–1740', *Transactions of Bristol and Gloucestershire Archaeological Society*, 98 (1980), pp. 135–54; M. Reed, 'Economic structure and change in

sector at least, the language of crisis and decline has a definite place, alongside that of boom and growth. Penelope Corfield rightly questions the tendency of both contemporaries and historians to use the growth of London to explain the fortunes of other towns. More significant was the prolonged instability of the British economy as it adjusted to a new position in European, indeed world, trade; the implications of this (as David Sacks shows in Ch. 11) were felt in the balance of power within towns as well as between them. The search for new trading patterns, as traditional north-western European contacts were disrupted by a century of post-Reformation warfare, meant some towns having to seek more distant trade, so perhaps strengthening the hold of the greater merchants. Other places settled for coastal trade or fishing, eroding (one might suppose) the dominance of local merchants (though, as Roger Howell shows in Ch. 10, this was not the case with the capital-intensive shipment of coal from Newcastle to London). In such conditions little distinction can be drawn between purely economic crises and those caused by warfare and piracy in British waters, intensifying the risks and sudden shifts of trade.

As the fortunes of individual towns are increasingly seen to depend on how well they could participate in broader economic trends, so the desire either to isolate the urban sector, or to rank towns in economic prosperity, has correspondingly declined. Rather than seeking an 'urban variable' in economic change, interest is turning to the changing nature of urban–rural economic relationships. We now recognize the key roles played by urban inns and carrier services in this process. But much remains to be discovered about how markets and fairs (still lying at the heart of towns, physically and in contemporary perceptions) adapted to change, including the growth of purely retail shops. Similarly we still lack detailed studies of how towns traded with each other, especially their relationships within a particular trade sector, such as the Channel or the Irish Sea.[17]

Despite the signs of growing sophistication in the economic analysis of towns, the most striking new developments in the study

seventeenth-century Ipswich', in Clark (ed.), *Country Towns*, pp. 87–141; R. Tittler, 'The vitality of an Elizabethan port: The economy of Poole *c.* 1550–1650', *Southern History*, 7 (1985), pp. 95–118; G. Talbut, 'Worcester as an industrial and commercial centre 1660–1750', *Transactions of Worcester Archaeological Society*, 10 (1986), pp. 91–102.

17. N. Goose, 'In search of the urban variable: Towns 1500–1650', *Economic History Review*, 39 (1986), pp. 165–85; Abrams and Wrigley (eds), *Towns*; P. Clark, *The English Alehouse* (1983); M. Spufford, *The Great Reclothing of Rural England* (1984); H. and I. H. Mui, *Shops and Shopkeeping in Eighteenth-Century England* (1989).

of the early modern town have derived from the work of social historians. Particularly influential has been the work of demographers associated with the Cambridge Group for the History of Population and Social Structure. The fundamental demographic characteristics of early modern towns were well established by 1976 and recent work has not altered the basic picture. Urban population levels responded, not to natural population growth, but to variations in mortality and the influx of migrants from the countryside and elsewhere. Generally speaking, towns found it hard to maintain their population levels; without migrants their populations would have stagnated or fallen rather than grown. This excess of mortality was the result of both endemic and epidemic diseases. A constantly high level of background mortality, especially of the very young, was supplemented by recurrent epidemics, of which plague was both the most notorious and the most often associated with towns. But plague's failure to recur after 1665 did not mean the end of urban epidemics, indeed the next half-century saw urban mortality at record levels.

The full significance of these fundamental facts, however, has come into sharper relief as a result of improved understanding of the broader demographic context. The emphasis on mortality in explaining *urban* population trends is highlighted by the new consensus that *rural* demography was determined largely by fertility trends, themselves dependent on changing marriage patterns. There is no clear evidence that urban fertility patterns varied significantly from rural, except for some intriguing indications that even quite small towns may have displayed a distinctively non-seasonal cycle of conceptions; whereas country people conceived their children in accord with the agricultural seasons, townspeople were affected by periods of festivity but little else.[18] In other respects, townspeople, most of them immigrants from the countryside anyway, shared rural behaviour, above all in their adherence to the so-called 'nuclear family', whereby young couples did not marry until they could establish their own household and support themselves. English towns lacked the extended households and dynasties of Renaissance Italian cities. Naturally this basic condition meant different things in town and countryside. Rather than waiting to inherit family land, young men and women in towns were waiting until they had served out apprenticeships, saved enough through service to start in business, or could inherit shops, houses or businesses. But the principle was the same and the effect, delayed marriage and a high rate of celibacy, also the same. None the less, the differential factor of

18. A. Dyer, 'The seasonality of baptisms: An urban approach', *Local Population Studies*, 27 (1981), pp. 26–34; E. A. Wrigley and R. Schofield, *The Population History of England 1540–1871* (1981).

urban mortality ensured that town and countryside played two very contrasting, though interdependent, roles in England's population history.

Until about 1650, the towns attracted the excess population of the countryside, as rural population almost doubled and land shortage, together with other agricultural changes, forced many to seek to establish a household outside their native parishes. But towns were only one possible destination; many moved into other rural areas, particularly pastoral districts where land and by-employments were more common. For many young men, especially after 1630, migration to town was a stepping-stone to emigration; Bristol and above all London shipped off hundreds of thousands to Ireland and the New World.[19] It is customary, and still helpful, to distinguish 'subsistence' migrants, pushed off the land into towns, from 'betterment' migrants. The latter were pulled into towns by economic opportunities and had clearly identified niches to occupy in town life. The distinction is useful, but the two categories are not of course mutually exclusive. The yeoman's second son, without a landed inheritance, who took an urban apprenticeship, was looking to the town for subsistence as well as betterment, and shared this characteristic with the humbler men and women who tramped into the town, usually as young unmarried people, in search of employment or charity. In both cases it was at a keypoint in their life cycle, between childhood and the establishment of a household, that migration to town most often took place.[20]

This introduces us to the two key concepts which have most changed the way we have looked at urban society since 1976: life cycle and household. Approaching towns with the questions that these two concepts lead us to raise has altered the character of urban historiography. The difference will be clear from contrasting Nigel Goose's piece on Cambridge reprinted as Chapter 4 with the pieces in *The Early Modern Town*, or even with Alan Beier's slightly ear-

19. P. Clark and D. Souden (eds), *Migration and Society in Early Modern England* (1987); J. Wareing, 'Migration to London and trans-Atlantic emigration 1683–1775', *Journal of Historical Geography*, 7 (1981), pp. 356–78.
20. J. R. Holman, 'Apprenticeship as a factor in migration: Bristol 1675–1726', *Transactions of Bristol and Gloucestershire Archaeological Society*, 97 (1979), pp. 85–92; A. Yarborough, 'Geographical and social origins of Bristol apprentices 1542–65', ibid., 98 (1980), pp. 113–30; E. Jones, 'The Welsh in London in the seventeenth and eighteenth centuries', *Welsh History Review*, 10 (1981), pp. 461–79; M. Siraut, 'Physical mobility in Elizabethan Cambridge', *Local Population Studies*, 27 (1981), pp. 65–70; D. M. Palliser, 'A regional capital as magnet: York 1477–1566', *Yorkshire Archaeological Journal*, 57 (1985), pp. 111–23; N. Alldridge, 'The mechanics of decline: Population, migration and economy in early modern Chester', in Reed (ed.), *English Towns* (no pagination); M. J. Kitch, 'Capital and kingdom: Migration to late Stuart London' in Beier and Finlay (eds), *London*, pp. 224–51.

lier article in this collection (Ch. 5). Common themes, such as migration and the social problems it created, appear very differently when examined through this approach. Most importantly, these concepts reinforce other trends away from the study of urban *structure* towards the examination of *processes* in urban society. Whereas the great strength of the first phase of urban history was its grasp of the overall structure of towns, the emphasis recently has been on reconsidering townspeople broken down, as the old joke has it, by age and sex, not to mention class. A group photograph and a video can both record the same event, but after seeing the video we may return to the group photograph less convinced that it captures the changing relationships between people. The emphasis has been on tracing what the changing experience of urban life meant to different people at different stages of their lives.

In many ways the most ambitious and successful study incorporating this approach is Charles Phythian-Adams's dissection of Coventry's period of crisis in the early and mid-sixteenth century. Using some uniquely full census and taxation materials, he reconstitutes the process of household formation in Coventry, showing how both the native-born population and immigrants could be integrated into urban life through apprenticeship and service, how they could progress to become independent householders and guild members and what was the typical *cursus honorum* of Coventry's governing class. At the same time, his study shows that this 'ideal type' was never the experience of the majority of Coventry people in this period. In part this was due to Coventry's particular economic crisis, which left it unable to recruit the necessary immigrants or to retain those wealthy householders who offered to others their chance of apprenticeship, service or employment once married. But in part it reflected the instability inherent in all urban life, where death, illness, old age, failure to marry or establish a household (each the problems of a small minority) served cumulatively to prevent most people, at some stage of their lives, from acting out the complete part laid down for the typical citizen.[21]

Phythian-Adams's work has remained unrivalled in the range of issues which it tackled for a complete town. Many of the points it covers have been examined in subsequent studies, but usually through the analysis either of specific topics or of sub-groups within the urban community. Even Goose's lengthy and wide ranging analysis of Cambridge makes no effort to tackle all the issues raised by life cycle and household. This is hardly surprising, given the absence of comparable sources and the incredible labour involved in such analysis, especially as the technical standards of demography have risen.

21. Phythian-Adams, *Desolation of a City*.

14

At one stage it looked as though London would never be amenable to such demographic study, given its sheer size and the problems of high population turnover caused by death, immigration and mobility between parishes. This was ironic, since one of the earliest fruits of the new demography was Wrigley's classic article 'A simple model of London's importance', which drew attention to the effect of London's excess mortality in slowing, and by the late seventeenth century even preventing, rural population growth, at least in the south. But it seemed as though London's impact on the national population would always be understood better than the history of London's own population. The last fifteen years, however, have seen an explosion of work on the capital, using studies of particular districts and sub-groups to establish hypotheses about the overall pattern.[22] Inevitably such studies, since they are based on samples, raise problems of representativeness. Are the districts analysed typical (whatever that might mean in such a varied city as London)? Are the sub-groups studied a random sample, or perhaps abnormal socially, economically or merely by virtue of their survival long enough to enter the written records? Without already knowing the answers we are seeking, how can we decide how to weigh the experience of natives and immigrants, residents of the inner city, West End and suburbs, rich and poor, young and old, men and women, in order to establish a balanced picture? In the end, then, we are forced to set the evidence of process in the context of structure, but an enormous amount can be learnt on the way.

Let us look first at mortality. A great deal has been done to get beyond the basic, but rather crude stress on high overall urban mortality, to an understanding of the varied character and implications of urban death rates. Identifying different causes of death and their differential impact by age, sex, occupation, wealth and district has not only explained more about changing overall populations, it has enabled analysis of death rates to illuminate other aspects both of

22. E. A. Wrigley, 'A simple model of London's importance', *Past and Present*, 37 (1967), pp. 17–40, reprinted in Clark (ed.), *Early Modern Town*, Abrams and Wrigley (eds), *Towns*, and Wrigley, *People, Cities and Wealth*. In addition to articles cited below see: T. R. Forbes, 'By what disease or casualty?: The changing face of death in London', in Webster (ed.), *Health, Medicine and Mortality*, pp. 117–40; R. W. Herlan, 'Aspects of population history in the London parish of St Olaves, Old Jewry 1645–67', *Guildhall Studies in London History*, 4(3). (1980), pp. 133–40; R. Finlay, *Population and Metropolis: The Demography of London 1580–1650* (Cambridge, 1981): P. R. Galloway, 'Annual variations in deaths by age, deaths by causes, prices and weather in London 1670–1830', *Population Studies*, 39 (1985), pp. 487–505; J. Landers, 'Mortality, weather and prices in London 1675–1825', *Journal of Historical Geography*, 12 (1986), pp. 347–64; *idem*, 'Mortality and metropolis; The case of London 1675–1825', *Population Studies*, 41 (1987), pp. 59–76; J. Boulton, *Neighbourhood and Society: A London Suburb in the Seventeenth Century* (1987).

urban experience and of urban–rural relationships. In one basic sense, most urban deaths seem to have been 'natural' not man-made, in that there is little evidence that towndwellers died directly of starvation or even as a result of malnutrition – surges in death rates rarely coincided with the highest food prices except in the mid-1590s. Even at such times, recent work suggests that the correlation may be an indirect consequence of rural starvation and bankruptcy during such periods, which brought to towns a large number of countrypeople, who were seeking food, charity and employment, but were vulnerable to urban diseases such as plague and smallpox.[23] The high mortality of recent migrants thus gave a social dimension to urban death rates; Alan Sharlin has suggested that a small rate of natural growth by native townspeople may be concealed within the parish registers, swamped by the deaths of those born elsewhere. This seems unlikely, given the high rates of infant mortality among all groups, but it offers a salutary reminder of the need to establish, if at all possible, exactly which groups in towns experienced specific forms of disease.[24] Equally, urban mortality caused two distinct but important flows of people from town to countryside which, being temporary, are often overlooked – namely the wet-nursing of urban children and the flight of townspeople from the city, especially during plague, but also in the summer months generally. Both these outward flows were confined largely to the better-off, though not exclusively to the rich. Disease and its prevention played a major part in urban life.[25]

The most intensive and imaginative work of this kind has been on the social history of plague. Though plague was a natural disaster, its character, course and consequences were shaped by urban society, and helped to shape it in turn. Plague's contemporary image as *the* scourge of urban life reflected the fact that it disrupted the whole of urban society – unlike some other equally virulent diseases it was recurrent but occasional and it struck not only the very young but those of all ages, possibly having an unusually marked effect on young adults. In this way it laid particularly bare the dependence of

23. A. Appleby, 'Nutrition and disease: the case of London 1550–1750', *Journal of Interdisciplinary History*, 6 (1975), pp. 1–22; Webster (ed.), *Health, Medicine and Mortality*; J. Landers, 'Burial seasonality and causes of death in London 1670–1819', *Population Studies*, 42 (1988), pp. 59–83.
24. A. J. Sharlin and R. Finlay, 'Natural decrease in early modern cities', *Past and Present*, 79 (1978), pp. 126–38 and 92 (1981), pp. 169–80; C. Cunningham 'Christ's Hospital: Infant and child mortality in the sixteenth century' *Local Population Studies*, 18 (1977), pp. 37–42.
25. G. Clark, 'A study of nurse children 1550–1760', *Local Population Studies*, 39 (1987), pp. 8–23; V. Fildes, 'The English wet-nurse', *Medical History*, 32 (1988), pp. 142–73; M. Pelling, 'Appearance and reality: Barber-Surgeons, the body and disease', in Beier and Finlay (eds), *London*, pp. 82–112.

town on countryside, as immigrants surged in after plague attacks to fill vacant niches in urban life. Temporary economic dislocation was succeeded by a distorted demographic profile, with many broken households to increase the burden of poverty. Moreover the link of plague with poverty grew ever closer and clearer, as plague's victims became increasingly restricted to those living in poorer housing, either in back alleys or suburbs. There is still room for doubt about the causal connection here – was it poverty as such, or bad housing and sanitation, or the inability to flee town that left the poor increasingly vulnerable? Whatever the cause, the result was to encourage urban authorities to tackle plague and poverty as linked ills, with an urgency that reflected the fact that the rulers of towns still suffered from plague in their purses and still dreaded that it might afflict their households. Plague management thus became a vital test of the character of government and class relations in towns, underlining tensions, though also offering opportunities for charity and communal solidarity in the face of crisis.[26]

Plague only accounted, however, for a small proportion of urban deaths, and even small towns, where plague struck very rarely, shared with larger towns a level of mortality (at least by the late seventeenth century) that set them off from rural areas.[27] Most of these deaths were of children, little noticed perhaps by the community at large. However, they served in the long term to restrict urban growth rates and prevent the survival of most urban families beyond a few generations, in direct line at least, which may have hindered the growth of urban dynasties and capital accumulation. This effect was much more obvious, however, when death broke up

26. I. G. Doolittle, 'The effects of plague in a provincial town', *Medical History*, 19 (1975), pp. 333–41; A. Dyer, 'The influence of bubonic plague in England 1500–1667', ibid., 28 (1978), pp. 308–26; A. Appleby, 'The disappearance of plague', *Economic History Review*, 33 (1980), pp. 161–73; P. Slack, *The Impact of Plague in Tudor and Stuart England* (1987). For plague in smaller towns see: R. Schofield, 'An anatomy of an epidemic: Colyton, November 1645 to November 1646', in P. Slack (ed.), *The Plague Reconsidered* (Matlock, 1977), pp. 95–126; T. S. Willan, 'The plague in perspective: the case of Manchester in 1605', *Transactions of the History Society of Lancashire and Cheshire*, 135 (1983), pp. 29–40; J. Taylor, 'Plague in the towns of Hampshire 1665', *Southern History*, 6 (1984), pp. 104–22; J. Howell, 'Haverfordwest and the plague 1652', *Welsh History Review*, 12 (1985), pp. 411–19.

27. C. E. Brent, 'Urban employment and population in Sussex 1550–1650', *Sussex Archaeological Collections*, 133 (1975), pp. 35–50; J. Skinner, 'Crisis mortality in Buckinghamshire 1600–1750', *Local Population Studies*, 28 (1982), pp. 67–73; J. R. Bignall, 'Epidemics in Tudor and Stuart Guildford', *Surrey Archaeological Collections*, 74 (1983), pp. 113–22; A. Dyer, 'Epidemics of measles in a seventeenth-century town', *Local Population Studies*, 34 (1985), pp. 35–45; G. Mayhew, 'Epidemic mortality in sixteenth-century Rye', *Sussex Archaeological Collections*, 124 (1986), pp. 157–77; R. Humphreys, 'Mortality crises in sixteenth-century Dorking', *Local Population Studies*, 29 (1987), pp. 46–53.

existing families. Wealth and poverty were both closely tied to the question of whether a particular householder could stay alive long enough to develop his business and shield his wife and children from widowhood and orphanhood.[28] Earlier marriage and lower mortality rates probably gave the advantage in both respects to the native-born, but the risks were high for all. As Phythian-Adams's ideal-type demonstrates, the ordering of urban society rested on the household as a means for integrating immigrants, training the young and placing women, children and employees in a secure position, but the household was itself a very insecure institution.

This point has been central to much of the recent work on urban inequality. Following Hoskins's pioneering work, the starting point for analysis used to be the great inequality of wealth revealed by tax returns, censuses of the poor and other data on cross-sections of the community at one moment in time. Those arguing the case for urban crisis have been prone to cite such evidence rather uncritically to suggest that the lives of many if not most urban dwellers were of unrelieved poverty. Recent work has stressed the intermittent character of most urban poverty. Many of those who were poor at any one moment, especially at the times of crisis which often prompted censuses and tax demands, were temporarily in distress due to economic depression or illness. A further group, as Alan Beier shows in Chapter 5, were those recent migrants unable to establish an immediate niche in urban society and unusually vulnerable to any fall in the demand for casual labour or rise in living costs. Lacking a household position they were easily labelled 'vagrants'. Special measures were taken to round them up, either to be ejected from town or to be put under the control of an institutional household until conditions improved and they could be fitted into urban life via service or employment. But the number of individuals experiencing long-term poverty was much more restricted, notably to those at certain points in the life cycle, or afflicted by the break-up of the household. Thus both private charity and public poor relief dealt largely with the long-term sick, orphans and widows,

28. C. Carlton, *The Court of Orphans* (Leicester, 1974); J. R. Holman, 'Orphans in pre-industrial towns: The case of Bristol', *Local Population Studies*, 15 (1975), pp. 40–4; T. Wales, 'Poverty, Poor Relief and the life-cycle: Some evidence from seventeenth-century Norfolk', in R. M. Smith (ed.), *Land, Kinship and Life-Cycle* (1985), pp. 351–404; P. Earle, 'Age and accumulation in the London business community 1665–1720', in N. McKendrick and R. B. Outhwaite (eds), *Business Life and Public Policy* (Cambridge, 1986), pp. 38–63. Alan Everitt suggests the late seventeenth century as a starting point for the growth of English urban dynasties in 'Dynasty and community since the seventeenth century' in his *Landscape and Community*, pp. 309–30.

both those left as single parents and those too old to support themselves.[29]

Such findings offer support both to optimistic and pessimistic accounts of urban inequality. The pessimists can rightly stress the ubiquity of broken households and the recurrent pressures of economic depression, notably in the troubled years of the late sixteenth and early seventeenth centuries, when high food prices left many townspeople very vulnerable, and when the pressure of subsistence migrants was at its greatest. Peter Clark's article on Gloucester (Ch. 9) seconds Beier in this interpretation, and Nigel Goose's Cambridge findings in Chapter 4 offer much supporting evidence. If the mid-seventeenth century was to see a fall in food prices and rural overpopulation, the short-term effects of the Civil War ensured a further spasm of urban misery in many places. On the other hand, as in many other troubled periods, the optimists can justly point to the limited character of poverty, at least for the 'typical' householder and family, and to the range of expediencies, such as changes in diet, by-employments and relief agencies, which enabled the poor to survive. The optimistic case has been put particularly strongly for London itself, not least in Valerie Pearl's article reprinted here as Chapter 6. The very general character of her argument and its concentration on the wealthier inner area of the City of London render it vulnerable to attack, but many of her points have been substantiated by others. Steven Rappaport has sought to exploit the life-cycle approach to demonstrate the reasonable expectations for upward mobility of the average London freeman, and questioned the timing and extent of the fall in real wages for London

---

29. R. Harvey, 'Recent research on poverty in Tudor and Stuart England' *International Review of Social History*, 24 (1979), pp. 237–52; R. W. Herlan, 'The social articulation and configuration of parochial poverty in London on the eve of the Restoration', *Guildhall Studies in London History*, 2 (1976), pp. 43–53; *idem*, 'Poor Relief in London during the English Revolution', *Journal of British Studies*, 18 (1979), pp. 30–51; *idem*, 'Relief of the poor in Bristol from Elizabethan times to the Restoration', *Proceedings of the American Philosophical Society*, 126 (1982), pp. 212–28; A. L. Beier, 'The social problems of an Elizabethan country town: Warwick, 1580–90', in Clark (ed.), *Country Towns*, pp. 45–85; *idem*, *Masterless Men* (1985); M. Pelling, 'Healing the sick poor: Norwich 1550–1640', *Medical History*, 29 (1985), pp. 115–37; J. J. Tronrud, 'Responses to poverty in three towns 1560–1640', *Histoire Sociale/Social History*, 18 (1985), pp. 9–28; *idem*, 'Dispelling the gloom: The extent of poverty in Tudor and Early Stuart towns: Some Kentish evidence', *Canadian Journal of History*, 20 (1985), pp. 1–21; S. McFarlane, 'Social policy and the poor in the late seventeenth century', in Beier and Finlay (eds), *London*, pp. 252–77; T. Arkell, 'The incidence of poverty in the late seventeenth century', *Social History*, 12 (1987), pp. 23–47; M. Pelling, 'Illness among the poor in an early modern English town: the Norwich census of 1570', *Continuity and Change*, 3 (1988), pp. 273–90; P. Slack, *Poverty and Policy in Tudor and Stuart England* (1988).

workers. Michael Power and Jeremy Boulton's studies have done much to correct images of undifferentiated suburban poverty.[30]

As the last examples suggest, the demographic approach has encouraged a greater sensitivity to the impact on inequality not just of age but also of *space*. Analysis of households leads rapidly to consideration of housing and this trend has been reinforced by the influence of historical geography. As John Langton explains in Chapter 7, geographers have been eager to test rival models of social space within the early modern town. His own analysis from hearth tax records confirms the impression of historians that the wealthiest still worked and resided in the town centre, while the least wealthy were concentrated on the peripheries and in the suburbs, although Langton rightly points to variations between towns and nuances within this simple model. Other analyses of social topography have reinforced this. As towns grew in population their housing patterns depended to a considerable extent on the pattern of vacant land available. In many places late medieval depopulation and the availability of monastic estates in prime urban sites allowed initial population growth to occur through fuller use of existing housing (often by subdivision) and in-filling (especially of poorer housing behind established streets). Where this was inadequate, however, suburban or peripheral building occurred, usually to house the poorer migrants.[31] In London, as nowhere else, these suburbs came rapidly to rival and then overshadow the established city, but although much of the new housing here was also low-grade building, the pattern was significantly modified. The poorer suburbs of south and east London contained many substantial enterprises, notably along the river and the roads, with quite wealthy residents, while in the West End the lure of power and culture led gradually to the development of a fashionable district, though not on any great scale

30. M. Power, 'Shadwell: the development of a London suburban community in the seventeenth century', *London Journal* 4 (1978), 29–44; V. Pearl, 'Social policy in early modern London', in H. Lloyd-Jones *et al.* (eds), *History and Imagination* (1981), pp. 115–31; S. Rappaport, 'Social structure and mobility in sixteenth-century London', *London Journal*, 9 (1983), pp. 107–35 and 10 (1984), pp. 107–34; Boulton, *Neighbourhood and Society*.

31. I. Roy and S. Porter, 'The social and economic structure of an early modern suburb: the tything at Worcester', *Bulletin of the Institute of Historical Research*, 53 (1980), pp. 203–17; *idem*, 'The population of Worcester in 1640', *Local Population Studies*, 28 (1982), pp. 32–43; J. and P. Clark, 'The society and economy of the Canterbury suburbs 1563', in A. Detsicas and N. Yates (eds), *Studies in Modern Kentish History* (1983), pp. 65–86; J. Hindson, 'The Marriage Duty Acts and the social topography of the early modern town: Shrewsbury 1695–8', *Local Population Studies*, 31 (1983), pp. 21–28.

until the mid-seventeenth century.[32] Other towns were beginning to follow this pattern by the later seventeenth century as their growth also led to the extension of better-class housing in the suburbs as well as the centre.

Recent work has also begun to examine housing patterns in finer detail, seeking to understand how different types of household used this housing stock. One immediate effect of this has been to cast some doubt on the assumption made by Langton and others that house size or value (as measured by numbers of hearths, taxes, etc.) necessarily correlates well with the overall wealth or social standing of the occupants. Nicholas Alldridge's work on Chester has shown how occupational requirements for space and changes in household size with age may have counted more than wealth in determining the numbers of hearths required. Studies of residence over time have shown rapid and extensive mobility between properties within a given area, often apparently to match house size to household needs. Almost all townspeople rented their houses, simplifying such movements. A range of accommodation types often existed in close proximity, notably in the contrast between substantial street-front properties and smaller ones behind them or in side-streets, while properties were often sub-leased or their space reorganized to fit changing needs and purses. All these factors render analysis at the level of the parish, the unit Langton uses, very crude. Paul Slack's studies of plague incidence, while revealing some differences at parish level, showed that a parish average could conceal marked differences between different types of housing within the parish.[33]

32. K. G. T. McDonnell, *Medieval London Suburbs* (Chichester, 1978); M. Power, 'East and West in early modern London', in E. W. Ives *et al.* (eds), *Wealth and Power in Tudor England* (1978), pp. 167–85; *idem*, 'John Stow and his London' *Journal of Historical Geography*, 11 (1985), pp. 1–20; *idem*, 'The social topography of Restoration London', in Beier and Finlay (eds), *London*, pp. 199–223; E. Jones, 'London in the early seventeenth century: An ecological approach', *London Journal*, 6 (1980), pp. 123–33; L. Stone, 'The residential development of the West End of London in the seventeenth century', in B. C. Malament (ed.), *After the Reformation* (*Manchester*, 1980), pp. 167–212; R. Finlay and B. Shearer, 'Population growth and suburban expansion', in Beier and Finlay (eds), *London*, pp. 37–59.
33. P. Slack, 'The local incidence of epidemic disease: The case of Bristol 1540–1650', in Slack (ed.), *Plague Reconsidered*, pp. 49–62; N. J. Alldridge, 'House and household in Restoration Chester', *Urban History Yearbook* (1983), pp. 39–52; D. Keene, 'A new study of London before the Great Fire', *Urban History Yearbook* (1984), pp. 11–21; J. Boulton, 'Residential mobility in seventeenth-century Southwark', *Urban History Yearbook* (1986), pp. 1–14; *idem*, 'Neighbourhood migration in early modern London', in Clark and Souden (eds), *Migration and Society*, pp. 107–49; S. Wright, 'Easter Books and Parish Rate Books', *Urban History Yearbook* (1985), pp. 30–45.

We are also beginning to learn more about the actual character of urban housing in general. The increased interest in vernacular architecture and the slow extension of urban archaeology into the early modern period, notably in Norwich, has resulted in the identification of various housing types.[34] This work can be corroborated by the findings from probate inventories. In principle these listings of household goods and other chattels, frequently recorded room by room, ought to offer an unrivalled picture of urban living. In fact such sources must be treated with caution: towns display great differences in housing types and the evidence is biased towards the more substantial households. But some general conclusions can be drawn. On the one hand the increasing pressure on urban space from the late sixteenth century is obvious from evolving house-types and the way houses are divided; on the other hand the growing range of household furnishings and other consumer goods, together with indications of specialized room functions and the search for privacy, suggest rising standards of living.[35]

An important next step will be to integrate this evidence with broader questions about the urban environment. What, for example, were the effects on urban health of the growth of separate kitchen and sleeping areas, the increase in chimneys, and changes in public and private water and sanitation facilities? David Palliser's impressionistic but thought-provoking observations on the environment of Tudor York (Ch. 8) are only gradually being followed up.[36] Many of the most characteristic aspects of *urban* experience, including high mortality, density of population, distinct types of building and

34. J. Schofield, *The Building of London from the Conquest to the Great Fire* (1984); *idem* and D. Palliser (eds), *Recent Archaeological Research in English Towns* (Council for British Archaeology, 1981); *idem* and R. Leech (eds), *Urban Archaeology in Britain* (Council for British Archaeology, 1987); R. Smith and A. Carter, 'Function and site: Aspects of Norwich buildings before 1700', *Vernacular Architecture*, 14 (1983), pp. 5–18; M. Laithwaite, 'Totnes houses 1500–1800', in Clark (ed.), *Transformation*, pp. 62–98.
35. R. Garrard, 'Probate inventories and their use for studying domestic interiors 1570–1700', *AAG Bijdragen*, 23 (1980), pp. 53–77; A. Dyer, 'Urban housing: Four Midland towns', *Post-Medieval Archaeology*, 15 (1981), pp. 207–18; U. Priestley and P. Corfield, 'Rooms and room use in Norwich housing 1580–1730', ibid., 16 (1982), pp. 93–123; P. Borsay, 'Culture, status and English urban landscape', *History*, 67 (1982), pp. 1–12; F. E. Brown, 'Continuity and change in the urban house: Developments in domestic space organisation in seventeenth-century London', *Comparative Studies in Society and History*, 28 (1986), pp. 558–90; Weatherill, *Consumer Behaviour*.
36. Notably by Mark Janner and Margaret Pelling at the Wellcome Unit for the History of Medicine, Oxford. Thought-provoking suggestions occur in E. L. Jones and M. E. Falkus, 'Urban improvement and the English economy in the seventeenth and eighteenth centuries', *Research in Economic Hist*, 4 (1979), pp. 195–233; M. Falkus, 'Lighting in the Dark Ages of English economic history', in D..C. Coleman and A. H. John (eds), *Trade, Government and Economy in Pre-Industrial England* (1976), pp. 248–73; E. L. Jones, S. Porter and M. Turner,

unique environmental problems, can only be analysed by pooling the skills of archaeologists, architectural historians, medical and demographic experts and so on. Interest in these questions will undoubtedly grow as historians begin to explore in more detail the role of women in towns, and consider their largely unrecorded contribution to feeding, cooking, cleaning and managing health, both within their own household and in the neighbourhood. There are many strong reasons for identifying gender distinctions in the early modern town. Gender was, for example, an important and shifting factor in migration to towns. The old emphasis on studying apprenticeship and freemen left unexplored the extent and methods of female recruitment into towns, but recent work on sex ratios in towns suggests interesting changes. London, and possibly other towns, had a male surplus around 1600, but by the late seventeenth century a wide range of towns had a marked female majority. Several reasons can be suggested for this, including heavy male emigration from port towns, but this in itself may reflect another factor, namely the growth in specifically female opportunities within urban life, notably in the retail and service areas. While rural population growth before 1650, followed by its stagnation or fall thereafter, may have affected the levels of *male* subsistence migration fairly straightforwardly, it is less clear whether female opportunities would follow the same pattern. It has been suggested that agrarian changes, especially a growing requirement for specifically male labour in arable-producing areas, may have left young countrywomen looking to urban employment. In turn, this shift may help to explain the apparent decline in long-distance migration to London and other southern towns after 1650, since young women may have travelled less far in search of work. In the pastoral north and west, where women's agricultural work and domestic industries both offered female employment in the countryside, the urban-rural relationship may have been different.[37]

A Gazetteer of English Urban Fire Disasters 1500–1900 (Historical Geography Research Series no. 13, 1984). On urban buildings outside the home see R. Tittler, 'The building of civic halls in Dorset *c*. 1560–1640', *Bulletin of the Institute of Historical Research*, 58 (1985), pp. 37–45 and Clark, *English Alehouse*.

37. J. Wareing, 'Changes in the geographical distribution of recruitment of apprentices in London Companies 1486–1750', *Journal of Historical Geography*, 6 (1980), pp. 241–50; D. Souden, 'Migrants and the population structure of later seventeenth-century provincial cities and market towns', in Clark (ed.), *Transformation*, pp. 133–68; *idem*, '"East, West – Home's Best"? Regional patterns in migration in early modern England', in Clark and Souden (eds), *Migration and Society*, pp. 292–332; P. J. P. Goldberg, 'Marriage, migration, servanthood and life-cycle in Yorkshire towns of the Later Middle Ages', *Continuity and Change*, 1 (1986), pp. 141–69; L. D. Schwarz, 'London apprentices in the seventeenth century: Some problems', *Local Population Studies*, 38 (1987), pp. 18–22; J. Dils, 'Deposition Books and the Urban Historian', *Local Historian*, 17 (1987), 269–76.

More is also being discovered about women's distinctive place in urban life, through studies of female employment and the position of widows and other single women. Harsh realities faced many of those female immigrants, who were much less likely than native London women to marry until their late twenties, if at all, and likely to marry less prosperous Londoners.[38] Once again we are brought back to the process of household formation, and the unequal resources of different groups in this process. Added importance is thus given to what has always been seen as a vital aspect of urban life, namely service and apprenticeship. Although apprenticeship evidence has always been used in the study of migration patterns, only recently have historians been returning to the agenda of an earlier generation and considering the character of relations between masters and their servants and apprentices. A familiar paradox emerges: both individuals and the urban community relied very strongly on the success of these relationships, and yet in a large minority of cases they broke down. Servant turnover was rapid, while disputes, illness, death, economic depression or other factors often prevented the completion of apprenticeship. Once trained, apprentices often found the expected niche in the urban environment was not available. Future research will surely focus on these tension points between civic ideals and realities, between standard urban careers and what individuals actually experienced.[39]

Efforts to gain a more complex understanding of the causes and courses of social inequality have also set urban government in a new light. While recent work has confirmed Clark and Slack's earlier stress on the 'oligarchic' character of urban magistracy, the significance of this concept has been modified. Oligarchy, the domination of town government by a small and usually self-perpetuating body of the richest citizens, has usually been portrayed as the inevitable result of extreme social inequality. Not only did

38. V. Brodsky Elliott, 'Single women in the London marriage market: Age, status and mobility 1598–1619', in R. B. Outhwaite (ed.), *Marriage and Society* (1981), pp. 81–100; *idem*, 'Widows in late Elizabethan London', in L. Bonfield *et al.* (eds), *The World We Have Gained* (1986), pp. 122–54; B. J. Todd, 'The remarrying widow: A stereotype reconsidered', in Prior (ed.), *Women*, pp. 54–92; and see n. 13 and 29.

39. A. Yarborough, 'Apprentices as adolescents in sixteenth-century Bristol', *Journal of Social History*, 13 (1979), pp. 67–82; S. Smith, 'The ideal and the real: Apprentice–master relationships in seventeenth-century London', *History of Educational Quarterly*, 21 (1981), pp. 449–60; M. K. McIntosh, 'Servants and the household unit in an Elizabethan English community: Elizabethan Romford', *Journal of Family History*, 9 (1984), pp. 3–23; M. Pelling, 'Child health as a social value in early modern England', *Social History of Medicine*, 1 (1988), pp. 135–64; T. K. Ben–Amos, 'Service and the coming of age of young men in seventeenth-century England', *Continuity and Change*, 3 (1988), pp. 41–64.

this give power to the rich, who alone could finance and find the time to run town affairs, but it also gave them the incentive to shoulder the burden of government, in order to control the unruly poor and avert the threat of social revolution. The assumption has tended to follow that these oligarchies then ruled their towns coercively, through their economic power and to their own benefit, paying little regard to the rest of the community, who were inevitably excluded from rule. This final assumption (a caricature of what Clark and Slack originally argued) does not, of course, necessarily follow. Much evidence has emerged to suggest a more complex view, with much more stress on the range of participation in urban government and its sensitivity to broader community opinion.[40] More fundamentally, revised views of urban social and economic relations have affected our views of the relationship between oligarchy and inequality.

As mentioned before, doubts have been cast, both about the reliability of the evidence for wealth distribution and its implications. Initial studies often drew on evidence from national taxation. But this was most often taken from a narrow taxbase, so creating a very strong impression of inequalities of wealth. Study of local rates, which often drew on a very wide range of the urban population, considerably modifies the picture of mass urban poverty.[41] Extremes of wealth and poverty certainly existed, but between them lay a spectrum of middling groups, probably comprising a majority of households. The life-cycle approach further modifies our outlook, encouraging us to consider oligarchy as a function of age (and of course gender) as well as wealth. If power at the top of urban government was the end of a *cursus honorum*, what proportion of those eligible to enter this race reached its finish? What were the reasons for failure – apart of course from the high risk of death?

40. Varying views of oligarchy can be found in: C. T. Hammer, 'Anatomy of an oligarchy? Oxford Town Council in the fifteenth and sixteenth centuries', *Journal of British Studies*, 18 (1978), pp. 1–27; J. T. Evans, *Seventeenth-Century Norwich: Politics, Religion and Government 1620–90* (Oxford, 1979); J. Goring, 'The Fellowship of the Twelve in Elizabethan Lewes', *Sussex Archaeological Collections*, 119 (1981), pp. 157–72; P. Clark, 'The civic leaders of Gloucester, 1580–1800', in Clark (ed.), *Transformation*, pp. 311–45; J. W. Kirby, 'Restoration Leeds and the aldermen of the Corporation 1661–1700', *Northern History*, 22 (1986), pp. 123–74. For oligarchies and social policy see: Tronrud, 'Responses to poverty'; P. Slack, 'Metropolitan government in crisis: The response to plague', in Beier and Finlay (eds), *London*, pp. 60–81; M. K. McIntosh, 'Local responses to the poor in late medieval and Tudor England', *Continuity and Change*, 3 (1988), 209–45.
41. See, for example: W. Champion, 'The Shrewsbury lay subsidy of 1525', *Transactions of Shropshire Archaeological Society*, 64 (1985), pp. 35–46; *idem*, 'The frankpledge population of Shrewsbury 1500–1720', *Local Population Studies*, 41 (1985), pp. 51–60; and references in n. 29 and 40.

25

Study of the steps to the top has drawn attention to the lower rungs of the civic ladder, the parochial, guild and minor civic posts which urban magistrates invariably held first. How many of these were there, who filled them and how much power did they have? Perforce we begin to see urban government more from the bottom up, or perhaps one should say from the middle outward, since the poorest are still firmly excluded.

Although Charles Phythian-Adams's work on Coventry opened up these issues, they have been pursued most thoroughly for London. The sheer size of the capital makes the concentration of power in the hands of the mayor and aldermen seem particularly extreme. But it has been for London that the strongest claims have been made for participatory and open government. Valerie Pearl's article (Ch. 6) emphasizes the range of representative institutions in Stuart London and the huge number of governmental posts to be filled. Like the Stuart Crown, she stresses the anti-authoritarian character of London's civic traditions, embodied in the freeman class, which still included the majority of male householders within the City of London proper. Pursuing the case back into the Tudor period, and exploiting the life-cycle argument, Steven Rappaport has underlined the claim that those apprentices who survived to claim their freedom could expect upward social mobility within their guilds and that a significant proportion would attain posts of responsibility. In more general terms Foster, Power, Lindley, Boulton and others have all portrayed a magistracy sensitive to the needs and opinions of the wider London community and highly reluctant to provoke its anger, even when pressurized to this effect by the Crown.[42]

Several factors make it difficult to generalize from this London evidence. Firstly, Pearl and Rappaport can be accused of portraying the City of London, with its long traditions of freeman and guild participation, as if its government was typical of the whole metropolis. Even the suburbs studied have not been typical of the majority of expanding parishes, which were larger than most provincial towns but usually still governed by the non-urban institutions of manor, parish and county. It can also be argued that the range of separate interest groups in the capital, ensuring that there would be

---

42. F. F. Foster, *The Politics of Stability: A Portrait of the Rulers in Elizabethan London* (1977); R. Ashton, *The City and the Court 1603–43* (Cambridge, 1979); R. M. Benbow, 'The Court of Aldermen and the Assizes: the policy of price control in Elizabethan London', *Guildhall Studies in London History*, 4 (1980), pp. 93–118; K. Lindley, 'Riot prevention and control in early Stuart London', *Transactions of the Royal Historical Society*, 5th ser., 33 (1983), pp. 109–26; H. J. Cook, 'Policing the health of London: The College of Physicians and the early Stuart monarchy', *Social History of Medicine*, 2 (1989), pp. 1–33; Rappaport, 'Social structure'; Power, 'London and control of crisis'; Boulton, *Neighbourhood and Society*.

many wealthy people with rival interests outside any conceivable governing body, encouraged competition for power rather than oligarchy. Recent work is showing the complexity of the power struggles within and between guilds, for example. Furthermore, as the centre of government and the focus of national political culture, Londoners were in a prime position to be politicized, both by the direct effects of government action on themselves and through the political struggles acted out in court, Parliament and on the streets of the capital.[43] Except during the Civil War, power was so centralized in the English State that no other English town (except York and Oxford on occasions) experienced similar conditions. So the debate over oligarchy in provincial towns cannot be settled by London.

Given the diverse character of provincial towns, no uniform answer can be given anyway. As we have seen, economic developments tending to concentrate urban fortunes in mercantile hands occurred in some places, while in others a range of crafts, professional groups and rival trading interests remained or emerged, discouraging any permanent concentration of power. The urban balance of power could also be affected by the intervention of the church or the surrounding gentry, especially in smaller towns. Again, these might support a monopoly of power or merely strengthen internal rivals. To add to these variables, the institutions of government within each town not only rested on potentially very varied precedents but also shifted wildly over this turbulent political period. The mid-Tudor period saw new charters and changes in urban government at a rate unprecedented since the thirteenth century, while the mid-Stuart period was no less unsettled, culminating in the notorious remodellings of borough government in the 1680s.

43. R. Brenner, 'The Civil War politics of London's merchant community', *Past and Present*, 58 (1973), 53–107; G. Ramsey, 'Industrial discontent in early Elizabethan London: Clothworkers and Merchant Adventures in conflict', *London Journal*, 1 (1975), pp. 227–39; *idem*, 'Clothworkers, Merchant Adventurers and Richard Hakluyt', *English Historical Review*, 92 (1977), pp. 504–21; D. Allen, 'Political clubs in Restoration London', *Historical Journal*, 19 (1976), pp. 561–80; B. Manning, *The English People and the English Revolution* (1976); J. E. Farnell, 'The social and intellectual basis of London's role in the English Civil Wars', *Journal of Modern History*, 49 (1977), pp. 641–60; S. Smith, 'Almost revolutionaries: London apprentices during the Civil Wars', *Huntingdon Library Quarterly*, 42 (1979), pp. 313–28; K. Lindley, 'London and popular freedom in the 1640s', in R. C. Richardson and G. M. Ridden (eds), *Freedom and the English Revolution* (Manchester, 1986), pp. 111–50; H. J. Cook, *The Decline of the Old Medical Regime in Stuart London* (Ithaca, 1986); D. Dean, 'Public or private? London, leather and legislation in Elizabethan England', *Historical Journal*, 31 (1988), pp. 525–48; F. Heal, 'The Crown, the gentry and London: the enforcement of proclamation 1596–1640', in C. Cross *et al.* (eds), *Law and Government under the Tudors* (1988), pp. 211–26; I. Archer, 'London lobbies in the later sixteenth century', *Historical Journal*, 31 (1988), pp. 17–45.

Generalizing wildly, one can suggest that the typical Tudor changes tended to strengthen the formal concentration of power within a fixed magistracy, although this was often merely regularizing a pre-existing reality. Seventeenth-century changes, however, cannot be so easily characterized – since successive governments might favour expanding or restricting public participation in town government according to circumstances. The sheer pace of changes after 1640 in itself ensured a substantial turnover in office, even if the magistracy remained limited in numbers. The growth of parliamentary politics, moreover, renders the notion of urban oligarchy more problematic: not only was the size of the electorate a random variable (ranging from all resident males to a few property-holders or the town councillors only) but participation in electoral politics gave new meaning to such privileges as town freedom without ensuring equivalent participation in purely local government. Yet the two were increasingly inseparable, not least in the eyes of Crown and Parliament.[44]

The interconnection between urban and national government has been one of the most important recent themes. Inevitably urban historians became drawn into the wider debate about court–country hostility and the significance of 'localism', especially in the origins and course of the Civil War.[45] Roger Howell's pioneering work in this area initially offered a picture of introverted towns more influenced by localism than interest in national issues, buffeted by national events rather than shaping them. As will be seen from Chapter 10, however, his arguments have modified, reflecting our growing understanding of how difficult it is to separate the local and the national. This is even clearer in the essays of Peter Clark and David Sacks on early Stuart Gloucester and Bristol respectively (Chs 9 and 11). Both of them emphasize the growing awareness, at least among urban élites, of the effect of national decisions on local affairs and portray the development of coherent attitudes to national political issues growing from such experience. Needless to say the Civil War, and the emergence of rival ideologies and parties that followed, only served to deepen this awareness, as studies of Restoration urban politics show very clearly. After 1640 poverty,

---

44. D. Hirst, *The Representative of the People?* (Cambridge, 1975); S. Bond and N. Evans, 'The process of granting charters to English boroughs 1547–1649', *English Historical Review*, 91 (1976), pp. 102–20; R. Tittler, 'The incorporation of boroughs 1540–58', *History*, 62 (1977), pp. 24–42; *idem*, 'The emergence of urban policy 1536–58', in J. Loach and R. Tittler (eds), *The Mid-Tudor Polity* (1980), pp. 74–93; Evans, *Seventeenth-Century Norwich*; J. Miller, 'The Crown and borough charters in the reign of Charles II', *English Historical Review*, 100 (1985), pp. 53–84; M. Kishlansky, *Parliamentary Selection* (Cambridge, 1986).
45. R. Howell, 'Neutralism, conservatism and political alignment: the case of the towns 1642–9', in J. Morrill (ed.), *Reactions to the English Civil War* (1982), pp. 67–89.

monopolies and extra-parliamentary taxation may no longer have posed towns such political problems, but increasing difficulties over loyalty to the regime, the growth of central bureaucracy and the concurrent increase in state taxation certainly compensated. In addition commercial disputes between provincial towns and with London always required the larger towns, at least, to maintain political contacts in the capital. Although London was the only decisive urban arena in the strongly centralized English State, this served, not to de-politicize other towns, but to force them to resolve their problems on the national stage.

These issues have brought back into prominence the role of the law in urban government. It has always been recognized that legal privileges, such as charters, determined the structure of most urban politics, and that urban rulers were above all *magistrates*, often ruling as justices of the peace for their borough (in some cases separate from county jurisdiction). In itself, of course, this legal framework brought the towns firmly into a national framework. They looked to Crown, Parliament and the law courts to establish, change or adjudicate on their legal position. Clashes between these national bodies caused problems for towns, but also left them room to play off one against another, possibly with different urban interests backing different sides. Opportunities abounded, for the legal position of towns was not only uniquely vulnerable, but also increasingly questionable. Governments anxious to ensure the proper enforcement of the law, and doubtful from the Reformation onwards about the loyalty of all local officials, were at least able to appoint rural magistrates and to destroy or bypass local rural jurisdictions, but they could never contemplate the same with towns. Towns chose their own magistrates and ran their own courts; no wonder that successive governments sought to ensure that this urban autonomy did not undermine their aims too seriously. Hence they supported the rule of those urban élites who owned most and owed most to governmental favour. Seventeenth-century governments became ever less patient with urban autonomy. But their interventions to alter the personnel of urban oligarchy rarely had the intended results; arguably they only revealed the resilience and hidden depths of urban politics.

For if urban magistrates were constantly made aware of their dependence on central government, legally and politically, they were equally aware of their dependence on support within the town, if they were to govern successfully. Town governments had few paid personnel, and relied on the amateur officials of wards, parishes and neighbourhoods to get things done. The legal framework of urban administration placed great weight on popular cooperation; without ordinary townspeople bringing offenses to court and returning verdicts in courts as jurymen, magistrates were unable to enforce their wishes. Magistrates certainly held the upper hand, but they could not prevent others from pursuing their interests and raising matters of public policy, for example in their presentments. The magistrates, especially in larger towns, also found it necessary to delegate much control to parishes and guilds, but once again this gave these bodies an important, if subordinate, influence in urban affairs.[46]

Between 1530 and 1688, and indeed beyond, the problem of religious uniformity lay at the heart of urban government, troubling relations both within each town and with national government. On the one hand, the Reformation intensified the concentration of urban power. In both religious and socio-economic legislation the Tudors sought to intensify the unity of Church and State within clearly established governmental structures and to weaken the voluntary, participatory aspects of urban life. This led to the abolition of fraternities and many communal celebrations and the granting of new duties and powers to parish notables and urban magistrates. Peter Clark's essay shows how urban oligarchs responded to this challenge to build a godly city – a theme which Patrick Collinson has now explored further. But urban uniformity proved a tricky goal to achieve. The Reformation had not, in fact, fully unified Church and State – points of tension abounded, between parish and town for example, or between town and cathedral. Studies of the varying experiences of such neighbouring towns as Hull, Leeds and York reveal how the progress of the Reformation was shaped by the varied character of the church, or churches, in each town. The voluntary tradition in religion persisted, not just in catholic and then protestant separatism, but also within the Church. The low value of most urban benefices required townspeople to provide voluntary support to attract preaching ministers, leading to urban lectureships and godly meetings, comparable to the activities of earlier fraternities. When first Elizabethan and then Laudian bishops opposed such necessary compromises to urban conditions, they set many urban magistrates against national authority, so convinced were the magistrates that religion's moral and spiritual discipline was needed to hold such unstable communities together. In such diverse

---

46. No study has yet brought together the evidence on this topic, which is scattered through the sources already cited. But see also: A. E. MacCampbell, 'London parish and London precinct 1640–60', *Guildhall Studies in London History*, 2 (1976), pp. 107–24; J. Boulton, 'The limits of formal religion: the administration of Holy Communion in late Elizabethan and early Stuart London', *London Journal*, 10 (1984), pp. 139–54; R. Tittler, 'The sequestration of juries in early modern England', *Historical Research*, 61 (1988), pp. 301–5; N. Alldridge, 'Loyalty and identity in Chester parishes 1540–1640', in S. Wright (ed.), *Parish, Church and People* (1988), pp. 85–124; J. Barry, 'The parish in civic life: Bristol and its churches 1640–1750', in ibid., pp. 152–78.

conditions even the search for religious unity served to create conflict.[47]

The unstable mixture exploded, of course, during the 1640s. Recent work, particularly on London, has shown the centrality of religion both in generating initial urban support for Parliament, and in creating first an anglican and then a presbyterian backlash in favour of religious uniformity and against that most unexpected, but profound, consequence of the war: the establishment of strong sectarian congregations, particularly in towns.[48] When reinforced by the presbyterians after 1662, these congregations posed an unprecedented problem for urban government. How, if at all, could nonconformists be integrated into parochial and civic institutions? When persecution was tried (and this varied enormously according to place and period) it became clear how hard it was for an urban oligarchy to enforce laws against a sizeable minority of citizens, many of them from the householder class and including a significant proportion of wealthy men who would normally be candidates for urban magistracy. The result was conflict and confusion at every level of urban government. Rival parties, each with support rooted

47. W. J. Sheils, 'Religion in provincial towns', in F. Heal and R. O'Day (eds), *Church and Society in England: Henry VIII to James I* (1977), pp. 156–76; P. Clark, 'Thomas Scott and the growth of urban opposition to the early Stuart regime', *Historical Journal*, 21 (1978), pp. 1–26; *idem*, 'Reformation and radicalism in Kentish towns *c*. 1500–1553', in W. J. Mommsen (ed.), *The Urban Classes, the Nobility and the Reformation* (Stuttgart, 1979), pp. 107–27; C. Cross, 'Parochial stucture and the dissemination of protestantism in sixteenth-century England: a tale of two cities', *Studies in Church History*, 16 (1979), pp. 269–78; *idem*, 'Priests into ministers: the establishment of protestant practice in the city of York 1530–1630', in P. N. Brooks (ed.), *Reformation Principles and Practice* (1980), pp. 203–25; *idem*, 'The incomes of the provincial urban clergy 1520–1645', in F. Heal and R. O'Day (eds), *Princes and Paupers in the English Church 1500–1800* (Leicester, 1981), pp. 65–90; *idem*, *Urban Magistrates and Ministers: Religion in Hull and Leeds from the Reformation to the Civil War* (Borthwick Papers no. 67, York, 1985); A. Fletcher, 'Factionalism in town and countryside: the significance of Puritanism and Arminianism', *Studies in Church History*, 16 (1979), pp. 291–300; P. Heath, 'Staffordshire towns and the Reformation', *North Staffordshire Journal of Field Studies*, 19 (1979), pp. 1–21; E. M. Shepperd, 'The Reformation and the citizens of Norwich', *Norfolk Archaeology*, 38 (1981), pp. 44–58; S. Brigden, 'Tithe controversies in Reformation London', *Journal of Ecclesiastical History*, 32 (1981), pp. 285–301; *idem*, 'Religion and social obligation in early sixteenth-century London', *Past and Present*, 103 (1984), pp. 67–112; G. Mayhew, 'Religion, faction and politics in Reformation Rye 1530–59', *Sussex Archaeological Collections*, 120 (1982), pp. 139–60; P. Collinson, 'The Protestant town', in his *Birthpangs of Protestant England* (1988), pp. 28–59.

48. M. Mahony, 'Presbyterianism in the City of London 1645–7', *Historical Journal*, 22 (1979), pp. 93–114; T. Gentles, 'The struggle for London in the Second Civil War', *ibid.*, 26 (1983), pp. 277–305; P. Seaver, *Wallington's World: A Puritan Artisan in Seventeenth-Century London* (1985); T. Liu, *Puritan London* (1986); E. S. More, 'Congregationalism in the social order', *Journal of Ecclesiastical History*, 38 (1978), pp. 210–35.

in church groupings, formed and fought to control office, to manipulate the courts and to control the streets. National government, alarmed in any case by the power of urban dissent and radicalism, sought to intervene, but could not find any formula for stability. Inconsistent Crown interventions merely boosted successive factions within towns and encouraged the growth of links between these factions and the emerging national parties – a process hastened by the prolonged electioneering of the Exclusion crisis and the subsequent intervention in town affairs throughout the 1680s. By 1688 the only agreed legacy of the Reformation in towns was anti-popery.[49]

In different ways the topics and approaches outlined above have all tended to emphasize variety and diversity within urban life. We have lost the clarity of the earlier work, with its emphasis on the characteristic identities of certain types of town, the overall structure of particular towns and the dominance within them of an oligarchy whose interests generated a coherent urban policy. Instead we have complex relationships between town and countryside, the local and the national, oligarchy and participation, unity and diversity. The emphasis on process helps us to understand how individuals and groups experienced urban life, but does it enable us to understand what towns were and what made them distinctive and so worth studying?

Many would argue that no such identity and urban distinctiveness existed. Not only can this be argued for urban history in general, but a particular case can be made for the Tudor and Stuart period. What characteristics could an emerging metropolis like London share with the puny provincial towns? Was London not now too large for a coherent identity, while the other towns remained too small, doomed to pay court to the capital or the surrounding

---

49. J. Hurwich, "'A Fanatick Town": The political influence of dissenters in Coventry 1660–1720', *Midland History*, 4 (1977), pp. 15–47; M. Watts, *The Dissenters: From the Reformation to the French Revolution* (Oxford, 1978); M. Mullett, "'Deprived of our Former Place": The internal politics of Bedford 1660–88', *Bedfordshire Historical Record Society*, 59 (1980), pp. 1–42; *idem*, 'Conflict, politics and elections in Lancaster 1660–88', *Northern History*, 19 (1983), pp. 61–86; *idem*, "'Men of Known Loyalty": the politics of the Lancashire borough of Clitheroe 1660–89', ibid., 21 (1984), pp. 106–31; *idem*, 'Catholicism and disorder in late seventeenth-century Wigan', *Catholic Historical Review*, 73 (1987), pp. 391–407; C. E. Brent, 'The neutering of the fellowship and the emergence of the Tory Party in Lewes 1663–88', *Sussex Archaeological Collections*, 121 (1983), pp. 95–107; Miller, 'Crown and borough charters'; T. Harris, *London Crowds in the Reign of Charles II* (1987); *idem*, 'Was the Tory reaction popular? Attitudes of Londoners towards the prosecution of dissent 1681–6', *London Journal*, 13 (1987–8), pp. 106–20; H. Horwitz, 'Party in a civic context: London from the exclusion crisis to the fall of Walpole', in Jones (ed.), *Britain in First Age of Party*, pp. 173–94.

countryside? Had not the Reformation dealt a fatal blow to an earlier, introverted model of urban culture, undermining the medieval articulation of urbanity through the Church and communal ritual? Struggling to overcome economic and social problems, did not urban oligarchs cling vainly to outdated traditions, while as individuals they aspired to gentry status and took their cultural models from the rural gentry? All of these cases have been persuasively argued for this period, although perhaps the most significant argument for the absence of a distinctive urban culture in this period has been that from silence. Few historians have bothered to examine urban culture outside the London of Shakespeare and Pepys.[50] The contrast with the period that follows could hardly be sharper, underlining Peter Borsay's claim that a new urban identity was forged during the 'urban renaissance' post-1688.[51]

This Introduction is hardly the place to construct a counter-argument for urban identity or to describe the distinctive urban culture of the period. To do so, however, would require the historian to recognize what contemporaries surely grasped, namely that it was in how the urban community responded to the complexity and fluidity of urban life that its identity lay. As the title of David Palliser's paper (Ch. 8) suggests, there was an 'urban mentality', if not a single urban culture. The characteristic institutions of the town were those intended to integrate the individual and the household into urban life and offer as much security as possible against the inevitable fragility of all personal relationships. The same might be said of the walls, gates, churches, town halls and other buildings that both visitors and residents saw as urban characteristics. Time and space, as Palliser shows, had to be ordered, and social relations constantly regulated. In practice, as our sources testify, order was never achieved. The individual's experience of these institutions or struc-

50. R. D. Altick, *The Shows of London* (1978); C. Phythian-Adams, 'Milk and soot: The changing vocabulary of a popular ritual in Stuart and Hanoverian London', in D. Fraser and A. Sutcliffe (eds), *The Pursuit of Urban History* (1983), pp. 83–104; R. Ashton, 'Popular entertainments and social control in late Elizabethan and early Stuart London', *London Journal*, 9 (1983), pp. 3–20; *idem*, 'Samuel Pepys' London', ibid., 11 (1985), pp. 75–87; P. Burke, 'Popular culture in seventeenth-century London', in B. Reay (ed.), *Popular Culture in Seventeenth-Century England* (1985), pp. 31–58; M. Berlin, 'Civic ceremony in early modern London', *Urban History Yearbook* (1986), pp. 15–27.

51. L. S. O'Connell, 'The Elizabethan bourgeois hero-tale', in Malament (ed.), *After the Reformation*, pp. 267–90; P. Clark, 'Visions of the urban community: Antiquarians and the English city before 1800', in D. Fraser and A. Sutcliffe (eds), *The Pursuit of Urban History* (1983), pp. 105–24; M. James, 'Ritual, drama and the social body in the late medieval English town', *Past and Present*, 98 (1983), pp. 1–29; J. Barry, 'Popular culture in seventeenth-century Bristol', in Reay (ed.), *Popular Culture*, pp. 59–90; D. Sacks, 'The demise of the martyrs: the feasts of St Clement and St Katherine in Bristol 1400–1600', *Social History*, 11 (1986), pp.141–69; Borsay, *English Urban Renaissance*.

tures was often fragmentary; the town itself neither achieved internal unity nor presented a united front to the outside world. But it is in understanding the efforts to establish such an identity, as well as the forces that worked against it, that we shall move forward to a fuller history of Tudor and Stuart towns and a better sense of their significance in shaping change in a rural society, which was itself increasingly faced with the same challenges.

Chapter 2

URBAN DEVELOPMENT IN ENGLAND AND WALES IN THE SIXTEENTH AND SEVENTEENTH CENTURIES[1]

Penelope Corfield

[from D. C. Coleman and A. H. John (eds), *Trade, Government and Economy in Pre-Industrial England* (London, 1976)]

This article appeared in a Festschrift *to the great economic historian F. J Fisher, whose work had highlighted the growth of Tudor and Stuart London. Corfield reviews the evidence for urban growth in this period and considers how far London's growth was at the expense of other towns. She draws primarily on population estimates and concentrates on those places, a minority of what were then classified as towns, whose populations reached 5000 by 1700. Within this group of larger towns, however, she identifies a number of different types, characterized by different rates of growth. Attention is also drawn to the surge of growth most larger towns experienced after 1650. The writer is conscious of many of the problems involved, both in establishing population totals in this period and of using them as a test of urban status. Equally problematic is the economic emphasis: as the opening paragraphs suggest contemporary ideas of urban development rarely focused on the purely economic, let alone the quantitative.*

The phenomenon of rapid growth is bound to attract controversy and discussion in almost any age. The myth of the big city is simplified but seductive, especially to the migrant from village or small-town society: bright lights, crowds, bustle, gaiety, opportunities for social and economic advancement; the big city is a magical place 'where all the streets are paved with gold, and all the maidens pretty.'[2] Yet no earthly city has ever lived up to such a

1. I would like to thank Peter Clark and Professor Donald Coleman for their helpful criticism of an early draft of this paper.
2. The refrain is sung in praise of London in George Colman's drama, *The Heir-at-Law* (Dublin, 1880), p. 14.

vision of splendour, and strictures upon the urban way of life and criticisms of the impact of rapid growth have also been many and eloquent, even if rarely powerful enough to halt the process they deplore.

In sixteenth- and seventeenth-century England there was considerable debate over the social, political and economic implications of urban development, particularly in relation to the dramatic growth of the capital city. The literature of the age abounds in references to the so-called craftiness, avarice and deceit of the townsman; but there was also a growing counter-tradition satirizing the alleged gullibility, boorishness and ignorance of the 'country bumpkin' (a phrase which first became current in the 1670s).[3] Local authorities and central government worried about the difficulties of feeding and controlling the growing urban population, but their efforts at restraint could not stop the surge of migration into the city.[4] There was also much disagreement over the economic consequences of urban expansion. Petty for example argued in the 1680s that the growth of cities was beneficial to the economy, as urban populations generated more demand for goods and services than did those who lived 'sordidly and inurbanely' in the countryside, through the greater pressures towards conspicuous consumption in the town. Yet there was a strong popular tradition criticizing London's growth as unhealthy and abnormal, a view summarized by Davenant (who disagreed with it) as 'the common and received notion that the growth of London is pernicious to England; that the kingdom is like a rickety body with a head too big for the other members'. Later, too, Andrew Fletcher of Saltoun presented in 1703 a more complex variant of this critique, with the observation that 'if, instead of one, we had twelve cities in these kingdoms possessed of equal ad-

3. 'Bumpkin', a word of Dutch origin, entered the English language in the later sixteenth century. *OED* does not record the use of the phrase 'country bumpkin' before the 1770s, but it was current at least a century before that, as a term of disparagement; see Sparkish in W. Wycherley's *The Country-Wife* (1675), p. 22: 'Why, d'ye think I'll seem to be jealous, like a Country Bumpkin?'
4. In the case of London, for example, growing concern at the difficulties of feeding its expanding population, plus fears of 'pestilence and riot', prompted the city authorities in 1580 to ask the Crown for assistance in regulating the capital's housing development by curbing the subletting of tenements and controlling the standards of new building. Regulations were promulgated by various proclamations between 1580 and 1661, and augmented for a brief period between 1593 and 1600 and in 1657 by Parliamentary statute. Proposals for fresh legislation were discussed in Parliament in 1675 and 1677 but not adopted. See E. J. Davis, 'The Transformation of London', in R. W. Seton Watson (ed.), *Tudor Studies* (1924), pp. 287-314; and especially N. G. Brett-James, *The Growth of Stuart London* (London, 1935), pp. 67-126, 296-308.

vantages, so many centres of men, riches and power would be more advantageous than one'.[5]

There are some interesting parallels between these arguments, formulated in the context of England's developing but still predominantly agrarian and pre-industrial economy, with the present-day debate over the implications of the growth of big cities in the agrarian economies of the Third World, where rapid urban expansion is currently provoking controversy. Whereas, in industrializing societies, urban growth is often seen as the joint harbinger and concomitant of economic growth, in a relatively backward and underdeveloped economy the correlation may not be so positive; and indeed in the context of an agrarian economy experiencing a population explosion, migration into the big cities might simply reflect the lack of development in the countryside rather than economic transformation in the town.[6]

The dimensions and significance of urban development in Tudor and Stuart England have been the subject of some discussion among historians in recent years. Particularly illuminating and important have been the magisterial studies by Professor Fisher into aspects of London's economic life.[7] His analysis of the functions of the capital city and its role in the long term as an 'engine of growth' in the seventeenth-century economy have been highly influential – not only directly, in that his conclusions have been accepted by others, but also indirectly, in that his writings have done much to establish the parameters and even some of the terminology of the debate. In

5. See C. H. Hull (ed.), *The Economic Writings of Sir William Petty* (Cambridge, 1899), p. 290. Davenant is cited in F. J. Fisher, 'The Sixteenth and Seventeenth Centuries: the Dark Ages in English Economic History?', *Economica*, N. S. 24 (1957), pp. 10–11. See also A. Fletcher, 'An Account of a Conversation Concerning a Right Regulation of Governments for the Common Good of Mankind . . . 1703', in *The Political Works of Andrew Fletcher, Esq.* (1732), pp. 443–4.
6. D. J. Dwyer (ed.), *The City in the Third World* (London, 1974), 'Introduction', pp. 11–12. See also B. J. L. Berry, 'Some Relations of Urbanisation and Basic Patterns of Economic Development', in F. R. Pitts (ed.), *Urban Systems and Economic Development* (Oregon 1962), pp. 1–15; for discussion of a specific example, the case of modern India, see B. F. Hoselitz, 'The Role of Urbanisation in Economic Development: Some International Comparisons', in *The City in the Third World*, pp. 169–90; and for the concept of 'pseudo-urbanization', see T. G. McGee, *The Southeast Asian City. A Social Geography of the Primate Cities of Southeast Asia* (London, 1967), pp. 15–22.
7. F. J. Fisher, 'The Development of the London Food Market, 1540–1640', *Econ. Hist. Rev.*, 5 (1934–5), pp. 46–64; 'The Development of London as a Centre for Conspicuous Consumption in the Sixteenth and Seventeenth Centuries', *Trans. R. Hist. Soc.*, 4th series, 30(1948), pp. 37–50; 'London's Export Trade in the Early Seventeenth Century', *Econ. Hist. Rev.*, 2nd ser., 3 (1950), pp. 151–61; and 'London as an "Engine of Economic Growth"', in J. S. Bromley and E. H. Kossman (eds), *Britain and the Netherlands*, vol. IV, *Metropolis, Dominion and Province* (The Hague, 1971), pp. 3–16.

tribute to his work, therefore, it might seem appropriate to consider another aspect of this theme, namely a comparison between London's growth rate and those of the provincial towns during the same period. It is acknowledged that London was both exceptionally large and fast-growing. But a penumbra of uncertainty still lies over the nature and extent of urban development outside the metropolitan area. Was London's experience the exemplar for the provincial urban centres, following in the steps of the capital city albeit on a smaller scale and at a respectful distance? Some authorities describe the period as one of general urban growth. Or was it the case, as contemporaries sometimes claimed (especially in periods of economic depression), that the provincial towns collectively were experiencing blight and decay? An Act to remedy the decay of the corporate towns in 1554 prognosticated gloomily that 'the same Cities Boroughes and Towns Corporate are like to come verie shortly to utter destruccion ruine and decaye . . .'. [8] These questions are of interest in themselves and they also throw light on the debate over the implications of London's rapid expansion, since one of the more specific allegations made against the capital city was that its growth was taking place at the expense of its smaller urban rivals. For example on a number of occasions the provincial outports complained bitterly of commercial competition from London, and provincial traders and dealers often expressed resentment at the spreading economic tentacles of the capital.

This essay sets out to review briefly the available evidence relating to long-term urban growth rates in sixteenth- and seventeenth-century England and Wales as a whole; and thence to reconsider the implications of big-city growth in the context of the overall pattern of urban development.

It is necessary however to begin with an admission. Accurate figures for the size of urban populations during these years are not available, and indeed absolutely precise totals may never be ob-

---

8. The view that the sixteenth century was a period of general urban growth is expressed by A. D. Dyer, *The City of Worcester in the Sixteenth Century* (Leicester, 1973), p. 11; while L. Clarkson, *The Pre-Industrial Economy in England, 1500–1750* (London, 1971), p. 47, describes the whole period from 1500 to 1750 as one of urbanization, referring not only to London but also to provincial towns. For complaints about decay among corporate towns (chiefly in the mid-sixteenth century) see R. H. Tawney and E. Power (eds), *Tudor Economic Documents* (London, 1924), I, pp. 119–21; and P. Ramsey, *Tudor Economic Problems* (London, 1963), pp. 102–3. For a wide-ranging view urging the sixteenth and seventeenth centuries as a period of 'critical economic problems' for English urban society, see P. Clark and P. Slack (eds), *Crisis and Order in English Towns, 1500–1700* (London, 1972), 'Introduction', pp. 10–16, 30–5 and 40–1.

tainable, even after further detailed research has been carried out. These are certainly among the obscurely illuminated, if not totally 'Dark Ages' of English demographic history. Yet although the quest for absolute certainty may be vain, it is possible to identify at least in outline the scale and dimensions of the country's urban development, especially if it is accepted that population figures deal with probable orders of magnitude rather than precise totals. The lack of reliable figures is of course a major and important problem for the discussion that follows, and the difficulties should not be glossed over. The focus here however is upon the long-term trend (whether the urban populations were rising, declining or holding steady), which can be more readily established than can the absolute figures and the short-term fluctuations in population size. There is in fact a considerable amount of very disparate information that can be pressed into service to calculate the size of urban populations from the 1520s onwards; the sources include tax lists, muster records, the ecclesiastical censuses, and, where available, local enumerations, which were taken with increasing frequency from the later seventeenth century onwards. All have to be supplemented with informed guesswork.[9]

What do the available estimates show? The single most prominent example of urban growth was undoubtedly that of the conurbation of London with Westminster and their suburban environs. It seems likely that the population of this greater London mushroomed from about 50 000 to 60 000 inhabitants in the 1520s, to some 200 000 by 1600, some 400 000 by 1650, and perhaps 575 000 by 1700.[10] It had thus grown about tenfold during the sixteenth and seventeenth

9. For ranking of English towns in terms of taxable wealth in the 1520s and 1660s, see W. G. Hoskins, *Local History in England* (London, 1972 ed), p. 239. These are illuminating but cannot be taken as an accurate guide to rankings in population terms. Records of freeman admissions, which provide much valuable data about the range of occupations in corporate towns, also have to be used with care in estimating trends in population growth, as municipal policy and enforcement could vary so much over time: see the pertinent remarks in R. B. Dobson, 'Admissions to the Freedom of the City of York in the Later Middle Ages', *Econ. Hist. Rev.*, 2nd ser., 26 (1973), pp. 1–22.

10. These figures are approximations only, based on historians' revision of contemporary estimates and other general evidence, but they seem to have commanded general agreement. See E. A. Wrigley, 'A Simple Model of London's Importance in Changing England's Society and Economy, 1650–1750', *Past and Present*, 37 (1967), pp. 44–5. Some earlier authorities have suggested rather higher totals for London's population in the seventeenth century: N. G. Brett-James, *Stuart London*, p. 512, estimated it at about 250 000 in 1600; and M. D. George, *London Life in the Eighteenth Century* (London, 1930), pp. 24, 329–30, suggested 674 500 inhabitants in 1700. It is probably safe to scale down these estimates, in line with the trend in recent demographic research. If adopted, however, they enhance rather than diminish the scale of the capital's growth during these years.

centuries together, and about threefold during the seventeenth century alone. In 1700 London was a large city even by modern standards, and it was one of the largest cities in the world at this time – the largest city in Western Europe, and surpassed in Eastern Europe only by Constantinople.[11] The growth of London had moreover taken place at a much faster pace than that of the population of England and Wales as a whole. Again estimates of the national population are imprecise and open to a certain margin of error.[12] But, however the estimates are juggled, it remains incontestable that the growth of London proportionately outstripped that of the total population, which did little more than double between the 1520s and 1700. Hence London's growth alone entailed a significant increase in the country's urbanized population, as London's share increased from approximately two per cent of the total population in the 1520s,[13]

11. London was the largest city in western Europe in 1700, followed by Paris with about 500 000 inhabitants, Naples with perhaps 300 000 and Amsterdam with about 200 000: Wrigley, 'London's Importance', p. 45. London was still however smaller than Constantinople, which had approximately 700 000 to 800 000 inhabitants in the later seventeenth century: R. Mantran, *Istanbul dans la seconde moitié du XVIIe siècle* (Paris, 1962), p. 46–7.

12. Useful summaries of the range of population estimates for England and Wales between 1500 and 1700 are found in Clarkson, *Pre-Industrial Economy in England*, p. 26; and for 1700 in B. R. Mitchell and P. Deane, *Abstract of British Historical Statistics* (Cambridge, 1962), p. 5.

   The most recent and up-to-date research suggests that the population of England and Wales had slightly more than doubled from about 2.5 million (perhaps 2.6) in the 1520s, to at least 5.2 million in 1700. The figure for the population in the 1520s is based on Cornwall's revised estimate of the population of England at 2.3 million: J. Cornwall, 'English Population in the Early Sixteenth Century', *Econ. Hist. Rev.*, 2nd ser., 23 (1970), pp. 32–44; with the addition of an estimated 200 000 inhabitants in Wales (eight per cent of the total population), which has been adopted for compatibility with a suggested 251 000 inhabitants there by the mid-sixteenth century: see J. Thirsk, 'The Farming Regions of Wales', in J. Thirsk (ed.), *The Agrarian History of England and Wales*, vol. IV, *1500–1640* (Cambridge 1967), pp. 142–3; other estimates put the population of Wales in the early sixteenth century at nearer 300 000, hence providing a total population for England and Wales together of 2.6 million.

   The figure for the total population in 1700 is based on the suggestion made by Professor Glass that Gregory King's estimate of the population at 5.5 million could be revised downwards to 5.2 million, a suggestion that does not seem to have been seriously challenged: see D. V. Glass, 'Two Papers on Gregory King', in D. V. Glass and D. E. C. Eversley (eds), *Population in History. Essays in Historical Demography* (London, 1965), pp. 203–4.

   Whatever the precise figures preferred, however, it now seems fairly well established that the total population did about double during the years between the 1520s and 1700, whether from 2.5–2.6 million to 5.2 million, or from 3 million to 6 million.

13. Calculated assuming the population of London to be 50 000 and that of England and Wales to be about 2.5 million. If a higher estimate for the country's population of about 3 million is adopted, then London's proportion falls slightly to 1.7 per cent.

to about five per cent in 1600,[14] about eight per cent in 1650,[15] and about eleven per cent in 1700.[16]

Two features of this pattern of growth need further comment. It is notable that London's expansion continued throughout the whole of the seventeenth century, both during the years before 1650 when the country's population as a whole was multiplying fairly rapidly, and during the second half of the century when the overall growth

14. Calculated assuming the population of London to be 200 000 and that of England and Wales to be about 4 million. If a higher estimate for the total population of 4.2 million is adopted, then London's proportion falls to 4.8 per cent.

   Until further research is done, estimates of the size of the country's population in 1600 must depend on calculations derived from the returns of the ecclesiastical census, which was conducted in the autumn of 1603 at a time of renewed discussion about the state of the church following the accession of James I: see R. G. Usher, *The Reconstruction of the Church of England* (London, 1910), I, pp. 158–9, 207, 309.

   The census listed a total of 2 313 898 adults over the age of communion (communicants of the Church of England, plus declared recusants) in England and Wales: B. L. Harley MSS 280, fos. 157–72. Hence the total population can be calculated at about 4 million: if the adults over the age of communion (usually 16 years of age, but could be as low as 14 years at this time) are taken to constitute 60 per cent of the population, then the total is 3 856 497; if they are taken to constitute 56 per cent only (as suggested by Gregory King for the 1690s) then the total population is higher at 4 131 961 inhabitants. The original census was clearly not an absolutely reliable survey (some of the diocesan returns of the number of communicants of the Church of England are presented in suspiciously rounded figures), but it provides a basis for calculating the probable order of magnitude of the country's population.

   These calculations tally with those recently made by Cornwall, who estimated the population of England alone in 1603 to be 3.5–3.75 million: Cornwall, 'English Population', pp. 43–4; but also include the addition of a population of 350 000–380 000 inhabitants in Wales (9 per cent of the total population of England and Wales together), as calculated from the ecclesiastical census returns. As Dr Cornwall has pointed out ('English Population', p. 32), the figure that is often quoted of 2 065 498 communicants in England and Wales, which was used by Professor Cox Russell in his pioneering studies of English population size, is in fact erroneous: see J. C. Russell, *British Mediaeval Population* (Albuquerque, 1948), p. 270, and G. S. L. Tucker, 'English Pre-Industrial Population Trends', *Econ. Hist. Rev.*, 2nd ser., 16 (1963/4), pp. 211–12.

15. Calculated assuming the population of London to be 400 000 and that of England and Wales to be 5 million. Wrigley, 'London's Importance', p. 45, suggests that London's population of 400 000 constituted only 7 per cent of the country's population in 1650, thus implying a total population of 5 714 285. It is probable however that such a population total is too high, and hence the proportionate size of London slightly underestimated. The population of England and Wales in 1700 was only about 5.2–5.5 million, and there is no evidence for an outright population decline between 1650 and 1700, although it is often accepted that there was relatively little new growth in these years. I have therefore preferred estimates of a total population of about 4 million in 1600, about 5 million in 1650 and 5.2–5.5 million in 1700.

16. Calculated assuming the population of London to be about 575 000 inhabitants and that of England and Wales to be 5.2 million. If a higher national total of 5.5 million is accepted, then London's proportion falls to 10.5 per cent.

rate had fallen very markedly.[17] But it is also clear that London's own rate of growth slowed down considerably in the later decades of the century, although not as sharply as did the growth of the total population: whereas the population of London had doubled between 1600 and 1650, between 1650 and 1700 it increased by less than half as much again. The capital city was thus not increasing at a continuously accelerating rate of growth, although in absolute terms of course its population was still expanding massively. Its great increase in population was fuelled completely by migration into the city from the countryside and from small towns – indeed so high were urban death rates at this time that considerable immigration was needed even to keep the population at par.

The emergence of one big city did not in itself entail any automatic consequences for other towns in the economy of the time: it did not spread a universal mantle of growth; nor equally did it spell automatic blight for smaller rivals. The factors promoting London's expansion were partly unique but partly generic. It was unique in that it was the political and administrative capital of a unifying nation-state; and its geographical location gave it a commanding (although not unrivalled) position in the all-important trade between England and the Netherlands. But London also functioned as an industrial centre, as a nodal point for inland trade, and as a service and social centre, none of which activities were intrinsically liable to be confined to the capital city – although it is true that as London expanded it tended to strengthen its dominance in some of these spheres simply by virtue of its size, in a cumulative and self-sustaining process. For instance the volume and variety of inland trade centring upon the capital city naturally multiplied through the need to supply London's inhabitants with food, drink and raw materials. It flourished as a manufacturing centre because it contained the largest single concentration of consumers in the country, in an age when much (though far from all) production was located close to consumer markets. And in the same way the vitality of London's social and cultural life in Tudor and Stuart times also reflected the growing size and prestige of the city, let alone the growing wealth and taste for conspicuous consumption of landed

17. It is postulated that the sixteenth- and early seventeenth-century population growth slackened throughout Europe in the middle years of the seventeenth century, possibly picking up only gradually in the last decades of the century: K. F. Helleiner, 'The Population of Europe from the Black Death to the Eve of the Vital Revolution', in E. E. Rich and C. H. Wilson (eds.), *The Cambridge Economic History of Europe*. vol. IV, *The Economy of Expanding Europe* (Cambridge, 1967), pp. 52–4. The nature and causes of this population 'pause' are at present only imperfectly understood, but for some interesting conjectures see E. A. Wrigley, 'Family Limitation in Pre-Industrial England', *Econ. Hist. Rev.*, 2nd ser., 19 (1966), pp. 82–109.

gentlemen (now gaining their town houses) and the affluent citizenry; hence London offered an expanding market for those with professional services to sell and a growing audience for those anxious to make a social splash. It produced a competitive and often ruthless society, where men learnt, in Ben Jonson's words 'to quarrel and live by their wits'.

However, other towns could also function as manufacturing, commercial or service centres, or with some combination of these roles, even if they could not emulate the sheer scale of London. What was happening therefore outside the capital city? The evidence relating to the demographic history of the provincial towns is patchy and far from perfect, but the overwhelming conclusion that stands out from even the most cursory glance at the picture is that there was no universal pattern in their development, whether of urban growth or of urban crisis. Far from all towns grew rapidly; far from all towns grew at the same pace as each other; and far from all towns grew continuously during these two centuries. To take some examples, it is likely that some provincial centres (it is not clear how many) were expanding in the fifteenth and early sixteenth centuries up until the 1520s: Coventry and Southampton were probably expanding in these years, only to slacken their rate of growth very markedly in the mid-sixteenth century.[18] Worcester, York, Ipswich and Colchester, by

18. Uncertainty over the size of urban population in the fifteenth century is very great indeed; it seems plausible to assume however that there was some selective urban growth in the course of the century, as both urban and rural populations recovered from the impact of the plagues and their aftermaths.

After experiencing some population decline in the later fourteenth century from a pre-plague population of about 2500 inhabitants, Southampton's population had recovered to a total of approximately 2000 by the early 1520s; after this however its population expanded only little, if at all, in the rest of the sixteenth century: see C. Platt, *Medieval Southampton. The Port and Trading Community, A. D. 1000–1600* (London, 1973), pp. 262–3; A. Ruddock, *Italian Merchants and Shipping in Southampton, 1270–1600* (Southampton, 1951), pp. 259–72; and O. Coleman, 'Trade and Prosperity in the Fifteenth Century: Some Aspects of the Trade of Southampton', *Econ. Hist. Rev.*, 2nd ser., 16 (1963/4), pp. 9–22. Southampton's population had however expanded subsequently to a total of 2939 inhabitants by 1696–7: A. Temple Patterson, *A History of Southampton, 1700–1914* (Southampton, 1966), I, p. 6.

Coventry's population history is slightly better documented than that of many towns, as it experienced various economic and demographic problems that prompted local attempts at enumeration. By the 1510s, it appears that Coventry's population had recovered considerably towards its estimated pre-plague population of about 8000, with an estimated population of about 7000 inhabitants in the 1510s (enumerated in 1520 at 6601); but the population declined by as much as 25 per cent in the course of the 1520s, and then replenished itself only gradually in the later sixteenth century; its population was later enumerated at 6502 inhabitants in 1586. It expanded somewhat in the early seventeenth century and in 1644 it was found to contain about 9500 people at the time of the Royalist siege (but the numbers at this date may have been inflated by refugees from the

contrast, were expanding quite vigorously from the mid-sixteenth to the mid-seventeenth centuries, but recruited population only very slowly in the following hundred years.[19] And others experienced several discrete spurts of population expansion, punctuated by periods of only sluggish growth. To take two very different examples, the textile city of Norwich expanded briskly between the 1570s and early 1620s from about 10 000 inhabitants to over 20 000 but then had a population 'pause' in the following four decades before resuming its upwards expansion to about 30 000 inhabitants by 1700; while the port and dockyard town of Plymouth experienced

countryside in time of civil war). A fourth local enumeration in 1694 found a population of 6710, suggesting that there had been virtually no long-term growth between the 1510s and 1700. See *V. C. H., Warwickshire*, vol. VIII, *The City of Coventry and the Borough of Warwick* (London, 1969), pp. 4–5; and W. Reader, *The History and Antiquities of the City of Coventry from the Earliest Authentic Period to the Present Time* (Coventry, 1810), pp. 51, 71, 86. Some sources suggest a higher population of about 8000–9000 inhabitants in early sixteenth-century Coventry: see C. Phythian Adams, 'Ceremony and the Citizen: the Communal Year at Coventry, 1450–1550', in *Crisis and Order*, p. 58. If this is adopted, then Coventry's later eclipse is even more marked.

19. The population of Worcester almost doubled from an estimated figure of 4250 inhabitants in 1563 to about 8000 inhabitants in 1546: Dyer, *The City of Worcester*, pp. 26–7. Its population subsequently remained at about 8000 or 9000 inhabitants in the later seventeenth century, rising gradually to about 10 000 by the mid-eighteenth century: C. W. Chalkin, *The Provincial Towns of Georgian England. A Study of the Building Process, 1740–1820* (London, 1974), p. 34; and C. M. Law, 'Some Notes on the Urban Population of England and Wales in the Eighteenth Century', *The Local Historian*, X (1972), p. 26.

The population of York grew from about 8000 (or perhaps rather less) in the 1520s to about 12 000 inhabitants by the mid-seventeenth century; in 1760 it still stood at approximately the same figure, rising subsequently to 16 800 by 1801: see *V. C. H., Yorkshire. The City of York* (London, 1961), pp. 121, 162–3, 212.

Ipswich was also expanding in population in the late sixteenth and early seventeenth century until the 1630s. The precise figures for the sixteenth century are not known, but it is unlikely to have contained more than 3000 or 4000 people in the 1520s. It had become a sizeable centre of 8000 inhabitants by the 1660s; it ceased to grow thereafter, however, and its population was enumerated at 7943 inhabitants in 1695: see J. Wodderspoon, *Memorials of the Ancient Town of Ipswich in the County of Suffolk* (London, 1850), pp. 198–205; J. Webb, *Great Tooley of Ipswich. Portrait of an Early Tudor Merchant* (Suffolk Record Society publication, 1962), pp. 24, 170; W. B. Stephens, 'The Cloth Exports of the Provincial Ports, 1600–1640', *Econ. Hist. Rev.*, 2nd ser., 22 (1969), pp. 238–9; J. E. Pilgrim, 'The Cloth Industry in Essex and Suffolk, 1558–1640' (unpublished M. A. thesis, London University 1938), pp. 186–8; and M. Reed. 'Ipswich in the Seventeenth Century' (unpublished Ph. D thesis, University of Leicester, 1973), pp. 91, 304. The figure sometimes quoted of 12 000 inhabitants in Ipswich in 1695 is based on an erroneous reading of the enumeration returns, an error apparently first made in the early nineteenth century and subsequently repeated: see for example G. R. Clarke, *The History and Description of the Town and Borough of Ipswich* (Ipswich, 1830), p. 68. (A contemporary copy of the 1695 enumeration totals is located in the Ipswich and East Suffolk Record Office, Edgar MSS. HA 247.)

a population boom in the later sixteenth century, increasing from about 4000 inhabitants in 1550 to over 7000 (perhaps 7800) by 1603, and then stagnated in the seventeenth century until the 1690s, when its population began to increase again, although less dramatically, to about 8400 residents by 1740.[20] The patterns of development were clearly then complex; and, as these examples show, the population growth, once embarked upon, was not necessarily continuous. Migration into the provincial towns (which usually, like London, relied on immigration for their expanding numbers rather than upon natural increase) was not an inexorable and invariable process.

The other major conclusion that is apparent from an initial scrutiny of the available population data is that no provincial town experienced a rate of growth that approached the tenfold increase of London and its environs during the sixteenth and seventeenth centuries as a whole, even although a few centres may have shown a faster proportionate expansion in some decades. Many of even the leading provincial towns in 1700 were still very small in absolute terms and they would have had to have been very small settlements

Colchester's population grew in the later sixteenth and early seventeenth centuries, with the assistance of an influx of Dutch refugees in Elizabeth's reign (again precise figures for the early sixteenth century are not available but its population in the 1520s was probably between about 3000 and 4000 inhabitants), and it had become one of the leading six or seven provincial centres in England and Wales by 1700. Its population may have reached a total of about 9500 by 1670 (although this calculation, based on imperfect hearth tax returns, might be on the high side), but does not seem to have expanded significantly thereafter, its population in 1775 being estimated at 10 000 and in 1801 enumerated at 12 000: see Chalklin, *Provincial Towns*, p. 14; Law, 'Some Notes on the Urban Population', p. 23; and *British Historical Statistics*, p. 24. Dr Chalkin considers that Colchester's population may have passed the total of 10 000 inhabitants by 1700, although not increasing significantly thereafter. A contemporary enumeration of 1692 however reportedly put the population of the city at only 6845, suggesting that its economic difficulties may have already arrested its growth before the end of the seventeenth century: see T. Cromwell, *History and Description of the Ancient Town and Borough of Colchester* (London, 1825), p. 402. The accuracy of this enumeration however awaits confirmation.

20. The population of Norwich expanded from approximately 10 000 or 12 000 inhabitants in the mid-sixteenth century to reach a total of about 20 000 by the early 1620s; and it increased in the later seventeenth century to a total of 30 000 inhabitants by 1700: see W. Hudson and J. C. Tingey, *The Records of the City of Norwich* (Norwich, 1910), II, cxxiii-cxxviii; J. F. Pound, 'The Social and Trade Structure of Norwich, 1525–75', *Past and Present*, 34 (1966), pp. 49–50; and P. Corfield, 'A Provincial Capital in the Late Seventeenth Century: the Case of Norwich', in *Crisis and Order*, pp. 263–7.

Plymouth expanded from about 4000 inhabitants in 1549 to about 7000 (perhaps 7800) by 1603; a further period of growth at the end of the seventeenth century brought its population up to 8400 inhabitants by 1740; see R. N. Worth, *History of Plymouth* (Plymouth, 1890), pp. 362–3; H. C. Darby (ed.), *A New Historical Geography of England* (Cambridge, 1973), pp. 297, 384: and Chalklin, Provincial Towns, pp. 23–4.

indeed in 1500 to have achieved a tenfold increase in the following two centuries. Whatever the state of uncertainty about the fortunes of the late medieval town,[21] it is not suggested that the populations of the leading provincial centres had fallen as low as 500 or 600 inhabitants, which represents one-tenth of the size of a medium-sized regional centre in 1700. Until further research is done, it is difficult in fact to know which individual provincial town experienced the fastest growth between the 1520s and 1700. One strong candidate however would seem to be Newcastle upon Tyne, 'the eye of the north', whose population showed a fourfold increase from about 4000 inhabitants in the early sixteenth century to about 16 000 in the 1690s.[22] And it is also likely that some of the newly emergent urban centres in the seventeenth century, such as Liverpool, Birmingham and Manchester, showed fairly brisk rates of expansion, chiefly on the strength of their growth from the 1670s onwards. These centres may each have multiplied about fivefold in the sixteenth and seventeenth centuries, although they were not yet quite in the front rank of the urban hierarchy by 1700 – Liverpool containing about 5000 inhabitants, Birmingham about 7000 or 8000, and Manchester perhaps 8000 or 9000.[23] Other than these examples,

21. The debate over the wealth and economic circumstances of the late medieval town, although interesting from many points of view, is not particularly helpful in calculating the size of urban populations, as the growth of taxable wealth does not necessarily correlate directly with growing population, or vice versa. Even the most pessimistic accounts of fifteenth-century population history however allow for an upturn in population from about the 1480s onwards, and many towns (although not all) had recovered to some extent, although in most cases not yet to their pre-plague levels: see Russell, *British Mediaeval Population*, pp. 282–306; and comments in *Crisis and Order*, pp. 8–10.

22. The population of Newcastle upon Tyne is estimated conjecturally at about 4000 inhabitants in the 1520s, rising to perhaps 5000 in 1549. This latter figure is calculated on the basis of a local muster list in that year, which recorded 1097 adult males (including servants) in the city who were capable of bearing arms; multiplied by 4, it gives a population of 4388 (the household multiplier is not relevant as the list is not confined to heads of households); and allowing for the old and sick and other non-combatants, it suggests a total of about 5000 inhabitants: see R. Welford, *History of Newcastle and Gateshead* (London, 1884–7), II, 173–4; and *Archaeologia Aeliana* O. S.4, pp. 124–35. Newcastle's population had increased to about 11 000–12 000 by the 1660s, and to about 16 000 by 1700: R. Howell, *Newcastle upon Tyne and the Puritan Revolution* (Oxford, 1967), pp 8–9; Chalklin, *Provincial Towns*, pp. 14–15. J. U. Nef, *The Rise of the British Coal Industry* (London, 1932), I, p. 107, also conjectured that Newcastle's population had trebled or quadrupled during the sixteenth and seventeenth centuries but did not cite any figures.

23. Birmingham grew about fivefold from about 1500 inhabitants in the mid-sixteenth century to about 7000 or 8000 by 1700; unfortunately very little is known of its early sixteenth-century history but it is not thought to have been developing very rapidly before the seventeenth century: see W. H. B. Court, *The Rise of the*

however, it seems probable that very few provincial towns experienced long-term rates of growth that were significantly higher than that of the population of the country as a whole. And this comment could be made even more strongly with reference to the century and a half before 1650. This is a key point to note, as evidence for urban growth looks more impressive out of context than it does when set against the figures for population growth in the country as a whole.

Thus some provincial towns in England and Wales were expanding, but much less rapidly than the growth of London. In 1700 as in 1500 the great majority of the country's population outside the capital city resided in very small village communities – Gregory King estimated in the 1690s that there were over 20 000 such villages containing on average about 180 inhabitants apiece[24] – serviced by a network of relatively small market towns that acted chiefly as local centres of commerce and distribution. There were probably some 810 market towns of this kind in early Tudor England and Wales[25] and two centuries later their numbers had hardly changed at all – again according to estimates made by the invaluable Gregory King in the 1690s there were some 794 places (excluding the capital city)

Midland Industries, 1600–1838 (Oxford, 1938), pp. 43–4, 47. The population figure sometimes cited for Birmingham in 1700 of 15 600 inhabitants is far too high, and not based on reliable evidence: see comments in Chalklin, *Provincial Towns*, p. 22, and Corfield, 'A Provincial Capital', p. 300.

Liverpool's population also rose about fivefold; its population was estimated at about 1000 inhabitants or less in the early sixteenth century (calculations based on a household listing in 1565 suggest a population of about 700, but the accuracy of the source is open to question). It rose subsequently to an estimated 5145 inhabitants at the end of the seventeenth century and to an estimated 8168 by 1710 (figures calculated on the bàsis of baptismal data, by Dr Enfield in 1773): see J. A. Picton, *Memorials of Liverpool, Historical and Topographical* (London, 1875), I, pp. 47, 55, 147, 159; T. Baines, *History of the Commerce and Town of Liverpool* (London, 1852), p. 492; and W. Enfield, *An Essay towards the History of Liverpool* (Warrington, 1773), pp. 19, 28.

Manchester's population is even more elusive than that of Liverpool or Birmingham: it probably contained about 1500–2000 inhabitants in the early sixteenth century, when Leland described it (in 1538) as 'the fairest, best buildid, quikest and most populos tounne of al Lancastreshire'; and it had probably expanded to about 6000 inhabitants by the 1660s and perhaps 8000–9000 by 1700: see E. Baines, *The History of the Country Palatine and Duchy of Lancaster* (London, 1889), II, p. 92; A. P. Wadsworth and J. de L. Mann, *The Cotton Trade and Industrial Manchester, 1600–1780* (Manchester, 1931), pp. 311–12, 509–11; and Chalklin, *Provincial Towns*, pp. 22, 36.

24. Glass, 'Two Papers on Gregory King', p. 178, Table 4: in calculation (a) King assumed that there were 20 333 'vills' in England and Wales, with an average of 45 houses apiece, at 3.993 inhabitants per house, and hence an average population of 180.

25. A. Everitt, 'The Marketing of Agricultural Produce', in *Agrarian History*, IV, p. 467.

that could be considered in contemporary eyes as 'towns', although some of these were very small in population terms.[26]

This raises the important question of what is meant by a town. In one sense the definition is simple: it refers to a 'relatively large, dense, and permanent settlement of socially heterogeneous individuals', whose economic functions are prevailingly non-agricultural.[27] A town is larger than a village; and large towns are further distinguished by the appellation of city, although the adjectival form of both town and city is 'urban'.[28] The difficulties come in ascertaining the dividing lines between the village and the town. Ideally it would be desirable to use multiple indices to measure size, density, social composition and occupational structure. For ease of comparison, however, and also because of the absence of the detailed information required for more complex calculations, demographers usually take a simple numerical index.

In the case of Tudor and Stuart England therefore it is possible to distinguish among the variety of settlements that were described by contemporaries as 'towns' and argue that the smallest of these, although important as market centres for their own local hinterlands, were not fully-fledged urban centres as they lacked at least one of the attributes in the definitions given above, namely a relatively large size. Most of the small market centres, which served hinterlands within a radius of between three and six miles, had populations

---

26. Glass, 'Two Papers on Gregory King', p. 186. King's figures were based on the contemporary listing provided by John Adam's *Index Villaris* (1680), with some amendments.

27. The quotation is from the seminal article by Louis Wirth, 'Urbanism as a Way of Life', *American Journal of Sociology*, 44 (1938), also available in P. K. Hatt and A. J. Reiss (eds.), *Cities and Society. The Revised Reader in Urban Sociology* (New York, 1951; reprinted 1968), p. 50. The expanded definition given here also draws upon the very helpful discussion in E. Jones, *Towns and Cities* (Oxford, 1966), pp. 1–12. It is possible to adopt a simpler definition-that a town is a community that people recognize as a town – which has the merit of taking account of changing contemporary attitudes over time, but it is far too subjective to be useful for comparative purposes.

28. Jones, *Towns and Cities*, pp. 4–5. In the sixteenth and seventeenth centuries, contemporaries used the term 'town' very widely to refer to a great variety of settlements (and indeed in its origin the term referred to any nucleated settlement or cluster of dwellings). Blackstone in the eighteenth century noted that: 'The word town or vill is . . . now become a generical term, comprehending under it the several species of cities, boroughs and common towns': W. Blackstone, *Commentaries on the Laws of England* (1765), I, pp. 110–11. The term 'city' in the sixteenth and seventeenth centuries was used to refer to a town that was also the seat of a bishopric; it was only in the nineteenth century and subsequently that it came to be used to refer simply to large towns. A borough was a town that possessed a municipal charter and/or sent representatives to Parliament; the cathedral cities that were also boroughs were usually referred to by the senior title of city. See definitions in *OED* and E. A. Freeman, 'City and Borough', *MacMillan's Magazine*, LX (1889), pp. 29–37.

of less than 2000 inhabitants at the end of the seventeenth century; a further forty to fifty that were minor regional centres had populations of between 2000 and 5000; and only about thirty-one or thirty-two leading provincial centres had more than 5000 residents in 1700[29] – and even that population total of course is still a fairly small figure in absolute terms. In a sense therefore there is a need for another descriptive term to convey the qualities of these small settlements with fewer than 5000 inhabitants: it is undeniable that many of them had at least some of the attributes of a town – namely an agglomerated settlement and a non-agricultural function, let alone in many cases also a borough charter and the framework of municipal government – but equally it is difficult to accord them the title of being fully 'urban', since their size was so small.[30] There is little point in protracted argument over the precise 'cut-off' point, but it is helpful to examine the growth of towns of above a certain size. It is notable that among the many agglomerated settlements defined by contemporaries in the seventeenth century as towns, there was a growing number of larger urban centres with populations of 5000 or more, and it was the emergence and development of these provincial towns that constituted one of the most significant long-term changes during the course of the sixteenth and seventeenth centuries.

In the 1520s there were perhaps fifteen or twenty major regional centres. They were headed by the city of Norwich, with about 10 000 to 12 000 inhabitants, followed closely by Bristol with 9500–10 000 residents, Exeter and Salisbury with populations of about 8000, Coventry and York with about 7000 inhabitants, and Worcester with possibly 4000–5000. After•these came a cluster of medium-sized

29. Chalklin, *Provincial Towns*, pp. 4–17, esp. p. 5, n. 2. Our estimates differ only very slightly in the number of towns that had surpassed the total of 5000 inhabitants, my total of 31–32 being similar to Dr Chalklin's of 30–31.
30. No happy term for these 'micro-urban' settlements springs readily to mind. For a discussion of the various numerical indices adopted currently in different societies to define a town, see Jones, *Towns and Cities*, pp. 3–5. He concludes: 'Above 5000 people there is less doubt that we are dealing with something urban, above 10 000 hardly any doubt at all' (p. 5). The author of the most comprehensive survey yet undertaken of European towns in the early modern period suggested the slightly lower 'cut-off' point of 4000 inhabitants, although warning against the dangers of adopting a fixed numerical definition: R. Mols, *Introduction à la démographie historique des villes d' Europe du XIVe au XVIIIe siècle* (Louvain 1954–6), I, pp. xxi–xxvi, esp. p. xxii.
   In an economy with as yet relatively little occupational specialization, there was considerable overlap between the range of activities carried on in the large village and small town: see J. Patten, 'Village and Town: An Occupational Study', *Agric. Hist. Rev.*, 20 (1972), pp. 1–16. As might be expected, the larger the settlement, the greater array of services and functions carried out. He argues that the dividing line between the village and the small town (my 'micro-urban' settlements) was about 1000 inhabitants.

settlements with populations of about 3000 to 4000 inhabitants apiece: these included places such as Gloucester, Shrewsbury, Taunton, Northampton, Leeds and Wakefield. It is in fact arguable that some of these population estimates err on the high side and should be scaled down by about twenty per cent; nonetheless they represent accurately enough the comparative size and ranking of these leading provincial towns.[31] Other middle-rank centres at this time also included Newcastle upon Tyne, Chester, Ipswich, Yarmouth, Colchester, King's Lynn, Oxford and Cambridge. The figures are too uncertain and too incomplete to know precisely how many centres had passed the total of 5000 inhabitants; there were at least six or seven in this category, but probably not many more. It is apparent that the combined populations of the seven provincial centres known to have passed this figure probably equalled or even surpassed the population of London: in aggregate their populations came to between 53 500 and 57 000, or about two per cent of the total population of England and Wales, compared with London's estimated 50 000–60 000 inhabitants. But their collective economic impact was much more diffuse than that of the nucleated population in the capital city.

By the end of the seventeenth century, however, there had been a perceptible increase in the number of towns with populations of over 5000, and they now constituted a larger proportion of the country's population as a whole. Estimates are still open to a margin of error, but it seems likely that of the thirty-one or thirty-two leading provincial centres outside London with more than 5000 inhabitants in 1700, at least six had populations of more than 10 000. The list was again headed by Norwich, now with 30 000 inhabitants, again followed by Bristol, with about 20 000 (or perhaps slightly more). These were followed in turn by Newcastle with about 16 000 inhabitants, Exeter with 14 000, York with about 12 000 and Great

31. W. G. Hoskins, 'English Provincial Towns in the Early Sixteenth Century', *Trans. R. Hist. Soc.*, 5th ser., 6 (1956), pp. 5–6. These estimates, which have been widely quoted, are based on calculations from surviving material in subsidy assessments, chantry certificates and other available sources. While the calculations reflect accurately enough the comparative size of these different provincial centres, it may be that the absolute size suggested is too high, as the estimates are based on a household multiplier of 6 whereas later research would suggest a lower multiplier of 4.5–4.75. See P. Laslett, 'Size and Structure of the Household in England over Three Centuries', *Population Studies*, 23 (1969), pp. 199–223, and J. T. Krause, 'The Mediaeval Household: large or small?', *Econ. Hist. Rev.*, 2nd ser., 9 (1956–7), pp. 420–32.

Incidentally, the practice followed by some historians of making an additional increase for servants and apprentices is not necessary, as these are included in the average household figure.

Yarmouth with a little over 10 000 inhabitants.[32] A crop of other large towns by the standards of the day with populations of between 8000 and 9000 also pressed on their heels, including centres such as Birmingham, Chester, Colchester, Ipswich, Manchester, Plymouth and Worcester.[33] And there were many others with populations of more than 5000: inland towns such as Bury St Edmunds, Cambridge, Canterbury, Coventry, Gloucester, Leeds, Leicester, Nottingham, Oxford, Salisbury, Shrewsbury and Tiverton; coastal towns such as Chatham, Hull, King's Lynn, Liverpool, Portsmouth and Sunderland.[34] Between them, the provincial urban centres of 5000 inhabitants or more now constituted about five per cent of the country's population, as compared with two per cent in the 1520s.[35]

Here then there are two slightly contradictory points to make. Firstly it is clear that the numerical importance of these leading provincial centres vis-à-vis London had declined. Not only did none of the provincial towns individually measure up to London (nineteen times the size of Norwich) but their aggregate population was much smaller than that of the capital city. But at the same time, it is also apparent that the provincial urban population was both expanding and diversifying in the long term. Hence the total 'urban' population living in centres of 5000 inhabitants or more by 1700 amounted to sixteen per cent of the population of England and Wales, of which just over two thirds lived in the capital city and one third in the leading provincial towns.

Can any discernible pattern be seen in the varying fortunes of the provincial towns in these years? One of the most interesting ways of looking at the pattern of changes in the urban hierarchy would be by a regional analysis, as it is plain that these developments were linked with the changing balance of economic and demographic forces between different regions, the growing economic importance of

32. Chalklin, *Provincial Towns*, pp. 13–16, and sources cited there. He also includes in the over 10 000 category the borough of Colchester, which in my view had not quite reached this total.
33. Chalklin, *Provincial Towns*, pp. 9–12, 18, and sources cited there.
34. All these centres can be confidently stated to have passed the figure of 5000 inhabitants, although precise totals are not available in all cases: my estimates, based on local source material, and calculations from figures presented in Chalklin, *Provincial Towns*, pp. 4–25, and Law, 'Some Notes on the Urban Population', pp. 22–6.
35. My calculation. The proportion of those living in all settlements with 2000 inhabitants or more was about 22–23 per cent, according to Dr Chalklin's estimates: see Chalklin, *Provincial Towns*, pp. 5, 16.
    Gregory King's well-known estimate that about 25 per cent of the population lived in towns therefore includes residents of a number of settlements with fewer than 2000 inhabitants: for his calculations, see Glass, 'Two Papers on Gregory King', p. 174.

the Midlands and the north of England being one of the most obvious of these. As yet however the material for a fully-fledged regional study of the English economy in the sixteenth and seventeenth centuries is not available, although some important work has been done by Dr Thirsk and her colleagues on the structure of agricultural regions.

Another way of looking at the process of urban change is by comparing the growth rates of individual towns against the general trend of population growth in the country as a whole. In this way, it is possible to pick out those towns whose growth more or less matched that of the total population, and also to identify those towns which exhibited unusual characteristics – either of unusually rapid growth or indeed of decline.

It seems in fact that many of the provincial towns, particularly the medium-sized inland market centres, were very much keeping pace with the growth of population in the country as a whole: a doubling of their population from (say) 2500 to 5000 people between the 1520s and 1700, or from 3000 to 6000. Nor had their economic functions changed very significantly during these years. They carried out a multiplicity of services within a regional hinterland, which might in turn contain within it several smaller market centres. Places which fell into the category of these medium-rank centres, reaching populations of 5000 or near that by 1700, included Bury St Edmunds, Gloucester, Hereford, Lancaster, Leicester, Northampton and Reading. Much of their importance stemmed from the fact that they were inland commercial centres; they contained a number of craft industries; they were often but not invariably the county towns, and centres for local political and administrative activity; and they were service centres and focuses for the social life of their agricultural hinterlands. Some even had miniature winter 'seasons' for the entertainment of local landed gentry who could not get to London, and many of them provided venues for balls, race meetings and other social gatherings in the summer months.

In many ways the gradual and unexceptional development of these centres reflects many elements of continuity in English economic life during these centuries. This is not to argue that they were all equally prosperous, or devoid of economic problems. A large proportion of the urban population were very poor, and the towns, like the countryside, suffered from problems of chronic under-employment, particularly in the sixteenth and early seventeenth centuries when employment opportunities in the economy as a whole were expanding less rapidly than was the total population.[36]

36. See D. C. Coleman, ' Labour in the English Economy of the Seventeenth Century', *Econ. Hist. Rev.*, 2nd ser., 8 (1956), pp. 280–95, and F. J. Fisher, 'Tawney's Century', in F. J. Fisher (ed.), *Essays on the Economic History*

But these towns were not falling into decline; nor were they expanding out of all recognition. An example of a modestly expanding local centre in this category was the Suffolk town of Bury St Edmunds, which was not an industrial centre of any importance, nor a county town, but which flourished as a commercial and social centre for the prospering agricultural region of west Suffolk. Bury in the early eighteenth century (when its population was about 5500 or 6000) was described by Defoe in the following terms: 'It is crouded with nobility and gentry, and all sorts of the most agreeable company; and as the company invites, so there is the appearance of pleasure upon the very situation; and they that live at Bury, are supposed to live there for the sake of it.'[37]

Yet the picture is not one of uniform or continuous growth. There were also a number of provincial centres that grew much less rapidly than the population as a whole, experiencing a relative eclipse or (more rarely) an outright decline in population. In fact examples of towns of any significant size that faced protracted loss of population are very rare in this period. Coventry's economic and demographic problems in the 1520s and 1530s are the best-documented instance of such a crisis, precipitated by problems in its staple textile industry. But even here Coventry had made good its losses in terms of population by the early years of Elizabeth's reign. A number of other provincial towns, such as York, Bristol, Norwich and Lincoln, also reported economic and financial difficulties in the mid-sixteenth century, and complained at empty and 'decayed' habitations. Indeed there seems a good case for regarding the years from about 1520 to 1560 as ones of some economic dislocation in a number of provincial towns.[38] But in the long term, these problems did not prove insuperable; or rather, did not prove insuperable in all cases, as Norwich, Bristol and York were all thriving in the later sixteenth century, even though Coventry and Lincoln were much less success-

of Tudor and Stuart England in Honour of R. H. Tawney (Cambridge, 1961), pp. 1–14.

37. D. Defoe, *A Tour through the Whole Island of Great Britain* (Everyman Ed., London 1962), I, p. 51. See also Chalklin, *Provincial Towns*, p. 9.

38. Ramsey, *Tudor Economic Problems*, pp. 102–3. There were a number of statutes enacted in the mid-sixteenth century in response to complaints about 'decayed town'. An Act of 27 Henry VIII cap. 1 (1526), for example, named Nottingham, Shrewsbury, Ludlow, Bridgnorth, Queenboro', Northampton and Gloucester as in need of repairs to the urban fabric; and an Act of 35 Henry VIII cap. 4 (1544) listed a number of small corporate towns (including Liverpool) that were described as 'fallen downe decayed and at this time unreedified,' ordering owners of dilapidated properties to refurbish them. In more general terms, an Act of 1 and 2 Philip and Mary cap. 7 (1554), enacted against the background of acute commercial depression in the mid-1550s, set out to give protection to retail traders in all the 'auncient Cities Boroughes Townes Corporate and Market Townes' against the allegedly unfair competition of tradesmen from outside the city.

ful. It is also noticeable that, despite the fact that this was a period when towns were subject to sudden and devastating attacks of plague, there were very few cases of prolonged population decline from this cause, as the urban populations were promptly replenished within only a few years by heightened migration from the countryside and increased urban birth rates.[39] Hence cases of outright decline (as opposed to relative eclipse) are very difficult to find in these years: indeed historically the lost city is about as rare as the lost villages are numerous.

On the other hand, a number of Tudor and Stuart towns did undergo a relative eclipse. Some were stranded by changes in their geographical environment, while others were marooned by shifting patterns of commercial and industrial life – changes as difficult to stem in their way as the more visible hazards of silt and sand. The most prominent example of geographical blight during these years was the silting up of the mouth of the river Dee and the eclipse of Chester as a major port for overseas trade in the later seventeenth century. Chester, with a population of about 9000 by 1700, remained a sizeable commercial centre for coastal traffic, and its population increased further in the early eighteenth century to about 13 000 people in 1750, but it was overhauled by Liverpool (5000 inhabitants in 1700, 22 000 in 1750) as the premier port in the region, dealing in both coastal shipping and in overseas trade with Ireland and the Atlantic colonies.[40] Examples of economic eclipse include the

These instances of legislation provide some grounds for claiming that some urban centres were facing economic problems in certain periods, but do not in themselves provide evidence for general urban decay. They show indeed that the towns were prompt to defend their positions against interlopers in times of economic stringency, and also that they could obtain government and Parliamentary support for their interests. How effectively any of this legislation was enforced is another matter: legislative fiat was usually inferior to economic forces in salvaging the fortunes of towns in this period.

39. To take two examples, the sixteenth- and seventeenth-century growth of both Norwich and Newcastle upon Tyne was punctuated by some devastating attacks of the plague, which nonetheless failed to curb their long-term growth. Norwich had epidemics in 1579–80 (when it was said to have lost as many as 5000 inhabitants), 1588, 1591, 1603, 1625, 1636, 1646, and 1665–6 (almost 3000 plague deaths): see P. Browne, *The History of Norwich* (Norwich, 1814), pp. 41–2, 44–5, 48, 51. And Newcastle upon Tyne had outbreaks of the disease in 1544, 1589, 1625, 1636 (when over 5000 people were said to have died in a 'tremendous visitation') and 1645: J. Brand, *The History and Antiquities of the Town and County of Newcastle upon Tyne* (London, 1789), II, pp. 438, 447, 453, 456, 470.

The economic problems of some late seventeenth-century towns (such as Ipswich) are sometimes attributed to their failure to recover from the impact of the 1665–6 plague epidemic, but it seems clear that this was rather the occasion than the cause of their slackening population growth.

40. For Chester, see Chalklin, *Provincial Towns*, pp. 9, 19; and T. S. Willan, *The English Coasting Trade, 1600–1760* (Manchester, 1938), pp. 180–1.

overshadowing of the ports of Southampton in the early sixteenth century and Ipswich in the later seventeenth century. In both cases contemporaries were wont to blame the successful commercial rivalry of London for the slackening in the growth of these two centres. Defoe claimed in a moment of exaggeration that London 'sucks the vitals of trade in this island to itself'. But an explanation based on proximity to London alone is clearly insufficient, as it does not explain the chronology of change: Ipswich for example had been flourishing in the later sixteenth and early seventeenth centuries at the same time as London's headlong expansion as a commercial centre; why should the challenge of London suddenly afflict it in the later decades of the seventeenth century?

In fact, it seems probable that the growth of London was the proximate rather than the root cause of the eclipse of both Ipswich and Southampton, and that the decline of the textile industries in their respective hinterlands, thus affecting the quantity of goods for export, was a much more significant factor.[41] It should be stressed too that the decline of both these centres was only a relative one. Neither disappeared or experienced a protracted loss of population. Ipswich in the eighteenth century, with a population of about 8000 inhabitants, was a centre for coastal trade and some fishing. And the much smaller Southampton, with a population of only 3000, enjoyed a modest vogue as a seaside resort in the eighteenth century: 'here are most of the conveniences and *agremens* of the town, without that perpetual thunder and clouds of smoke which blind and deafen those who have not quite lost their senses', claimed a *Southampton Guide* in 1775. Some of the smaller inland towns too were experiencing a relative eclipse or failure to expand during these years. Winchester, with a population of about 4000 in the 1520s, perhaps 3100 in 1604 and 4000 in 1700, was a long-established centre struggling to keep its ground. And Lincoln, with a population of some 2000 in 1500, increased only modestly to 2460 in 1700.[42] Their slowness to expand reflected in both cases the fact that their respective agricultural hinterlands were relatively sparsely populated and thus did not generate a great amount of business, and neither had any

41. Southampton's eclipse is often attributed to the loss of the Anglo-Italian trade, which migrated to London as improved navigation aids in the early sixteenth century made access to the port of London easier for the big ocean-going galleys from the Mediterranean: Ruddock, *Italian Merchants*, pp. 262–6. But it was also linked with changes in the industrial fortunes and organization of the Salisbury textiles industry, for which Southampton had traditionally acted as distribution centre.

For Ipswich and the economic decline of the Suffolk broadcloths industry, for which Ipswich had previously been a major port of export, see Defoe, *Tour*, I, p. 43; and Reed, 'Seventeenth Century Ipswich,' pp. 24–86.

42. See T. Atkinson, *Elizabethan Winchester* (London, 1963), pp. 29–33, 250–1; and J. W. F. Hill, *Tudor and Stuart Lincoln* (Cambridge, 1956), pp. 22–3, 88–9, 210.

specialized economic function in addition to their market activities that might promote growth.

Finally, there were the provincial towns that were either exceptionally large or fast-growing in the sixteenth and seventeenth centuries. Urban expansion that was more rapid than the overall population growth was usually associated with some specialized function or trade which enabled the town to attract and sustain an increasing population, although all of these specialized centres also combined a market function with their other roles. In this period the major specializations were textiles, trade (especially overseas trade) and shipping. It should however be stressed that specialization did not in itself guarantee permanent or continuous growth, as changing economic circumstances could bypass a large town, which might then find its economic problems worsened by its earlier dependence upon one industry or trade. Hence the size and rank order of these leading provincial centres was liable to vary over time, their changing fortunes closely reflecting the fluctuations in English trade and industry in these years.

In the century and a half before 1650, expansion could be seen in a number of special categories of towns. One such group were the larger industrial towns, such as Norwich, Colchester, Worcester and Exeter, and some smaller but expanding centres such as Leeds or Halifax. It is true that much industry was carried out in the countryside in Tudor and Stuart times, in a search for lower production costs.[43] But most textile manufacturing areas generated and sustained within their ranks one or more larger urban centre, which carried out some of the production processes and also acted as the nodal point for the finishing and distribution stages. Certainly this was the case with Norwich as the organizational centre for the production of the 'new draperies'; with Exeter as focal point for the Devonshire serge-manufactures; and Worcester as one of the centres for the West Country broadcloth industry. On the whole, the more important the finishing processes were to the completed article, the larger the size of the organizing urban centre, as the advantages of relative geographical concentration in those circumstances began to outweigh those of dispersal. Another important urban specialization was in coastal and overseas trade. Any transshipment stage in a transportation network tends to generate a certain concentration of population; and in this period expanding trade laid the basis for the growth of a number of provincial ports. These included Newcastle upon Tyne, the purveyor of seacoals for London, and undoubtedly the fastest growing provincial town in the years between 1500 and 1650, Chester and Bristol as centres of Anglo-Irish trade, Yarmouth

43. See Darby, *New Historical Geography*, p. 297; and on the location of industries, see Clarkson, *The Pre-Industrial Economy*, pp. 48–97.

as the port of Norwich and home of the herring fishing industry, and Ipswich as the port of outlet for the Suffolk broadcloth industry.[44] Yet a third category to expand briskly were the dockyard and naval centres, including in this period most notably Plymouth and to a lesser extent Portsmouth and Chatham. These dockyard towns in particular were very closely tied to their one specialized function, their expansion being associated with periods of naval warfare, and their social characteristics resembling those of nineteenth-century single-industry towns.[45]

There was also one example of provincial urban expansion based upon an administrative and political function: the growth of the city of York, which was the seat of the Council of the North until its abolition in 1641. At the height of the political importance of pacifying the north in Elizabeth's reign, York increased in population quite rapidly from about 8000 inhabitants to nearer 12 000 by the 1630s. This was a sizeable enough growth over a relatively short period, especially in the light of the fact that York had ceased by this time to be a centre for the Yorkshire textiles industry. In the long term, however, York did not long sustain such a rapid rate of growth, as the political problems of the north became less acute and the administrative business generated in York flagged. It remained a very important trading centre in its economic region, but this function alone did not promote much population growth. Thus between the 1520s and 1700 as a whole York's expansion (from about 7000 to 12 000) was not impressive, being less than that of the country's population as a whole.[46]

In all, there had certainly been some significant provincial urban expansion in the century and a half before 1650, even though the evidence does not suggest an exceptionally rapid surge of growth. Unfortunately it is extremely difficult to detect the point at which provincial urban growth began to take off. It is unlikely that the populations of the leading provincial towns in aggregate had exceeded three per cent of the country's population by 1650, but at some stage in the mid-seventeenth century the pattern began to change and the pace of provincial urban growth accelerated.

Thus despite the fact that the overall rate of population growth had slackened by the later seventeenth century, these decades were a period of vigorous urban growth among a number of provincial

44. Willian, *Coasting Trade*, pp. 111–88, and G. D. Ramsay, *English Overseas Trade in the Centuries of Emergence* (London, 1957), esp. pp. 6–10, 132–60.
45. Darby, *New Historical Geography*, pp. 297–8; *Crisis and Order*, p. 31. See also D. C. Coleman, 'The Economy of Kent under the later Stuarts' (unpublished Ph. D. thesis, University of London 1951), pp. 245–71.
46. *V. C. H., Yorkshire*, pp. 162, 166–70; and D. M. Palliser, 'York under the Tudors; The Trading Life of the Northern Capital,' in A. Everitt (ed.), *Perspectives in English Urban History* (London, 1973), pp. 39–59.

towns, including not only some of the long-established urban centres but also some other 'new' towns. From about the 1670s onwards (or perhaps earlier) something of the configuration of modern urban England began to emerge at least in outline. The range of urban specializations also began to become more broadly based, as the domestic economy began to diversify its production. Expanding industrial centres included not only textile towns such as Manchester, Leeds, Nottingham and Derby, but also metal-working towns such as Birmingham and Sheffield. There were also a number of fast-growing ports such as Liverpool, Hull, Bristol and Newcastle; and a number of the dockyard towns including Portsmouth, Plymouth and Chatham experienced further expansion, especially in the war years under William III and Anne. There were also some early signs of the specialized spa-towns: Bath began to gain its reputation as a resort and social centre in these years, although it was still quite small, with not more than 3000 inhabitants in 1700.[47]

Gradually, a more complex and polycentric urban society was emerging, with a concomitant growth in the number of large towns and a broadening range of economic specializations. Not all was simply preparation for later industrial society, however; two of the leading provincial centres in the later seventeenth century, the textile towns of Norwich and Exeter, which were in many ways at the height of their relative economic importance at this time, were subsequently to be eclipsed in the eighteenth century. Exeter ran into economic problems in the 1720s, aided partly by competition from the Norwich textiles industry, and Norwich in turn lost its position as the largest provincial town when it was overtaken by Bristol in the 1730s or 1740s.[48] And it was not only the older towns that were liable to reversals of fortune. The Cumberland town of Whitehaven sprang up overnight (with magnate patronage) in the later seventeenth century but also became comparatively economically isolated in the later years of the following century, although it remained a minor regional capital.[49] Overall, however, there had begun in the

47. An excellent survey of urban growth in the later seventeenth century is contained in Chalklin, *Provincial Towns*, pp. 17–25.
48. For the growth of Norwich, see Corfield, 'A Provincial Capital,' pp. 263–310; there is some debate over the timing of the eventual disappearance of the Norwich worsted weaving industry in the nineteenth century, but the relative overhauling of Norwich by other more rapidly-growing towns had commenced by the mid-eighteenth century.

    For late seventeenth-century Exeter, see Chalklin, *Provincial Towns*, pp. 14, 20; and W.G. Hoskins, *Industry, Trade and People in Exeter, 1688–1800* (Manchester, 1935), pp. 11–110. Exeter's industrial importance languished from the 1720s onwards but it remained an important regional trading, financial and social centre.
49. Whitehaven was promoted in the later seventeenth century by the Cumberland landowner Sir John Lowther, to export coal mined on his estates. It expanded

later seventeenth century the expansion of the provincial 'urban' population (resident in towns of 5000 inhabitants or more) that was to be such a feature of the eighteenth century. And some of the more rapidly growing provincial centres, whose growth rates in these years surpassed that of London, had also begun the long process of eating into the massive lead in population terms established by the capital city during the sixteenth and early seventeenth centuries.

A survey of long-term trends is bound to miss some of the short-term complexities of urban development. But some general conclusions can perhaps be drawn. The major point that emerges is that the experience of different towns was very varied. There were differences over time, differences between regions within the national economy, and differences between individual towns. It is fruitless to look for one urban experience – particularly so if it is deemed to refer to the whole range of nucleated settlements from a small market centre of (say) 1500 inhabitants via a provincial capital of 10 000 people through to the capital city with over half a million residents in 1700.

A second conclusion therefore is that it is useful to classify the settlements, known as towns by contemporaries in Tudor and Stuart times, by size. Adopting a definition of the 'urban' population as those living in settlements of 5000 inhabitants or more, it can be seen that there were some significant changes during these years. The total 'urban' population expanded between the 1520s and 1700 – chiefly as the result of the dramatic growth of London, but in the later seventeenth century augmented by an appreciable, if selective, growth of the provincial urban population. By 1700 about sixteen per cent of the population were urban residents, making England and Wales one of the more highly urbanized areas in the whole of Europe at this date.[50]

Within the hierarchy of the provincial towns, there were also fluctuations in the fortunes of the individual centres, and consequently changes in their respective rank order. Migrants from

from about 2000 inhabitants in the 1690s to over 9000 in the 1760s, when it was at the 'height of its prosperity,' but ceased to grow at the same pace thereafter: Chalklin, *Provincial Towns*, p. 19.

50. Comparative statistics of urbanization are difficult to obtain. In the later medieval period, the most densely urbanized areas of Europe were the industrial-commercial complexes of Northern Italy and the Low Countries: see J. C. Russell, *Medieval Regions and their Cities* (Newton Abbot, 1972), pp. 27, 39–51, 62–76, 112–21. By 1700, the most highly urbanized area of Europe was that of the United Provinces, led by the province of Holland; but England and Wales were also coming to the fore: Rich and Wilson, *Cambridge Economic History*, pp. 45–7, 50–3, 81–3. See also for statistics on the Dutch provinces of Holland, Friesland and Groningen, J. De Vries, *The Dutch Rural Economy in the Golden Age, 1500–1700* (London, 1974), pp. 81–7, 103, 107.

the countryside moved into some towns rather than others, and in different numbers at different times, in response to changing employment opportunities. This is not to argue that all urban residents, whether migrant or native-born, found themselves in full employment at all times. Clearly such was not the case, and many towns were seriously troubled by the extent of urban underemployment and mendicancy. The Norwich orders for the poor in 1571 referred disapprovingly to the great number of 'Persons whoe for the most parte went dayely abroad from dore to dore, counterfeattinge a kinde of worke but indeede dyd verie lyttle or none at all'.[51] But in the long term, rates of expansion were correlated with economic viability.

Hence the growth of a larger and more diversified urban population in the later seventeenth century was a sign of economic growth in the economy as a whole. Urban development depended upon an increasingly efficient and productive agricultural system; it was linked with the growth of inland trade and the great expansion of England's overseas trade in the later seventeenth century; and it also reflected the strengthening of the country's manufacturing base. It is important to insist on this latter point, since so much attention has been devoted to the more readily quantifiable evidence for expanding commercial life. 'Thus People make Trade, Trade builds Towns and Cities, and Produces every Thing that is good and great in a Nation,' exclaimed Defoe in dithyrambic vein in 1728. But his own analysis was careful to note that the country's 'populous towns' included a number of inland manufacturing and commercial centres as well as the big seaports.[52]

In this context, the growth of London cannot be regarded as the prototype of urban development in provincial England, since the urban experience was so diverse. Nor can it be accused of shedding general blight and decay over other towns. Some centres were possibly overshadowed by London's expansion; some were positively stimulated, such as the growth of Newcastle upon Tyne; and many others expanded or declined due to factors that were not directly linked to London at all. The most vocal critics of London's dominance were the provincial outports, envious of the capital's overseas trade and hostile to the powers of the London-dominated trading companies. Complaints were however usually most loudly voiced in periods of commercial depression, such as the 1550s, 1586–

---

51. Tawney and Power, *Tudor Economic Documents*, II, pp. 316–17. See also discussion in J. F. Pound, *Poverty and Vagrancy in Tudor England* (1971), pp. 25–36.
52. D. Defoe, *A Plan of the English Commerce* (1728), pp. 27, 84–5. He also added: 'Trade, like Religion, is what everybody talks of, but few understand' (p. 1).

7, and the early 1620s.[53] And it simply was not the case in the long term that all the outports (or even a majority of them) were experiencing economic difficulties through the growth of London. Exeter, Bristol, Newcastle, Chester and Yarmouth, for example, were all independent trading centres, and were all reasonably flourishing during these years. And some of the smaller ports, like King's Lynn, that complained at loss of their overseas trade, were at the same time developing a brisk coastal trade in agricultural produce to feed the voracious appetites of the London consumer.

Thus it seems difficult to argue that London's growth was harmful to other towns, or even to other ports, in the long term. Many of the accusations thrown at it were exaggerated or misdirected – mistaking the symptoms of change for the cause. If at all, there was probably most case for arguing that the expansion of London was in itself based on unhealthy foundations at the end of the sixteenth century. At this time the population of London was expanding fairly rapidly (it had increased fourfold since the 1520s); it contained many casually and semi-employed labourers, many of them engaged in tertiary sector activities, and some scarcely absorbed into a regular work discipline;[54] the city's earlier reliance upon the important trading axis with Antwerp, which had been sharply disrupted by economic

53. For example, Hull complained at London merchants taking over their trades in the mid-1550s; and Bristol argued the same in 1619. A memorandum written in 1598 also claimed that outports adversely affected by London included eight provincial ports, Newcastle, Hull, Boston, Lynn, Southampton, Poole, Weymouth and Chester; see Ramsay, *English Overseas Trade*, pp. 9, 132–7; Stephens, 'The Cloth Exports', pp. 241–3; and Clark and Slack, *Crisis and Order*, pp. 12–13.

54. Surprisingly little work has been done as yet on the occupational structure of Tudor and Stuart London. However, in London at this time there were undoubtedly a large number of casually and semi-employed workers characteristic of a very large city. But most contemporary estimates of the numbers of the out-and-out vagrant population were greatly exaggerated: see F. Aydelotte, *Elizabethan Rogues and Vagabonds* (Oxford, 1913), p. 31. The number of those not in regular employment, however, may have been substantial. In 1602, it was claimed that there were in the capital city as many as 30 000 'idle persons and masterless men': C. Hill, *Reformation to Industrial Revolution. A Social and Economic History of Britain, 1530–1780* (London, 1967), p. 31. This total is almost certainly exaggerated and the description is vague: those described as 'masterless men' presumably included a number of day labourers and others casually employed, who could not in fact be simply equated with the 'idle' rogues and vagabonds. But if the figure in the estimate is scaled down by half to a total of 15 000 men, and taken to refer simply to those not in regular employment, it still refers to approximately 30 per cent of the adult male population in a city of 200 000 inhabitants. These estimates, like the data on which they are based, are purely speculative; they illustrate only the difficulty presented to contemporaries and also to historians in establishing how the multitudinous population of early seventeenth-century London made a living.

and political crises on the continent in the preceding decades, had not been replaced with satisfactory alternative markets; and in the mid-1590s there was a run of bad harvests which forced the city to rely upon imported grain, thus incidentally worsening the country's balance of payments position. It is not surprising therefore that it was in this decade that Parliamentary support was forthcoming for attempts to regulate and curb the expansion of the capital by statute. But the threatened economic and social crisis in London did not ensue, nor did its growth halt, either then or in the early 1620s, another period of commercial crisis that produced severe economic depression in the city. The urban economies of expanding boom towns often have a greater resilience than the horrified observers of their 'insensate' growth allow.

Thus the sixteenth and seventeenth centuries were a period of some urban growth, seen initially and most spectacularly in the growth of London, and subsequently, as the economy became stronger and more diversified, in a number of provincial urban centres. Parallels with the accelerating urban growth in the present-day Third World are thought-provoking but not exact, as Tudor and Stuart England was not experiencing the same explosion of population induced by modern medical technology. The significance of urban growth depends upon its context. It was a sign of increased economic strength that there had been a perceptible growth in the size of the urban population in the sixteenth and seventeenth centuries, despite the fact that levels of urban mortality were still shockingly high. In 1700 a greater number of English men and women than ever before were pursuing the crock of gold at the end of the urban rainbow.

Editorial suggestions for further reading

C. G. A. Clay, *Economic Expansion and Social Change* (2 vols, Cambridge, 1984), vol I, pp. 165–213.

A. Dyer and C. Phythian-Adams, 'Growth and decay in English towns 1500–1700', *Urban History Yearbook* (1979), pp. 60–76.

E. A. Wrigley, 'Urban growth and agricultural change', *Journal of Interdisciplinary History*, 15 (1985), pp. 683–728.

Chapter 3

ENGLISH PRE-INDUSTRIAL
URBAN ECONOMIES

Nigel Goose

[from the *Urban History Yearbook* (Leicester, 1982)]

This brief discussion criticizes, on both evidential and theoretical grounds, the characterization of pre-industrial urban economies as 'unspecialized'. Although certain basic services were common to all towns, the key features of a particular town's economy were often quite specific, so that the town's overall fortunes followed that of its specialism. In addition to the more skilled and capital-intensive aspects of manufacturing, such specialisms included distributive roles and, in some towns, a concentration on providing services to a wider market than the town and its immediate hinterland. The article seeks to redress an imbalance caused by a rather caricatured contrast of Tudor and Stuart towns with their industrial successors; its own emphasis on key economic functions must be balanced by awareness of the common stock of occupations that shaped the social history of all towns. Recent work suggests that the standard sources, rather than concealing workers in manufacturing, may underestimate what Goose calls the 'support sector', especially women's contribution to this.

In an attempt to define how pre-industrial towns are differentiated from their counterparts in industrial societies, some (though not all) historians have emphasized the unspecialized nature of their economies. Of Elizabethan Leicester, Hoskins wrote 'The special interest of Leicester to the economic and social historian is that it had no industry worth speaking of. Here was a community of some three thousand people, the largest and wealthiest town between the Trent and the Thames, which had no obvious means of livelihood ... Towns which had no marked industrial character (such as Leicester) greatly outnumbered those which had (such as Coventry).'[1] Recently this argument has been developed by Patten,

1. W. G. Hoskins, *Provincial England* (1965), 88.

63

who writes 'far from having "no obvious means of livelihood" at the time, Leicester had an urban superstructure as typical of Stuart and Restoration towns as it was of Elizabethan towns. The activities of building, brewing, provisioning, tailoring, weaving and the like in pre-industrial Leicester supported the basic economy of every pre-industrial town. Specialities in the manufactures of the day – usually textiles, iron and leather goods – were invariable additions rather than the basis of their economies . . . To look at the pre-industrial town is thus to look at an unspecialized economy . . . In dealing with the non-specialized urban economy we are dealing with the majority of English pre-industrial towns.'[2] The case is forcefully put, but does it stand up to scrutiny?

There is one aspect of this argument to which no exception can be taken. It has become commonplace to suppose that a substantial proportion of all urban populations were engaged in the provision of what might be described as 'the basic necessities of life'. On the basis of his analysis of the occupational structure of Coventry, Northampton and Leicester in the early sixteenth century, Hoskins concluded that 'in any English provincial town with the rudiments of an urban character, some 35 to 40 per cent of the population were employed in three fundamental groups of trades' – that is, food and drink, clothing and building.[3] From his analysis of Norwich trades in 1525 Pound found that just over 30 per cent of the freeman class were engaged in these same occupations.[4] More recently Palliser, relying heavily upon figures compiled by Phythian-Adams, has argued that 'In all eleven towns [Bristol, Chester, Coventry, Exeter, Hull, Leicester, Lynn, Northampton, Norwich, Worcester and York] the basic victualling, clothing, and building trades loomed large.'[5] My own research on Colchester and Reading, based upon will evidence, suggests that Hoskins' figure might be a little too high for some towns; but still, at various periods during the sixteenth and seventeenth centuries, between 23 and 33 per cent of the occupational samples for these two towns were employed in these fundamental occupations.

The 'basic necessities of life' was bound to involve a relatively large percentage of urban populations in a society lacking the advantages of modern mass production. Not only did urban populations have to feed, clothe and house themselves, but they also provided a proportion of goods and services required by their hinterlands.[6]

2. J. Patten, *English Towns 1500–1700* (1978), 148, 163, 165.
3. Hoskins, op. cit. 80.
4. J. Pound, 'The social and trade structure of Norwich 1525–1575' in P. Clark (ed.) *The Early Modern Town* (1976), 135.
5. D. Palliser, *Tudor York* (1979), 155.
6. Ibid. C. Phythian-Adams, in *The Fabric of the Traditional Community* (1977), 20–1.

Certain rather basic – and certainly not export-orientated – occupations appear time and again amongst the leading trades of provincial towns: bakers, butchers, brewers, shoemakers and tailors in particular.[7] However, it is also true that towns could differ markedly in this respect, to the extent that in some towns the proportion engaged in basic occupations could be double that in others. In sixteenth-century Cambridge, for instance, roughly 50 per cent were so employed,[8] as were 46 per cent in early sixteenth-century York.[9] This would seem to imply that there was something rather different about these towns, the figures reflecting a substantially different economic bias.

Given the fact that a substantial proportion of urban populations even in textile towns such as Colchester or Coventry were engaged in supplying the town itself or its region with food, clothing and shelter, one must not ignore the fundamental importance of towns above the level of the simple market town as centres of manufacture – albeit of a variety of different products. Of 13 towns for which occupational information is readily available for the sixteenth century (Bristol, Cambridge, Chester, Colchester, Coventry, Exeter, Hull, Leicester, Lynn, Norwich, Reading, Worcester and York), only four had less than 50 per cent of their occupied populations engaged in manufacturing.[10] One came close to the 50 per cent mark, whilst the figures for Lynn may well be distorted by the under-representation of worsted weaving in the sources.[11] In the other two, Cambridge and Hull, the figure stood at 35 and 37 per cent respectively. At this level in the urban hierarchy, therefore, as Phythian-Adams has emphasized,[12] manufacturing was of central importance in most urban economies, and of substantial importance in the rest. The fact that these towns performed other roles as well – processing and distributing agricultural produce, operating as marketing centres, and selling a range of more specialized services – should not blind us to this, for it was one of the distinguishing features of more developed urban economies.

This is not to argue that manufacturing in itself represents a specialism, although on the basis of these figures one might quibble

7. See Phythian-Adams, op. cit. 17. The same is also true of Cambridge, Colchester and Reading.
8. This figure comes from a sample of 653 individuals' occupations taken from wills for the period 1500–1619.
9. Phythian-Adams, op. cit. fig. 5, p. 16. The figure for Oxford was even higher still: see A. Crossley (ed.), *Victoria County History of Oxfordshire*, IV, 105.
10. Phythian-Adams, ibid. A. Dyer, *The City of Worcester in the Sixteenth Century* (1973), 84; the figures for Cambridge, Colchester and Reading will be presented in my forthcoming thesis, 'Economic and social aspects of provincial towns 1500–1700: Cambridge, Colchester and Reading'.
11. Phythian-Adams, op. cit. 15.
12. Ibid. 16–18.

with Hoskins' assertion that most towns had 'no marked industrial character'. But some historians seem to want to go further; hence Patten refers to 'the lack of *any* really specialized urban economies' (my italics).[13] Even in the case of towns possessing large textile industries, the high proportion of the population that was employed in *other* activities is often emphasized. Pound, for instance, writes that 'almost 70 per cent of the Norwich freemen were employed in trades other than textiles and even if the clothing trades are considered to be closely allied more than six people in every ten were engaged in different spheres.'[14] There are a number of points to be made here. Firstly, one must remember the biases involved in the records used to determine the occupational structure of pre-industrial towns, whether they be freeman's lists or wills, for they obscure both the poorer members of the community and part-time employment. Not all textile workers were poor men, though there is evidence to suggest that many were. Although writing about the industry in a rural area, Ramsay concluded that 'Most weavers lived from hand to mouth upon the meagre wages of the clothier', and quotes references to 'the thousands of poore people that doe only live upon clothing'.[15] A substantial percentage of those listed in the Norwich census of the poor of 1570 as being in gainful employment were textile workers.[16] For Colchester, James I's letter patent of 1612 to the Dutch Congregation congratulated them on providing employment for many of his poorer subjects,[17] whilst Cromwell's argument that the inhabitants of the town's suburbs were 'chiefly poor weavers' is supported by my own research.[18] A petition from the Colchester weavers of 1715 sought the abolition of the use of cheap labour, particularly of women and boys, in the industry.[19] Pre-industrial cloth production was a highly labour intensive industry, whether traditional cloth or the 'new draperies', and much of the employment it provided is likely to be hidden behind the source material available. Apart from full-time cloth workers whose poverty excludes them from the records used, one must also take account of part-time employment as well as the numerous women and children who played an essential role in domestic textile production.

13. Patten, op. cit. 22.
14. Pound, op. cit. 134.
15. G. D. Ramsay, *The Wiltshire Woollen Industry in the Sixteenth and Seventeenth Centuries* (1943), 16.
16. J. Pound, 'The Norwich census of the poor, 1570', *Norfolk Record Soc.* XL (1971), 16.
17. Quoted in T. Cromwell, *History and Description of the Ancient Town and Borough of Colchester* (1825), II, 287.
18. Cromwell, op. cit. I, 108.
19. K. H. Burley, 'A note on a labour dispute in early eighteenth-century Colchester', *Bulletin Inst. Hist. Research*, XXIX (1956), 228.

Phythian-Adams, for instance, has emphasized the importance of women as thread-makers, spinners and knitters in early sixteenth-century Coventry, going so far as to argue that 'Without them, the textile and clothing industries would have collapsed'.[20] The point is accepted by Patten, who writes that 'far from all of those involved in the cloth producing trade, with its myriad of components and network of domestic and part-time workers were likely to be Freemen'.[21] The figures produced from these sources do, therefore, result in under-estimation of the textile industry as a source of employment, and hence also in under-estimation of the degree of specialization achieved in textile producing towns such as Colchester, Norwich, Reading or Worcester.

A second point relates to the proportion of the population required to be employed in a particular industry before it amounts to a specialism. Figures for Colchester and Reading from will evidence produce proportions of between 22 and 38 per cent for different periods between 1500 and 1700, though if distributors of cloth are included they rise to between 26 and 43 per cent. In Norwich and Coventry the proportion was about one-third, and only in late sixteenth- and early seventeenth-century Worcester did it reach one-half.[22] Taking the above argument into account, these figures must be regarded as minima. But given that of necessity, due to low productivity levels, large numbers were involved in providing food, clothing and shelter for the urban inhabitants themselves, surely these figures represent a considerable degree of specialization. Only 28 per cent of my occupational sample for sixteenth-century Reading were engaged in textile production, but Leland still thought that 'the town chiefly standeth by clothing'.[23] Even when the Colchester industry had started to decline, Defoe could still argue that 'The town may be said chiefly to subsist by the trade of making bays.'[24] Even in an urban economy that we would not hesitate to describe as highly specialized, that of nineteenth-century Sheffield, almost 50 per cent of the male population were engaged in occupations other than the staple metal trades.[25] Furthermore, a very similar percentage had been so employed in the middle to late seventeenth century, whilst in Birmingham as early as *c.* 1540 a 'grate parte of

20. C. Phythian-Adams, *Desolation of a City* (1979), 88.
21. J. Patten, 'Urban occupations in pre-industrial England', *Trans. Inst. Brit. Geog.* N. S. II (1977), 299.
22. Dyer, op. cit. 82.
23. L. Toulmin-Smith (ed.) *Leland's Itinerary in England (c. 1535–43)*, (1907), I, 111.
24. D. Defoe, *A Tour Through the Whole Island of Great Britain* (Penguin edn, 1971), 58.
25. S. Pollard, *A History of Labour in Sheffield* (1959), 6.

the towne' was said to be 'mayntayned by smiths'.[26] In Preston in 1851, only 32 per cent of men aged 20 and over were engaged in cotton manufacturing, whilst other prominent occupations were those commonly to be found amongst the leading occupations of many *pre*-industrial towns, such as shoemakers, tailors and smiths.[27] And if the economy of Preston was particularly susceptible to the effects of the trade cycle upon its staple industry, depression of trade could have an equally severe impact upon pre-industrial Reading, as the pages of the Corporation Diary for the 1620s and 1630s reveal.

A similar degree of specialization is evident in a number of other nineteenth-century Lancashire boroughs. In 1861 the percentages of males employed in cotton textiles in Manchester and Salford, Bolton, Oldham and Blackburn were 7, 21, 26 and 35 respectively. If, to allow comparison with the published Preston evidence, only males aged 20 and over are considered, the figures rise slightly to 9, 28, 31 and 43, but these percentages are all of a similar order of magnitude to those which relate to pre-industrial textile towns, cited above.[28] Further analysis of the occupational structures of nineteenth-century towns might provide a better context for the consideration of the nature of pre-industrial urban economies, and might well reveal that in *numerical* terms their specialisms were not *overwhelmingly* important, whilst the size of what might be termed the 'support' sector was often quite considerable.

A final point relating to urban textile production is that such towns were often specialized in another sense. Although the cloth industry was anything but an urban preserve, many towns concentrated upon the production of cloth of a particularly high quality. In the early seventeenth century, as Pilgrim writes, Colchester bays and says 'had an uncommonly high reputation',[29] whilst in the 1720s Defoe informs us that Colchester bays were known by name 'over most of the trading parts of Europe'.[30] The kersies produced in sixteenth-century Reading also enjoyed a reputation for their fineness,[31] whilst the industry in Worcester produced broadcloth of a very high standard.[32] Furthermore, even when much of the produc-

26. L. A. Clarkson, *The Pre-Industrial Economy in England 1500–1750* (1971), Table 2, 88–9; J. Langton, 'Industry and towns 1500–1730', in R. A. Dodgshon and R. A. Butlin (eds.) *An historical geography of England and Wales* (1978), 180, and sources cited therein.

27. M. Anderson, *Family Structure in Nineteenth Century Lancashire* (1971), p. 25 and n. 22.

28. These figures, taken from the 1861 census, were kindly supplied by Paul Laxton.

29. J. E. Pilgrim, 'The rise of the "new draperies" in Essex', *Uni. Birmingham Hist. J.* vii (1959–60), 49–50.

30. Defoe, op. cit. 58.

31. P. J. Bowden, *The Wool Trade in Tudor and Stuart England* (1971), 50–1.

32. Dyer, op. cit. 93.

tive process was carried out in the countryside, towns often acted as organizing centres for large regions, were often important as finishing centres, and also acted as centres of distribution, whether by direct export or by transportation to the capital for export from there. During the depression of the 1620s, the Corporation of Reading ordered that the clothiers of the town 'shall not henceforth put the weaving, burling or dressing of any their cloth into the country'. Of Essex Defoe wrote 'the whole county, large as it is, may be said to be employed, and in part maintained, by the spinning of wool for the bay trade of Colchester, and its adjacent towns'.[33] By the early seventeenth century Exeter's main importance lay in its cloth markets, which had attained regional significance, and in its cloth finishing industry and export trade, whilst Taunton and Tiverton also developed as finishing centres for the textile industry of the region.[34] A cursory glance at the occupational structure of Exeter in the early seventeenth century is unlikely to lead to the conclusion that it was a specialist cloth town, but if one takes into account the various facets of the cloth trade in which its inhabitants were involved, then this is exactly what it was.[35]

Textile production was not the only specialism to be found in English pre-industrial towns. Hoskins' figures for early sixteenth-century Northampton and Leicester show that 23 and 19 per cent respectively of his occupational samples were engaged in leather processing and manufacture.[36] These figures are probably under-estimates, for a number of general categories are excluded who would have been 'fairly evenly distributed among the principal crafts and trades of the town'.[37] If, in accordance with the argument employed above regarding textile towns, a lower threshold is set before we feel able to think in terms of specialization, it remains difficult to view either of these towns as unspecialized urban economies. Hoskins himself argues that Northampton 'showed a decided bent towards specialization in the leather trades',[38] but surely this was true of Leicester as well. And if it was the case, as Hoskins suspected, that the numerous butchers of the town were 'More interested in providing hides for the local tanners than meat for the townspeople',[39] then Leicester stands out even more clearly as a specialist leather town.

Even when a town did not contain a particular specialist *industry*, it often had another rôle to play that might be regarded as a

33. Defoe, op. cit. 58.
34. W. B. Stephens, *Seventeenth Century Exeter* (1958), 6, 12, 135.
35. W. T. MacCaffrey, *Exeter 1540–1640* (2nd edn, 1975), 162–5.
36. Hoskins, op. cit. 80.
37. Ibid. 79, n. 1.
38. Ibid. 80.
39. Ibid. 81.

specialism. All towns played a part in inland trade, acting as centres of exchange and distribution, and there is some indication that the larger towns were becoming increasingly important in this respect towards the end of the sixteenth century.[40] But it is also true that some were of far greater importance than were others. King's Lynn, for instance, was ideally situated to control the traffic passing along three great rivers, the Ouse, Nene and Welland, and hence rose to prominence as a centre of trade, particularly for the trade in corn. This rôle is clearly reflected in the town's occupational structure.[41] Following the decline of its textile industry, York was reborn in the sixteenth century as a trading and administrative centre.[42] Cambridge was another town the geographical location of which encouraged its growth as a centre of trade, corn predominating on a regular basis and wool and hops assuming particular importance at that great national gathering, Stourbridge Fair. The merchant community of Cambridge itself may have been small, but the importance of this rôle is clearly reflected in the size of the town's service and transport sector. Here we find one explanation of the relatively high proportion of the occupied population of this town who were engaged in the provision of certain 'basic necessities', particularly food, drink and accommodation. This was not, of course, all there was to the economy of Cambridge, any more than in the case of York or Lynn, and the existence of the captive (and growing) university market was another reason for the town's growth and prosperity in the later sixteenth and early seventeenth centuries. But all of these towns played a key rôle in internal trade which, although they lacked a dominant industry, can be seen as a specialist *function*. The same is also true of seaports, whether they were primarily concerned with coastal or with overseas trade. It may be true that the merchants and mariners in such towns did not constitute a majority of the occupied populations, but this does not allow us to think of them as unspecialized urban economies.

The importance of specialist functions to English pre-industrial urban economies is demonstrated clearly by consideration of the rise and fall of towns in this period. It may be true that, after the fifteenth century, it was rare for the larger towns to decline in absolute terms, but they clearly did change position relative to one another, and so often this was related to the loss or growth of a particular specialist rôle. To cite just a few examples, the decline of Coventry in the earlier sixteenth century was intimately linked with the decline of its textile industry, whilst the relative decline of Reading (as well as its rise in the later Middle Ages) can also be related to the health

40. A. Everitt, 'The market towns', in Clark, op. cit. 194.
41. See Phythian-Adams, *Traditional Community*, 16.
42. Palliser, op. cit. 271.

of its staple industry. The rise, fall and revival of York can be explained in terms of the rise and fall of its cloth industry and its subsequent development as a trading and administrative centre. Southampton in the sixteenth century suffered the loss of its importance as a port due to shifts in international trade, and declined as a result. And the rise of Boston in the Middle Ages cannot be understood without reference to its growth as an international trading port. The list could be extended almost indefinitely. The point has already been emphasized by Corfield, particularly for the seventeenth century.[43] Those towns which grew fastest during this period were usually associated with a particular specialist function or trade, including the industrial centres of Norwich, Colchester, Worcester and Exeter, the provincial ports of Newcastle, Bristol and Yarmouth and the naval and dockyard towns of Plymouth, Portsmouth and Chatham. If we look at the list of leading towns for the later seventeenth century, specialist functions abound; but the same is also true for the early sixteenth century, and indeed for the early fourteenth century.[44]

In all periods of history towns had certain common characteristics, as Braudel pointed out. One of the most obvious common features of English pre-industrial towns was their rôle as market places, and, in general, the larger the town the wider its market region. Foodstuffs loomed large in the internal trade of the period, but man does not live by bread alone, and a marketing centre was the ideal place within which the manufacturer of consumer goods could ply his trade. These are both aspects of the 'basic' sector of urban economies, involving the provision of goods and services to customers living outside the town itself. In certain favourable circumstances, perhaps related to geographical location, or to the ready availability of a particular raw material, one aspect of this 'basic' sector might become of special importance, resulting in the development of a specialist industrial or commercial bias. But besides this all towns require a 'non-basic' sector, concerned with meeting the needs of the town's own inhabitants, and in any urban community this sector was always likely to be an important source of employment. Due to the prevailing low level of productivity, this would be particularly true of pre-industrial towns. This division is, of course, an abstraction, for many townsmen had a part to play in both of these sectors. It does, however, serve to show why one should not *expect* to find an overwhelmingly high proportion of a town's occupied population within one specialist occupational category, and why it is so easy to find features common to all pre-industrial towns. By concentrating upon these common features, historians such as Patten have reached the conclusion that the great majority of pre-industrial towns in England were unspecialized. But if we ignore for a moment the necessarily large 'support' sector, then a very different picture emerges, and urban specialisms, in industry or in trade, stand out more clearly. Furthermore, in terms of the amount of wealth generated, these specialisms assume even greater importance. It was not the various bakers or tailors who stood at the head of the subsidy lists for Colchester and Reading in the 1520s, but the clothiers and mercers of these towns. And given the very unequal distribution of wealth in these and other pre-industrial towns, their contribution to the total wealth of their communities was of overwhelming importance.

The emphasis here has been placed upon towns above the level of the 'simple market town'. These smaller communities have received relatively little attention from urban historians of the period, partly, no doubt, because they left fewer records. Even here, however, one can find many examples of specialization, whilst the central importance of marketing to so many of these towns might itself be regarded as a specialist function.[45] But it might also be argued that it is *necessary* to consider separately towns at different levels in the urban hierarchy, otherwise any judgment about the essential nature of their economies is always likely to come up with the lowest common denominator. And as both Hoskins and Patten use the town of Leicester as an example, there is a certain justification for concentrating upon towns of this stature. At this level in the urban hierarchy, research to date reveals a considerable degree of specialization, whether in a particular industry (usually textiles or leather) or in internal or maritime trade. A substantial proportion of the population of these towns was, it is true, employed in other activities, and all exhibited a great diversity of different trades. But such diversity was also found in nineteenth-century Birmingham and Leeds,[46] whilst the example of Preston has already been cited above. Some towns possessed a dual specialism, as in the case of early sixteenth-century Chester,[47] but then so did nineteenth-century Leeds.[48] Exeter was both a textile producing town and a marketing centre for the cloth produced in its region, but so was nineteenth-century Manchester.[49] The comparison with industrial England

45. For Sussex market towns see Patten, *English Towns*, 170–1.
46. A. Briggs, *Victorian Cities* (Penguin edn, 1971), 151, 186.
47. See Phythian-Adams, *Traditional Community*, 16.
48. Briggs, op. cit. 151.
49. Ibid. 106–8.

72

cannot be taken further until more occupational figures have been produced for this period, but there is enough to suggest that whilst all towns in pre-industrial England possessed certain common features, many of these were common to towns at *all* times. And it is by concentrating upon key functions, rather than common features, that most insight is likely to be gained into the nature of pre-industrial urban economies and the reasons for their rise or decline.

Editorial suggestions for further reading

L. Charles and L. Duffin (eds), *Women and Work in Pre-Industrial England* (1985).

A. Everitt, 'Country, county and town', *Transactions of the Royal Historical Society,* 5th ser., 29 (1979), pp. 79–108.

N. Goose, 'In search of the urban variable: Towns 1500–1650', *Economic History Review*, 39 (1986), pp. 165–85.

J. Patten, 'Urban occupations in pre-industrial England', *Transactions of the Institute of British Geographers*, 3 (1977), pp. 296–313.

W. R. Prest (ed.), *Professions in Early Modern England* (1987).

Chapter 4

HOUSEHOLD SIZE AND STRUCTURE IN EARLY-STUART CAMBRIDGE

Nigel Goose

[*Social History*, 5 (1980)]

This article serves as an excellent introduction to both the advantages and the complexities brought to urban history by the demographic approach. Government concern at the tripling of population in a university town led to the compilation of household listings for five parishes, whose statistical analysis forms the core of the paper. These findings are compared with similar studies for other towns and rural communities. They reinforce the general belief that most urban and rural people of the period lived in small households, swollen in towns by lodgers and among the better-off by servants and apprentices. But Goose also brings out the fluidity and variation within and between towns. He seeks to correlate his findings with the pressing urban problems of overcrowding, poverty and plague, especially in peripheral areas, which produced the listings in the first place. As he admits, this is hard to prove without further evidence covering the whole town and showing how its members' conditions changed over their lifetimes. Demographic analysis thus serves rather to generate questions than to provide clear answers to the urban historian.

Since the publication of Laslett's seminal article in 1969, relatively little progress has been made in the study of household structure in pre-industrial England.[1] In this article Laslett presented the statistical findings of an analysis of 100 communities over a period of 300 years. No attempt was made to consider variations over time within these three centuries which might have resulted from changing economic, social and demographic conditions. Nor was any attempt made to consider differences between *types* of community. The ex-

---

1. P. Laslett, 'Size and structure of the household in England over three centuries', *Population Studies*, XXIII (1969).

istence of an urban/rural contrast is an obvious candidate for consideration. Recent analysis of medieval and Renaissance Italy has shown a marked difference between the structure of households in urban and rural areas.[2] But even within the agrarian sector, dif-- ferent agricultural economies, the existence of rural industry or contrasting inheritance patterns may well have resulted in variations in household composition. Laslett's statistics take no account of these possibilities, whilst even his breakdowns by social group utilize only very broad and vague categories. This is not to deny the value of this pioneering work. It does provide a useful average, though not a carefully weighted one, which can be used as a yardstick by those conducting studies more firmly fixed in time and space. And, of course, we have Laslett and the Cambridge Group to thank for introducing a completely new area of historical research. But in order to invest a census study with more significance, one has to step outside the listings themselves and consider other historical evidence which can be used to add some flesh and blood to the bare bones of statistical analysis. In this way the numerous factors which might have influenced the composition of the household and family can be considered, and historical explanation offered.

The documents upon which such studies are based (referred to here as 'listings') are, or purport to be, complete enumerations of particular communities. The reasons for their compilation are diverse, and the amount of detail they provide about household composition highly variable. Apart from Laslett's survey, there are a handful of studies which attempt to analyse household structure at a more local level, some of which make use of evidence apart from the listings themselves.[3] But so often the same criticism can be applied. The contextual matter is dealt with all too briefly and little attempt is made to link this context with the results of analysis. The range of subsidiary sources used tends to be narrow. In other cases the lack of detail provided in a particular listing prevents the analysis

---

2. Fiumi, *Demografia,* citied in D. O. Hughes, 'Urban growth and family structure in medieval Genoa', in P. Abrams and E. A. Wrigley (eds), *Towns in Societies* (Cambridge, 1978), 106.
3. For pre-industrial England: P. Laslett and J. Harrison, 'Clayworth and Cogenhoe', re-printed with revisions in P. Laslett (ed.), *Family Life and Illicit Love in Earlier Generations* (Cambridge, 1977); eighteenth century: N. L. Tranter, 'Population and social structure in a Bedfordshire parish: the Cardington listing, 1782', *Population Studies*, XXI (1967); H. Medick, 'The proto-industrial family economy: the structural function of household and family during the transition from peasant society to industrial capitalism', *Social History*, III (1976) – this relies heavily upon the work of D. Levine; J. M. Martin, 'An investigation into the small size of the household as exemplified by Stratford-on-Avon', *Local Population Studies*, XIX (1977); L. A. Clarkson, 'Household and family structure in Armagh City, 1770', *Local Population Studies*, XX (1978).

being taken very far.[4] Here a fairly wide range of evidence has been used to shed light on the social and occupational structure and the main features of the demography of Cambridge in the early seventeenth century.[5] I have tried to present Cambridge as a *type* of community at a particular point in time and, as many of the social and demographic features of the town were common to many other large provincial towns in this period, would argue that the results found here might have a more general relevance. The date of the Cambridge listings adds to their value. Very few community listings survive for so early a period and the number that relate to truly urban communities, prior to those produced by the taxation of the 1690s, can be counted on the fingers of one hand.[6] Furthermore, *perhaps* with the exception of the Coventry census of the 1520s, these listings are unique in the wealth of detailed information they provide.[7] In this paper this detailed information has been used in conjunction with a number of other sources in an attempt to *explain* some of the features of household and family size and structure in early seventeenth-century Cambridge, particularly where these features differ from the 'averages' presented by Laslett for pre-industrial society in general.

There are essentially two different approaches to a multi-source, community-based study. One is via an elaborate system of record linkage of the type at present being conducted on Earles Colne by Macfarlane and his team.[8] Where the results of interest are primarily demographic, as with the study of the family and household, this would have to be based upon complete reconstitution of all available parish registers.[9] This approach has been rejected here for several reasons. First, such a study would take a research *team* several years

4. This is true to a certain extent of Martin op. cit. The article by Medick is a good demonstration of what can be achieved by the placing of findings in context.

5. Sources used include parish registers, wills and inventories, corporation minute books, depositions, exchequer subsidies and hearth taxes, and contemporary maps. More detail about the economy and society of Cambridge in this period will be presented in my forthcoming thesis, 'Economic and Social Aspects of Provincial Towns 1500–1700: Cambridge, Colchester and Reading'.

6. A list is available at the offices of the Cambridge Group for the History of Population and Social Structure.

7. This has been used by C. Phythian-Adams in his *Desolation of a City: Coventry and the Urban Crisis of the Late Middle Ages* (Cambridge, 1979).

8. See A. Macfarlane, *Reconstructing Historical Communities* (Cambridge, 1977).

9. Cambridge parish registers survive for most, but not all, of the town's parishes from the later sixteenth century; those that do survive have the usual shortcomings in terms of completeness. Their reconstitution would be an extremely lengthy process, and would be hampered by the effects of migration. For a good discussion of the problems involved in family reconstitution see R. Schofield, 'Representativeness and family reconstitution', *Trans. Royal Historical Society* (1971), 121–5.

to complete.[10] Second, a wealth of different types of documentary evidence, all of the best quality, would be needed. The evidence available for Cambridge is quite substantial, but still has its shortcomings. And third, the fluidity of urban communities in this period was so marked that the use of techniques such as record linkage and family reconstitution is extremely difficult.[11] The second possible approach, and that used here, is to link the results gained from an analysis of different types of document by hypothesis. Here the historical background of the community has first been described, partly by the use of independent sources and partly through the use of documentation relating to the drawing up of the census. This context has then been used in attempting to explain certain features of family and household size and structure derived from statistical analysis of the listings themselves. The conclusions drawn will not, of course, be watertight. But in view of the virtual impossibility of using the alternative approach outlined above, might be regarded as the best that can be achieved.

The listings of inhabitants upon which this paper is based date from the years *c.* 1619–32, and were the product of a long period of concern over the problem of overcrowding in the town.[12] As early as 1584, in response to a petition from the town and university, the Privy Council first ordered that a census be taken.[13] A Privy Council letter of June that year read as follows:

> Whereas we are given to understand that divers of the inhabitants of the Town of Cambridge, seeking their own private gain with the public hurt and incommodity of the whole University and Town, have heretofore accustomed to build and erect upon sundry spare grounds in and about the said Town; but of late and at this present especially, they do not only increase and continue the same, but do more usually divide one house into many small tenements (for the rudeness and straitness of them not fit to harbour any other than of the poorest sort) are a means, (as we are informed) whereby the University and Town are overburthened in yearly allowance towards the maintenance of the poor, and that inconvenience not unlikely to be accompanied with a further mischief and danger if any plague or other infection should happen within the Town, by reason that so many poor people are so narrowly and unwholesomely thrust and thronged together in diverse places.

10. See the warnings in Macfarlane, op. cit., 207–14.
11. The difficulty caused by the fluidity of town populations was demonstrated to me by my attempts to link hearth tax returns with probate inventories. Surprisingly few names could be matched from these two sources. See, however, R. A. P. Finlay, 'The accuracy of the London parish registers 1580–1653', *Population Studies*, XXXII (1978), 111–12.
12. The listings used here have no date on them, and were dated as precisely as possible by the use of wills and parish registers.
13. Cambridge University Archives: C.U.R. Town 37.3, doc. 124.

For redress of this situation the Vice-Chancellor and Mayor were to

> immediately upon receipt hereof cause speedy and diligent enquiry to
> be had what number of tenements have been erected within the
> liberties of the University and Town, and how many of them or of
> any other houses formerly built have been and are divided into
> tenements within the compass of ten years last past, and what
> number of inmates are bestowed and do inhabit in them and every of
> them . . . .[14]

This letter has been quoted at some length because it outlines the
central social problems of the town in the later sixteenth century:
overcrowding, poverty and plague.

In typical sixteenth-century fashion the administrative machinery
was slow to move. Concern about the same problems was still occasionally voiced, however, and it was perhaps as a result of an
intensification of these problems in the early seventeenth century
that a new Privy Council order was issued in June 1619.[15] This differed very little from that of 1584, though it also mentioned the fire
hazard caused by the erection of houses and cottages thatched with
reed and straw. Again 'speedy and diligent enquiry' was to be made
as to

> what number of tenements have been erected within the liberties of
> the University and Town, and how many of them, or of any other
> houses formerly built have of late years been divided into tenements,
> and what number of inmates do inhabit in them and every of them,
> and how long they have continued there and from whence they came.

Here we see the connection being firmly drawn between the problem of the housing of poor 'inmates' in divided tenements and
immigration into the town. But it was only after a further Privy
Council order of May 1623 that concerted action was taken.[16] The
complete listings of all inhabitants, which survive for five of the
town's fourteen parishes, can be attributed to the mid-1620s or early
1630s.[17] Detailed lists of the households of those presented for offending the injunctions against taking of inmates also survive for five
parishes, these being clearly dated June 1632.[18] But all this activity
appears to have been to little avail. In January 1636 a further order
was received which stated that 'a multitude of poor people have
been received out of the Countrie Towns adjoining and divers other
parts of this Kingdom . . .'.[19] Apart from a petition later the same

14. C. H. Cooper, *Annals of Cambridge*, II (Cambridge, 1843), 398.
15. Cambridge University Archives: C.U.R. town 37.7, doc 1a.
16. Ibid., C.U.R. Town 37.7, doc. 1b.
17. Ibid., C.U.R. Town 37.3, docs. 110, 111, 114, 115 and 116.
18. Ibid., C.U.R. Town 37.3, docs. 128, 129 and 130; C.U.R. Town 37.5, doc. 37;
C.U.R. Town 37.7 doc. 22.
19. Cooper, op. cit., III 272.

year which complained about the erection of cottages and taking of
inmates by wealthy citizens, this is the last surviving piece of
evidence of anxiety over this problem in Cambridge.[20]

To place Cambridge within the urban hierarchy of early-modern
England, it could be described as one of the 100 or so 'second-rank'
provincial centres.[21] All other towns in this period were dwarfed
by London, both in terms of size and in terms of economic importance and complexity.[22] Below London can be placed the provincial
capitals such as Bristol and Norwich, whose role as regional centres
set them apart from other county towns.[23] But most counties contained one town, sometimes two or even three, that can be
distinguished from the simple market town in terms of size, judicial
and administrative functions, central marketing role and the ability
to offer a relatively wide range of services.[24] This picture is, of course,
an over-simplified one. There is still little published research
on the regional influence of towns of different sizes, and still less on
the ways in which the urban hierarchy influenced, and was influenced by, the economy and society of the region or county in
which it stood.[25] In counties such as Hertfordshire or Devon, so well
endowed with simple market towns, one might expect the role of
the county centre to differ somewhat from a town like Cambridge,
situated in a county of relatively few market centres.[26] Clearly, many
of these towns which fit into the category of 'second-rank' provincial
centres differed markedly from each other, not only in terms of their
relative size and importance, but also in terms of their economic
structure. Some, of course, were ports; and despite the variegated
nature of urban economies in this period could be strongly affected
by shifts in international trade, as is evidenced by the case of
sixteenth-century Southampton.[27] Others, such as Worcester and

20. Ibid., 274.
21. P. Clark and P. Slack, *English Towns in Transition 1500–1700* (Oxford, 1976),
    25–32.
22. Clark and Slack, op. cit.. 62; E. A. Wrigley, 'A simple model of London's im-
    portance in changing English society and economy 1650–1750', *Past and Present*,
    XXXVII (1967), 44–70.
23. Clark and Slack, op. cit., 46–61.
24. It was not invariably the case that all these criteria were to be found together.
    In Essex, for instance, Colchester was without doubt the largest and most
    economically active town; but although it possessed its own borough courts,
    Chelmsford remained the administrative centre of the county.
25. But see J. Patten, *English Towns 1500–1700* (Folkestone, 1978), ch. 6, which is
    based upon his Cambridge Ph.D. thesis.
26. A. Everitt, 'The market town', reprinted in P. Clark (ed.), *The Early Modern
    Town* (1976), 168–204.
27. A. A. Ruddock, 'London capitalists and the decline of Southampton in the early
    Tudor period', *Economic History Review*, 2nd Series, II (1949–50), 137–51.

Reading, contained large textile industries.[28] Colchester performed both of these roles.[29] The seventeenth century sees the rise of a number of highly specialized dockyard towns, such as Chatham and Portsmouth.[30] Still others concentrated heavily upon internal trade, examples including Bury St Edmunds and Gloucester.[31] It is, perhaps, this variety of emphases that makes it so difficult to generalize about the fate of these 'second-rank' towns as a whole during this period, and it might even be suggested that attempts to do so are misguided.[32] Cambridge itself had never possessed a large manufacturing sector, and in the sixteenth and seventeenth centuries depended heavily upon its role as a trading centre and a supplier of services to the university. Stourbridge Fair, held under the town's municipal authority in a nearby field every September, was clearly of some importance to its economy. But Cambridge also fulfilled the role of an inland port. Nevertheless, it was probably the captive market provided by the university that gave a living to the majority of the small craftsmen and tradesmen of the town, as is evidenced by the distress that could result from the withdrawal of the university population.[33] An occupational sample from Cambridge for the period 1580–1640 is presented in Table 2.

Despite this variety amongst towns of the second-rank, they did possess common features. Notwithstanding the existence of economic specializations, Hoskins has pointed towards the large proportion of urban populations that were engaged in the provision of the basic necessities of life: food, clothing and shelter.[34] Available evidence suggests that wealth in such towns was heavily concentrated in a few hands; a small wealthy elite existed side by side with a large mass who were at least relatively poor.[35] In this respect Cambridge was no exception. Although in comparison with towns such as Colchester and Reading there appear to have been relatively

---

28. For Worcester, see A. D. Dyer, *Worcester in the Sixteenth Century* (Leicester, 1973). Historians have paid scant attention to the town of Reading, which is at present the subject of my research.
29. Patten, op. cit., 173, 234.
30. D. C. Coleman, 'Naval dockyards under the later Stuarts', *Economic History Review*, 2nd Series VI (1953).
31. P. Corfield, 'Economic growth and change in seventeenth century English towns', in *The Traditional Community Under Stress* (Milton Keynes, 1977), 53–4.
32. For the main arguments in this debate see C. Phythian-Adams, 'Urban crisis or urban change?', in *The Traditional Community* . . ., 9–29.
33. Cooper, op. cit., III, 222–8.
34. W. G. Hopkins, 'English provincial towns in the early sixteenth century', reprinted in Clark (ed.), op. cit., 99.
35. Clark and Slack, op. cit., 111–12; but see also C. Phythian-Adams, 'The economic and social structure', in *The Fabric of the Traditional Community* (Milton Keynes, 1977), 34–5.

TABLE 1   Cambridge population (excluding colleges)

Date	Source	Approx. no.
1524–5	Exchequer Lay Subsidies	2600
1563	Ecclesiastical Census	2400
1587	Vice-Chancellor's estimate	5000
1620s	Inmate Census	7750
1674	Hearth Tax	8000

few men in 1524–5 who could be described as 'wealthy', the Exchequer Lay Subsidies of these years reveal that less than 12 per cent of the town's taxable population owned nearly 60 per cent of the total taxable wealth. The bottom 83 per cent owned only 35 per cent of all taxable wealth.[36] In 1674, including those exempt from taxation by certificate but *excluding* paupers, 13 per cent of the town's population lived in households with six or more hearths, whilst nearly 60 per cent possessed only one or two hearths.[37] At both dates the suburban areas of the town tended to contain more than their share of poorer inhabitants.[38] But apart from these 'static' elements that appear to have been common to the larger towns of pre-industrial England, many of them in the later sixteenth century appear to have been developing similar social problems which are of particular relevance to the Cambridge census of the 1620s.

The later sixteenth and early seventeenth centuries were a period of growth for many of the larger provincial centres, including Cambridge.[39] The figures presented in Table 1, which it must be stressed are approximations only, suggest stability in the early sixteenth century followed by rapid expansion thereafter. The bases for the calculation of these various figures are discussed in Appendix A. Non-statistical evidence gives no indication of prolonged decay into the sixteenth century.[40] In its Paving Act of 1544 Cambridge was described as 'well inhabited and replenished with people both in the university . . . [and] also with sundry and diverse artificers and other inhabitants . . .',[41] and whilst Oxford appears in the list

36. Results from analysis of the exchequer subsidies of 1524–5: Public Record Office, E 179 81/133 and E 179 81/144.
37. From the analysis of the hearth tax return of this year: Public Record Office, E 179/244/23.
38. Comparison between the two dates is difficult, due to the fact that the subsidies of the 1520s were compiled by wards, whereas the hearth tax lists are arranged by parish. Nevertheless, it appears that the suburbs contained a slightly higher proportion of poor at the later date.
39. Phythian-Adams, 'Urban crisis or urban change?', in *The Traditional Community* . . ., 19.
40. Cf. Phythian-Adams, 'Urban decay in late Medieval England', in Abrams and Wrigley (eds.), op. cit.
41. British Library, Add. MSS. 5821, fo. 91.

81

of towns in need of 're-edification' in the statute of 1540, Cambridge is notably absent.[42] Between the 1560s and the 1620s its population roughly trebled, and this without any expansion in the actual area of the town.[43] Some of the listings produced in the 1620s indicate the extent of new building, whilst a comparison of Braun's map of 1575 with Fuller's map of 1634 shows that many streets had been extended during these sixty years, and many open spaces had been filled in.[44] This was reflected in the University's complaint of 1616 that it was the policy of the town to 'build and pester every Lane and Corner with unwholesome and base cottages'.[45]

This rapid growth appears to have been essentially the product of large-scale immigration, as is suggested in the Privy Council letters quoted above. John Mere in his diary for 1533 gives an account of a mayoral speech in which foreigners were welcomed and urged to become freemen.[46] Figures provided by Mary Siraut show that only 30 per cent of freemen admitted between 1545 and 1582 were born in Cambridge, whilst of 861 deponents in the University Commissary Court, the Vice-Chancellor's Court and the Ely Consistory Court over the period 1560–1603, only 17 per cent had been born in the town.[47] In 1576 it was ruled that every freeman might have all his sons free for a mere 4d. apiece,[48] and in 1585 fines for 'foreigners' seeking the freedom of the town were raised substantially.[49] But still, of the 242 freemen admitted between 1608 and 1630, only 31 per cent are stated to have been, or can be assumed to have been (as sons of freemen or ex-freemen) indigenous. 50 per cent were born elsewhere, whilst of the 19 per cent of unstated origins the majority were probably born outside Cambridge.[50]

At the same time the Cambridge parish registers show a substantial natural decrease over the period 1580–1630, with a deficit of well over 600 occurring between 1616 and 1630.[51] One must, of

42. *Statutes of the Realm 1225–1713*, III (reprinted London, 1963), 459–60.
43. M. D. Lobel (ed.), *Historic Towns Atlas*, II (1975), 19.
44. Copies of these maps can be seen in the Map Room of the University Library, Cambridge.
45. Copper, op. cit., III 110.
46. Quoted in M. C. Siraut, 'Some Aspects of the Economic and Social History of Cambridge Under Elizabeth I', Unpubl. M. Litt. thesis, Cambridge, 1978, 284.
47. Ibid., 284–6.
48. Ibid., 284.
49. Cooper, op. cit., II, 409.
50. Cambridge County Record Office, Book of Orders 1608–11, Common Day Book no. 7.
51. Of the 14 Cambridge parishes, the registers survive for the whole of this period for 10, most of which are at the Cambridge C.R.O. Those for St Peter, St Giles and St Botolph are still in the parishes. For Barnwell and Gt St Andrew the bishops' transcripts, which survive from the late sixteenth century, have been used (Cambridge University Archives, EDR H₃). Gaps in the St Giles (pre-

course, remember the problems involved in the use of parish registers as a source, particularly in the case of populations as fluid as those of early-modern towns.[52] It has recently been argued that urban burial figures are inflated in this period due to the *temporary* migration to towns of young, unmarried people.[53] These temporary migrants, so the argument runs, would substantially increase the urban population subject to the risk of death, hence swelling burial totals, but would not themselves have been baptised in the town concerned; and nor would they contribute towards the birth-rate by staying in the town during the early, most fertile years of marriage. By-passing the point that the exact age and marital structure of the migrant population needs more detailed examination, this thesis rests fundamentally upon the argument that the majority of urban immigrants were strictly temporary. The English evidence to date does not allow this conclusion to be drawn. Migration from town to countryside has received little attention, but available evidence does suggest that most migrants moved only once in their lives.[54] Furthermore, on *a priori* grounds, it seems unlikely that young migrants entering towns to receive training in urban occupations and to establish the necessary connections to enable them to set up in business would then immediately retire again to the countryside. Thus, although immigration certainly would supply a number of people destined to die in a town who had not been born there, it is likely that the more youthful age structure produced by the surviving migrants might also inflate the number of births. Furthermore, the migrant played such a fundamental role in urban communities in this period that any attempt to abstract a 'stable element' is a denial of historical reality.[55] In Cambridge, parishes such as St Giles, St Botolph and Holy Trinity were clearly substantial consumers of men, and the authorities were quite correct in seeing a connection

1610) and St Peter (pre-1585) registers have been filled by using figures extracted by Bowtell in the eighteenth century before these earlier registers were lost (Bowtell MSS, Downing College Library, Cambridge). Thus my figures, which will be presented in my forthcoming thesis, cover 12 parishes from 1580, and the whole town from 1600.

52. This problem has led one writer to conclude that the vital rates produced from parish register counts for the town of Maldon 'are the chance products of a mobile population': W. J. Petchey, 'The Borough of Maldon, Essex, 1500–1680', Ph.D. Leicester, 1972, 76.

53. A Sharlin, 'Natural decrease in early modern cities: a reconsideration', *Past and Present*, LXXIX (1978), 126–38.

54. P. Clark, 'The migrant in Kentish towns 1580–1640', in P. Clark and P. Slack (eds), *Crisis and Order in English Towns 1500–1700* (1972), 123–4.

55. Even amongst the more 'respectable' townsmen, that is, those who appear in freeman admissions lists and court depositions, a remarkably high percentage were born outside the town in question.

between plague sensitivity and overcrowding. As the population density of the town increased in the late sixteenth and early seventeenth centuries, so did the impact of periodic epidemics. Parishes with a high proportion of 'inmates' relative to their total populations particularly suffered in this respect.[56]

Evidence from letters, adjournments of the university and references in parish registers and other sources show that plague was active in Cambridge in 1574, 1577, 1580, 1593, 1603, 1605, 1608, 1610, 1625, and 1630–1.[57] Apart from these plague years, crisis mortalities, as defined by Schofield,[58] occurred in a number of the town's parishes in the years 1588, 1595, 1616–17 and 1619–20. Many of these outbreaks were relatively mild, and none was as vehement as, for instance, that which affected Shrewsbury in 1592–3 or York in 1604.[59] But the scale of mortality in years such as 1610, 1625 and 1630–1 was far from insignificant, with death-rates of between two and six times the annual average being reached in many parishes.

The relationship between overcrowding, *poverty* and plague stands out quite clearly in the Cambridge records. In 1599 it was ordered by the Vice-Chancellor and Mayor that the parishes of Great St Andrew, St Giles and Holy Trinity, which were overburdened with poor, should receive contributions from the other parishes.[60] It cannot be coincidental that these parishes suffered particularly from regular, quite violent, outbreaks of disease, whereas the central and more wealthy parish of Great St Mary suffered markedly less. Also, the listings of those presented for offending the injunctions against the taking of inmates of June 1632 reveal that St Giles and Great St Andrew were two parishes with the highest proportion of inmates relative to their total populations amongst those parishes for which evidence survives. But not only did poverty and overcrowding tend to encourage plague – the relationship also worked in reverse. The economic structure of the town, so dependent upon its role as a trading centre and a supplier of services to the university, rendered it particularly vulnerable to economic dis-

56. This was particularly true of the suburban parish of St Giles. It is, however, virtually impossible to assess the relative contributions of overcrowding and poverty as the two went hand in hand.
57. Cooper, op. cit., II, 321–4, 357, 373, 426, 522–3; III, 3, 19, 30, 40–1, 179–81, 222–9. These outbreaks are confirmed by notes in various of the Cambridge parish registers for 1603, 1605, 1610 and 1630. In their histories of plague both Creighton and Shrewsbury usually quote Cooper as their source when referring to Cambridge: C. Creighton, *A History of Epidemics in Britain*, I (Cambridge, 1891); J. F. D. Shrewsbury, *A History of Bubonic Plague in the British Isles* (Cambridge, 1970).
58. R. Schofield, 'Crisis mortality', *Local Population Studies* IX, (1972), 10–22.
59. Creighton, op. cit., I, 357, 498.
60. Cambridge University Archives, T.X. 1(b).

location in times of plague.[61] The cancellation of Midsummer and Stourbridge Fairs and the university population's exodus could and did cause severe distress. A document of 1630 stated that the number of families likely to require relief because of the plague visitation was 839, or 2825 persons: 338 of these were in the one parish of St Giles, the total population of which was only 584.[62] In this year local rates and contributions were insufficient to deal with the problem. In a letter to Lord Coventry the Vice-Chancellor stated that 'there are five thousand poor and not one hundred who can assist in relieving them', whilst a royal brief calling for a national collection to relieve the town estimated that the total charge to relieve the poor, *apart* from those visited with plague, would amount to £150 per week at the least, 'which charge the university and town are noe wayes able to disburse there not being above seven score of the said inhabitants that are able any longer to contribute towards their relief'.[63] A further letter from Whitehall dated 11 May 1631 stated that the number of poor and 'visited' was 'about 4000', costing £200 per week in relief.[64] Possibly as much as £5000 was contributed by London and elsewhere towards the relief of the town in this year.[65]

The poverty problem was not confined to years in which the town's economy was disrupted by plague. In 1579 the corporation had attempted to enclose Jesus Green with a view to putting the money raised towards a hospital for the relief of the poor, although the plan was foiled by university opposition.[66] Several attempts were made to prevent the setting up of unlicensed trades by those who were poor and lacked the necessary training.[67] In 1594 one Richard Wilkinson was engaged to set the poor on work in the weaving of fustians, although once again the plan failed to materialize.[68] Eight 'collectors and governers' of the poor were appointed by the Vice-Chancellor and Mayor in 1597 to organize a stock to set the poor on work, and a house at Newnham mills was allocated as a house of correction. The collectors and governors were authorized to expel disreputable persons from the town, and none was to come to inhabit in Cambridge unless their landlord entered into a sufficient

61. For some general remarks about the effect of plague on urban economies see A. D. Dyer, 'The influence of bubonic plague in England 1500–1667', *Medical History*, XXII (1978), 308–26.
62. Cambridge University Archives, C.U.R. Town 37.5, doc. 39.
63. Cooper, op. cit., III, 223–7.
64. Cambridge University Archives, T.X. 1(a).
65. Shrewsbury, op. cit., 359.
66. Cooper, op. cit., II 369–70.
67. For instance, Cooper, op. cit., II, 484; Cambridge University Archives, T.X. 1(a).
68. Cooper, op. cit., II, 579.

bond to ensure that their new tenants would not become a charge upon the parish. At the same time the town constables were urged diligently to seek out beggars and rogues.[69] But if this scheme operated at all its life must have been fairly short, for in 1628 the famous Cambridge carrier Thomas Hobson endowed the town with funds for the very same purpose – to build a workhouse and house of correction.[70] In the previous year an agreement had been made between the town and university and one Charles Raye, clothier, late of Woodbridge in Suffolk, according to which he was to instruct twenty poor people each month at his house in the spinning and dressing of woollen yarn. He was then to provide them with the means to continue this work in their own homes. But whilst there is evidence that this tuition was actually given, very few continued to practise their new trade.[71]

Thus a variety of different kinds of evidence can be produced to show that the related problems of immigration, overcrowding, poverty and plague, repeatedly stressed in Privy Council orders, were very much a feature of the town of Cambridge in the late sixteenth and early seventeenth centuries. But, as argued above, Cambridge was by no means exceptional in experiencing these problems at this time. It would appear that in general urban immigration was particularly marked in this period.[72] Overcrowding was severe in the rapidly expanding suburbs of the capital,[73] and an act of 1593 referring to London complained that 'great mischiefs daily grow and increase by reason of pestering the houses with diverse families, harbouring of inmates, and converting great houses into several tenements'.[74] But the same problem was also to be found in many other provincial towns, of which Worcester and York are just two examples.[75] The influx of poor into towns, and the consequent erection of small cottages and division of existing tenements to house them, was a cause for consternation amongst various urban authorities. At Sandwich in Kent in 1578 the governing body prohibited inhabitants from subdividing houses and offering rooms to newcomers.[76] At Winchester in the early seventeenth century 'inmates' or illegal lodgers were

69. Cambridge University Archives, C.U.R. Town 37.7, doc. 91.
70. Cooper, op. cit., III, 204–5.
71. Cambridge University Archives, C.U.R. Town 37.7, doc. 92 *etr seq.*
72. Clark, in Clark and Slack (eds), op. cit.; Patten, op. cit., 83, 130.
73. M. J. Power, 'The east and west in early modern London', in E. W. Ives *et al.* (eds), *Wealth and Power in Tudor England: Essays Presented to S. T. Bindoff.*
74. Quoted by W. Minchinton, 'Patterns and structure of demand', being Chapter 2 of C. Cipolla (ed.), *The Fontana Economic History of Europe* II, 136.
75. Dyer, *Worcester . . .*, 163–4; D. R. Palliser, 'Epidemics in Tudor York', *Northern History*, VIII (1973), 46.
76. Clark, in Clark and Slack (eds), op. cit., 142.

presented at every session of the town court.[77] In Worcester in 1609 it was claimed that 'there are of late many small cottages erected and built within the city and suburbs', and the authorities were concerned that their occupiers would add to the burden of poor relief.[78] Three special surveys of the poor and vagrants were ordered in early seventeenth-century Chester, and concerted attempts were made to stop inhabitants taking in lodgers who might be a burden to the city.[79] In 1606 Oxford joined with Cambridge to petition for an act for taking down all cottages which had been erected within a certain time, the main reasons given being that the taking in of 'foreign' inmates caused an increase of plague, and an increase in the number of poor.[80] Slack's study of a number of provincial towns clearly points to the relationship between suburban growth, poverty and plague.[81] Indeed, the plague became known in this period as the 'poors' plague';[82] and given this, it is not surprising that it was particularly virulent in town suburbs.

Many large towns were clearly expanding in this period, and a proportion of their inhabitants were achieving relative prosperity from the expansion of internal trade and perhaps also from increased demand from farmers and landowners. Available probate inventory evidence certainly suggests this was the case.[83] But this very expansion also brought an intensification of social problems with which urban authorities were scarcely able to cope. At times the arrival of plague could result in a complete halt to economic activity, which in the long run could only serve to hinder economic development.[84] Stability was lacking. Urban populations themselves were inherently fluid, and this appears to have been true of the more respectable tradesmen as well as of the poorer sections of the community.[85] At the same time, the scale of the poverty problem was increasing, and

77. A. B. Rosen, 'Economic and Social Aspects of Winchester 1520–1670', unpubl. D. Phil. thesis, Oxford, 1975.
78. Dyer, *Worcester . . .*, 163.
79. A. M. Johnson, ' Some Aspects of the Political, Constitutional, Social and Economic History of the City of Chester, 1500–1662', D, Phil., Oxford, 1970, 204.
80. Cooper, op. cit., III, 22. Other examples could also be cited: for Reading, for instance, see J. M. Guilding (ed.), *Reading Records: Diary of the Corporation*, III (1895), 15.
81. Slack's findings are quoted in Patten, op. cit., 145; also P. Slack, 'Social problems and policies', in *The Traditional Community . . .*, 88.
82. C. Cipolla, ' The plague and the pre-Malthus Malthusians', *Journal of European Economic History*, III, 2 (1974), 277–84.
83. See, for instance, W. G. Hoskins, *Essays in Leicestershire History* (Liverpool, 1950), 135.
84. Dyer, 'The influence of bubonic plague. . .', 319.
85. See fn. 55.

what appears to have been happening in the larger towns is simply a more extreme and more obvious example of what was happening in English society in general at this time: a growing polarization between rich and poor.[86] The political implications of this have been spelt out for the capital city by Fisher.[87] The hearth taxes for Cambridge and for other towns (though admittedly these come from a slightly later date) show that whilst there was a tendency for the rich to congregate in the centre of towns with more heavy concentrations of the poor in the suburbs, there was never anything approaching complete segregation.[88] Most towns were still too small in area for physical separation to take place. Furthermore, municipal charity was on the increase, as were private benefactions from townsmen.[89] From this point of view, many of the 'subsistence' migrants to towns may well have deemed themselves relatively well off. The failure of townsmen to establish long-standing 'dynasties', which could act as a focus for resentment, might also be relevant.[90] We are not dealing here with a city with a great 'merchant aristocracy' like medieval Genoa; and in this respect it is interesting that, as we shall see below, although the households of the wealthier members of the community were relatively large in early seventeenth-century Cambridge, they show none of the complexity of the households of Genoa, which were designed with an eye to the maintenance of the economic position of the family.[91] But the fact that there was a degree of socio-economic polarization in English towns in this period remains, and this implies a degree of demographic polarization, which one might expect to see reflected in household size and structure.

THE CAMBRIDGE LISTINGS

Despite the fact that in many other towns overcrowding was in evidence, poverty was just as much a problem,[92] plague outbreaks

86. Clark and Slack, op. cit., 125; Patten, op. cit., 145 and sources cited therein; L. Stone, 'Social mobility in England 1500–1700', *Past and Present*, XXXIII (1966), 16–55.
87. F. J. Fisher, 'The growth of London' in E. W.Ives (ed.), *The English Revolution 1600–60* (1968), 78–80.
88. See fn. 38.
89. Clark and Slack, op. cit., 123.
90. Hoskins, 'English provincial towns . . .', 96.
91. Hughes, in Abrams and Wrigley (eds), op. cit., 127; see also F. W. Kent, *Household and Lineage in Renaissance Florence: the Family Life of the Capponi, Ginori and Rucellai* (Princeton, 1977).
92. For some general remarks on urban poverty see Patten, op. cit., 34–5; also P. Slack, 'Poverty and politics in Salisbury 1597–1666', in Clark and Slack

were often more violent, and the economic dislocation caused by the combination of these factors could be just as severe,[93] it was in the case of Cambridge, not York or Salisbury or any of these other towns, that the Privy Council called for a census to be taken. The only other example where such concern is apparent is in the case of Oxford.[94] The existence of a special relationship between the Vice-Chancellors of these university towns and the Privy Council, and the fact that they were the resort of many sons of the gentry and nobility for much of the year, was clearly behind such exceptional concern.

The listings produced as a result of concern over these problems provide a wealth of information. The very best returns give details of the size and structure of households, including numbers of children, servants and apprentices, occupations of household heads, indication of whether an individual was 'foreign' or town born, and the names of landlords. Some even give information regarding the number of cows and horses kept. The five complete listings of inhabitants analysed here claim to be, and give a strong impression that they are, comprehensive in their coverage. In each case they are signed at the bottom, and the information given could only have been collected by a house-to-house survey. Furthermore, the population totals they provide produce acceptable vital rates when set alongside the decadal averages of baptisms and burials for the 1620s.

THE SAMPLE OF PARISHES

The parishes upon which this study is based are St Peter, St Michael, St Botolph, Barnwell and St Giles. Before proceeding to the analysis of these listings, it remains to be determined whether or not these five parishes for which complete lists survive are representative of the town as a whole. In Figure 1 a sketch map of Cambridge shows their position.[95] Of these, Barnwell and St Giles were essentially suburban parishes, with the other three lying closer to the town's centre. But unfortunately the central parish of Great St Mary, which housed the town's main market, the Guildhall and many of the wealthier inhabitants of the town, is not included in our sample.[96]

(eds), op. cit., 164–94; J. F. Pound, *The Norwich Census of the Poor 1570*, Norfolk Record Society XL (1971). J. Pound, *Poverty and Vagrancy in Tudor England* (1971).

93. See particularly Slack, 'Poverty and politics . . .'; also the account of plague in Salisbury in 1627 in P. Slack (ed.), *Poverty in Early Stuart Salisbury*, Wilts. Record Society, XXXI (1975), 117–19; for the impact of plague of 1586–7 on Lincoln, J W. F. Hill, *Tudor and Stuart Lincoln* (Cambridge, 1956), 91.

94. *Ex. inf.* Alan Crossely (ed. VCH Oxford).

95. Based upon maps in Lobel (ed.), op. cit.,

96. The relative wealth of Great St Mary is evident from the the hearth tax returns of the later seventeenth century, and also from will and inventory evidence.

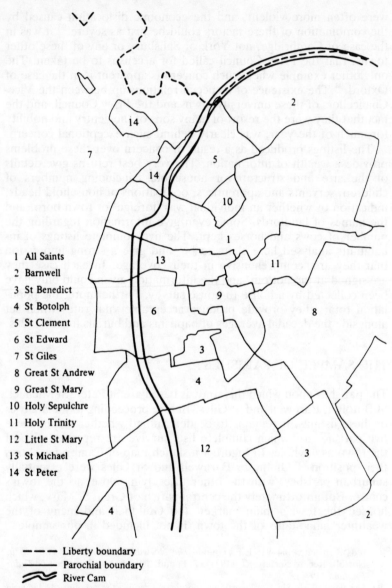

1 All Saints
2 Barnwell
3 St Benedict
4 St Botolph
5 St Clement
6 St Edward
7 St Giles
8 Great St Andrew
9 Great St Mary
10 Holy Sepulchre
11 Holy Trinity
12 Little St Mary
13 St Michael
14 St Peter

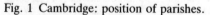

--- Liberty boundary
――― Parochial boundary
≈≈≈ River Cam

Fig. 1 Cambridge: position of parishes.

TABLE 2   Cambridge occupational structure

	Whole town 1580–1640		5 census parishes, 1620s	
	No.	%	No.	%
Gentleman	56	5.82	8	2.33
Prof./official	124	12.88	11	3.20
Merchant/retail	111	11.53	9	2.62
Food/drink	177	18.38	45	13.08
Service/transport	59	6.13	44	12.80
Textiles	6	0.62	4	1.16
Clothing	140	14.54	58	16.86
Leather	23	2.39	4	1.16
Metal	25	2.60	13	3.78
Woodwork	24	2.49	20	5.81
Building	44	4.57	20	5.81
Rural	86	8.93	8	2.33
Labourer	36	3.74	93	27.03
Miscellaneous	52	5.40	7	2.03
	963	100.02	344	100.00

This inclusion of the two most suburban parishes, and the omission of the most central one, is reflected in the occupational structure of our sample. In Table 2 the occupational structure of these five parishes is compared with a sample of 963 individuals from the whole town in the late sixteenth and early seventeenth centuries drawn from wills and inventories.

The bases for these classifications are discussed in Appendix B. The sample from wills and inventories will have certain inbuilt biases. The very poor tended less often to leave a will, or if they did leave one, to have it registered.[97] Thus labourers, and perhaps also the more lowly members of the service and transport sector (tapsters, porters and the like) will be under-represented. Scriveners, public notaries and clergy (included in the professional/official category) will be greatly over-represented in this sample, for their names commonly appear at the bottom of wills as witnesses. Those deemed to be of 'gentleman' status might also be over-represented, partly because they were more likely to be called upon to execute or oversee a will, and partly because a wealthy townsman might be expected to want to emphasize his status in so important a document as his last will and testament. The term 'yeoman' was also used as a status category in early modern towns, and thus a number of those

97. R. S. Gottfried, *Epidemic Disease in Fifteenth Century England* (Leicester, 1978), 22.

TABLE 3   Assessments for Ship Money, 1635[a]

Parish	Census pop.	No. taxed	% taxed	Av. assessment	Tax per head
St Peter	262	19	7.3	53d.	3.8d.
St Michael	293	31	10.6	33d.	3.5d.
St Botolph	528	40	7.6	34d.	2.5d.
Barnwell[b]	265	20	7.5	47d.	3.5d.
St Giles	584	36	6.2	41d.	2.5d.

[a] Cambridge University Archives: C.U.R. Town 36.1, doc 21. Apart from the fact that the exchequer lay subsidies are poor in coverage and unreal in the levels of assessment by this period, Cambridge lists were compiled by ward rather than by parish, so they cannot be used to determine relative parochial levels of wealth.
[b] The Barnwell figures are distorted by the inclusion of two individuals taxed at the very high level of 18 shillings.

included in the 'rural' category in Table 2 might well have had no connection with farming whatsoever.[98]

Taking the above considerations into account, two major discrepancies stand out: the low percentage of merchants and retailers in the census sample, and the high percentage of labourers. This is as one would expect given the geographical positioning of our five parishes discussed above. The former feature is due to the absence of the parish of Great St Mary from our sample. The low percentage of labourers in the figures for the whole town is partly due to the bias inherent in the sources used here, but the much higher figure of 27 per cent for the five census parishes is produced by the inclusion of the two semi-agricultural, suburban parishes of Barnwell and St Giles. Thus whilst both relatively wealthy and relatively poor are represented in these documents, the balance is weighted in favour of the latter.

Independent, though rather crude, evidence of the level of wealth of these five parishes is provided by the Ship Money assessments of 1635, presented in Table 3, and this tends to support the conclusions drawn from their respective socio-occupational structures (see Table 7, below). Whilst no parish was monopolized by either the rich or poor, St Michael and St Peter appear to have stood out above the others in terms of *overall* wealth.

98. College butlers, for instance, were sometimes also described as 'yeomen'; on these problems see J. Patten 'Urban occupations in pre-industrial England', *Trans. Inst. Brit. Geog.*, N.S., II (1977), 296–313.

PROBLEMS OF DEFINITION AND DELINEATION

Although the documents used here are generally remarkable in their clarity, certain terms require careful definition. The term 'sojourner' means a temporary resident, and appears to have been used as such by the compilers of the listings. Those so described are occasionally relatives of particular households, presumably caught in the census whilst making a family visit. Others may have been staying in the town on business. But whatever the reason for their presence, they are clearly marked out as being in a different category to 'inmates' and 'lodgers', and will be regarded as non-residents of the town.[99] Lodgers and boarders in the lists are usually unmarried individuals, and some are described as living-out servants or university students. They appear to be strictly temporary members of particular households, sharing the facilities of that household without being in any real sense part of it. They will therefore be treated, in accordance with Laslett's usage, as belonging to no household grouping, and will be analysed separately.[100]

Due to the nature of the census inmates figure prominently in the listings. But the term is not used entirely consistently. Whilst they *usually* constitute a clear, separate household, merely sharing a physical housing structure, occasionally they are subsumed under other household groups. The course followed here is to place faith in the compilers of the listings. When a group described as inmates is marked out in a listing as a separate household, they will be treated as such here. It is difficult to agree with Laslett's argument that 'since they do not occupy dwellings they should not in strictness be called households' despite the fact that they are 'parallel in definition to types of household'.[101] The layout of the listings would appear to indicate that they function as a household group. As noted above (see p. 78), the authorities equated inmates with poor immigrants; thus to exclude them from the analysis would only serve to bias our findings away from the less well established households in the community. Where inmates are included as part of another household, they will be regarded as lodgers.

99. M. Spufford noted that the term sojourner was used 'to cover the wandering and rootless', although she also seems to suggest that it referred to retired parents who lived with their children: M. C. Spufford, 'Peasant inheritance customs and land distribution in Cambridgeshire from the sixteenth to the eighteenth centuries', in J. Goody, J. Thirsk and E. P. Thompson (eds), *Family and Inheritance* (Cambridge, 1976), 174. None of the sojourners in the Cambridge lists could be identified as a parent of the household head.
100. P. Laslett and R. Wall (eds), *Household and Family in Past Time* (Cambridge, 1972), 26–7, 34–6.
101. Ibid., 87.

MEAN HOUSEHOLD SIZE IN CAMBRIDGE

The mean household size of a number of pre-industrial English towns, including Cambridge, is presented in Table 4.[102]

TABLE 4   English pre-industrial urban household sizes

Date	Town	Population	*Mean household size*
1574	Poole, Dorset	1 357	6.05
1622	Stafford, Staffs.	1 551	4.05
1619–32	Cambridge, Cambs. (5 parishes)	1 932	4.13
1645	Chester, Cheshire	3 701	5.62
1693	Whitehaven, Cumberland	2 272	5.04
1695	Bilston, Staffs.	1 006	4.01
1695–6	Exeter, Devon (2 parishes)	2 263	6.98
1696	Gloucester, Gloucs.	4 756	4.22
1695–6	Lichfield, Staffs.	3 038	4.63
1696	London (18 parishes)	32 499	4.87
1696	Norwich, Norfolk (18 parishes)	15 445	4.23
1695–6	Shrewsbury, Salop. (1 ward)	935	4.21
1695–7	Southampton, Hants. (5 parishes)	1 816	4.03[a]
1695	Tiverton, Devon	7 351	4.54

[a] This figure is an average of the mean household sizes of the various Southampton parishes presented by Laslett.

These figures, ranging between 4 and 7 with Cambridge towards the lower limit, give a clear warning against the careless use of multipliers to estimate total populations from numbers of households. Even between urban communities at similar dates marked variations existed.

There are numerous possible explanations of such differences. Demographic and migrational trends might partially explain differences over time. Rapid immigration was a prominent feature of many provincial towns in the late sixteenth and early seventeenth centuries, with young men and women figuring prominently amongst the migrants. Of the migrants in Mary Siraut's sample of Cambridge deponents 69 per cent were between the ages of 10 and 29 when they entered the town.[103] This would affect the age and marital structure of the town concerned, and might in part account for the low figures for Cambridge and Stafford in the 1620s. The influx of

102. Taken from Laslett, op. cit., 204; Laslett and Wall (eds), op. cit., 174–89.
103. Siraut, op. cit., 289.

TABLE 5   Mean household sizes of Cambridge parishes

Parish	Population	Mean household size
St Peter	262	4.64
St Michael	293	4.61
St Botolph	528	4.04
Barnwell	265	3.95
St Giles	584	3.89
Combined	1932	4.13

poor into towns would also tend to depress mean household sizes, for available evidence suggests a strong positive relationship between household sizes and wealth.[104] Recurrent plagues, or other diseases, might produce similar results by constantly interrupting the natural growth of families. Different economic, and hence social and occupational structures, might be expected to result in differences in average household sizes. Furthermore, most censuses cover only parts of each town, and might easily be biased towards either the poor or the rich. The biases in the Cambridge sample of parishes have already been noted. With a range in Norwich between parishes of 3.67 to 5.40, and in London of 4.00 to 6.32, one wonders if the two Exeter parishes or the one Shrewsbury ward in Table 4 are likely to be representative of the town as a whole.[105] All this serves to underline the central argument of this article. More detailed analyses of individual listings and sets of listings within the context of the history of the communities concerned are necessary if any attempt is to be made to explain variations (or similarities) between different places and between different periods.[106]

104. Laslett. op. cit., 220–1; see also E. Shorter, *The Making of the Modern Family* (1976), 24; Phythian-Adams in *The Fabric of the Traditional Community* 25.

105. R. Wall, in Laslett and Wall (eds), op. cit., 183, 185–6.

106. A further problem is lack of consistency in the way different listings have been analysed. I have already discussed some of the terminological problems. Also some listings are of better quality than others, and it is sometimes difficult to distinguish between the 'household' and the 'houseful'. This is why Laslett's original analysis of the London parishes differs from Wall's: cf. Laslett, op. cit., 204, and Laslett and Wall (eds), op cit., 183.

MEAN HOUSEHOLD SIZE IN CAMBRIDGE BY PARISH

Of the five Cambridge parishes the two semi-rural suburban parishes of St Giles and Barnwell, the relative overall poverty of which is suggested by their occupational structures and the Ship Money assessments, exhibit the lowest averages. The highest averages were in the two wealthier parishes – the centrally situated St Michael and the riverside parish of St Peter. If comparison is made with the five parishes for which listings of *inmates only* are available for the year 1632 (that is St Clement, St Giles again, Holy Trinity, Little St Mary and Great St Andrew), one finds, as would be expected, a generally lower average. But the wealthier, more central parish of St Clements stands out, having a mean household size amongst its inmate population of 4.07.

A more detailed breakdown is given in Table 6. These figures strongly support the now orthodox view that the majority of households in pre-industrial English communities were quite small. In every listing over 50 per cent of households had between three and five members, whilst in every listing apart from St Peter's over 50 per cent of the population lived in households of this size. But despite the predominance of medium-size households, 39 per cent of the population lived in households of six or more members, this total lying midway between the two figures calculated by Laslett and Harrison for Clayworth in 1676 and 1688.[107] The percentage of the population in very small households, with one to three members, was 26 per cent for the five Cambridge parishes, which is also comparable to the Clayworth figures of 29 per cent and 22 per cent.

Comparison with Laslett's 100 communities can only be made in terms of the percentage of *households* of a particular size. The major contrast to be noticed is in the higher percentage of small households in early seventeenth-century Cambridge, and the correspondingly lower percentage of large ones.[108] The bias in the Cambridge sample towards the poorer areas of the town is obviously influential here, and one might also suggest (as argued above) that rapid immigration of young adults and the effects of recurrent plagues might also have helped produce these results.

While in all five Cambridge parishes much the same percentage of households are to be found in the middle range, the parishes of St Michael and St Peter stand out as having a lower percentage of small households and a higher percentage of large ones. Once again the greater overall wealth of these two parishes immediately comes

---

107. Laslett and Harrison, in Laslett (ed.), op. cit., 87.
108. Laslett, op. cit., 216.

TABLE 6 Household sizes in five Cambridge parishes

(a) Number and percentage of households size 1–13

Household size	Barnwell		St Botolph		St Giles		St Michael		St Peter		Combined	
	No.	%	No.	%	No.	%	No.	%	No.	%	No.	%
1	4	6.15	8	6.40	15	10.14	1	1.69	–	–	28	6.19
2	16	24.62	23	18.40	27	18.24	8	13.56	10	18.18	84	18.58
3	13	20.00	27	21.60	35	23.65	10	16.95	11	20.00	96	21.24
4	10	15.38	24	19.20	27	18.24	12	20.34	9	16.36	82	18.14
5	12	18.46	17	13.60	16	10.81	13	22.03	8	14.55	66	14.60
6	1	1.54	12	9.60	8	5.41	3	5.08	6	10.91	30	6.64
7	5	7.69	6	4.80	10	6.76	6	10.17	5	9.09	32	7.08
8	1	1.54	2	1.60	2	1.35	4	6.78	2	3.64	11	2.43
9	1	1.54	3	2.40	2	1.35	1	1.69	2	3.64	9	1.99
10	–	–	1	0.80	4	2.70	–	–	1	1.82	6	1.33
11	1	1.54	2	1.60	2	1.35	1	1.69	1	1.82	7	1.55
12	–	–	–	–	–	–	–	–	–	–	–	–
13	1	1.54	–	–	–	–	–	–	–	–	1	0.22
Total	65	100.00	125	100.00	148	100.00	59	100.00	55	100.00	452	100.00

Table 6 (cont.)

(b) Number and percentage of persons in households size 1–13

Household size	Barnwell		St Botolph		St Giles		St Michael		St Peter		Combined	
	No.	%	No.	%	No.	%	No.	%	No.	%	No.	%
1	4	1.56	8	1.58	15	2.60	1	0.37	–	–	28	1.50
2	32	12.45	46	9.11	54	9.38	16	5.88	20	7.84	168	9.01
3	39	15.18	81	16.04	105	18.23	30	11.03	33	12.94	288	15.44
4	40	15.57	96	19.01	108	18.75	48	17.65	36	14.12	328	17.59
5	60	23.35	85	16.83	80	13.88	65	23.89	40	15.69	330	17.69
6	6	2.33	72	14.26	48	8.33	18	6.62	36	14.12	180	9.65
7	35	13.62	42	8.32	70	12.15	42	15.44	35	13.73	224	12.01
8	8	3.11	16	3.17	16	2.78	32	11.76	16	6.27	88	4.72
9	9	3.50	27	5.35	18	3.13	9	3.31	18	7.06	81	4.34
10	–	–	10	1.98	40	6.94	–	–	10	3.92	60	3.22
11	11	4.28	22	4.36	22	3.82	11	4.04	11	4.31	77	4.13
12	–	–	–	–	–	–	–	–	–	–	–	–
13	13	5.06	–	–	–	–	–	–	–	–	13	0.70
Total	257	100.00	505	100.00	576	100.00	272	100.00	255	100.00	1,865[a]	100.00

[a] The discrepancy between this total and that in Table 5 is due to the exclusion here of lodgers, etc., of those resident in institutions.

to mind. But if these inter-parochial differences are to be explained in less general terms, each listing requires more detailed consideration in terms of the influence of factors such as varying occupational structures, sizes of child groups, proportion of widows, and so on.

HOUSEHOLD SIZE BY SOCIO-OCCUPATIONAL GROUP

A breakdown by occupational group is presented in Table 7. The divisions used here are essentially, though not entirely, based upon trades, and thus only partially reflect differences in socio-economic status.[109] Hence the categories are not entirely satisfactory. Under 'textiles', for instance, a clothier is included together with the presumably more humble cloth workers. Under 'service and transport' innkeepers are grouped together with porters and ostlers. These are extreme examples, but serve to show that anomalies exist regarding the homogeneity of our categories as *socio*-occupational groups, even with the large number of divisions employed here. But nor is it feasible to break down these groupings any further. Already the small numbers in many of the categories in Table 7 prevent realistic comparison between parishes. Furthermore, only a rough outline of the socio-occupational ranking in Cambridge and other pre-industrial towns is yet known. Hence the divisions used in Table 7 are a compromise between a division into trades and a division into socio-economic groups.

Notwithstanding the small numbers in the higher status groups, there is a clear distinction between the average size of households of those described as gentlemen and those of the various merchants and artisans. Professionals and officials occupied a half-way position. It is possible that, had the merchants and retailers from the parish of Great St Mary been included in the analysis, the average household size of this category would also have been noticeably larger than that of many of the craft groups. *Within* certain categories there is some indication that household size increased with occupational status and hence wealth. Thus under 'food and drink', the average household size of brewers was larger than that of other trades in this group. Within 'service and transport' inn-

109. See fn. 98. Also the term 'gentleman', particularly in towns, was essentially a description of status rather than occupation. The title 'generosus' generally accompanied achievement of the mayoralty in sixteenth- and seventeenth-century Reading.

TABLE 7 Mean household sizes by socio-occupational group

	Barnwell		St Botolph		St Giles		St Michael		St Peter		Combined	
	Size	No. of entries	Size	No. of entries	Size	No. of entries	Size	No. of entries	Size	No. of entries	Size	No. of entries
Gentleman	–		10.00	(2)	10.00	(4)	2.00	(1)	7.00	(1)	8.63	(8)
Prof./offic.	–		5.67	(6)	–		5.00	(5)	–		5.36	(11)
Merch./ret.	–		5.00	(3)	–		4.00	(4)	6.00	(2)	4.78	(9)
Food/drink	6.67	(3)	4.10	(20)	4.83	(12)	5.40	(5)	6.80	(5)	4.91	(45)
Serv./trans.	4.00	(3)	4.00	(6)	5.55	(11)	3.91	(11)	4.08	(13)	4.39	(44)
Textiles	3.00	(1)	1.50	(2)	–		5.00	(1)	–		2.75	(4)
Clothing	4.67	(3)	4.32	(22)	4.23	(13)	5.06	(16)	3.25	(4)	4.45	(58)
Leather	–		2.00	(1)	5.50	(2)	4.00	(1)	–		4.24	(4)
Metal	6.00	(2)	3.00	(5)	5.00	(1)	4.00	(4)	4.00	(1)	4.31	(13)
Woodwork	4.50	(4)	4.60	(5)	3.67	(3)	3.80	(5)	5.00	(3)	4.30	(20)
Building	4.33	(3)	4.22	(9)	4.50	(4)	4.50	(2)	8.00	(2)	4.70	(20)
Rural	6.83	(6)	1.00	(1)	5.00	(1)	–		–		5.88	(8)
Labourer	3.84	(19)	3.25	(4)	3.70	(59)	–		3.45	(11)	3.65	(93)
Misc.	–		5.67	(3)	3.00	(1)	11.00	(1)	5.50	(2)	6.00	(7)
Not stated	3.08	(13)	3.44	(18)	3.00	(6)	5.00	(1)	6.33	(3)	3.51	(44)
Widow(er)	1.71	(7)	3.28	(25)	2.70	(40)	3.67	(6)	4.00	(10)	3.51[a]	

[a] No total has been calculated for widow(er)s as the Barnwell list provides insufficient information for the identification of widowers.

keepers stand out as having a notably higher average household size, with such as porters, ostlers and tapsters at the other end of the scale. Although the numbers involved are small, the evidence does suggest a positive relationship between occupational status and wealth, and the size of households.

Further support is provided by the smaller average size of labourers' households. As most of these are to be found in the semi-rural parishes of St Giles and Barnwell, they were probably in the main agricultural labourers. If, as seems likely given the amount of information the compilers of the listings were able to provide, many of those whose trades are not stated were paupers, then a positive relationship between occupational/economic status and household size stands out even more clearly.

The *ranking* of household sizes by occupation is similar to Laslett's 100 communities. But while the average figure for 'trades and crafts' combined is much the same, labouring households in early seventeenth-century Cambridge were significantly smaller (3.65 as compared with 4.51).[110] Perhaps this is a reflection of the extent of poverty amongst the lowest social groups in urban communities at this time. Or it could be that recurrent epidemics of plague, which (as noted above) was often described by contemporaries as the 'poor's plague' and was usually particularly vehement in over-crowded town suburbs, took its toll amongst the labouring households of early seventeenth-century Cambridge.[111] Interestingly, most of the widowers in St Giles *were* labourers. A further poss-ibility is that newly arrived immigrants, a high percentage of whom were young adults, and particularly the 'subsistence' rather than the 'betterment' migrants, may have gravitated towards unskilled labouring jobs, creating a bias in our figures for labourers towards more recently formed households (see also below, p. 103). Unfor-tunately no satisfactory information regarding place of birth is given in the Barnwell or St Giles lists.

Obviously these hypotheses cannot be tested without detailed biographical information about the individual families in our lists – information which is probably not recoverable from surviving documentation. But at least the influence of occupational structure upon the differences in mean household size between the five Cambridge parishes is now clearer. The abundance of labourers in St Giles was an important cause of the low overall average here. Most labouring households consisted of only two or three members, the average being buoyed up by a smattering of larger ones. The presence of a small group of gentry families served to enhance the percentage of persons in larger households in this parish. But just

110. Laslett, op. cit., 221.
111. See above, p. 84–5.

as noticeable is the large number of widow and widower households and their small mean household size. Here, it would seem, is one effect of recurrent epidemics within a generally poor suburban parish.

In Barnwell, the combination of the presence of a significant number of labourers and a large group who were probably paupers served to keep the mean household size low. In St Botolph the large number of pauper and widow households tended to produce the same effect. As noted above, St Botolph was, like St Giles, particularly hard hit by recurrent epidemics. But even within particular trades, although the numbers involved are very small, household sizes in St Peter and St Michael often tended to be larger. Perhaps this is an indication that the wealthier and longer established tradesmen were more commonly found in some parishes than in others.[112]

Thus we can conclude that differing occupational structures played an essential part in producing variations in mean household sizes between parishes, but that this cannot be divorced from the general poverty of particular parishes and the allied varying incidence of epidemic disease between them.

CHILDREN

Information regarding children is only available for four of the five parishes, and this is presented in Table 8. Mean size of groups of children varied little from parish to parish, and there is no obvious relationship between mean household size and the average size of child groups within particular parishes. We are, of course, dealing only with averages, but the figures do show that the average size of child groups was not the crucial variable behind differences in *mean* household size. A similar lack of variation is evident for percentages of households with children.

In St Giles, and to a lesser extent in St Botolph, children formed a slightly higher proportion of the total population. In St Giles, particularly in comparison with St Michael, this is partially a reflection of the *slightly* higher average child group size in the former parish, though this would be offset to some extent by the slightly higher percentage of households with children in St Michael. In St Giles as compared with St Peter, there was a lower overall percentage of households composed of childless couples. But perhaps a more im-

112. For a similar argument for Newcastle, based upon more substantial evidence, see J. Langton, 'Residential patterns in pre-industrial cities', *Transactions of the Institute of British Geographers*, LXV (1975), 21.

TABLE 8   Children, by parish

	Av. size child groups	% Households with children	Children as % of pop.	No. childless couples (and % of total no. of households)
St Botolph	2.27	72.00	39.77	21 (16.80)
St Giles	2.37	74.32	45.03	19 (12.84)
St Michael	2.24	77.97	35.15	8 (13.56)
St Peter	2.27	74.55	35.88	11 (20.00)
Combined	2.30	74.16	40.19	59 (15.25)

portant explanation, which holds good for both St Giles and St Botolph, is that in these parishes there was a higher percentage of widows, widowers and one-person families, which would serve to raise the number of children as a proportion of the total population. This is evident from Table 6 (above) and Table 13 (below). Interestingly, Laslett also found a negative correlation, though in his study a very strong one, between mean household size and the proportion of children in the population.[113]

Our four parishes combined give an average child group size roughly 0.5 lower than for Laslett's 100 communities. The percentage of households with children is almost identical, while the number of children as a percentage of the total population is again slightly lower for Cambridge.[114]

Table 9 presents the sizes of child groups by occupation. A slight positive relationship between occupational status and child group size is apparent, though this is less marked than was the case for mean *household* size by occupation. Here we are at variance with Laslett's results for 100 communities.[115] But the correlation is only slight, and the problems with our occupational classifications have already been noted. But gentlemen, professionals and officials do stand above the rest in this respect, while sizes of child groups in labouring households were significantly smaller than for some trades and crafts, and slightly smaller than for others.

Possibly the fact that a high proportion of labouring households were childless supports the idea of a positive relationship between occupational status and numbers of children. But the figures in Table 9 are averages which present a picture at one point in time only, and reveal nothing about *completed* family sizes. Some indi-

113. Laslett, op. cit., 216.
114. Ibid., 217.
115. Ibid., 221–2.

TABLE 9 Sizes of groups of children by occupation

	St Botolph		St Giles		St Michael		St Peter		Combined	
	Size	No. of entries	Size	No. of entries	Size	No. of entries	Size	No. of entries	Size	No. of entries
Gentleman	5.50	(2)	4.25	(4)	–		–		4.67	(6)
Prof./offic.	3.50	(4)	–		2.60	(5)	–		3.00	(9)
Merch./ret.	3.50	(2)	–		2.00	(3)	2.50	(2)	2.57	(7)
Food/drink	2.07	(14)	3.11	(9)	3.75	(4)	4.50	(2)	2.90	(31)
Serv./trans.	1.20	(5)	3.18	(11)	1.38	(8)	1.60	(10)	2.00	(34)
Textiles	–		–		–		2.00	(1)	2.00	(1)
Clothing	2.19	(16)	3.00	(8)	2.55	(11)	2.50	(2)	2.49	(37)
Leather	–		8.00	(1)	1.00	(1)	–		4.50	(2)
Metal	3.00	(1)	3.00	(1)	2.33	(3)	2.00	(1)	2.50	(6)
Woodwork	3.00	(4)	1.00	(3)	1.80	(5)	3.33	(3)	2.27	(15)
Building	1.56	(9)	2.00	(3)	1.50	(2)	4.00	(1)	1.87	(15)
Rural	–		2.00	(1)	–		–		2.00	(1)
Labourer	2.00	(1)	1.96	(48)	–		1.88	(8)	1.95	(57)
Misc.	4.50	(2)	–		7.00	(1)	2.00	(2)	4.00	(5)
Not stated	2.44	(9)	1.75	(4)	1.00	(1)	2.00	(2)	1.94	(16)
Widow(er)	2.15	(20)	2.00	(27)	1.40	(5)	2.00	(8)	2.00	(60)

cation of the potential influence of the length of time a family had been formed has recently been provided for Stratford in 1765 by Martin, although the lack of detail in the listing he used prevented the analysis from being taken very far.[116] If, as I have suggested as a possibility, many of the labourers in our sample were young immigrants, this in itself could explain the relatively small average size of groups of children for this occupation, rather than it being an intrinsic feature of the occupation itself. A further factor to be considered is the high rate of infant mortality within urban communities, which may well have exerted a particular impact upon the families of the lower social groups.[117] Or it might be that a higher proportion of labourers' children left home at an early age, due to parental inability to support them, and became servants in the households of others. In his study of Swindon in 1697, Cardington in 1782 and Colyton in 1841, Richard Wall found that a significantly higher proportion of children aged 15 and over were still resident in the households of tradesmen than was the case for labourers.[118] And Tranter on Cardington noticed that whilst labouring families had on average five children, no more than two were resident within the parental household.[119] These studies do, of course, deal with very different communities at a much later period. But they do show that only *age-specific* information will reveal just why it was that labouring families in early seventeenth-century Cambridge tended to contain fewer children than higher socio-occupational groups.

In general the numbers are too small, or the occupational subgroups too difficult to compare, to allow the drawing of conclusions about differences between parishes by occupation. All that can be said is that it was *not* invariably the case that the smallest child groups in particular categories were to be found in the poorer parishes. Interestingly, some occupational categories which exhibit a relatively high child group size in the parish of St Giles tend less frequently to contain servants or apprentices. For instance, the size of child groups is higher in the clothing trades in St Giles than it is in St Michael or St Botolph, but a much lower percentage of the St Giles households in this category contained either servants or apprentices. Thus a tendency for children to perform the role of servants or apprentices in poorer parishes is clearly a possibility.

116. Martin, op. cit.
117. Patten, op. cit., 144; Clarkson, 'Household and family . . .', op. cit., 24 and fn. 34.
118. R. Wall, 'The age at leaving home', *Journal of Family History*, III, 2 (1978), 195–6.
119. Tranter, op. cit., 272, 278. Early death, besides leaving home, also contributed towards this result. Tranter also noticed the differences in family size according to the age of the household head: at Cardington the largest family size occurred when the family head was aged between 31 and 40 (273).

SERVANTS AND APPRENTICES

There is still much to be learnt about servants and apprentices in early-modern England. Laslett's averages for 100 communities remains the only major study of the differing tendencies of various socio-occupational groups to keep servants and apprentices (his 'servants' do in fact include apprentices). And there is still a need for more detailed breakdown within particular contexts. Within towns, for instance, some trades had more use for apprentices whilst some had more use for servants. This throws suspicion upon apprenticeship figures as accurate reflections of urban occupational structures. Furthermore, there is a little evidence that the dividing line between servants and apprentices may on occasions have been thin. From his analysis of the London lists of 1695 David Glass concluded that servants and apprentices were not entirely distinct categories, and that some servants may have been assistants serving in something comparable to an apprenticeship role.[120] There are a few individuals described as both a servant and an apprentice amongst the Cambridge lists, and further examples appear in Cambridge wills. On the other hand, a high proportion of the servants in the Cambridge lists were female, which, although female apprentices were not unknown, does suggest a domestic role. Given the present state of knowledge, here servants and apprentices will be treated as distinct categories.

Table 10 presents statistical information regarding servants and apprentices. The percentage of households containing servants and/or apprentices varies markedly between parishes, as did their numbers as a percentage of the total population. These figures clearly underline the importance of servants and apprentices in the determination of mean household size. The figures for St Michael and St Peter as compared with St Giles show that this feature had a far greater influence than did the proportion of children or the average size of child groups.

In all parishes only a small percentage of households contained both servants *and* apprentices,[121] whilst very few indeed included journeymen. It should be noted that only those journeymen who lived within the household of a trade or craftsman are distinguished in the lists. It is possible that some of the heads of household listed were 'living-out' journeymen. Still, the low number of 'living-in'

---

120. D. V. Glass, 'Notes on the demography of London at the end of the seventeenth century', *Daedalus*, LXXXXVII (1968), 2.
121. A listing of the High Ward in Reading of 1584, although it only includes males, similarly shows that very few households contained both a servant and an apprentice.

TABLE 10 Servants and apprentices by parish

	St Botolph	St Giles	St Michael	St Peter	Combined
% households with servants	24.00	11.48	23.73	32.73	20.41
Av. size servant groups	1.53	1.94	1.14	1.94	1.65
% servants in pop.	8.71	5.65	5.80	13.36	7.86
% households with apprentices	16.80	12.84	39.98	12.73	18.09
Av. size apprentice groups	1.19	1.32	1.48	1.29	1.33
% apprentices in pop.	4.73	4.28	12.20	3.44	5.70
% households with either	37.60	23.13	54.24	41.82	35.23
% households with both	3.20	1.35	8.47	3.64	3.36
% households with journeymen	–	–	3.39	1.82	0.78
Sex of servants[a] (% female)	83.33	?	94.12	72.73	?
Sex of apprentices[a] (% male)	92.00	100.00	77.78	100.00	89.47
% servants 'foreign'	78.26	72.73	?	77.42	?
% apprentices 'foreign'	64.00	68.00	?	57.14	?

[a] Assummed to be male unless otherwise stated

journeymen remains of interest. The relative cost of retaining either a journeyman or an apprentice at a time of abundant labour is an interesting question. A complaint by the Vice-Chancellor and mayor in the early 1630s about 'the multiplying of tradesmen and the retaining of apprentices from other towns by persons of small or no ability',[122] along with the complaints about the setting up of unlicensed trades cited above (see pp. 85–6), might be taken as an indication that, in a town where craft gilds were a dead letter by the seventeenth century,[123] the 'classical' master craftsman/journeyman/apprentice set-up was no longer the norm. The high percentage of servants and apprentices designated 'foreigner' in the lists (and particularly servants) confirms the importance of these roles as a means of entry into urban society.

Our combined totals are substantially higher than Laslett's findings for 100 communities.[124] He found that 28.5 per cent of all

122. Cambridge University Archives: T.X. 1a.
123. Siraut, op. cit., 242.
124. Laslett, op. cit., 219.

TABLE 11   Servants and apprentices by occupation (4 parishes)

No.	Occupation	% households with servants	% households with apprentices	% households with either	Both as % population in house- holds
8	Gentlemen	87.50	25.00	100.00	37.68
7	Professional	14.29	–	14.29	8.11
4	Official	75.00	25.00	75.00	31.82
9	Merch./retail	44.44	33.33	55.56	18.18
42	Food/drink	33.33	14.29	45.24	12.94
41	Serv./trans.	41.46	4.88	43.90	14.36
3	Textiles	–	–	–	–
55	Clothing	12.73	41.82	47.27	17.21
4	Leather	–	25.00	25.00	5.88
11	Metal	18.18	27.27	36.36	18.18
16	Woodwork	6.25	31.25	37.50	8.82
17	Building	11.76	35.29	64.71	16.05
2	Rural	–	50.00	50.00	16.67
74	Labourer	10.81	4.05	13.51	5.58
7	Miscellaneous	28.57	57.14	71.43	16.67
28	Not stated	14.29	7.14	21.43	15.84
58	Widow(er)s	12.07	10.34	22.41	10.24

households included either a servant or an apprentice, compared with 35.23 per cent in the Cambridge sample. And had more wealthy Cambridge parishes been included in the sample our figures would have been even higher still. This difference might be expected of an urban population compared with a predominantly agrarian one.

In Table 11 servants and apprentices are analysed by occupation. A positive relationship between socio-occupational status and the percentage of households with either servants or apprentices stands out very strongly, though with one or two exceptions. But it was still far from uncommon for the lower occupational groups to keep servants, though as one might expect few apprentices are to be found in labouring households. There is a clear tendency for particular trades to favour servants (as in service and transport), while in others (particularly the craft trades) apprentices predominate.

Compared with Laslett's figures for percentages of households with servants or apprentices in the 'gentleman', 'trade and craftsman' and 'labourer' categories, the Cambridge results are significantly higher, and to an increasing extent further down the social scale.[125] Whether or not this was generally the case in pre-industrial

125. Ibid., 222.

towns is not known, though one might expect these results given the evident pull that towns exerted coupled with the fact that service and apprenticeship were common means of entry. It might also suggest that the complaints about poor townsmen taking in servants and apprentices in Cambridge cited above had some foundation in fact.

KIN

As the table 12 shows, the percentage of households with resident kin was small and their effect on mean household size minimal.

TABLE 12   Resident kin

	Number of entries	% households with resident kin	% of population
St Botolph	4	2.40	0.76
St Giles	4	2.03	0.68
St Michael	3	5.05	1.02
St Peter	5	5.45	1.91
Combined	16	3.10	0.96

There is little sign here of the complexity of the households of Italian cities such as medieval Genoa or Renaissance Florence.[126] This contrast was noticed by contemporaries such as Fynes Moryson who wrote, 'Never did I observe brothers to live in such unity as in Italy, so as the father being dead, many of them ordinarily live in one house together, not dividing their patrimony, but having all goods in common . . .'.[127] It would seem that the advice of William Whately was already being heeded by the inhabitants of early seventeenth-century Cambridge: 'When thou art married, if it may be, live of thy self with thy wife, in a family of thine own, and not with another, in one family, as it were, betwixt you both . . .'.[128] Although, as a Quaker bachelor, he may well be untypical, a similarly individualistic attitude is expressed in the diary of William Stout of Lancaster.[129] Furthermore, will evidence for Cambridge,

126. See above, p. 88; Hughes, op. cit.; Kent, op. cit.
127. Quoted in C. Cipolla, 'Four centuries of Italian demographic development', in D. V. Glass and D. E. C. Eversley (eds), *Population in History* (1965), 578.
128. Quoted in A. MacFarlane, *The Origins of English Individualism* (Oxford, 1978), 75.
129. J. D. Marshall (ed.), *The Diary of William Stout of Lancaster, 1665–1752* (Manchester, 1967).

Colchester and Reading suggests that it was rare for property to be left to children in common. This picture fits well with our knowledge regarding the relatively short duration of family businesses in English provincial towns at this time.[130]

In agreement with Laslett, kin were more commonly found in larger households,[131] and a positive relationship between the overall wealth of a parish, its mean household size and the percentage of households with kin is evident. There is no sign here of pauperization leading to family extension.[132] The most common category of kin to be found was a brother or sister of the household head or his wife.[133]

In Laslett's study roughly 10 per cent of households contained resident kin, forming almost $3\frac{1}{2}$ per cent of the total population, figures which are substantially higher than even the wealthier Cambridge parishes.[134] In late seventeenth-century Southampton, Shrewsbury and London, the percentages were 7.4, 8.3 and 8.3 respectively,[135] while in mid-nineteenth-century York as many as 22 per cent of households contained kin.[236] Thus, even in comparison with other towns, the Cambridge figures are low, and it might be suggested that this was a product of the marked fluidity of towns at this time, and partly also a result of the bias towards the poorer areas of the town in the Cambridge sample of parishes. What seems clear is that *intra*-urban variation could itself be substantial.[137]

---

130. See above, p. 88 and fn. 90.
131. Laslett, op. cit., 218.
132. Medick, op. cit., 308.
133. One problem here is that some of the servants and apprentices listed may also have been kin, though it is impossible to identify them as such. A number of such cases occur in Cambridge wills, but no reliable quantification is possible. William Stout of Lancaster certainly made good use of his nephews and nieces as servants and apprentices: Marshall (ed.), op. cit., *passim*.
134. Laslett, op. cit., 218.
135. This information was kindly supplied by Richard Wall, whose paper on regional and temporal variations in English household structure is awaiting publication. The London figures were taken from a balanced sample of rich and poor parishes, the whole town of Southampton is included but for two parishes, whilst the Shrewsbury list omits part of the suburban area.
136. W. A. Armstrong, 'A note on the household structure of mid-nineteenth-century York in comparative perspective', in Laslett and Wall (eds), op. cit., 210–11.
137. E. Shorter, though on the basis of only slight evidence, has suggested that pre-industrial rural households were generally more complex that urban ones, and also notes that intra-urban differences were marked: Shorter, op. cit., 23–5. Richard Wall's forthcoming article should throw more light on this question of rural-urban variation for the late seventeenth-century. But it is also possible that changes may have taken place within urban communities during the course of this period of 200 years which we term 'pre-industrial'. Paucity of early urban listings makes further investigation difficult. It is interesting, however, that Charles Phythian-Adams found so few kin in early sixteenth-century Coventry: Phythian-Adams, *The Fabric of the Traditional Community*, 25.

TABLE 13   Widowed persons

	St Botolph	*St Giles*	*St Michael*	*St Peter*	*Combined*
% households headed by widow(er)	20.00	27.03	10.17	18.18	20.93
% households with co-residing widow(er)	–	1.35	–	1.82	0.78
% households with solitary widow(er)	1.60	6.76	–	–	3.10
Sex ratio(% female)	95.83	76.21	57.14	81.82	81.81
% widow(er)s in population	5.68	7.19	2.39	4.20	5.10
Av. size widow(er) households	3.28	2.70	3.67	4.00	3.11

WIDOWS AND WIDOWERS

In all parishes a significant proportion of households were headed by widowed persons, as Table 13 shows, with a generally higher proportion in the less wealthy parishes. This possibly reflects the greater effect of plague and other diseases, particularly in the case of St Giles.

Solitary widows were quite rare, though once again more common in the poorer suburban parishes. The mean size of widow(er) households varies quite markedly, and a positive relationship existed between the average size of households of widowed persons and the wealth (and MHS) of the various parishes. The influence that a high percentage of widow(er) households could have on the mean household size of a particular parish is clearly shown, this being largely due to the simple numerical effect of the loss of one household head.

The figure of 20.93 for the percentage of households headed by widowed persons is a little higher than for Laslett's 100 communities,[138] though not so much as might be expected given our sample of parishes and the virulence of plague in towns at this time. Possibly these factors were counterbalanced to some extent by a lower age structure due to immigration of young adults and (at one remove) the effect on the population as a whole of a long period of population growth. But it is also probable that some widowed persons have escaped inclusion in Table 13. No solitary widow*ers* were found in the lists, which is probably simply because they were

138. Laslett, op. cit., 216.

not described as such. In fact, the word is only found in one of the lists of those presented in 1632, referring to a man who was shortly to be remarried. Thus widowers have been identified by the absence of a wife in households composed of a male head and children, and it is possible that some of the solitary males in our lists were in fact widowers, though it is impossible to identify them as such.

ORPHANS

Orphans in Table 14 have been defined as children who had lost at least one of their parents. As might be expected, the figures are higher for the poorer parishes.

Surprisingly, given our sample of parishes, the combined total is slightly lower than the average calculated by Laslett for 19 English communities between 1599 and 1811, although this might be explained by the fact that Laslett's figures include children living with a remarried parent.[139] John Holman's calculations for late seventeenth-century Bristol produce a notably higher percentage of orphans than in early seventeenth-century Cambridge.[140] Nevertheless, it remains the case that, in these four Cambridge parishes, almost one-fifth of all children had suffered the loss of one of their parents.[141]

LODGERS AND SOJOURNERS

As in respect of inmates my definition differs from that of Laslett,[142] the percentage of households with lodgers has also been calculated in terms of his definition, with inmates and sojourners being treated as if they were lodgers (def. 2 in Table 15).

139. P. Laslett, 'Parental deprivation in the past', in Laslett (ed.), *Family Life* . . ., 166–8.
140. J. R. Holman, 'Orphans in pre-industrial towns – the case of Bristol in the late seventeenth century', *Local Population Studies*, XV (1975), 40–4.
141. To describe children who had lost just one of their parents as 'orphans' may seem odd, and perhaps it is better to use the phrase 'parentally deprived'. The problem is that one is rarely able to identify children who had lost both their parents, for of necessity these would have tended to join other households to be included in the listings as simply 'children' or as resident kin. It should also be remembered that it is not possible to analyse the extent of parental deprivation amongst servants and apprentices (see Laslett, 'Parental deprivation . . .', 165).
142. See above, p. 93.

TABLE 14   'Orphans', as a percentage of all children

St Botolph	St Giles	St Michael	St Peter	Combined
23.33	19.92	6.80	15.05	18.29

TABLE 15   Lodgers and sojourners

	% house-holds with lodgers	% in population	% sojourners in population	% house-holds with lodgers (def.2)	% in population
Barnwell	3.08	1.91	1.15	21.05	10.57
St Botolph	3.20	0.95	–	11.21	5.30
St Giles	1.35	0.34	1.20	14.60	5.82
St Michael	8.47	3.75	–	14.29	6.48
St Peter	–	–	2.67	20.83[a]	12.60
Combined	3.54	1.61	0.91	17.87	7.35

[a] The relatively small number of households in St Peter tends to enhance the percentage influence of just a few 'inmate' households and hence also the figure for 'lodgers' using this definition. Three of these were in fact 'sojourners'; two more were a tapster and an ostler who lived at the inn where they worked. These figures, and those for occupations by parish, do show, however, that the strictly suburban parishes had no monopoly of the town's poorer residents. Nevertheless, the average size of inmate households in St Peter was significantly larger than in St Giles.

With the definition in use here, lodgers and sojourners form a very small proportion of the total population, though they were noticeably more common in St Michael than in the other parishes.

When inmates are included as lodgers the percentages at once soar, as one might expect given the reason behind the preparation of the Cambridge census. Many who were simply sharing a house will be included in these figures. This is why the percentages are so much higher than Laslett's average for his 100 communities.[143] It would seem that the special nature of the Cambridge census resulted in a more all-embracing use of the term inmate, which in other listings was perhaps used more restrictively.

Nevertheless, inmate households did tend to be smaller, probably because they were likely to include many of the poorer and least well-established households in the community.[144] But even if inmates are not treated as households, the mean household size for our five parishes is raised by only 0.13, and the ranking of the parishes is unchanged.

143. See, however, Laslett and Wall (eds), op. cit., 134.
144. See above, p. 93.

SUMMARY AND CONCLUSION

In these five Cambridge parishes in the early seventeenth century the small nuclear household predominated, although nearly 40 per cent of the population lived in households of six or more persons. There was a higher proportion of small households than in Laslett's 100 communities, which might be explained in terms of the nature of our sample of parishes, recurrent plague and large-scale immigration. A clear positive relationship existed between socio-occupational status and household size, though it was not possible to differentiate between craft groupings. Mean household size by occupational group was comparable to Laslett's findings, although labouring households were smaller. This could have been due to the depth of their poverty, to the greater impact of disease upon the more lowly social groups, or to the likelihood that more of them were recent immigrants.

Differences in mean household size between parishes were a product of their differing occupational structures, in conjunction with variations in the overall levels of wealth between parishes. The sizes of groups of children were not positively related to the mean household size of a parish, although a slight positive relationship existed between the size of child groups and socio-occupational status. In particular occupational categories it was *not* invariably true that the smallest groups of children were to be found in the poorer parishes. While the proportion of households with children is similar to Laslett's findings, the mean size of child groups in Cambridge was a little smaller, and they formed a lower percentage of the total population. It is possible that rapid immigration of young adults could have produced these differences.

A strong positive relationship was noticed between the mean household size of the various parishes and the proportions of households with servants and apprentices. This was equally true regarding occupational status. Few households possessed both a servant and an apprentice, and only a tiny number housed living-in journeymen. The figures for servants and apprentices were higher than Laslett's, and would have been even more so given a more representative group of parishes. Where a broad occupational group could be compared with Laslett's results, the Cambridge figures were noticeably higher, particularly lower down the social scale. This might well be a feature of urban societies at this time, where apprenticeship or going into service was a common means of entry, though the taking in of servants and apprentices by those too poor to maintain them seems to have been a particular problem in Cambridge.

Very few households possessed co-residing kin, far fewer than in Laslett's study, and there is some indication that they were more commonly found in larger households and in the wealthier parishes.

More widowed persons were to be found in the poorer parishes, probably due to the greater impact of plague here, and in such parishes their household size was on average smaller. Despite the nature of our sample of parishes, the figures are similar to Laslett's. This might partly be due to an underestimation of the number of widowed males, and perhaps also to the age structure of the town. Surprisingly, although a higher percentage of children were parentally deprived in the poorer parishes in Cambridge, the overall figures are slightly lower than in comparable research.

Finally, only 5 per cent of all households contained lodgers or sojourners, a figure similar to Laslett's, and there is some indication that they were more commonly found in wealthier parishes.

From the foregoing it is quite clear that there were differences regarding household size and structure between different social groups in early seventeenth-century Cambridge and hence also, given at least a degree of concentration of relatively rich and relatively poor, differences between particular areas within the town. The nature of these variations, and their possible causes, have been outlined above. In many respects, however, they were *relatively* small, and are more in the nature of a difference in degree rather than in kind. The same might be said of the Cambridge results in comparison with Laslett's average for 100 communities. Despite variations of detail, family and household structure was not of a different *kind* to that which appears to have obtained in general in English society during this period. So from asking the question as to why aspects of household size and structure in early seventeenth-century Cambridge were dissimilar in certain respects to the English 'average', we find ourselves asking just why the basic structure should be so very much the same. This much bigger question, which lies outside the scope of the present paper, is just now beginning to attract the attention of historians.[145]

In conclusion, it should perhaps be remembered that a listing of inhabitants, in spite of its obvious value, presents a picture of a community at one point in time only, and ignores the possible existence of a developmental cycle. Here I have asserted that in five parishes in early seventeenth-century Cambridge the small nuclear household predominated. However, in his study of the Austrian peasant household in the eighteenth century, Berkner argued that a census 'takes a cross-section and gives a static picture of households and families that the historian or sociologist can sort into types . . . But

145. MacFarlane, *The Origins of . . .*, *passim.*

rather than being types these may simply be phases in the developmental cycle of a single family organization'.[146] And while in the Waldviertel census of 1763 only 25 per cent of all peasant households included any kin, by examining the types of family whilst controlling for the age of the head of household 'the extended family emerges as a normal phase in the developmental cycle of the peasant household'.[147] This point was later taken up by Lawrence Stone in *The Family, Sex and Marriage in England*.[148] Here he argued that the European family expanded and contracted like a concertina, moving from the extended family stem to the nuclear and back again. Thus a couple might live with their parents for a year or two, then move out on their own. Subsequently widowed mother might come to live with them. Their eldest son might also marry and live with them with his wife for a while. The mother would eventually die, and the son eventually move out.

It is, however, possible to exaggerate the likelihood of the occurrence of this chain of events. The European marriage pattern, involving delay of marriage for the majority of the population until their late 20s, was very much a feature of pre-industrial England.[149] At the same time the expectation of life was low, particularly in the less healthy areas of towns.[150] These demographic and biological facts would in themselves severely curtail the chances of such developmental cycles taking place.[151] Furthermore, migratory tendencies amongst young adults, into service, apprenticeship or simply in search of a job, by removing them from the place of origin of their families, might also lessen the chances of the formation of an extended family household. And while Stone notes that the generation-extended family was not uncommon amongst the wealthier landed gentry, he also argues that the relatively poor simply could not afford it.

The English evidence supports this theoretical view. In criticizing Laslett, Berkner fails to appreciate that *even at a point in time* there was a *far* higher proportion of households containing kin amongst

---

146. L. K. Berkner, 'The stem family and the development cycle of the peasant household: an eighteenth century Austrian example', *American Historical Review*, LXXVII (1972), 105.
147. Berkner, op. cit., 406.
148. L. Stone, *The Family, Sex and Marriage in England 1500–1800* (1977), 23–6.
149. J. Hajnal, 'European marriage patterns in perspective', in Glass and Eversley (eds), op. cit., 101–43; E. A. Wrigley, *Population in History* (1965), 118; P. Laslett, 'Characteristic of the western family considered over time', Table 1.4 in Laslett (ed.), *Family Life . . .*, 132.
150. Patten, op. cit., 135–9, and sources cited therein.
151. See A. J. Coale. 'Estimates of average household size', and L. A. Fallers, 'The range of variation in actual family size', in A. J. Coale *et al.*, *Aspects of the Analysis of Family Structure* (Princeton, 1965); Wrigley, op. cit., 132.

his Austrian peasants than was the case for Laslett's sample,[152] while the overall mean household size was also significantly higher in Austria.[153] As Laslett writes, the infrequency of extended and multiple households in England and the colonial United States makes it very difficult 'to make a case for an institution like the stem family as an *established, ongoing feature* of pre-industrial English society'[154] (my italics). Nor is it *necessarily* the case that the existence of the extended family is hidden by the static picture provided by a census: a recent study of three American urban communities shows only a moderate degree of variation in nuclearity between the families of one age cohort and another.[155] One must, of course, allow for the possibility of regional variations even within England. From her analysis of Midlands wills Cicely Howell concluded that the extended family was quite common, although the 'three-generation phase in the developmental cycle of the family was on average only 3 to 5 years . . .'.[156] Alan Macfarlane, however, has suggested that evidence from wills and manorial documents cannot be taken at its face value,[157] and from his study of Lipton and Killingworth in Cumbria concludes that the extended family was almost entirely absent.[158]

The Cambridge evidence shows quite clearly that here the developmental cycle did not prevail. We have seen (in Table 12) the very low percentage of households with resident kin, and noted that even amongst these a brother or sister of the household head or his wife was the most common relation. The high percentage of households *headed* by widows and the very low percentage of households containing a co-residing widow (Table 13) shows how rare it was for a widowed person to join the household of one of their married children.[159] Even at one point in time, if the extended family was at all common, one would expect more evidence of it than this. In fact, in the four Cambridge parishes of St Michael, St Peter, St Botolph and St Giles, containing a total of 387 households, only 6 were *vertically* extended.[160] Furthermore, as argued above

---

152. Cf. Berkner, op. cit., 406, 417, and Laslett, op. cit., 218.
153. Berkner, op. cit., 417.
154. Laslett, in Laslett and Wall (eds), op. cit., 150.
155. Stuart M. Blumin, 'Rip Van Winkle's grandchildren: family and household in the Hudson Valley, 1800–60', in T. K. Hareven (ed.), *Family and Kin in Urban Communities, 1700–1930* (New York, 1977), 113.
156. C. Howell, 'Peasant inheritance, customs in the Midlands 1280–1700', in Goody, Thirk and Thompson (eds), op. cit., 145.
157. MacFarlane, *The Origins of* . . ., 138.
158. Ibid., 74.
159. See 'The history of aging and the aged', in Laslett (ed.), *Family Life* . . ., 198–9.
160. The absence of the extended family was also a notable feature of early sixteenth-century Coventry: Phythian-Adams in the *The Fabric of* . . ., 25.

(p. 110) will evidence for the towns of Cambridge, Colchester and Reading in the sixteenth and seventeenth centuries leaves the distinct impression that married children were very rarely to be found within the parental home, while the division of a house to accommodate both the testator's widowed spouse and the family of one of his children was a highly infrequent occurrence.

In this paper I have attempted to compare and contrast features of the size and structure of households in a group of early seventeenth-century Cambridge parishes, both between themselves and between Cambridge and an average for 100 other pre-industrial communities. One of the main criticisms of Laslett's pioneering study is that his results lacked context. Here I have tried to place my findings within the general history of the town at this time, and have suggested that the main differentiating factors were the socio-occupational structure of a particular parish or group of parishes, the relative incidence of plague (or other diseases) and the extent of recent immigration (via its effects on the age structure of the community). Socio-economic and hence also demographic differences within the town and between Cambridge and other areas clearly did affect aspects of household size and structure, though not to the extent of producing essentially different types of household. More detailed studies of both urban and rural communities would provide interesting comparisons with the conclusions drawn here, and might provide some test for those which are more conjectural.

APPENDIX A. SOURCES FOR POPULATION FIGURES IN TABLE 1

The figure for 1524–5 is based on a correlation of the two subsidy lists for these years, excluding the women taxed, which can be regarded as indicating the size of the taxable male population over the age of 15. This figure was multiplied by 2 to allow for women, and 40 per cent was added to allow for children under 16. Ten per cent was allowed for those too poor to be taxed. This minimum figure was chosen for the following reasons: less than half of those taxed in either 1524 or 1525 are listed in both years. Partly this must have been the result of attempts to overcome omissions and avoidance in the first taxation, and there is some indication that efforts were made to spread the tax burden more widely in 1525 (without changes in the geographical area assessed). But this procedure of correlating tax lists from consecutive years means that: *(a)* those who left the town between the two subsidies as well as those who migrated *to* Cambridge will be included; and *(b)* those who died between the two subsidies as well as those who came to taxable age will be included. The importance of such factors has recently been stressed by Bruce Campbell of Queen's University, Belfast, in a paper presented to the Historical Geography Research Group. Thus the minimum figure of ten per cent for the 'poor' was chosen to compensate for any possible exaggeration of the male population over 15 in any one year. The subsidies are to be found in the Public Record Office, E 179 81/133 and E 179 81/144.

For 1563 the number of 'houseling people' in the ecclesiastical census of this year (British Library, Harl. MSS. 594, fo. 196) was multiplied by 4.5, an estimated figure for household size higher than the known one in the 1620s to allow for the bias in the 1620s sample of parishes.

The Vice-Chancellor's estimate, produced by concern over food supplies, is to be found in the British Library, Lansd. MSS. li fo. 144. The scholars and masters of the university were numbered at 1500.

For the 1674 figure the number of households listed in the hearth tax of this year (P.R.O. E 179/244/23) was multiplied by 4.5, and 5 per cent added to allow for the omission of paupers. I agree with Hoskins that the hearth tax figures must represent households and not houses – see W. G. Hoskins, 'Exeter in the seventeenth century: tax and rate assessments 1602–99', *Devon and Cornwall Record Society,* N.S., II (1957), xvii.

All the figures arrived at as described above have been rounded off. The numerous uncertainties in these calculations mean that, as Table 1 states, these figures can only be regarded as rough approximations.

APPENDIX B. BASIS OF OCCUPATIONAL CLASSIFICATIONS IN TABLE 2

The occupational classifications used are loosely based upon those used by Clarkson (L. A. Clarkson, The *Pre-Industrial Economy in England 1500–1700* (1971), 90–1). The 'Professional/official' category includes musicians, registers, notaries, butlers and parish clerks; 'Food/drink' includes millers and maltsters; 'Building' includes plumbers, glaziers, thatchers and carpenters, but joiners are included under 'Woodwork'; 'Clothing' includes glovers, shoemakers, cordwainers, cobblers and buttonmakers; 'Rural' includes those described as yeomen, husbandmen, shepherds and plowrights: 'Miscellaneous' includes all those for which no other category seemed suitable – barbers, bedmakers, basketmakers, gardeners, potters, etc. A useful discussion of the problems of occupational classification at this time is J. Patten, 'Urban occupations in pre-industrial England', *Inst. Brit. Geographers Trans.*, N.S., II, no 3 (1977), 296–313.

Editorial suggestions for further reading

P. Clark (ed.), *Country Towns in Pre-Industrial England* (Leicester, 1981).

P. Clark and D. Souden (eds), *Migration and Society in Early Modern England* (1987).

C. Phythian-Adams, *Desolation of a City: Coventry and the Urban Crisis of the Late Middle Ages* (Cambridge, 1979).

I. Roy and S. Porter, 'The social and economic structure of an early modern suburb: The tything at Worcester', *Bulletin of the Institute of Historical Research*, 53 (1980), pp. 203–17.

P. Slack, *The Impact of Plague in Tudor and Stuart England* (1987).

E. A. Wrigley and R. Schofield, *The Population History of England 1540–1871* (1981).

Chapter 5

SOCIAL PROBLEMS IN ELIZABETHAN LONDON[1]

A. L. Beier

[*Journal of Interdisciplinary History*, 9 (1978–9)]

Rapid growth in the rural population combined with high urban mortality made the period 1550–1640 one of great mobility. The clearest manifestation of this was the massive influx of people into London, and particularly into its suburbs. Here Alan Beier explores the fate of the losers in this process, those whose poverty and failure to establish a secure place in urban society led them to be labelled vagrants. After examining the factors which explain the growth of vagrancy he considers briefly the measures taken to deal with the problem, where good intentions without adequate resources left punishment and expulsion as typical solutions. Vagrants and their supposed criminality fascinated contemporaries, and Beier's emphasis on the uprooted young male adds force to his comparison with the modern Third-world city, but these vagrants were only a small section of the poor in Tudor and Stuart towns. An alternative critique of those who, like Beier, concentrate on London's social problems is provided by Pearl in Chapter 6.

Frances Palmer, a vagrant sent in by Mr. Dale's warrant out of Southwark, having two children begotten and born in whoredom, says that one Thomas Wood, servant with Sir Edward Wotton, is the father of them, and the place where she was delivered was openly in the street, two or three doors off from the Cross Keys, and they died and were buried in Allhallows parish in Gracious Street, and she was after her delivery taken into the Cross Keys. Ordered to be punished and delivered.[2]

1. The author wishes to thank Anthony Salerno and Lawrence Stone for their comments on early drafts of the article. Research for the article was aided by grants from the Social Science Research Council (United Kingdom) for a study of the vagrant poor in Tudor and early Stuart England.
2. Court Book, Bridewell Hospital, 1597–1604, fol. 337b (18 May 1603); for Gracious read Gracechurch (other spelling modernized). I wish to thank the

The growth of London is recognized to be one of the major developments of the Tudor and Stuart period. The economic and demographic aspects of that growth have been explored in some depth, but much less is known about the crime and poverty that accompanied it. This article examines one group of the London poor, people arrested for vagrancy and sent to Bridewell hospital for judgment and punishment, and charts the growth of vagrancy and its causes. Bridewell was the chief institution dealing with vagrants in London and its suburbs up to 1649. The Bridewell offenders therefore provide evidence of long-term changes in vagrancy in London, although they do not represent the numbers actually on the streets because it is improbable that all vagrants were caught. After 1614, moreover, the Bridewell figures are minimum ones to which we would have to add the unknown number dealt with in houses of correction established from that date in Middlesex, Surrey, and Westminster.[3]

The evidence of Bridewell's Court Books suggests a massive increase in London vagrancy between 1560 and 1625. There were 69 vagrants dealt with by the Court of Governors in 1560–1, 209 in 1578–9, 555 in 1600–1, and 815 in 1624–5. Thus we have an eight-fold increase by 1601 and almost a twelve-fold rise by 1625. London's rise to the position of a great city evidently included a huge increase in its social problems.[4]

Governors of Bridewell Royal Hospital and Lt. Colonel Alan Faith, Clerk to the Governors, for permission to quote from the Court Books (located at King Edward School, Witley, Surrey) and for agreeing to have a microfilm made of them for the period from 1559 to 1660. Earlier historians consulted the Court Books of Bridewell, but not systematically: E. M. Leonard, *The Early History of English Poor Relief* (Cambridge, 1900), 38; E. G. O'Donoghue, *Bridewell Hospital* . . . (London, 1923–1929), 2 v.

3. For vagrancy and poor relief policies, Leonard, *English Poor Relief*, 23–40; Charles Pendrill, *Old Parish Life in London* (London, 1937), 133–205. Estimates of numbers on the streets range from 200 'ydell vagabondes' in Edward VI's reign to 30 000 'idle persons and maisterles men' in 1602. Both come from official sources, but are probably inaccurate. Eileen Power and R. H. Tawney (eds), *Tudor Economic Documents* (London, 1924), III, 417–418; John Bruce (ed.), *Diary of John Manningham,* . . . *Barrister-at-Law, 1602–3* (1868), 72–73. For other houses of correction in London's suburbs, Leonard, *English Poor Relief*, 227–228; the Middlesex house at Clerkenwell – Journal 29, fol. 295a (1614), Court of Common Council, Corporation of London Records Office (hereafter 'Jnl.'); the Westminster house – John Edward Smith, *A Catalogue of Westminster Records* . . . (London, 1900), 52. There was a plan for a Westminster house of correction in 1561, but no evidence has been found of one operating before 1622. Cf. S. A. Peyton, 'The Houses of Correction at Maidstone and Westminster', *English Historical Review*, XLII (1927), 251–261.

4. The increase of all Bridewell offenders was more sluggish than for vagrants (445 in 1560–1, 586 in 1578–9, 899 in 1600–1, and 1639 in 1624–5). Non-vagrants included a great variety of offenders – prostitutes, adulterers, bigamists, drunks, thieves, swearers, slanderers, dice-players, runaway servants and apprentices, and

What caused the increase in vagrancy? It is unlikely to have been due solely to greater efforts and efficiency at catching vagrants by the authorities.[5] Recent national studies have put forward a number of explanations – the growth of England's population, roughly doubling from 1520 to 1620 and causing population pressure and migration; underemployment and unemployment in a backward economy; the unsettling effect of migration from open-field to forest/pastoral areas and to towns; and the unstable positions of servants and apprentices, large groups in the workforce.[6] These facts help us to understand vagrancy nationally, but London was exceptional. It was the largest city in Britain and experienced rates of immigration and population growth that far outstripped the rest of the country.

Mid-Tudor London and its suburbs contained from 80 000 to 90 000 people. In 1605 they may have held a quarter of a million, in 1625 perhaps 320 000, and in 1650, 400 000.[7] If vagrancy kept pace with London's population between 1560 and 1625 it might have increased four-fold. Bridewell's records suggest that vagrancy rose at a far faster rate than the city's population. Hence other factors

many simply 'sent in' with no offence stated – whom it would be dubious to lump together with vagrants. The reasons for the slower rate of increase among non-vagrants are unclear. The sample years here are calculated from March to March (e.g. 25 March 1560 to 24 March 1561) because this was the method used by the Governors. Periods of bad harvest and trade depression were avoided, although in 1600–1 half the year may have been affected by a bad harvest: C. J. Harrison, 'Grain Price Analysis and Harvest Qualities, 1465–1634', *Agricultural History Review*, XIX (1971), 154; cf. W. G. Hoskins, 'Harvest Fluctuations and English Economic History, 1480–1619', ibid., XII (1964), 46.

5. Increased detection was perhaps one factor behind increased 'recidivism' in the early seventeenth century (see below). The only major change in the arrest system was the appointment of 'marshals' from 1570. But they do not appear as arresting officers in the Bridewell records with any frequency until after 1589 when provost-marshals were appointed. *Their* appointment was in response to an increase in vagrants, in particular sailors and soldiers. See Lindsay Boynton, 'The Tudor Provost-Marshal', *English Historical Review*, LXXVII (1962), 442–446; Jnl. 22, fol. 347b. Legal definitions of vagrancy did not change in ways that would increase arrests; if anything, they became more restricted from 1597; see 39 Elizabeth I, *cap.* 4 repr. in *Tudor Econ. Docs.*, II, 354–355; cf. 14 Elizabeth I, *cap.* 5, *Statutes of the Realm*, IV (i) (London, 1963; orig. pub. 1819), 591.

6. A. L. Beier, 'Vagrants and the Social Order in Elizabethan England', *Past & Present*, 64 (1974), 12–13, 21–26; Paul A. Slack, 'Vagrants and Vagrancy in England, 1598–1664', *Economic History Review*, XXVII (1974), 374–376. For an overview – Lawrence Stone, 'Social Mobility in England, 1500–1700', *Past & Present*, 33 (1966), 29–31.

7. Figures (all rough estimates) from Norman G. Brett-James, *The Growth of Stuart London* (London, 1935), 495–503, 512; J. C. Russell, *British Medieval Population* (Albuquerque, 1948), 298–300; E. A. Wrigley, 'A Simple Model of London's Importance in Changing English Society and Economy, 1650–1750', *Past & Present*, 37 (1967), 44.

TABLE 1   Vagrants in London of local origin and residence, 1516–1642

	Number of cases	From London area (%)[a]	From southeast (%)[b]
1516–66	35	22.9	37.0
1574–9	102	29.4	44.1
1597–1604	267	51.7	64.0
1604–10	327	47.0	58.7
1620–1	156	50.0	62.8
1634–42	129	44.2	56.6

Sources: Bridewell Court Books. 1559–1642; Jnls, Court of Common Council, and Repertories (hereafter 'Rep'), Court of Aldermen, 1516–1566, Corporation of London Records Office.
[a] London area = London and suburbs, Southwark, Middlesex.
[b] Southeast = London, Middlesex, Kent, Beds., Herts., Surrey, Sussex.

besides population growth must be considered to understand London vagrancy.

London grew to be a great city on the basis of immigration. Vast numbers were needed to fuel the city's growth in early modern times because deaths usually far outnumbered births. From 1650 to 1750 about 8000 immigrants per year were necessary to sustain London's growth. Assuming, as one writer did, that deaths outnumbered births by 2080 in London in 1607 and applying this figure to the years from 1560 to 1625 (though in reality it would be lower at the start and higher at the end), then London's growth between those dates required an influx of 367 280 people, or about 5600 each year. Immigration on this scale might cause problems in a modern city of similar size. In the London of 1600 the difficulties proved enormous.[8]

Where did vagrants originate? Were they mainly long-distance migrants to London as contemporaries thought?[9] The majority of London vagrants in the sixteenth and early seventeenth centuries were from outside the London area (defined as London and its suburbs, Southwark, and Middlesex). Places sending large contingents who ended up as vagrants in London were East Anglia, Yorkshire,

8. Ibid., 46; 1607 figure from 'A Consideration of the Cause in Question before the Lords Touching Depopulation', British Library, Cottonian Mss. Titus F.iv, fol. 322–3, repr. in Eric Kerridge, *Agrarian Problems in the Sixteenth Century and After* (London, 1969), 203. London's population is assumed here to be 90 000 in 1560 and 320 000 in 1625; see note 7 for sources.
9. E.g. William Fleetwood, Recorder of London, in *Tudor Economic Documents*, II, 336; James F. Larkin and Paul L. Hughes (eds), *Tudor Royal Proclamations* (New Haven, 1969), II, 415–417.

TABLE 2   Vagrants from within ten miles of London Bridge, 1516–1642

	Number of cases	% From within ten miles
1516–66	35	25.7
1574–9	102	35.3
1597–1604	261	55.9
1604–10	329	48.0
1620–1	158	48.1
1634–42	123	47.9

Sources: See Table 1.

the counties between London and Bristol, and from 1600, Ireland.[10] However, the assumption that vagrants were 'foreign' to the London area lost validity in the period, as more and more of them came from London and southeastern England (see Table 1). Until 1580 vagrants claiming to be born or last resident in the London area formed 20 to 30 percent of the total and those from the southeast as a whole about 40 percent. But after 1600 about 50 percent were from the London area, and 60 percent from the southeast. Thus the late Elizabethan years saw increases in vagrants from the London area and the southeast of 100 and 50 percent, respectively.

Looking at vagrants' origins from the standpoint of distance, those coming from within ten miles of London Bridge more than doubled in the century. By 1600 about half of all vagrants stating a place of origin fell into this category (see Table 2). Finally, there is evidence that the migratory patterns of vagrants were similar to those of apprentices and working-men in London. A rising share of apprentices to city companies also came from the southeast in the period, and, among a group of East London working-men who gave church court depositions between 1580 and 1639, 30 percent were born in London and the southeast. By comparison, when the Bridewell authorities listed birthplaces from 1597 to 1604, 30 percent of vagrants were also born in London and the southeast.[11]

Two points must be made about the above evidence. First, although majorities of vagrants claimed to be born or resident in London and the southeast, many of them were immigrants. From 1597 to 1604, 30 percent claimed to be born in the area, but 52

10. Space does not allow a full breakdown of the regional origins of London vagrants, but for some evidence for the southeast see Beier, 'Vagrants and Social Order', 19–20; Slack, 'Vagrants and Vagrancy', 379.
11. Stone, 'Mobility in England', 31–2; Steven R. Smith, 'The Social and Geographical Origins of the London Apprentices, 1630–1660', *The Guildhall Miscellany*, IV (1973), no. 4, 202–206; David Cressy, 'Occupations, Migration and Literacy in East London, 1580–1640', *Local Population Studies*, 5 (1970), 55–59 (figures on 58 reworked to cover the southeast as defined in Table 1.

percent said that they originated there. The difference between the figures must be explained by immigration. Second, the rising numbers of vagrants originating locally might be due to London's growing share of England's population, which roughly doubled from 1545 to 1605.[12] Despite these qualifications, conclusions can be drawn about London vagrants as migrants. First, the similarities between vagrants, apprentices, and working-men suggest that vagrants were part of general tendencies in migration; that in this respect vagrants were not a 'culture' apart from society as portrayed in the literature of roguery. Second, that London vagrants increasingly originated in London and the southeast suggests that, whether they were born there or not, *the experience of living in a rapidly urbanizing area brought about vagrancy*. In other words, vagrants did not come to London as vagrants but *became* vagrants in London because of conditions there.

Why was London unable to assimilate all its immigrants? One answer lies in the places in London where vagrants were born or lived. By three to one these were in suburbs that nearly encircled London within the walls – Southwark, south of the Thames; St Katherine's by the Tower and Whitechapel in the east; St Giles without Cripplegate, Clerkenwell, and St Sepulchre's in the north; and St Giles in the Fields, Holborn, Fleet Street, and Westminster in the west. The suburban origins of vagrants are not surprising: these areas were growing faster than the city within the walls; it was common in early modern cities for the poor to be in the suburbs and the rich in the center. What is more, London's suburbs were especially afflicted with disease, poverty, and slum housing. Mortality rates were higher there. Poverty was greater, too: from the 1560s the Court of Aldermen ordered that parishes with great numbers of poor in the suburbs were to receive assistance from wealthier parishes within the walls. Westminster itself was the scene of incredible poverty. The records of St. Margaret's parish overseers and of the Court of Burgesses show people living, having children, and dying in the streets and in cellars. With such conditions on their doorstep, it is little wonder that Parliament and the Privy Council were concerned about vagrants and London's growth.[13]

---

12. London's share of England's population rose from 3 to 6½% from 1545 to 1605, assuming the city to number 80 000 and the nation 2.8 million at the first date, and 250 000 and 3.75 million, respectively, by the second. Figures from Russell, *British Medieval Population*, 298; Brett-James, *Growth of Stuart London*, 497–498; Julian Cornwall, 'English Population in the Early Sixteenth Century', *Economic History Review*, XXIII (1970), 43–44.

13. Peter Clark and Paul Slack (eds), *Crisis and Order in English Towns, 1500–1700* (London, 1972), 18, 34; Brett-James, *Growth of Stuart London*, 496–497; Rep. 17, fols. 425a–426a, 446a (1573); no. 32, fols. 157a–b (1615); no. 41, fols. 151a–b (1627); Archives Department, Westminster Public Libraries.

Housing was terrible in these slums. Landlords divided houses for multiple occupation, crammed people into cellars, and threw up hovels in alleys. By 1570 the space left by the dissolution of the monasteries was filled. By 1580 slum housing reached crisis proportions, and the authorities acted to halt its further spread. Governments continued to call for action, for example in the statute of 1589 against new buildings without four acres of land, and in numerous actions under the early Stuarts. However, by the 1590s it is clear that the suburbs were centers of crime and poverty. Parts of Southwark were described then as 'nurseries and seminary places of the begging poor that swarm within the City'. In 1598 the Privy Council wrote to the Justices of the Peace for Middlesex about landlords who let tenements to 'base people and to lewd persons that do keep evil rule, and harbor thieves, rogues and vagabonds' in Shoreditch, St Giles without Cripplegate, and Clerkenwell. In his *A Survey of London* (London, 1598) John Stow described slums springing up in Southwark, Whitechapel and Houndsditch. Housing may have improved in some parts of seventeenth-century London, but whether these slums saw much improvement seems doubtful. George found that many of them were still centers of poverty, crime, and disease in the eighteenth and early nineteenth centuries.[14]

Who were the vagrants of Elizabethan London? They were mainly young and male. Their youth is suggested by a list of 'Vagrants in the House' at Bridewell in 1602: of thirty-seven whose ages were listed, thirty were between the ages of eleven and twenty, and only one was over the age of twenty-one. Although a small sample, the youth of vagrants in London is seen elsewhere, for example, at Norwich. Vagrants were also overwhelmingly male. In samples between 1516 and 1625 males accounted for about 70 percent, a higher proportion than in the provinces, which is probably explained by London's great attraction of apprentices and male servants.[15]

14. Brett-James, *Growth of Stuart London, passim* (still the best study of London's growth); Remembrancia, II, items 74, 102, Corporation Records Office; John R. Dasent (ed.), *Acts of the Privy Council of England, 1597–1598*, n.s. (London, 1904), XXVIII, 427–428; John Stow, *A Survey of London* (London, 1598; repr. 1956), 116, 150, 365, 376. Cf. M. J. Power, 'East London Housing in the Seventeenth Century', in Clark and Slack, *Crisis and Order*, 240–241, 258–259; M. Dorothy George, *London Life in the Eighteenth Century* (Harmondsworth, 1965; orig. pub. 1925), 78, 91–94.
15. Bridewell Court Book, 1597–1604, fols. 322b—324b. At Norwich 33 out of 46 vagrants with ages listed, 1595–1609, were below age twenty-one: Proceedings in the Mayor's Court, 1595–1603 and 1603–14, *passim*, Norfolk Record Office. Cf. Beier, 'Vagrants and Social Order', 9–10. Males varied from 56 to 80% of London vagrants depending on the period; the reasons for variations are unclear. Sources as in Table 1. Cf. ibid, 6–7; Slack, 'Vagrants and Vagrancy', 366.

Bridewell's Court Books leave no doubt that by 1600 London's streets were filled with vagrant young men. They begged; sold ballads, brooms, and pamphlets; shined shoes; and hung around the streets, shops, and market stalls. They were caught stealing from shops and stalls, from the purses and pockets of passers-by; taking lead from roofs, including St Paul's; and being idle and 'masterless'. London by 1600 was experiencing large-scale juvenile delinquency. It would be no exaggeration to compare the situation to ghetto areas of Western cities today. The authorities feared these young men as makers of riots and disorders.[16]

What were the economic and social origins of London vagrancy? Surprisingly little is known about some aspects of London's economy: the industrial sector, the occupations of Londoners, and the supply of work for immigrants. By contrast, London's rise to a monopoly position in English cloth exports and as a center for consumption between 1500 and 1650 is well known. In industry some growth areas in the period were leather, brewing, soap-making, shipbuilding and the docks, silk-throwing, and frame-work knitting.[17] How much new employment was provided by the growth of trade and industry is difficult to determine, for there are few figures available. In agricultural trade there was probably a growth in jobs as middlemen, market and transport workers, and market-gardeners. The numbers employed in trades involving conspicuous consumption are also likely to have increased, but by how much remains uncertain.

In the industrial sector the evidence is sparse, when not ambiguous. Of cloth-workers it was reported in 1634 that 2000 of them lived by dressing cloth bought in the open market, but whether this represents an increase over earlier periods is unclear and perhaps doubtful in the crisis-ridden 1630s. Even assuming that some industries grew in the period, to know, for example, that there were 400 frames for knitting stockings in 1660 does not tell us how far this industry was taking up labor from a depressed one such as woollen cloth. Finally, in our preoccupation with growth, we may ignore the size of operations and their impact on the larger economy. For example, people employed in privately-owned ship-building 'multiplied several times over' from 1540 to 1640, according to Nef. The

---

16. For example on Shrove Tuesday, the first of May, and at plays: Alfred Harbage, *Shakespeare's Audience* (New York, 1941), 81–83.
17. J. D. Gould. *The Great Debasement* (Oxford, 1970), 125; F. J. Fisher, 'The Development of the London Food Market, 1540–1640', in E. M. Carus-Wilson (ed.), *Essays in Economic History* (London, 1954), I, 142–150; Fisher, 'The Development of London as a Centre of Conspicuous Consumption in the Sixteenth and Seventeenth Centuries', in ibid., II, 197–207.

statement may be strictly true, but the operations of London ship-builders remained small ones, none of them employing over a hundred men in peacetime. The growth of London's docks also involved small-scale operations up to 1660.[18]

How far was the occupational distribution of Londoners changed by economic growth? Parish registers yield some clues, although the evidence thus far collected for East London parishes is of limited use. First, it concerns short periods, so that the extent of long-term changes in the size of occupational groups cannot be gauged. Second, it is based on the occupations of men whose children were baptized, and leaves out women and others who were not supposed to marry and have children before a certain age, living-in servants, and apprentices.[19]

Burial registers also have limitations, but they provide a fuller picture of occupations than baptismal records.[20] An analysis of three London parishes' burial records suggests that no radical changes took place in occupational distribution from the mid-sixteenth to the mid-seventeenth century (see Table 3). There were variations between parishes. St Peter's, Cornhill, had a high concentration of people in victualling trades, and St Helen's, Bishopsgate, large numbers in leather trades. But the largest group in all three parishes were 'servants', comprising between 34 and 47 percent depending upon period and parish. Moreover, all three parishes had sizeable stakes in the manufacture and sale of cloth, and taken together 'servants' and people working with cloth accounted for the majority of positions from 1548 to 1652. The term 'servant' in the registers appears to include apprentices but, even if it were possible to assign

18. E. Lipson, *The Economic History of England* (London, 1934; 2nd ed.), II, 3, 106; J. U. Nef, 'The Progress of Technology and the Growth of Large-scale Industry in Great Britain, 1540–1640', in Carus-Wilson, *Essay*, I, 104; Ralph Davis, *The Rise of the English Shipping Industry in the Seventeenth and Eighteenth Centuries* (London, 1962), 55–56; Charles Wilson, *England's Apprenticeship, 1603–1763* (New York, 1965), 273.

19. Thomas R. Forbes, *Chronicle from Aldgate. Life and Death in Shakespeare's London* (New Haven, 1971), 9–10; East London Population Study Group, 'The Population of Stepney in the Early Seventeenth Century', *Local Population Studies*, 3 (1969), 50. Consistory Court depositions are likely to be even less reliable as records of occupations: Cressy, 'Occupations, Migration and Literacy in East London', ibid., 5, 54–55.

20. Besides contemporaries' imprecision in attributing occupations and status and the practice of affiliating to city companies without actively practicing the trades of the companies, which would affect most types of record, the value of burial records is also limited by registering people's occupations at the end of their working lives, so that the results are not indicative of the active population of the time. The force of this argument is limited by the high mortality rates in London, which meant that many working people were struck down.

TABLE 3 Occupations and status of people buried in three London parishes, 1548–1652

| | St Michael, Bassishaw | | | | St Peter's, Cornhill | | | | St Helen's, Bishopsgate | | | |
| | 1548–1598 | | 1599–1649 | | 1571–1611 | | 1612–1652 | | 1575–1610 | | 1611–1646 | |
	No.	%	No.	%	No.	%	No.	%	No.	%	No.	%
'Servants'	156	47.4	211	42.4	107	34.7	157	42.4	98	40.7	95	37.6
Cloth-making & sale	47	14.3	81	16.2	50	16.2	47	12.7	30	12.4	42	16.6
Victualling	24	7.3	22	4.4	57	18.5	66	17.8	8	3.3	11	4.4
Building	23	6.9	24	4.8	7	2.3	8	2.2	8	3.3	10	3.9
Distributive	13	4.0	35	7.0	9	2.9	8	2.2	5	2.1	4	1.6
Professions	12	3.7	21	4.2	9	2.9	11	2.9	13	5.4	10	3.9
Metal	12	3.7	26	5.2	17	5.5	19	5.1	13	5.4	7	2.8
Gentlemen	10	3.0	8	1.6	6	2.0	8	2.2	16	6.6	15	5.9
Leather	6	1.8	19	3.8	16	5.2	25	6.8	31	12.9	27	10.7
'Merchants'[a]	3	0.9	17	3.4	2	0.7	7	1.9	6	2.5	16	6.3
Miscellaneous	23	7.0	35	7.0	28	9.1	14	3.8	13	5.4	16	6.3
Totals	329	100.0	499	100.0	308	100.0	370	100.0	241	100.0	253	100.0

Sources: A. W. Hughes Clarke (ed.), The Registers of St Mary Magdalen Milk Street, 1558–1666, and St Michael Bassishaw, 1538–1735 (London, 1942–4), LXXII–LXXXIII, pts. 1–2; Granville W. G. Leveson Gower (ed.), The Registers of St. Peter's Cornhill (London, 1877), I; W. Bruce Bannerman (ed.), The Registers of St Helen's, Bishopsgate, 1575–1837 (London, 1904), XXXI. These parishes were selected because their registers were in print and because two of them (St. Michael and St. Helen's) differed in social structure later in the period: D. V. Glass, London Inhabitants Within the Walls, 1695 (London, 1966), maps on xxii–xxiii.

[a] Merchants to whom a particular area of trade is not attributed ('merchant tailors' included in category of cloth-making and sale.)

130

them to crafts, it seems doubtful that any single trade would out-number domestic servants.[21]

Three parishes cannot speak for all London; only further research will show whether these were typical. Certainly they may not prove typical of parishes outside the city walls, where there was less corporate control and greater room for expansion, or of parishes along the Thames, which would have more workers involved in sea and river trades. Nevertheless, the evidence of these parishes suggests doubts about how far London's economy was transformed by the growth of new industries and trade before 1650.

A final piece of economic evidence is that labor in pre-industrial England was underemployed and subject to crises causing unemployment.[22] Workers in London may have been worse off in these respects than elsewhere. Underemployment was caused by primitive methods of production that made it difficult to keep labor regularly employed. Thus all sectors remained subject to the intervention of bad weather and poor harvests. Underemployment was also caused by the age-structure of the population. The life-expectancy was only about half of what it is today, so that working lives were shorter. This situation was worse in London because of higher mortality rates. There was also a higher proportion of young people than today, with roughly 40 percent of the population below age fifteen. Even granting that the young were put to work early and could do the work of an adult from the age of twelve, they were probably less disciplined workers than adults because they were new, often unwilling recruits to the labor market, were less tied down by family responsibilities, and were at or near the restless age of puberty. London's population was probably especially young due to the large numbers of young immigrants. Unemployment in trade and industry was caused by poor harvests, wars, and government interventions such as the Cockayne project. The cloth industry was especially prone to such setbacks, which occurred in 1562 to 1564, 1571 to 1573, 1586 to 1587, and frequently after 1614. London, with its large stake in cloth, was likely to suffer during these crises.[23]

21. In the late seventeenth century, when servants and apprentices made up nearly 50% of the 'primary taxpayers' in a dozen London parishes, servants outnumbered apprentices by 10 to 1: D. V. Glass, 'Socioeconomic Status and Occupations in the City of London at the End of the Seventeenth Century', in A. E. J. Hollaender and W. Kellaway (eds), *Studies in London History* (London, 1969), 379–381.
22. D. C. Coleman, 'Labour in the English Economy of the Seventeenth Century', in Carus-Wilson, *Essays*, II, 291–308, *passim*; F. J. Fisher, 'The Growth of London', in E. W. Ives (ed.), *The English Revolution, 1600–1660* (London, 1968), 78.
23. Fisher, 'Commercial Trends and Policy in Sixteenth-century England', in Carus-Wilson, *Essays*, I, 153; Gould, 'The Crisis in the Export Trade, 1586–7', *English Historical Review*, LXXI (1956), 212–222; Barry E. Supple, *Commercial Crisis*

How does this economic evidence help us to understand vagrancy in London? First, in such a backward economy it is certain that some of the many immigrants to London would end up unemployed or underemployed (in contemporary terms, 'idle', 'masterless', or a vagrant). Second, the small scale of economic operations and continued importance of the cloth industry, servants, and apprentices are significant. They suggest that the economy was not transformed in the period, that 'face to face' relations remained the norm with employers, and that the latter were unlikely to have sufficient capital to keep workers employed in times of crisis, which frequently afflicted the cloth trade and industry.

The socioeconomic groups in London most prone to vagrancy were servants and apprentices. Between 1597 and 1608 almost three quarters of vagrants of London origin with occupations listed were servants and apprentices (forty-seven of sixty-five cases). London drew great numbers of both because of the presence of the Court, a high concentration of aristocratic, gentry, and middle-class households, the growing popularity among the landed upper classes of spending the winter 'season' in London, and the attraction of the city companies. We know that servants and apprentices made up a third to a half of the labor force according to the burial records of three parishes. Apprentices are thought to have numbered 20 000 in London between 1640 and 1660, and domestic servants were probably several times more numerous.[24]

Their numbers alone, however, do not explain why servants and apprentices made frequent appearances in Bridewell, for they appeared there far more often than warranted by their numbers in the working population. It seems that these positions contained inherent instabilities. One problem was that both tended to be short-term and subject to lay-offs. Servants were generally employed by the year, but the contract could be terminated at a quarter's notice, sometimes less. If a master died or left town, a servant could be out of work overnight and without a testimonial. Apprenticeships were

---

and Change in England, 1600–1642 (Cambridge, 1959), 39–40, 42–43, 52–53, 102, 118, 122–123 (crises); 57, 101 (non-quantitative evidence of unemployment and poverty among London cloth-workers in the crises of 1622 and 1625). From 1516 to 1642 a fifth of vagrants with trades listed were in some branch of cloth trade or manufacture, which is higher than in the population in general according to burial records (sources as in Table 1).

24. Smith, 'Origins of London Apprentices', 195–198. Glass, 'Socioeconomic Status and Occupations', 386, estimates that there were 11 000 apprentices in London in 1690 at a minimum. If servants outnumbered apprentices by 10 to 1 (1768 and 176, respectively, among 'primary' taxpayers: ibid., 379–381), then the two groups may have accounted for 121 000 people in the 1690s, or about a fifth of London's total population.

supposed to last a minimum of seven years, but there were many violations. A contemporary singled out short apprenticeships and early marriages as causes of poverty and vagrancy. Evasion of the seven-year term was prevalent in London's suburbs according to a memorandum of 1610. Lay-offs among apprentices were caused by trade slumps. John Howes, writing during the crisis in the cloth trade in 1586–7, said that poor masters in London let apprentices go during depressions or mistreated them so that they would leave. Vagrancy among apprentices and journeymen also resulted from strict enforcement of settlement regulations in times of depression, for example at Norwich in the 1630s.[25]

The leading causes of vagrancy among servants and apprentices were conflicts with their masters. Most servants and apprentices were in low-paid, menial positions. They had rights that could be (and were) defended by the law, but in general the master held the whip hand. He had the right to dispose of his charge's time and labor, to determine his living conditions, and to discipline him. That labor was cheap and abundant between 1540 and 1640 compounded the weakness of servants and apprentices in relation to masters.[26]

Conflicts took a number of forms – mistreatment by masters in denying their charges food, lodging, and proper training; rebelliousness, refusals to work, and flight by menials; thefts from masters and mistresses; and physical violence, sometimes with terrible results. Illicit sexual relations were also common sources of conflicts. Most servants and apprentices were young and unmarried and therefore, in theory, supposed to abstain from sexual intercourse. Most were probably also at or near the age of puberty. Celibacy and sexual abstinence were written into apprenticeship indentures, and among servants it appears to have been exceptional, if not unheard of, for them to marry and have children while in service. Female

---

25. Since we lack studies of the working conditions of servants and apprentices in the period, material has been gleaned from Margaret Gay Davies, *The Enforcement of English Apprenticeship, 1563–1642* (Cambridge, Mass., 1956), 6–7, 194–197, 224–225, 231–234; J. Jean Hecht, *The Domestic Servant Class in Eighteenth-Century England* (London, 1956), 12–14, 27–28, 33–34, 81–82; Dorothy Marshall, *The English Domestic Servant in History* (London, 1949), 10–11; 'The Statute of Artificers', 5 Elizabeth I, *cap.* 4, repr. in *Tudor Economic Documents*, I, esp. 340–341, on length of service, testimonials, etc. References above to *Tudor Economic Documents*, I, 356–360; British Library, Lansdowne Ms. 169/130–131; *Tudor Economic Documents*, III, 430; William L. Sachse (ed.), *Minutes of the Norwich Court of Mayoralty, 1630–1631*, Norfolk Record Society (1942), XV, 154–155, 158.

26. Marshall, *Domestic Servant*, 10; Hecht, *Domestic Servant Class*, 77–78; Ivy Pinchbeck and Margaret Hewitt, *Children in English Society, I, From Tudor Times to the Eighteenth Century* (London, 1969), 227–228; Steven R. Smith, 'The London Apprentices as Seventeenth-Century Adolescents', *Past & Present*, 61 (1973), 152–154.

servants were the targets of sexual advances by the master of the house, his sons, apprentices, and male servants. Even in respectable circles female menials were fair game, to judge by Pepys' pursuit of his maids. For the girl the results were often disastrous – pregnancy without marriage, dismissal from service, a child she could not support, homelessness, vagrancy, and prostitution. For males the results were generally less grave – possibly a bastardy case which, if lost, involved a financial burden; for servants and apprentices, possible dismissal, flights to escape prosecution, and vagrancy.[27]

Masters were by no means always at fault. The burden of looking after children besides one's own could clearly be a heavy one. One can sympathize, for example, with the master whose servant 'beat him and broke his . . . head and scratched him by the face and beat his mistress and locked his master and mistress out of doors one night'. These conflicts between masters and menials included mistreatment, violence, and sexual relations, and resulted in vagrancy, prostitution, and even death. Such conflicts, which are regular features of county quarter sessions as well as Bridewell's Court of Governors, raise serious doubts about how harmonious and stable the 'patriarchal household' really was.[28]

The foregoing discussion suggests that London experienced unprecedented social problems in the late Elizabethan period. By 1600 slums were mushrooming in the suburbs, and hundreds of young, male vagrants, increasingly recruited from the London area itself, were loitering around the streets. It seems fair to trace the origins of the rookeries of the 'Great Wen' to this period in London's history. The origins of the problem lay chiefly in massive immigration, which a backward economic and social system was unable to absorb into the regular workforce.

How did London's institutions cope with the problems of rapid urbanization? The city's hospitals were 'allreadie overcharged' in 1587 according to John Howes. 'All London is but an hospitall', he said. Vagrants were a major problem, and Bridewell was the least effective of London's hospitals and contributed to the growth of crime and vagrancy by its failings. Persons in need and out of work through no fault of their own were 'packte up and punnyshed alyke in Brydewell with roges, beggers, strompets and pylfering theves'. No distinction was made between 'bonum and malum', and so the

---

27. Examples of conflicts – Pinchbeck and Hewitt, *Children in English Society*, 230–232. Sexual regulation – Peter Laslett, *The World We Have Lost* (London, 1971; 2nd ed), 2–3. The epigraph to this essay, for an example of a servant not practicing abstinence. Henry B. Wheatley (ed.), *The Diary of Samuel Pepys, M.A., F.R.S.* (London, 1918), VIII, 131–133, 145, 148ff. (the case of Deb Willet).
28. Court Book, 1597–1604, fol. 174a (23 July, 1600); for views of patriarchalism different from this see Laslett, *World We Have Lost*, 1–6; cf. John R. Gillis, *Youth and History* (New York, 1974), 21–22.

good were soon corrupted: 'the very name of Brydewell is in the eares of the people so odyous that it kylleth the creadit for ever'; 'a thousande to one if ever he or shee comme to any preferment, having tasted of that soyle'; 'nothing is to be learned but lewdenes amoungest that generacion'.[29]

Howes' criticisms of Bridewell had some foundation. It is doubtful whether the hospital gave practical training to more than a minority of offenders after 1600, although the original aim of Bridewell's founders was to set the able-bodied vagrant and prostitute to work. By 1600 most offenders were sent on their way after judgment and punishment by the Governors; the hospital's chief functions had become judicial and penal. There is also some evidence to show that Bridewell corrupted rather than corrected its charges. Rates of 'recidivism' were high and grew worse in the early seventeenth century: in 1602 one in 4.6 offenders was in Bridewell on a previous occasion; by 1631 the figure was one in 3.4. Return visits were sometimes astonishingly frequent: in 1602 one vagrant, John Gurnet, was said to have been arrested on *forty* previous occasions; another, Thomas Careles, twelve years of age, was in Bridewell eight or ten times before.[30]

These criticisms of Bridewell must nevertheless be put in perspective. It is possible that Howes' criticisms were motivated by self-interest. He was a 'sometime renter and gatherer of legacies' for Christ's hospital; the London hospitals being one corporation, he may have hoped to gain some of Bridewell's revenues for his own institution. In addition, Bridewell faced a staggering task as the chief institution dealing with vagrants in London, Middlesex, and Surrey until 1614. By 1590 the strain was taking its toll upon the hospital's finances. In March the Court of Aldermen appointed a committee to investigate the problem. It found that the hospital was 'more charged than before' because the Justices of the Peace for Middlesex and others sent in many prisoners and vagrants. In June Bridewell was granted further funding but, despite this stop-gap measure, the hospital experienced another crisis in 1605 and in 1631 was again in financial trouble.[31]

29. *Tudor Economic Documents*, III, 431, 439.
30. Of an average annual intake of 862 in 19 selected years from 1634 to 1694, 154 vagrants on average were still in Bridewell at the time of the Easter report. The proportion kept rose to 37% between 1704 and 1718, but fell to 22% from 1728 to 1734. Esmond S. de Beer, 'The London Hospitals in the Seventeenth Century', *Notes and Queries* (Nov. 18, 1939); John Stow (ed. J. Strype), *A Survey of London* (London, 1720) I, 191; William Maitland, *The History and Survey of London* (London, 1756), II, 1290. In Oct. 1602, 9 out of 41 vagrants were in Bridewell previously; in Feb. 1631, 25 out of 85; Gurnet and Careles appear in the Court Book for 1597–1604 at fols. 322b, 323b.
31. Rep. 22, fols. 151b, 154b, 155a, 163b–164a, 184b; Jnl. 26, fols. 336b, 337b, 338a; W. K. Jordan, *The Charities of London, 1480–1660* (London, 1960), 377.

The sixteenth century was the first to incarcerate and set the poor to work in institutions such as Bridewell. The intentions were to relieve and reform them, but also to remove them, as a source of disorder, from society. Setting the poor to work made some sense in conditions of unemployment and underemployment. The problem with these institutions was that they required generous financing and careful administration, which early modern states were not always able or willing to provide. In Bridewell's case the hospital lacked resources to meet the rising tide of vagrancy. It was out of the question that it could keep and employ a thousand inmates, which was the number the Governors were dealing with in their Court by the early seventeenth century. The only options were to judge, punish, and send away offenders forthwith, as was done; or, as also happened, to establish more houses of correction in the London area.

A final indication of London's inability to cope with its growing population was that the authorities were obliged to use measures to rid the city and England of vagrants by transporting them to the American colonies and by impressing them for foreign wars. Transportation is the better known of the two policies, although it requires further study. The first instance of large-scale transportation took place in 1618–19 when ninety-nine children between the ages of eight and sixteen were sent to Virginia. The action was initiated by the Virginia Company, James I, and the Court of Common Council. It was executed by the Governors of Bridewell. This and the later transportations to Virginia until 1622 are well known to historians. What is not well known is that transportation of London vagrants continued on a large scale after 1622. Bridewell's Court Books are peppered with references to vagrants sent to Bermuda, Barbados, Virginia, and 'to sea'. Questions remain to be answered about transportation in seventeenth-century London – how many were sent, who was sent, and to which colonies – but a more thorough analysis of the records will be required than heretofore and than is possible here.[32]

Impressment of vagrants to be soldiers also helped rid the city of undesirables. Impressment of London vagrants went back at least to the reign of Mary, but the Bridewell evidence shows that it increased considerably in the late Elizabethan years. It continued under the early Stuarts despite the peace with Spain in 1604, and once the Thirty Years War began vagrants were used to supply Bohemia and Count Mansfeld with troops. Precise statistics have still to be com-

---

32. Abbot Emerson Smith, *Colonists in Bondage. White Servitude and Convict Labor in America, 1607–1776* (Gloucester, Mass., 1965; orig. pub. 1947), ch. 7, esp. 139–141; Robert C. Johnson, 'The Transportation of Vagrant Children from London to Virginia, 1618–1622', in Howard S. Reinmuth (ed.), *Early Stuart Studies. Essays in Honor of David Harris Willson* (Minneapolis, 1970), 137–151.

piled for the numbers of London vagrants disposed of in these ways. The *impression* is that a minimum of several hundred were involved. Whatever the final tally, both policies underline the failure of London's institutions to cope with its social problems.[33]

The evidence of increasing vagrancy in London shows that contemporary outcries against vagrants had a basis in reality, whether or not one accepts their authors' presuppositions. Thus it is no coincidence that production of the literature of roguery appears to reach a peak in the 1590s and early 1600s. What about the assumptions of contemporaries such as the rogue writers that vagrants were typically professional criminals organized in gangs? There is an organization reported in Recorder Fleetwood's letter to Lord Burghley about a Fagin-type character running a school for cutpurses in an alehouse near Billingsgate. There are also occasional references in the Bridewell Court Books to thieves meeting at certain alehouses. No evidence has been found, however, of the organized hierarchies of the rogue literature. The typical London vagrant appears to have been alone in his 'crime'. Professional crime also appears to be exceptional among London vagrants, most of whom were listed as vagrants in the Court Books and who, when they committed other crimes, were typically petty thieves and confidence men.[34]

Apart from the writings of Robert Greene and Thomas Dekker, evidence is lacking to show that London vagrants typically had a 'culture' of their own. No evidence has been found of the canting language that vagrants were supposed to use. Moreover, in some respects London vagrants clearly did not have a culture apart. As immigrants they showed similarities to apprentices and working-men in London. They were also predominantly young, which was probably true of most immigrants to London. Finally, vagrants were mainly servants and apprentices, which were the most common positions in London's labor force at this time. Even in London it seems that the rogue writers' stories about organized criminality and a subculture among vagrants were largely unfounded.[35]

33. Rep. 13 (i), fol. 148a (9 April, 1554).
34. William Fleetwood's letter, *Tudor Economic Documents*, II, 337–339. Vagrants in gangs might have been arrested less *because they were organized*. But considering the authorities' notorious fear of conspiracies in this period, there is still a marked paucity of gangs in otherwise voluminous records. It is true that Bridewell did not see many capital offenders, who went to Newgate, and it cannot be denied that the great increase in vagrancy would breed felons.
35. Perhaps the best known piece of the literature is Thomas Harman's *A Caveat or Warning for Common Cursitors, Vulgarly called Vagabonds* (London, 1566: S.T.C. 12787), repr. in Gamini Salgādo (ed.), *Cony-Catchers and Bawdy Baskets* (Harmondsworth, 1972), 85–86 (cant language), 89–138 (orders of rogues;

In conclusion, London's example suggests an hypothesis about urban growth and social problems in the early modern period. It seems that social problems in urban centers of this period resulted from three conditions – rapid growth based on massive immigration; the type of immigrant that they attracted; and the likelihood that work was irregular, when not wholly lacking. To become urban giants early modern cities required great numbers of immigrants because deaths far outstripped births in the cramped and dirty conditions. The immigrants were predominantly young, male, and single; uprooted from families and local communities; and employed in low-paid, transient jobs (if at all). Finally, these young men were periodically involved in organized violence, for example the London apprentices in the Evil May Day riots of 1517, a number of affrays under Elizabeth, and in the revolutionary agitation of 1640. Urban growth therefore resulted in conditions that we would associate with ghettos in Western cities and places such as Calcutta. Institutions such as Bridewell were established to deal with these problems, but whether they provided long-term solutions is doubtful.[36]

Editorial suggestions for further reading

A. L. Beier, *Masterless Men* (1985).
P. Slack, *Poverty and Policy in Tudor and Stuart England* (1988).

criminal activities). For a debate touching the accuracy of this literature see J. F. Pound and A. L. Beier, 'Vagrants and the Social Order in Elizabethan England', *Past & Present*, 71 (1976), 128, 131. Cf. Peter Burke, 'Popular Culture in Seventeenth-century London', *The London Journal*, III (1977), 143.

36. Demographic evidence in Roger Mols, *Introduction à la Démographie historique des Villes d'Europe* (Louvain, 1955), II, 205–207, 209, 213–217 (predominance of males up to roughly age 20), 333 (mortality); John Patten, 'Rural-Urban Migration in Pre-Industrial England', Oxford Univ. School of Geography, Research Papers 6, 1973, 16–17; Roger S. Schofield, 'Age-specific Mobility in an Eighteenth-Century Rural English Parish', *Annales de Démographic historique* (1970), 266, 271, 273. For the social consequences a most suggestive study is David Herlihy, 'Some Psychological and Social Roots of Violence in the Tuscan Cities', in Lauro Martines (ed.), *Violence and Civil Disorder in Italian Cities, 1200–1500* (Berkeley, 1972), esp. 135–145. *Tudor Economic Documents*, III, 85–86; Thomas Wright (ed.), *Queen Elizabeth and Her Times, a Series of Original Letters* . . . (London, 1838), II, 227, 308; Valerie Pearl, *London and the Outbreak of the Puritan Revolution* (Oxford, 1961), 107–108. Cf. urban social problems in modernizing countries of the twentieth century: Robert C. Cook, 'The World's Great Cities: Evolution or Devolution?' repr. in Paul Meadows and Ephraim H. Mizruchi (eds), *Urbanism, Urbanization, and Change: Comparative Perspectives* (London, 1969), 43 (Calcutta in the 1950s); S. Kirson Weinberg, 'Urbanization and Male Delinquency in Ghana', repr. in ibid., 370 (Accra in the 1960s).

Chapter 6

CHANGE AND STABILITY IN SEVENTEENTH-CENTURY LONDON

Valerie Pearl

[*London Journal*, 5 (1979)]

Professor Pearl used her inaugural lecture to challenge pessimistic accounts of London society, building on her own work on the politics and poor relief measures of the City of London. Her main concern is to argue that the City remained a 'responsive and stable political community', offering both responsibility and reward to the majority of heads of household. More controversial are her claims that the male freemen of the City of London proper constituted London's typical inhabitants until the later seventeenth century. The latest work suggests that the suburban population overtook that of the City earlier than she allows, and adult male householders were by definition those who had survived the dangerous phases of immigration and job seeking and found a stable niche in society. None the less they did form the stable core of urban society and Pearl's evocation of their activities as freemen and guild members throws precious light on civic mentality and aspirations. The lecture has sparked off a lively controversy, with several subsequent attempts to offer stronger evidence from the suburbs and from social history to reinforce Pearl's primarily political material.

It seems appropriate for an inaugural lecture[1] to begin with a survey of recent scholarship in the field, in my case seventeenth-century London. While some aspects of the century have been excellently illuminated, there has been very little scholarly work of synthesis: the last but not the best was published some seventy years ago – the posthumous work of Sir Walter Besant, one of the early protagonists of the LCC. We are not likely to see his kind again and I will not

1. Delivered at University College London, 26 October 1978. I wish to thank Professor Donald Coleman and Miss Betty Masters for reading this essay. For the views expressed I alone am responsible.

be able to emulate him: among other things he wrote a novel a year for twenty years, each one 'of the regulation length' says the *DNB*, and he inspired the foundation of both the People's Palace and what was to become Queen Mary College.

The rigorous method and the synoptic vision demanded nowadays make the writing of such a history a formidable task – the work of perhaps teams of people if we use the approach of the *Annales* school. In the early modern period, London has probably the finest archives of any great city of the world, certainly the largest in bulk, of which only a very small part has been systematically examined and an even smaller fraction edited and published. The City's letter books calendared up to 1495 thereafter remain unprinted. There are literally hundreds of *series* of manuscript sources in the Guildhall Library and Corporation Record Office, nearly all comprising within each series thousands of folios; the single most voluminous record, the repertories of the aldermanic bench, contains about 400 folios for each year. A team working for a generation or two might recover all the information buried there, although such a labour would be incomplete without sifting also the enormous outpourings of the seventeenth-century press and the archives of national government. In contrast, the records of the city of Westminster and the surrounding townships and parishes of Middlesex and Surrey with their multifarious and overlapping local authorities are either fragmentary or laconically formal and require the most sensitive skills of interpretation – a task that has not yet begun.

Notwithstanding such difficulties, generalisation about the role of London abounds; indeed without it no account of the nation's economy or politics would stand. The new school of urban history in this country has in my view presented an incomplete account of town life, shaped partly by sociological theories and by what has been called the philosophy of 'doom and gloom'. Despite excellent individual work, the general presentation of urban history and, sometimes of London also at this time, places an overriding emphasis on crisis, conflict and social polarisation. Prompted by seemingly analogous social and economic conditions, some urban historians see close parallels between seventeenth-century towns and third world cities today. Stuart Lincoln, for example, has been compared with present day Ibadan.[2] Let me sum up some judgements about London which may soon become received orthodoxy. We are told that the rapid growth of the city in the early modern period, sustained by high immigration levels, created some of the problems of a modern shanty town. A large masterless population living on or below the poverty line and physically segregated into poor areas, is said to have erupted into food riots in the sixteenth century and

2. P. Clark, 'Lincoln: urban context' Open University Film A 322/01.

political disorder in the seventeenth. The City, outnumbered by the suburbs, was unable to solve the problems of poverty or of order. The rulers, it is claimed, became more oligarchic and elitist, while medieval commensality, as expressed in craft and consumer control, was eroded and disappeared.

These generalisations are not drawn from a particular work but sum up what is found in a number of recent histories.[3] They have become common currency and few, perhaps, would dissent from them. Yet the picture of London which I have formed is different. The view of the city dissolving into administrative chaos, conflict and economic anarchy, is too stark and simplistic. It can give rise to a distorted image of a totally dangerous, primitive but huge city. Furthermore, some of the similarities discerned between London then and third world cities today seem less substantial on closer view. Compared with many towns in subsistence economies, seventeenth-century London, despite periods of hardship for the poor, was a rich place; as many as 17 per cent of householders living within her walls, for example, were paying a kind of 'surtax' or higher income and property tax by the end of the century, notwithstanding the exodus of some of the richest men into the fashionable western suburbs.[4] Her independence and her range of goods and services, specialist and entrepreneurial skills placed her, in common with other great European cities, in a luxury class compared with most towns of the time or with some cities of the third world today. Some of the contrasts in cultural and political traditions between these twentieth-century towns and seventeenth-century London are reflected in her social administration which although primitive by our standards was more sophisticated and effective than exists in many underdeveloped countries. Take poor relief. The poor flocked to the growing metropolis. In contrast with the haphazard, sometimes chaotic conditions of the suburbs London provided for the poor with greater sensitivity to need than has been recognised. Its system of poor relief, far in advance of most of England, provided for some poor housekeepers and their children (not just freemen as is sometimes suggested) not only the statutory weekly

---

3. P. Clark and P. Slack, eds, *Crisis and Order in English Towns 1500–1700* (1972), 35–8; C. Hill, *The World Turned Upside Down* (1972), 33; P. Clark and P. Slack, *English Towns in Transition 1500–1700* (1976), 69; F. Braudel, *Capitalism and Material Life 1400–1800* quoted in P. Clark, *The Early Modern Town* (1976), 83. Contrast the view of London's 'shanty' building given by Braudel with M. Power's reconstruction of the housing of the artisan hamlet of Shadwell: 'Shadwell: the Development of a London Suburban Community in the seventeenth century', *London Journal*, IV, i (1978), 29–49; M. Power, 'East London housing in the seventeenth century', P. Clark and P. Slack, eds, *Crisis and Order*, 237–63.
4. D. V. Glass, *London Inhabitants within the Walls 1695*, London Record Soc. (1966), ixxxxviii.

doles from the parish, but also pensions from the guilds and charitable handouts in money and kind from parochial and ward fines and parish fees; it must be remembered that before the setting up of modern systems of relief, charities consisted of small sums from a variety of sources. Some rich and 'middling' rich parishes provided free education for their foundlings and free housing for pensioners. Exceptional provision was made for orphans, and a rate equalisation scheme, presaging later rating systems, was established. Of course, unlicensed immigrants into the parish were debarred from relief, and harsh obligations, sometimes tyrannically paternal, of a kind totally unacceptable today were often imposed on pensioners.[5] Yet at the time these conditions aroused few protests. Such provision, unusually caring by the standards of the day, suggests that the study of poor relief for London, at least, needs sharper definition and deeper examination than it sometimes receives.

May I also touch briefly on the ambiguity of another of the characteristics of London often emphasised, or sometimes over-emphasised: urban disorder. Historians and interpreters of English literature habitually present a picture of a city constantly close to riot, a place in which criminality was endemic and the underworld pervasive. Of course, there was a serious problem of crime and serious riots occurred but such one-sided accounts largely drawn from the colourful sources of pamphlets and plays are misleading – as misleading as a future account of present-day American society would be if it were drawn entirely from the exploits of Starsky and Hutch. Dorothy George, one of London's greatest social historians, wrote that London in the eighteenth century combined turbulence with fundamental orderliness.[6] Her judgment is even more apt for the previous period. Since the seventeenth century was an age of political revolution, the paradox which she described is sharpened.

5. V. Pearl, 'Puritans and Poor Relief: the London Workhouse 1649–1660' in D. Penington and K. Thomas, eds, *Puritans and Revolutionaries* (1978), 206–32; R. W. Herlan, 'Poor Relief during the Great Civil War and Interregnum 1642–1660', Ph.D. thesis, State Univ. New York, Buffalo (1973); R. W. Herlan, 'Poor Relief in the London Parish of Antholin's Budge Row, 1638–1664', *Guildhall Studies in London History*, ii, 4 (1977), 179–99; R. W. Herlan, 'Social Articulation and Parochial Poverty on the eve of the Restoration', ibid., ii, 2 (1976), 47; E. Freshfield's edns of *The Vestry Minute Book of the Parish of St Margaret Lothbury in the City of London 1571–1677* (1887), *The Account Book of the Parish of St Bartholomew Exchange in the City of London 1596–1678* (1895), and *The Vestry Minute Books of the Parish of St Bartholomew Exchange in the City of London 1567–1676* (1890), *passim*. For the rate equalisation scheme, see The Booke of the Poores Accompts, St Andrew by the Wardrobe 1613–68, Guildhall Library (GL) MS 2089: I, Churchwardens' Poor's Account for Portsoken Ward 1622–78, GLMS 9237, Annual Accounts, St Botolph Bishopsgate, GLMS 4525: 2.
6. M. D. George, *London Life in the Eighteenth Century*, 1965 edn, 9.

Around 1640, a striking phenomenon had appeared, unknown in the rest of Europe: the rise of mass political activity of a new kind, accompanied by demonstrations in the streets and petitions. Yet frightening though some found them, there was a sense of containment in these London évènements: there was often a strong element of political direction and discipline in such popular manifestations: occasionally there was manipulation by their betters; hence the lack, hitherto unremarked, of prosecutions for riot among the sessions records and the absence of attacks on private property, contrasting sharply with the behaviour of eighteenth-century city mobs.[7] The silences of historians are sometimes more eloquent than their words. It is surely a matter deserving of more comment than it has received that London should have remained without a popular uprising, even without significant bloodshed, during some of the most disturbed years in English history – decades which saw constant changes in government, including the abolition of the monarchy, and widespread public debate among classes outside the political elite. The point was not lost on the French ambassador: blood would certainly have flowed in the streets of Paris, he wrote in 1642, if similar events had happened there.[8] Even more individual forms of violence – such as mugging, street brawls and vandalism – appear to have been less common in London before the 1670s than they were to become.

I do not think that it is sufficient to explain this pattern of behaviour and these individual and collective responses by abstract concepts of the power of authority, by the deference of Englishmen at this time, or by the 'godly discipline' of a patriarchal puritan society, important though these factors are. Opposed to them, after all, were new and countervailing freedoms. The city in the middle of the seventeenth century astonished and horrified well-thinking

---

7. The sessions records for the City are not extant between 1640–1660. I refer to the records for Middlesex and Westminster where most political riots took place. They have been calendared by J. C. Jeaffreson, ed., *Middlesex County Records*, reprinted 1974, iii, *passim*. A fuller calendar is contained in typescripts compiled by W. J. Hardy (1900–10), vols. 1638–44, 1644–52, *passim*. British Library, 10360 t. 1. Barely a handful of cases refer to political riot. For a discussion of the 'disciplined' nature of the London crowd, see R. Yarlott, 'The Long Parliament and the Fear of Popular Pressure 1640–1643', M. A. thesis Leeds 1963; V. Pearl, 'London's Counter-Revolution' in G. E. Aylmer, ed., *The Interregnum: The Quest for Settlement 1646–1660* (1972), 49–56. Cf. B. Manning, *The English People and the English Revolution 1640–1649* (1976), chaps. 1–3. For the much more violent City mobs of the eighteenth-century, see G. Rudé, *The Crowd in History* (1964), G. Holmes, 'The Sacheverell Riots', *Past and Present*, 72, 56–85; N. Rogers, 'Popular protest in early Hanoverian London' *Past and Present*, 79, 70–100.

8. V. Pearl, *London and the Outbreak of the Puritan Revolution* (Oxford, 1961), 279.

Europe by its political liberty. One opponent of change wrote of London: 'All the world was now run into one trade, and that was state-mending and church modelling. . . [so] that every little blue-apron boy behind the counter undertakes as boldly as if he had served an apprenticeship at the council board.'[9]

Politics were openly debated by societies meeting in ward-clubs and in taverns and coffee houses, the 'penny universities', as they would be called, where gentry, shopkeepers and artisans not yet segregated into separate clubs, mingled freely. Like all great cities, London itself was an educator. Not that formal education did not thrive. There were probably more grammar and private schools in the city and surrounding villages at that time than would exist again before the twentieth century.[10] A European scholar and educationalist, Johann Comenius, visiting London in 1641, was astonished by the sight of a large part of a London congregation taking notes in shorthand during the sermon; not one note-taker, but half a churchfull. Even if we see the seventeenth-century sermon as roughly equivalent to today's university extension lecture it is still astonishing. He was amazed too by the great number of bookshops, more probably per head of population than today.[11] Encouraged by the absence of censorship, writers, printers and booksellers combined to produce a flood of newspapers and pamphlets, containing some of the most radical literature ever published in this country. Moreover, this sudden freedom followed a time of tight censorship, of very rapid immigration with the attendant social strains, and some of the worst outbreaks of plague in the history of the city.[12] So perhaps the more searching question is not why there was disorder but why, given some of the pre-conditions for a popular uprising, London society proved stable.

Our view of London society in the seventeenth century must depend on how far population growth and economic change had destroyed the social and civic character of the earlier city. It is also affected by a further consideration: whether the spirit of capitalist

9. John Nalson, *An Impartial Collection* (1682–3), ii, 775–6.
10. S. M. Wide and J. A. Morris, 'The episcopal licensing of schoolmasters in the diocese of London, 1627–1685', *Guildhall Miscellany* (1968), 402–6. J. W. Adamson, 'Literacy in England during the Fifteenth and Sixteenth Centuries', *The Illiterate Anglo-Saxon and other Essays* (1946), 44–61.
11. R. F. Young, ed., *Comenius in England* (1936), 65; C. Bridenbaugh, *Vexed and Troubled Englishmen 1590–1642* (Oxford, 1968), 342.
12. The statement by W. G. Bell in *The great plague in London in 1665* (1924), 5, that only four years of the first half of the century were free of plague is not borne out by Ian Sutherland, 'When was the Great Plague? Mortality in London, 1563–1665', in D. V. Glass and Roger Revelle, eds, *Population and Social Change* (1972), 306. The relative mortality in the plagues of 1603 and 1625 was higher than in the famous outbreak of 1665.

enterprise, undeniably more pronounced in seventeenth-century London than hitherto, produced a harsher and less homogeneous society as some historians allege, a view which may contribute, for example, to the failure to take seriously such features of social amelioration as the many-sided provisions of London's Poor Law to which I referred earlier. The argument also depends on the quality of the city's civic life: whether the traditional polity at the ground level of parish, ward and precinct continued into the seventeenth century to provide a responsive and stable political community, the topic which comprises the main theme of this lecture.

Many lines of enquiry into social history are germane to my argument but I shall touch briefly on three. First, it is sometimes implied that by the mid-seventeenth century the suburban area of London had overwhelmed and outstripped in population the area of the ancient City. We cannot work out accurate population totals because our sources are derived from burials and christenings rather than from numbers of deaths and births,[13] but we can compare the size of the City with the outparishes. From the Bills of Mortality we can discover totals of burials and christenings in the area of the city under the Lord Mayor's jurisdiction and we can compare these figures with the outparishes beyond. Leaving aside the separate city and government of Westminster, the comparison makes plain that there were more people living under the Lord Mayor's jurisdiction down to the Great Fire than living outside it and that the balance is not finally weighted in favour of the outer parishes until well into the 1670s.[14] Even if we include in our calculation the City of Westminster with all the outparishes and villages, the municipality was not surpassed in population until the 1650s. Such a comparison also emphasises that the rough total population figures with which historians work do not apply to a monolithic urban area or block as might first appear. They apply to the conurbation of greater London included within the Bills of Mortality, an area which was extended from time to time during the century to take in the growing

13. The most satisfactory analysis of London's population in the seventeenth century is contained in Sutherland, op. cit., 310. He suggests figures for the years 1600–50 considerably lower than those given by E. A. Wrigley, 'A simple model of London's importance in changing English society and economy 1650–1750', in P. Abrams and E. A. Wrigley, *Towns in Societies* (1978), 215 n. 1.

14. Calculated from the tables of burials and christenings in London in *A Collection of the Yearly Bills of Mortality from 1657–1758* (1759) and from J. Graunt, *Natural and Political Observations upon the Bills of Mortality* (1662) which is appended to it. According to Graunt, roughly two-thirds of the sixteen parishes described in the second column as 'outside the walls' were included within the jurisdiction of the municipality. Assuming it was so (and there is no means of checking the fraction) it is necessary to subtract one-third of the figures under the sixteen parishes and add that sum to the totals given under the out-parishes. See Sutherland, op. cit., 307.

townships which surrounded the city. This larger region artificially inflated the population of the *urban* area, particularly after 1636 when the territory covered by the Bills was extended to include the six rural townships of Hackney, Islington, Stepney, Lambeth, Kensington and Rotherhithe.[15] They would not form a continuous link with the city until the time of Defoe. Thus, in the London conurbation, the ancient City with its web of interlocking administrative councils and committees was still predominant, at least until the Restoration and perhaps for another decade.

Second, how far had the social and economic patterns of medieval London society collapsed by the seventeenth century? The question suggests many areas of research yet untouched, but a study of social topography reveals that one medieval feature, the social intermingling of rich and poor not yet segregated into clearly distinguished neighbourhoods, was retained well into the century. We are fortunate in having data which enable a rough kind of property valuation to be computed for most of the City in 1638: a list of tithe rentals in which evidence is extant for 93 out of 113 parishes.[16] A study of this material shows that social segregation into *rigidly* divided rich and poor quarters within London had not developed.[17] Even in the richest parishes, there were considerable enclaves of poor dwellings. In the nine most highly rated parishes, more than 10 per cent of the houses were assessed at values below the average rent for the city. In as many as 86 out of 93 parishes, between one-tenth and one-third of rentals were below the city average, revealing a very wide dispersal of low rents throughout the city. The impression of social intermixing is strengthened by the very small size of parishes, few within the walls containing more than 200 houses. Allhallows Barking was a poor wallside parish where the mean rent was below average and most people lived in alleys containing some of the lowest rents in the city. Yet even here one-fifth of the houses was occupied by rich merchants dwelling in three of the prominent lanes. The 1638 list confirms that the parishes hugging the city walls were usually poor areas, as were the riverside parishes on the north Thames bank, though they would be partially rehabilitated after the Fire. The rich were more concentrated in the centre as was the normal pattern in pre-industrial towns, but this area in the case of

15. J. Graunt, op. cit., 7.
16. T. C. Dale, *The Inhabitants of London in 1638: edited from ms 272 in the Lambeth Palace Library* (1931). This is a list of 'moderated' rents, i.e. rents which were 75 per cent of real rents without fines.
17. I am grateful to my student Dr Gregg Carr for the analysis contained in his thesis 'Residence and social status: the development of Seventeenth Century London', Ph.D. Sociology, Harvard (1974), chapters IV and V *passim*.

London stretched east and west to cover at least two wealthy districts on the city's extremities.[18] The general picture is not so exclusively divided into rich and poor quarters as has been claimed, but presents rather a continued pattern of medieval infilling, much as it had long been, with the rich in the main thoroughfares and the poor in alleys and courts immediately behind them.

The third area of research relates to the gilds, which provided one of the most important bonds in the medieval city, arguably even more crucial to social and political life than to the economy. It is often said that surburban growth and the hostility of common lawyers to trade restrictions destroyed the gilds' powers of regulation and search. It is doubtful, however, whether either factor produced any sudden or dramatic change. London's gilds never enjoyed a complete monopoly of the classic kind once postulated by economic historians. By the so-called 'custom of London', anyone free of a buying and selling gild could practise any other trade, thus providing both an invitation and a means for entrepreneurs to expand without the restraints of company regulations. It is inappropriate to speak of collapse of government in these crafts because economic regulation had always been flexible. The manual trades, in contrast, were more strictly controlled. A policy developed in many of the 'mechanical' crafts from the late sixteenth century, for a man engaged in a different trade from his gild's to come under the regulation and search of the trade he practised.[19] Here, therefore, the custom of London had only a limited application, despite Sir Edward Coke's attempt to extend the principle to manual gilds in the famous case of John Tolley. Much quoted in error since by historians as having destroyed the power of the gilds, it has largely escaped notice that the judgment was modified in favour of manual

18. St Dunstan's in the West, the rich legal quarter, and St Dunstan's in the East, described by Stow as 'a great parish of many rich merchants', are revealed also in D. V. Glass, *London Inhabitants*, as among the city's wealthy parishes. For the beginnings of social differentiation in the western suburbs, see M. Power, 'The East and West in early-modern London', in E. W. Ives, R. J. Knecht, and J. J. Scarisbrick, *Wealth and Power in Tudor England* (1978), 167–85, Clark and Slack, *English Towns in Transition*, 69. Cf. the social decline of Covent Garden from the 1670s, F. H. W. Sheppard, Gen. Ed., *Survey of London*, xxxvi, *The Parish of St Paul Covent Garden* (1970), 34–7.

19. S. Thrupp, *A Short History of the Worshipful Company of Bakers of London* (1933), 66–9; T. C. Barker, *The Girdlers' Company* (1957), 93–4; A. Plummer, *The London Weaver's Company 1600–1900* (1972), 92; A. Crawford, *A History of the Vintners' Company* (1977), 55 ff; C. Blagden, *The Stationers' Company: A History 1403–1959* (1960), 114–5; G. Unwin, *The Gilds and Companies of London* (1908), 262–6; C. M. Clode, *Memorials of the Gild of Merchant Taylors* (1875), 532; A. H. Johnson, *History of the Drapers' Company* (1915), ii, 166–7; Goldsmiths' Court Book V (1639–42), f. 37.

trades twenty years later.[20] The collecting of citizens in certain crafts into their proper trades was supported by the City government to a lesser or greater degree for much of the seventeenth century, and even on occasion into the eighteenth; as late as 1778 twenty-two City crafts were reaffirming their right to compel enrolment or translation of workers in their trade.[21] In some companies, efforts to impose supervision and standards were as vigorous in the mid-seventeenth century as they had been at any time during the previous hundred years. Naturally, success was limited particularly in the rapidly growing suburbs. Yet we should not infer that industrial control had never extended to the suburban areas. It has not always been realised that most gild charters granted after 1600 placed areas of from two to ten miles of the city within the purview of the companies' search, though we may doubt whether it was ever operated very efficiently so far afield. The role of the 'mercantile' or greater crafts should not be sought solely or even mainly in the sphere of economic regulation. In the seventeenth century as in the medieval period, their life still found expression in an intricate formality of fraternal social organisation and in a close integration with the city's political life.

An extraordinary feature of the London gilds was that the number of freeman was as high in the third quarter of the seventeenth century as it had been earlier even though the power of the gilds was declining and the freedom in some ways less attractive. Perhaps one of the most misleading statements made about London in the seventeenth century is that the freemen of the city were a small elite class superimposed 'upon a mass of labouring poor', as a recent

---

20. W. Bohun, *Privilegia Londini: or the Laws Customs and Privileges of the City of London* (1702), 115 ; Appleton *against* Stoughton, *Croke's Reports*, 1638, 516–17; R. Monier-Williams, *The Tallow-Chandlers of London* (1977), iv, 206–7. For prosecutions carried out under the Statute of Apprentices against members of companies practising trades other than their own, see ibid. 215–16; and S. Thrupp, *Bakers of London*, 69.

21. The City government encouraged voluntary translation to collect men into their proper companies but their view on the use of compulsion varied from time to time during the century. If the interests of the big twelve companies were affected they would normally oppose it, W. H. Overall and H. C. Overall, eds, *Analytical Index to . . . the Remembrancia 1579–1664* (1878), 108. From 1639 to 1658, and again in the late seventeenth and early eighteenth centuries, the City supported the claims of the victualling and smaller 'mechanical' crafts, W. E. Alford and T. C. Barker, *A history of the Carpenters' Company* (1969), 82; Plummer, *London Weavers*, 92–3; R. Monier-Williams, *Tallow-Chandlers*, iv, 208–13; Repertories of the Aldermanic Bench, 61, ff 15 v, 16, Rep. 63 ff 257 v–8, Rep. 64 ff 151–2, 213 v, 409; J. R. Kellett, 'The breakdown of gild and corporation control over the handicraft and retail trade in London', *Econ. Hist. Rev.*, 2nd series, X, 390. Vigorous maintenance of the search and of apprenticeship regulations is found in some of the manual crafts, for example the Pewterers, J. Hatcher and T. C. Barker, *A History of British Pewter* (1974), 176–7, 202–3.

thesis put it.[22] Our authorities present a figure of between 10 000 and 12 000[23] in the second half of the seventeenth century in a population of about 200 000 which suggests that around one-third of male householders were freemen. I shall show that this is an absurd under-estimate. We shall never have an exact count though we can get nearer to the total after 1675 when the Chamberlain's admission lists are extant. We can find fairly precise figures for individual companies for which there are freemen and quarterage lists (the latter being affiliation fees), but we must estimate figures for others, a tricky business because of the great variations in company structure and size. From such a computation, it is clear that there must have been at least 30 000 freemen, that is over twice as many as previously thought. It would be tedious to give each separate figure for 79 companies but I will sum it up by saying that there were more than 20 000 freemen in five of the 79 companies, those covering the weaving, tailoring, clothing, haberdashery and portering trades; approximately 8000 in twenty of the larger companies; and perhaps 3000 in the remaining 54.[24] Allowing for some freemen having settled elsewhere, it suggests that around mid-century roughly three-quaters of the adult male house-holders in the City were

22. A. M. Dingle, 'The role of the householder in early Stuart London *c.* 1603– *c.* 1630', M. Phil. thesis, London (1974), 35.
23. S. and B. Webb, *English Local Government . . . The Manor and the Borough* (1908), iii, 579. The Webbs, whose work on London was mainly based on research into the eighteenth century, may well have drawn their figures from contemporary estimates of the freemen electorate. See *Historical Register* X (1725), 84–5, for a reference to 10,850 City freemen: presumably freemen who were also £10 householders in accordance with the Act of 1725. There is no doubt that the total number of freemen was much greater. For the view that the number of freemen was already growing faster *pro rata* than the population in the middle of the sixteenth century, see C. Carlton, *The Court of Orphans* (Leicester, 1974), 33. A. G. Smith, 'London and the Crown 1681–1685', Ph.D. thesis, Wisconsin (1967), 205, speculated that the number of freemen in the 1680s might be about 20 000.
24. In these calculations, I am trying merely to establish an order of magnitude.

Merchant Taylors' Co. GL MS Microfilm 302, 303		*c.* 8000
Clothworkers' Co. Quarter & Renter Warden Accounts, Clothworkers Hall	based on average decennial enrolment figures for freemen using a multiplier of 31.8. See below, n. 26	*c.* 3900
Haberdashers' Co. Quarterage Book 1642–1772 GL MS 15857: 2		*c.* 4300
Weavers' Company (approx. figure extrapolated from A. Plummer, London Weavers)		*c.* 4500
Porters' Co. (an Act of common Council, 1946, mentions over 3000 ticket porters alone)		*c.* 4000
Drapers' Co. (given by A. H. Johnson, *Drapers' Company*, ii, 236)		1300
		c. 26 000

freemen, an even higher proportion than in Norwich or York which themselves stood out as two of the most 'liberal' boroughs in England in respect of franchise. It is even more remarkable that in the 1670s when freemen's lists begin, about 1700 freemen were enrolled annually.[25] If one rates a life expectancy for newly enrolled freemen aged 24 at 31.8 years,[26] it suggests that the total roll was then in the region of 50 000. You may think that it is too neat a confirmation of my calculations that the City government, as part

Goldsmiths' Co. (actual quarterage figures from 1620s)	767
W. S. Prideaux, *Memorials of the Goldsmiths' Company* (1986), i, 132	
Coppers' Co. (actual quarterage figures from 1640s) GL MS 5614: 3	1100
Girdlers' Co. (figure quoted by T. C. Barker, *Girdlers' Company*)	600
Cordwainers' Co. (actual quartage figure in 1664) GL MS 7358:1	773
Leathersellers' Co. (estimated for c. 1640 by Dr Richard Grassby to whom I am grateful)	1500
Fishmongers' Co. (estimated from freemen enrolments) GL MS 5576: 1	c.1100
Grocers' Co. (estimated from freemen enrolments) GL MS 11 593: 1	c.1260
Stationers' Co. (estimated by C. Blagden, Stationers' Company)	c.600
Ironmongers' Co. (estimated from freemen enrolments) GL MS 16 987: 3	c.400
Mercers' Co. (estimated from freemen enrolments)	c.300
Carpenters' Co. (estimated by Alford and Barker, *Carpenters' Company*)	c.500
	c. 8900

3000 for the 54 small companies is possibly an under-estimate. The total here of over 38 000 needs to be reduced because it includes some aliens and foreigners paying quarterage. It is doubtful if they would number more than 5000 in all (only those totals mentioned here which are taken from quarterage figures would need scaling down). The Coopers' Company for which we have a quarterage book breaks down the membership into householders, journeymen and foreign and alien householders and journeymen. About one-fifth of the total is described as either foreign or alien. The typescript edited by T. C. Dale in 1931 of Exchequer Papers E. 1179/251 and 272 (Public Record Office), 'The Members of the City Companies in 1641 as set forth in Returns for the Poll Tax' contains only a fragment of the total returns. There are no returns at all for seven of the largest City companies and the Coopers' Company which we know had over 1000 members at the time is represented by only 304 names.

25. Accounts of fees received for freedom, 1675–84 City of London Record Office 39A, hereafter CLRO. It is possible to work out rough numbers of freemen enrolled form the City's cash records. The average income from this source in the 1630s was just under £1100. Since the fine paid by new freemen was 13s. 4d., the numbers appear comparable with those being enrolled in the 1680s.

26. Calculation based on figures derived from A. J. Coale and P. Demeney, *Regional Model Life Tables and Stable Populations* (Princeton, 1966), 182, $e^0 = 32.484$ years; page 8, e_x^0 with $_x$ at 24 years = 24.0 + 31.8 = 55.8 years. There are numerous problems involved in basing estimates of life expectation in a pre-industrial society on later more reliable data, in which low growth of population is postulated. Such information derived from a hypothetical stable population can only be inferential. See a similar application, J. J. Spengler, 'Demographic factors and early modern economic development' in D. V. Glass and R. Revelle, *Population and Social Change* (1972), 93–4.

of its polemics against the Crown in the *Quo Warranto* crisis of 1682, put the total at much the same figure as mine – however I am not dismayed by this apparent correlation with the City's guesstimates – if they were such. Enumeration was often wildly wrong in the seventeenth century but the City, at least, had considerable experience in listing and census-taking.[27] The total is even more remarkable because it was a period when traders were widely said to be deserting the City. Of course, some freemen would have served their time to achieve the status and skills associated with London gilds and then moved to the provinces for a variety of reasons, among them family ties and marriage, but the number is not likely to have been very large, if only because of the financial liabilities involved in taking up the freedom. Also, of course, by this late period in the century, a considerable number (we have no means of knowing how many) would be residing and trading in the suburbs.

Nevertheless, it is plain that the freemen, far from being the élite constituted the great majority of male householders in the city. The presence in the middle of the century in any one year about 20 000 apprentices extends even further the existence of widespread privilege in London.[28] One of our most eminent seventeenth-century historians states that the poorer sort of men were excluded from becoming citizens because of the limitation of apprenticeship to the sons of forty shilling freeholders as provided in the Statute of Apprentices of 1563. This limitation, however, did not apply to London, which was expressly excluded from the provision by clause 33 of the same Act.[29] For many quite humble men, seventeenth-century London must have appeared as a land of opportunity – an El Dorado where the Dick Whittingtons and the Simon Eyres of the day could achieve fame and fortune. It was no accident that both at this time became folk heroes and that from the late sixteenth century myths about their careers entwined with fact gained wide currency. Of course, I am not implying that all freemen were rich or even substantial men. There were plenty of poor freemen who were badly

27. W. Maitland, *The History of London from its foundation to the present time* (1756), i, 478. Lists of inhabitants drawn up by the Lord Mayor and Aldermen at the request of the Privy Council to illuminate a great variety of social problems are scattered throughout the State Papers for the sixteenth and seventeenth centuries.
28. S. Smith, 'The Social and Geographical Origins of the London Apprentices 1630–1660', *Guildhall Miscellany*, iv, 4, 198. Cf. D. V. Glass, 'Socio-economic Status and Occupations in the City of London at the End of the Seventeenth Century' in A. E. J. Hollaender and W. Kellaway, eds, *Studies in London History* (1969), 386, where a figure of 11 000 for the 1690s is suggested.
29. C. Hill, *The World Turned Upside Down*, 33; *Statutes of the Realm* (1819), 4, pt. 1, 421.

housed, who suffered deprivation of many kinds, and who may also have been alienated from their fellows. Nevertheless, they were not deprived of the privileges of the city; I shall attempt shortly to show what this meant in terms of participation in government. The wide diffusion of privilege helps explain why the Levellers, despite their defence of the underdog, never claimed that the freedom should be extended or, more significantly, rarely spoke of the problems of the non-free, even in pamphlets wholly devoted to London's government and liberties.[30] Presumably, they saw non-free status as equivalent to economic dependence, the league in which personal servants, women and children were placed; perhaps too the class of non-free was not large or vociferous enough within the city to claim attention. It also explains why in London the term 'housekeeper' (or 'head of household' today) tended to become synonymous in the sixteenth and seventeenth centuries with the word 'householder' which up to that time meant strictly a freeman of a company who had become a master. The two terms became interchangeable because to a greater extent than historians have realised housekeepers were also householders.[31]

How was this large class of privileged freemen governed? The government of London consisted of a multitude of overlapping courts and jurisdictions in which the citizens and housekeepers were either represented or took part in person. The Webbs enumerated seventeen separate 'courts' which divided among them the electoral, executive, judicial and legislative business of the Corporation. The top layer of government was oligarchical, dominated by the Court of Lord Mayor and Aldermen, although uncharacteristically for towns in this period Common Council claimed sovereignty for two short periods during the century. At the roots of this elaborate organisation, government was more diverse and pluralistic. There were 79 craft gilds exercising administrative, governmental and in some cases electoral powers. The primary units of City government for

---

30. J. Lilburne, *The Charter of London*, 1646. In *London's Liberty in Chains discovered* (1646) Lilburne estimated that there were 300 freemen to every liveryman, p. 52. Since there were then in the region of 4000 liverymen, his arithmetic would have produced the preposterous figure of more than a million freemen.

31. One of our main areas of ignorance about seventeenth-century London relates to the position of the small master. Most histories suggest that the number of small masters declined rapidly with the rise of merchant capitalism. The quarterage books of the Coopers' Company for the seventeenth century provide a breakdown of the membership of the Company into householders and journeymen. It shows that the proportion of masters to journeymen was much higher than is usually thought; in 1635–36, there were 444 free householders and 586 free journeymen; in 1643–44, 654 free householders and 735 free journeymen. GLMS 5614: 3 n. p. The Drapers' Company also contained a large number of freemen masters in the 1620s, Johnson, *Drapers' Company*, ii, 194.

police, taxation and electoral purposes were the wards, which were themselves divided into as many as 242 precincts. Alongside, but not coincident in boundaries, were 111 parishes which were increasingly involved in local administration; indeed, since the parish administered the considerable sums of money received for the poor, it complemented the ward as a centre of local power. These tiny units of government overlapped in authority and in boundaries, yet still partly preserved separate identity. Their miniscule area has not been fully appreciated. The City comprised 677 acres. Each precinct was on the average under three acres in size – that is, equivalent to a square one side of which measured only 120 yards – and every parish on average four and a half acres in extent. A man could cross a precinct on foot from one side to the other in a few minutes or so. The term 'parochial' takes on a deeper significance when one studies such miniature authorities. I do not want to suggest that London precincts and parishes were like fratricidal Italian hill towns but sometimes their quarrels about boundaries, precedency, and powers do sound as though here were walled cities contending. Even as late as the 1670s, the wards were divided from each other, at times of disorder, by chains and posts stored in the Inquest House or in the church and erected when there was need.[32]

The parish was run by a vestry of householders elected by part of the ratepayers or, occasionally, by all of them. Sometimes, officers were simply selected by previous office-holders in what were known as closed vestries, although I believe historians have exaggerated their extent in seventeenth-century London. There was a long tradition in the city, surviving into the eighteenth century, by which vestries were open to a large assembly of the ratepayers, particularly if the business in hand affected the *precinct* (it was then termed a 'general vestry' or a 'public' meeting of parishioners); for other purposes it was confined to a group of ten to twenty when it was called a 'select vestry'.[33] The ward or wardmote, however, was

32. Cornhill Wardmote Inquest book. GLMS 4069: 2, f 336v.
33. 59 of 109 parishes were listed as having select vestries in 1638. Many of these were thrown open in or after 1641 and became 'closed' again after 1660. But the select vestry did not usually exclude the general body of parishioners from precinct meetings and from electing lecturers. Many parishes had both a select and general vestry, the latter assembling to elect precinct and sometimes also parochial officers, A. E. McCampbell, 'The London Parish and the London Precinct 1640–1660', *Guildhall Studies in London History*, ii, 3, 109–18. Even when the vestry was 'select', the notion remained that business was to be done 'as if we are all personally present', as the parishioners of St Botolph Aldersgate insisted, GLMS 1453: 1 n.p. The Webbs found select vestries in the eighteenth century in only just over one quarter of the metropolitan parishes between 1689 and 1835, S. and B. Webb, *English Local Government . . . the Parish and the County* (1906), 174 n. 1.

a more genuinely popular as well as populous assembly. It enjoined attendance by *all* householders, permitting them in some respects and in certain favoured neighbourhoods a remarkable degree of participation in local affairs. In sixteenth- and seventeenth-century London, the growth in political consciousness endowed the precinct and ward with a new vigour, and with a community role which may have become more pronounced than it was in the medieval period.[34] As I shall show, the wardmote came to provide an arena for public opinion – a platform from which popular views could be put before the Court of the Lord Mayor and Aldermen. The Webbs alone among historians treat at length of the wardmote, but they deal only with a period when the institution was in very rapid decline. They do not point out, for example, how high was the proportion of elected officials to rate-paying householders, a feature that was unique not only in England but almost certainly in Europe too. The elected officers of each ward numbered between 100 and 300 according to its size. In a small ward like Cornhill, for instance, there were in the 1640s, 118 officers elected annually (if we include jurors), to serve 267 householders in a population of around 1800, that is, one officer for about sixteen people or one for under three householders. Cornhill ward was served by six Common Councilmen, four scavengers, one raker, sixteen inquestmen, four constables, one beadle, twenty-six watchmen and around sixty jurymen elected to sit in the Mayor's and Sheriff's Courts. Even in the largest extra-mural ward, Farringdon Without, there were in the 1640s 300 elected officials for perhaps 27 000 people, one for every 90 inhabitants or 18 householders.[35]

Of course, not all these offices were sought after. Privileges entailed tiresome duties and obligations. Some offices (such as scavenger and watchmen, who were normally paid) were onerous and disagreeable, avoided by all but the poorest.[36] Others, such as

---

34. The origin of the precinct is unknown. So far no record of its existence has been found in the medieval period. Its existence is plain in wardmote inquest books and vestry minute books from the sixteenth century. It is also mentioned in John Mountgomery, 'A Booke containing the manner and order of the watch to be used in the City of London' (1585), CLRO 3 6c f. 3v –4. The role of the precinct became more evident in the seventeenth century perhaps as a result of the 'politicising' of the City.

35. The size of wards is based on a population count of 1631 which gives totals for each ward (total, 130,178), J. Graunt, *Observations*, 42. To arrive at figures for 1640, I have allowed 15 per cent for under-enumeration and 10 per cent for increases in population. Cornhill Ward Inquest Book GLMS 4069: 1.

36. F. Foster in *The Politics of Stability* (1977), 57–60, suggests that office avoidance by paying a fine was well established in the late sixteenth century. In the seventeenth century, while wealthy people skipped the lowest rungs, avoidance of office was less common than has been thought, particularly for higher posts. A. M. Dingle, thesis, 130 ff. for a study of office-holding in St Dunstan's in the

foreman (or as we would say chairman) of the inquest and Common Councilman, were usually much striven for. In theory, they were filled in open election at a meeting of the wardmote which all householders were obliged to attend;[37] only freeman householders normally voted for Common Councilmen, choosing one of the two names presented by the precinct, but all ratepayers were supposed to vote for every other post. In practice, a panel presented by the outgoing officers or drawn up by a general vestry was usually accepted, naming those best qualified for the posts by rank, wealth and seniority in a well-established *cursus honorum*. One sees here shades of the hundred court and hints of modern democratic centralism with attendant suggestions of consensus politics. Occasionally, such lists would be challenged because precedence had been disturbed by someone being promoted out of turn or because a small clique in the vestry had usurped the nomination. Also the Alderman or his deputy, who presided over the wardmote, could intervene at the annual election meeting on St Thomas's day to remove candidates who seemed to him unqualified or unsuitable. It would be a mistake to see modern self-governing procedures in a body more akin to the tithing and the hundred court.

Not democratic in our sense, the wardmote nevertheless provided a degree of citizen participation in local matters and of communal obligation which has rarely if ever existed since. The amount of rotatory office-holding was indeed extraordinarily high – there were also numerous gild and parish officers – and only occasional pluralism to offset it. In these tight communities in London, minute in size, everyone knew everyone else and primitive 'democratic' directives flourished – what one may term 'your turn to be scavenger but not Common Councilman'. Nothing passed unnoticed. It was the 'inquisitorial' function of the wardmote 'inquest' to see that it did not. To assist the inquest, one of the prime functions of both constable and beadle was the keeping of lists of householders with their craft and rank, the names of lodgers and aliens with the dates of their arrival in the precinct and their length of stay (a long visit

West between 1603 and 1630. Of 616 offices filled, fines were paid on only 91 occasions. Throughout the century, it was difficult to escape the obligation to serve, or the fine for office, records being kept in every precinct of each man's liability. See the office book of St Michael Bassishaw, GLMS 2501: 1 *passim*.

37. Precinct book of St Christopher le Stocks, GLMS 4426: 1, p. 2 (Rules drawn up in 1670) stating 'That all the Inhabitants being housekeepers (and not inmates or lodgers) shall be summoned to the precinct assemblies', Strype, op. cit, ii, 313 ff. James Howell, *Londinopolis* (1657), 391 ff. As late as 1687, Cornhill Wardmote defined the office of pricker, one of the named officers of the inquest, as 'to note the appearance of every householder in the Ward and the absence of every dweller on St Thomas day before the Aldermen'. GMLS 4069: 2, f. 369.

required a licence), and the names of inmates (that is, lodger families who were not householders).[38] The origins of this intense, self-imposed registration and watch on inhabitants go back a long way in European history. They were not, as one might suppose, a creation of Puritan society, although theocratic presbyterian regulation would attempt to make them more all-embracing. We are here at a great distance from the complete lack of registration and control that was to become a characteristic feature of town life in England from the eighteenth century. Perhaps we can find today closer echoes of such bureaucratic listings and *dossiers* in the *commissariats de police* of much of Europe and even in the block wardens further east.

Be that as it may, registration was intended for a purpose. The 46 articles of the inquest, set out by the municipality for every ward, were intended to be read out annually and enumerated a great number of offences ranging from moral backslidings to failure to perform communal obligations and the contravention of market, housing and environmental regulations. Sexual misdemeanours bulked large for in municipalities in the sixteenth and seventeenth centuries immorality was punished in secular as well as in ecclesiastical courts. Also penalised were scolding and nagging, offences curiously confined to women but dear to the heart of a male-dominated society. We find in the account of these meetings a vivid portrayal of urban society and its *mores* and of the minute control which they tried to exercise. Apart from the usual cases of street sellers and coachmen who obstruct the traffic, and charges of drunkenness and immorality, we read of a householder who had a suspicious lodger and another who put up a Portuguese, a clothworker whose hot press shook the next door house and endangered the whole street, an upholsterer who filled the nostrils of his neighbours with feathers, a trader who took an unfair advantage over his fellows by hanging his goods too far over the road, and even woman fruit sellers who were said to be too much of an attraction for flirtatious young men in the evenings.[39] Naturally, there were always some who found insufferable the snooping and prying entailed in these public inquisitions – as did Thomas Bott in 1629, reported in Cornhill Wardmote for 'speaking unfitting words in scorne and contempt of us of the Inquest'. What is remarkable is that organised opposition to such authority is fairly rare. Perhaps a policy of partially lenient law enforcement by the City and its local officers, noticeable particularly from the early seventeenth century in delaying prosecutions (some offenders appear in the records in successive years), may have blunted the edge

38. GLMS 4069: 1, *passim*; GLMS 3018: 1, *passim*.
39. GLMS 4069: 1, *passim*.

of local animosities.[40] 'Face to face' societies can involve great personal rivalries, rancour and persecution. It is tempting to see their lack of expression in precinct and ward records as due to an unusual degree of social harmony and acceptance. Cornhill itself, however, for which we have the best surviving inquest book, was a reasonably prosperous and unusually small ward.[41] If such good sources had survived for larger and poorer areas more subject to social stress, we would almost certainly find stronger evidence for resentment and revolt.

Participation by the adult population was, of course, far from complete even in the more favoured wards because it excluded non-ratepaying householders from voting, though not from attending. But this was a small class as far as we know: records are not complete but in well-to-do parishes they numbered less than 10 per cent, and perhaps 25 per cent in less wealthy areas; for the poorest parishes, the nature of the evidence makes any general estimate much more difficult to establish.[42] Also excluded from both atten-

40. The tendency noticeable late in the sixteenth century for offenders to be presented in successive years grows in the seventeenth century. The absence of continuous records for the Lord Mayor's Court for these years makes it difficult to judge how efficiently and promptly offenders were dealt with, but one suspects a great decline. Cornhill Ward introduced a system of fining by the inquest, appropriately scaled to match the gravity of the offence. Three cases of protest to the Privy Council against presentments by the wardmote inquest occur in *Remembrancia*, 267–9. A. M. Dingle, thesis, concluded however, that there was not much abuse of office in the City in the early seventeenth century.

41. Three of the 26 wards were smaller than Cornhill: Bassishaw, Lime and Walbrook. See population count of 1631, J. Graunt, *Observations*. The evidence for numbers of households and householders which I have only sampled is a major task for future research.

42. These figures are estimated from the numbers of householders paying charges for the rakers, which unlike the poor rate were paid by all householders who were not in need. I have compared them with the population figures for the wards provided by the count of 1631, see n. 35. In Cornhill Ward in 1631, 276 householders were paying to the raker in a population of between 1500 and 1600, A. M. Dingle, thesis, 139. St Margaret Lothbury was a socially mixed parish, Carr, thesis, 111. In 1631, about 75 per cent of householders paid poor rate, Freshfield, 66–7; Dale, *Inhabitants*, 98. According to the tithe list of 1638, there were 97 titheable units in St Bartholomew Exchange. 92 householders were rated to the poor in this year, suggesting that in a rich parish, as this was, a very high proportion of householders paid towards the poor rate. Freshfield, 132; Carr, thesis, 100. The survival of records for the poorest parishes is fragmentary; they are therefore more difficult to asses. Around one quarter of City parishes had rents below the mean according to the tithe list of 1638. Cf. R. W. Herlan, 'Social Articulation and Parish Poverty on the eve of the Restoration', *Guildhall Studies in London History*, ii, 2 (1976), 49, for figures showing 20 of 113 parishes having serious pockets of poverty. For some poorer parishes where lists of ratepayers are extant, the relationship between numbers of householders and ratepayers appears to be comparable with medium rich areas. See St Alban Wood Street, GLMS 7674: 1 1628 list; St John Zachary, MS 590: 1, 1611 list; St

dance · and the franchise were women, servants (but not journeymen), apprentices, lodgers, inmates and vagrants. Poor almsmen who had once been householders were in a special category and may well have been allowed to vote.[43] An Act of Common Council of 1692 excluded them, however, by reaffirming that the franchise for electing Aldermen and Common Councilmen was vested in freemen who were also householders paying Scot and Lot.[44]

Nevertheless, for those qualified, if one could rise above the lack of privacy and the pressures for conformity (we may doubt whether these were widely felt grievances of the time), the wardmote provided a close-knit and enduring society with degrees of belonging, of neighbourliness, of recognition, and of security of property that were highly valued: qualities now recognised by all of us as desirable. The system engendered alongside much spirited turbulence, community-imposed obedience and stability of government. The government of London in the seventeenth century was greatly admired by John Graunt, one of the most perceptive thinkers of the time and the father of the social sciences. He pointed out in 1662 that the incidence of violence and murder in the London of his day was remarkably small, even in the time of the Revolution. He explained it by the obligation of citizens to serve each other in turn: 'The Government and Guard of the City was by Citizens themselves and that alternately; no man settling into a trade for that employment'.[45] Henry Robinson, probably the most outstanding writer on trade during the Puritan Revolution, considered that London was preserved from the harmful effect of too rapid growth only by her 'good government'.[46] James Howell, who was something of an authority on towns, having written a history of Venice, emphasised that element of inquisition or over-government which I have mentioned. London's second outstanding virtue, after her lo-

Andrew Hubbard, MS. 1278: 1, 1630 list; St Katherine Coleman, MS. 1124: 1 1615 list; St Leonard Foster Lane, MS. 9801 1672 list; St Olave Silver Street, MS. 1262, 1676/7 list; St Michael Queenhithe, MS. 4875: 1 1642 list. Perhaps a half only of householders were ratepayers in St Bride's Fleet Street in 1687/8, MS. 6614, which may have been more typical for poor extra-mural parishes.

43. By servant is meant here 'personal servant'. The word was also used synonymously with 'journeyman'. In St Bartholomew Exchange, eight out of ten pensioners were rated to pay the raker in 1607, Freshfield, 55–60. See D. Hirst, *The Representative of the People?* (1975), 100–03 for cases of almsmen voting in Parliamentary elections. K. Thomas, 'The Levellers and the franchise', in G. E. Aylmer, ed., *The Interregnum: the Quest for Settlement . . . 1646–1660* (1972), 64–6.

44. Journal of Common Council (hereafter J. Co. Co.) 51, f. 161, 167, 167v; Maitland, i, 495–6.

45. J. Graunt, *Observations*, 12.

46. Henry Robinson, *England's Safety in Trades encrease* (1641), 5.

cation, was, he wrote, 'her strict and punctual government; . . . there's no City goes beyond her, nor indeed equals her, take night or day together; for there is not the least misdemeanour or inconvenience that can be, but there be officers in every corner of the City to pry unto them and find them out'.[47]

Was there really such a 'strict and punctual government'? Or was this for the most part a medieval survival, under which offenders were presented but not punished and obligations existed only in name? One must be wary of accounts which are puffed up with civic pride, as Howell's tends to be, but we have several surviving records for this time which give some support to his claim. They include records of six precincts and five wardmote inquest books,[48] one of which is very full and contains not only lists of officers and of proceedings, but also of presentments, that is, names of those accused of offences and details of their misdemeanours. That record, to which I have already referred, is of Cornhill, a small socially mixed ward containing the Royal Exchange, but also a maze of narrow twisting alleys not more than eight feet across, their extent still visible today between office blocks. It provides most unusual testimony of community behaviour among ordinary citizens. Officers chosen annually in a precinct meeting at the vestry were confirmed by the wardmote. These officers perambulated the ward monthly in the 1630s and also imposed fines on offenders;[49] even in the early eighteenth century, they were still searching but at less frequent intervals. Besides raising city taxes, they enjoyed the power to levy rates to pay scavengers and watchmen, a right which the Webbs wrongly confined to parishes.[50] They organised the watch through constable and beadle. They also preserved the ward's arms for use by the Trained Bands: for in the seventeenth century it was the householders of the precinct who formed the militia – that citizenry in arms, so beloved by later American democrats.

From the ceremonies which surrounded it we catch a glimpse of an elaborate ritual that had come to be attached to the wardmote and which still provided it with a social function and an institutional form. Even as late as the 1670s, Cornhill Ward possessed its own

47. *Londinopolis*, 391.
48. Wardmote Books exist for Cornhill, Portsoken, Bridge Within, Aldersgate and Bassishaw. Precinct Books for St Dunstans in the West, St Christopher le Stocks, St Sepulchre Holborn, St Ann Blackfriars, St Peter Westcheap, St Martin Ludgate. A number of parish vestry books also contain precinct business, usually names of annually nominated officers and sometimes other matter belonging to the ratepayers organised as a precinct rather than as a parish.
49. See above, n. 40, GLMS 4069: 1 f. 161v.
50. S. and B. Webb, *English local government. . . . The parish and the county*, 1, 39.

heavy silver mace, symbol of authority and constitutionality.[51] Paraded with appropriate ceremony, we may see it as a pattern, *multum in parvo*, of the powers of court, parliament, and lord mayor. Other traces exist of an established and complicated system of social roles. Reminders are found in the naming of sixteen strangely titled officers. In Cornhill and other wards there were still chosen annually prickers, benchers, blackbookmen, fewellers, scribes within and scribes without, a halter-cutter, introducers, upperspeakers and underspeakers, butlers, porters and even a gentleman entertainer.[52] One ward elected annually what was termed a 'Young Man'. Perhaps we have here an equivalent of our 'statutory student' or 'woman', a useful reinforcement for seventeenth-century Londoners no doubt of the civic concept of *communitas*.[53] When we look at the rules and observances governing the conduct of wardmote inquests we find still in existence in the middle seventeenth century an elaborate code which also reveals something of the sense of discipline, the spirit of fellowship and of clubbish ritual. A list of rules sets out a remarkable scale of behavioural standards in which we can measure, by means of the fines imposed, the monetary values of offences against the social code of this ruling committee: a 'backbiter' or slanderer was fined one shilling; one not wearing an inquestman's gown at the meeting fourpence; one showing 'needless courtesy' as it was called, meaning an unnecessary and excessive or exaggerated politeness such as taking off his hat during the meeting had to pay twopence.[54] All this suggests a ritual which would make its members feel part of a solemn, superior and selected group.

We may ask why such a close-knit community did not develop *public* ward festivals like the *quartieri* of Florence, for example, and similar ceremonials found elsewhere in Europe. London as a whole still enjoyed many public festivals and processions, with scripts written by poets and poetasters, and colourful shows staged by impresarios, but public ward festivals do not appear to have been organised. Perhaps the release of tension, said to be one purpose of civic jollifications, was less necessary in the community-conscious City. More likely, the smallness of the wards made them impractical. Perhaps, even, English weather had something to do with it. In London, ward festivals tended to be private boozing parties. In Cornhill, celebrations were confined to the inquest who hired a quest room

---

51. GLMS 4069: 2, 336v. Even today a number of wards still possess their ancient maces.
52. S. and B. Webb, *The Manor and the Borough*, iii, 599–600.
53. GLMS 877: 1, f. 87. c.f. as rank-symbols the probable deviation from yeoman and 'young man' as a term widely used in the gilds.
54. GLMS 3461: 1, f. 1. iv.

appropriately furnished for periodic feasts and convivial evenings to round off the solid labours which I have described. It is reported that the ensuing dicing and card-playing horrified local puritans.[55]

The work of the wardmotes in the eighteenth century, as described by the Webbs, was mainly concerned with the oversight of weights and measures, of paving and lighting, and with the control of traffic. In the earlier period, however, they fulfilled community functions of which only a shadow remained later. There are instances in Cornhill when they acted to reconcile local disputes. When a man complained about the nuisance caused by a neighbour's pigeons,[56] the wardmote reconciled the parties in the way that the gilds were accustomed to do without going to law. Perhaps we get an echo of its power to act as a force for social unity in the Leveller demand that disputes between neighbours should be settled by local people, two, three or twelve of them, rather than by recourse to lawyers. No less significant was the part it played as a forum for public opinion and for expressing radical demands or social policies of a kind which historians, wrongly in my view, confine to the period of the Puritan Revolution. The Webbs noticed the survival of such common action in the eighteenth century, but the records show that its role was most marked in the late Elizabethan period, a time of the worst successive harvests in English history. Then the Cornhill wardmote pronounced on some of the great social issues of the day, and sent their views in the form of a remonstrance to the Lord Mayor and Aldermen. In 1573, a year of very high bread prices, they made a protest, familiar enough to modern ears, against provincial and foreign immigrants who allegedly caused housing and food shortages and appeared to take away jobs and trade. A few years later, the social conscience of these ordinary citizens was aroused by the 'poor boys and girls lying in the street very pitifully'. On other occasions, they protested against the failure in the brewers to provide small enough casks for poor people and about colliers who sold under weight.

More striking, because it has an echo of earlier schemes for public enterprise in the 1520s, was a demand in 1582 (again a time of high corn prices) for a municipal brewhouse which would provide good beer at a reasonable price in small containers; the profits, it was suggested, should go to Christ's Hospital, the orphanage for poor children. This demand commanded support beyond the confines of Cornhill because a municipal brewhouse was indeed established to the great chagrin of the Brewers; it was still standing when John Stow perambulated the southern bank of the Thames near to Bridgehouse in 1598. Even more impressive was the persistent na-

55. GLMS 4069: 1, f. 104.
56. Ibid., 1, f. 25v.

ture of the campaign begun in the wardmote in 1595, the year of the worst bread shortage in two centuries, for provision for the poor who were said to 'lye in the streets'. Every year until 1598, they renewed their petition, demanding also the building of municipal mills for grinding corn which the livery companies had long supplied for the poor at heavily subsidised prices in times of shortage.[57] It is not too fanciful to see this as part of a campaign bearing fruit ultimately in the great Poor Law legislation of 1598 and 1601, which strengthened parochial responsibility for the poor, the obligation to apprentice poor children, and the setting of the unemployed to work. There are many cases in sixteenth-century and seventeenth-century England of merchants and gentry lobbying the House of Commons in pursuit of their interests. This is the first occasion known to me when a group of ordinary citizens in their local neighbourhood attempted a similar campaign.

Strangely in the century of radical change which followed, there are few instances of humane public concern to match these examples. The wardmote's role of public forum declined earlier than some of its other activities. Perhaps the religious and political 'parties' of the revolutionary period replaced them for a time as the venue for radical protests and policies. Or perhaps improving living conditions made their intervention less urgent or necessary. The union of white and brown bakers in 1645 (prematurely in view of the shortages in the years immediately following) showed that cheap black bread was no longer in general demand, indicating, according to Sylvia Thrupp, that London had the highest living standard in the country;[58] white bread would not become general everywhere until the late eighteenth century. After 1651, London wage earners enjoyed for a period the highest *real* wage for more than a century, and, contrary to Miss Lennard and Professor Tawney, bread prices were as regularly set and even some market controls as strictly upheld in the 1640s and 1650s as before.[59]

At the same time the disciplinary character of the inquest began to lessen. Its busy-bodying interference with morals and personal conduct began to decline in the 1630s, diminished most noticeably

---

57. Ibid. 1, ff. iiv–12, 18v, 33v, 65, 67, 71v, 83; Bankes Papers, Bodleian Library, 6/5; C. L. Kingsford, *John Stow A Survey of London* (1908), ii, 66.
58. Thrupp, *Bakers of London*, 128–9.
59. W. E. Alford and T. C. Barker, *Carpenters' Company*, 90–1. Between 1600–70, Carpenters' real wages rose by 25 per cent; 'the strongest impression of full wage packets is gained from the 1650s and 1660s'. See Act of Common Council 1646, which strengthened market regulations aimed at keeping a steady supply of cheap food, Strype, ii, 411. See Repertories of the Aldermanic Bench, vols. 59–65 *passim* for setting of the assize of bread. Rep. 64, f. 168 for declaration by the Lord Mayor and Aldermen of their right to set the price of victuals and fuels in the City.

in the 1650s and was almost unknown by the end of the century. That the decline comes as early as it does is puzzling if we expect puritanism to have reinforced an all-pervasive control. No longer do we hear after mid-century of unfortunate women like Ellen Davison being presented for 'receiving company into her lodging at unlawful hours in the night and for being of very ill behaviour and a scold'.[60] Henceforth, only those moral offences like open brothel-keeping which caused public brawls were complained of by the wardmote. Three other types of 'offence' declined. Numbers of presentments for industrial nuisance decreased partly perhaps because of new, more individualistic, attitudes but also because of the migration of noisome trades to the outer areas, a move hastened by the Fire and by greater opportunities in outlying districts. Cases of religious non-conformity also diminished. Men were presented in Cornhill Wardmote on two separate occasions in the late sixteenth century for being of 'no church', and in 1643 Nicholas Tewe was presented for 'admitting assemblies into his private house', and for 'being of the separation'.[61] After 1650, the only people in trouble with the wardmote over religion were papists. The prohibition on taking 'inmates' (lodger families who it was feared would be a charge on the rates) was constantly reiterated in this period, partly because of the threatened burden and partly because the taking in of inmates contradicted the notion, strongly held in London's civic community and implicit in the role of the householder in local government, that every house should be inhabited by a single householder. That policy, inevitably always more evident in the breaking than the keeping, was to be greatly undermined by two developments that weakened the City's independence: the effects of the Great Fire and the competition of the western suburbs. The challenge of the suburbs brought the City face to face with the dilemma sharply expressed later by Sir Josiah Child: 'you must allow inmates, or have a city of cottages'. The last complaint in Cornhill against inmates was in 1650.[62] Within a matter of months the first formal protests were made in Common Council about competition from suburban traders and against excessive taxes, contrasting unfavourably with those of Middlesex.[63]

For the wardmote as for the City and the nation, the period between 1650 and 1660 was in many ways a watershed. On the one hand there was a loosening of restraints on individual behaviour

60. GLMS 4069: 1, fol. 147v. Cf. L. Stone, *The Family, Sex and Marriage in England 1500–1800* (1977), 93.
61. Ibid., f. 29, 228v.
62. Ibid., f. 246; Sir J. Child, *A Method concerning the Relief and the Employment of the Poor* (1672), 8.
63. J. Co. Co. 41, f. 46v.

resulting from the great flood of new ideas released during the Puritan Revolution, attitudes towards church and society involving greater toleration and individualism. On the other hand, in the period between 1660 and 1730 moves were taking place towards a greater centralisation in London in the organisation of municipal services, that is, of paving, lighting and the watch. A newly emerging small committee of Aldermen and Common Councilmen of each ward took over at least one of the functions of the ward, while others were absorbed into committees of sewers, lighting and additional services.[64] In some ways it was indeed a move towards oligarchy and a greater bureaucracy in that the citizen's role in a direct sense was undoubtedly reduced. That role was not abrogated however. The Common Councilmen of the wards were elected officers who represented the citizens in the legislative body of Common Council, nearly 270 strong in the seventeenth century. The new committees for providing essential services were responsible to it. After a set-back early in the next century, instead of having its power whittled away (the common experience of many boroughs in England at the time), Common Council finally achieved legislative sovereignty over the Court of Aldermen. Its access of power is demonstrated by its championship of the party of John Wilkes, a role in which it assumed a national dimension. It came to enjoy what seventeenth-century radicals had inaccurately claimed for it – equivalence with the House of Commons in London's municipality.

It is difficult in some ways not to lament the passing of these tiny authorities and to see them as components of a pluralistic society resembling neighbourhood associations of today but enjoying real powers. But I confess it is difficult to see how the City would ever have got a system of uniform lighting, paving, drainage, police, and other services if their rule had continued. It was a system which was incompatible with improving urban standards. The greater centralisation of the late seventeenth and early eighteenth centuries produced such remarkable results that by the 1750s, London, from being a city that was indifferently paved, drained and lit became one of the best in Europe. From the 1670s the adjoining parishes began to exceed the population of the ancient City and to grow far more rapidly, so that, by 1750, three-quarters of the metropolitan population was resident outside the old walls. The evolution of the hundred and the manorial courts in the ancient townships and villages of Middlesex, Surrey, Essex and Kent into organisations like the city precinct would have been unthinkable. They lacked civic values and tradition. They were also simply too populous. It was a system which could only operate below a certain size. The ward and precinct were unsuited to the eighteenth-century metropolis, which

64. S. and B. Webb, *The Manor and the Borough*, iii, 607–9.

had far-reaching interests, with new goals like banking, world commerce and empire. In industry the looser traditions which as I have shown were always associated with the London gilds would ease the transition to a freer economy.

Historians have rightly lamented the failure of the City government to meet the challenge of the growing metropolis in the seventeenth century. But no one has commented on how much of the fabric of the earlier society was retained and how it alleviated the pangs of the new order. The amelioration of the 'moral economy' helped preserve the social peace in London. Moreover the experience of parish, precinct and ward, as of the seventeenth-century yeomanry, may have helped to make negotiation, bargaining, mediation and elected officials, all ingredients of a modern democratic society, appear traditional and appropriate. It is not unreasonable to account for the absence of social upheaval in London in a time of political revolution by the existence of such officials. Ellen Wilkinson once explained the reformist nature of English society and politics in words that encompass part of my theme. 'English revolutions are bloodless,' she said, 'because they are always led by English churchwardens'.[65] Similarly, I believe, we can see in the survival of such tiny pluralistic authorities and their officials a force for political stability in the great city at a time of rapid change.

Editorial suggestions for further reading

A. L. Beier and R. Finlay (eds), *London 1500–1700* (1986).

J. Boulton, *Neighbourhood and Society: A London Suburb in the Seventeenth Century* (1987).

T. Harris, *London Crowds in the Reign of Charles II* (1987).

M. Power, 'London and the control of the crisis of the 1590s', *History*, 70 (1985), pp. 371–85.

65. I wish to thank Lord Beaumont of Whitley for pointing out this remark.

Chapter 7

RESIDENTIAL PATTERNS IN PRE-INDUSTRIAL CITIES: SOME CASE STUDIES FROM SEVENTEENTH-CENTURY BRITAIN

John Langton

[*Transactions of the Institute of British Geographers*, 65 (1975)]

Addressed primarily to fellow geographers, this article explores various theories of urban space and illustrates these with numerous maps. But its theme, the relationship of urban housing to the distribution of wealth, power and occupations, has been of great concern to historians of the Tudor and Stuart town. A detailed study of Newcastle is supplemented by briefer accounts of Exeter and Dublin, each based on the late seventeenth-century hearth tax returns. The general conclusion, that those of greater wealth and higher status occupations resided in the town centres, has been reinforced by many other studies, though all have echoed Langton's point about local variations caused by topography and the character of the land and housing market. There are considerable problems with using hearth tax figures as guides to relative wealth and with analysing towns at the level of ward or parish, rather than by street. Recent work has also begun to reveal more about the seventeenth-century housing market, but the main conclusions reached here seem unlikely to be significantly revised.

In the literature of urban geography, little space is devoted to pre-nineteenth-century cities. When the subject is discussed it is usually treated with a bland lack of controversy: textbooks, and monographs and papers on historical and modern cities are alike in their exclusive and uncritical presentation of Sjoberg's generalizations about what he termed the 'pre-industrial city'.[1] The reasons for this situation are not, of course, hard to find. Until recently, this was the only set of generalizations available, and the continents in which much of the recent work in urban social geography has been done have no great fund of pre-nineteenth-century urban experience. The

1. Sjoberg, G. (1960) *The pre-industrial city, past and present* (Glencoe, Ill.).

current preoccupation of urban social geographers with techniques of analysis which require large arrays of data, and with theories which link urbanism with industrialization or modernization, and thus define the pre-nineteenth-century city out of consideration, also contribute to this end. Moreover, the ease with which the processes which destroyed the 'pre-industrial city' can be thought of as synonymous with those which created the modern city has contributed to the development of the concept of 'ecological transition', and this fusion seems only to have bolstered the confidence of urban geographers in Sjoberg's monolithic ideas about the nature of cities before the transition occurred.[2] The result is a general agreement that urban society was segregated by wealth or status, with the rich and powerful living near to the centre and the poor and powerless on the periphery of cities before industrialization, or modernization. Afterwards, class-based segregation became manifest, and the social geography of cities, in terms of these two gross categories, was reversed.

It is time to question forcefully the basis of this certitude about the early stage of this sequence. Such questioning has been begun by Vance,[3] who recently introduced a welcome note of controversy into the geographical literature. It can be taken a stage further by examining the differences between the conclusions of Sjoberg and Vance, and the reasons for their differences. This should help to bring more sharply into focus the fact that there is not, yet, any set of acceptable generalizations about the social geography of pre-nineteenth-century cities. An attempt to relate the assumptions and conclusions of Sjoberg and Vance to a reasonably sound body of empirical evidence is also necessary, not only because of their differences, but also because each of them employed a methodology in which the formulation and verification of hypotheses were inextricably mixed, so that neither can really be said to have tested his own conclusions.

Such a compound exercise should at least indicate that attempts to generalize and explain the complexity of the social geographies

---

2. Schnore, L. F. (1965) 'On the spatial structure of cities in the two Americas' in Hauser, P. M. and Schnore, L. F. (eds) *The study of urbanization*, 347–98 (New York). Schnore considered that the patterns of wealthy centre and poor periphery, which he found in Latin American cities, and poor centre and wealthy periphery, which characterizes North American cities, were 'both special cases more adequately subsumed under a more general theory of residential land uses in urban areas'. His work, and that of Sjoberg whose conclusions he quotes, form the basis of the meagre treatment of pre-nineteenth-century cities given in the two major recent textbooks of urban social geography by Johnston and Herbert. Johnston, R. J. (1971) *Urban residential patterns* (London) and Herbert, D. T. (1971) *Urban geography: a social perspective* (Newton Abbot).
3. Vance Jr., J. E. (1971) 'Land assignment in pre-capitalist, capitalist and post-capitalist cities', *Econ. Geogr.* 47, 101–20.

of pre-nineteenth-century cities are enmeshed in some fundamental difficulties: it might too contribute, across the bridge of the ecological transition, something which is relevant to the major preoccupations of contemporary urban geographers.

SJOBERG'S IDEAS

THE PRE-INDUSTRIAL CITY

Sjoberg postulated that social order ultimately flowed from technology. He dichotomized the sweep of technical progress into pre-industrial and industrial periods, the change occurring when inanimate sources of energy were used to power tools.[4] Before this, society was 'feudal', comprising an élite, which was small, and much larger lower-class and outcast groups.[5] Functionally, the feudal city was dominated by religious, political, administrative and social (i.e. educational, ceremonial and entertainment) activities and the élite achieved its dominance by controlling these functions.[6] Economic activities were, of course, present, but they were of much lower status, and even wealthy merchants were excluded from the élite because a 'preoccupation with money-making and other mundane pursuits ran counter to the religious-philosophical value system of the dominant group',[7] whose authority was entrenched in traditional and absolute criteria which were often founded upon religious codes of practice and doctrine.

It was the spatial expression of this marked social cleavage between the élite and the remainder of society which produced the geographical hallmark of the pre-industrial city – its wealthy and exclusive central core. This was surrounded by a much larger area over which status diminished outwards, the poor living beneath and beyond the walls.[8]

The élite group was not attracted to the centre of the city because it was an economic focus, a place of business and exchange. Such functions may have been performed in the centre, but they were subservient to the administrative, religious, political, ceremonial and educational activities which were also carried on there, and it was to these non-materialistic attractions that the élite responded in its residential choice. This response produced an exclusive, high-status

4. Sjoberg, op. cit., p. 8.
5. Ibid., p. 110.
6. Ibid., p. 97.
7. Ibid., p. 83.
8. Ibid., pp. 95–8.

core. Tight segregation was further encouraged by primitive transport technology, bad road surfaces, a street system designed more for house access than intra-city travel, the physical repulsiveness of the garbage-strewn, poorly built and crowded non-central area, and the tightly knit structure of élite society, which was often reinforced by bonds of kinship and intermarriage. 'The highly valued residence, then, [was] where full advantage [could] be taken of the city's strategic facilities; in turn, these latter [had] come to be tightly bunched for the convenience of the élite.'[9]

Over the remainder of the city there were 'certain minor differences according to ethnic, occupational and family ties.'[10] Foreign and minority religious groups were alienated from feudal society and lived in spatially segregated quarters. Occupational zoning was the product of poor transport facilities, coupled with the external economies to be derived from spatial association by handicraftsmen-retailers, and reinforced by social organizations such as gilds, which fostered both the spatial propinquity and the group cohesion of members.[11] The lowest status groups of all lived on the outskirts of the city 'through the efforts of the élite to minimize contact with them'.[12] This group included those employed in malodorous jobs, such as tanners and butchers, as well as those who formed what Engels called the 'surplus army' of urban labour, 'which [kept] body and soul together by begging, stealing, street sweeping, collecting manure, pushing hand-carts, driving donkeys, peddling or performing, occasional small jobs'.[13] As Jones[14] has vividly demonstrated, it was intermittency of work which produced a large army of this type, and in Sjoberg's city, where the major functions were subject to seasonal cycles, and where the élite might follow these cycles in periodic urban residence, this army would be a large one. Indeed, Sjoberg considered that the possibility of adding part-time agricultural earnings to the fluctuating income derived from urban occupations was a supplementary factor in the location of the houses of the poor in the outer areas of the city.[15]

9. Ibid., p. 99.
10. Ibid., pp. 95–6.
11. Ibid., p. 101.
12. Ibid., p. 99.
13. Engels, F. (1892) *The condition of the working-class in 1844*, p. 95, 1952 edn (London).
14. Jones, G. S. (1971) *Outcast London* (Oxford).
15. Sjoberg, op. cit., p. 100.

VANCE'S IDEAS

THE PRE-CAPITALIST CITY

Vance based his social order not on the technology used in production, but on the means of organizing production. Because the emergence of capitalism caused this to change before the Industrial Revolution, so did the prevailing social order change, and so, too, did the residential patterns which were based upon it. Capitalism brought with it a fundamental alteration in attitudes to land holding: in capitalist society 'men no longer held, they owned' land, and this change in attitude ushered in the emergence of the capitalist city at 'some time in the sixteenth century'.[16]

Vance's pre-capitalist society was, like that of the pre-industrial city, characterized by its recognition of immutable proportion and order, based on traditional, absolute and non-material criteria. And, in medieval times, 'city air made men free'. These two aspects of medieval urban life were interlaced in the evaluation of urban land plots according to the social intercourse it was possible to derive from a residence upon them, rather than in terms of the monetary rental income that they might produce. This attitude to urban land, the recognition of the need to regulate behaviour to achieve immutable order, and the needs of an urban economic base of craft production for local or regional hinterlands became embodied in, and exemplified by, the gilds. The gild was the archetypal social institution and structure of the pre-capitalist urban economy. City freedom, necessary before a craft could be practised, the holding of burgages, participation in city government and gild membership were inextricably entwined: the last was at once the avenue of access to, and the reason for, the possession of city land and the freedom it conferred.

Gild membership merely required, besides the profession of Christianity, the possession of the requisite skills and the right to burgage property, and as this often existed in minute parcels its ownership was not limited to the rich. The membership of any gild in a city provided the same opportunities, rights, duties and privileges. The result of this free access to institutions, which conferred equal rights and opportunities, was 'a society governing itself and establishing standards on what come rather close to our current notion of "one-man-one-vote" . . . there is little question that medieval urban life was popular rather than patrician. So long as a man was an artisan of accomplishment, a responsible citizen, and a defender of the commonwealth and faith, he might enjoy true par-

16. Vance, op. cit., p. 107.

ticipation in civil control'.[17] Gilds were, then, instruments of access to participation in civic life and exemplars of the completely enmeshed relationships between economic and social organization and functioning in the pre-capitalist city. Not surprisingly, 'gild associations were among the most powerful forces shaping the morphology of the medieval town'.[18]

Indeed, the social geography of the pre-capitalist city was dominated by the gild system: because he based his model of social structure on economic organization the gild became, for Vance, the pre-eminent ecological agency in the city, whereas for Sjoberg it was only a minor contributor to the secondary details of social geographical patterns. Because man used rather than possessed land, his valuation of it was a functional rather than a capitalist one. In such a context, locations were not relative, but absolute; to exist within a gild area was necessary for the proper practice of a trade and for the receipt of the social beneficence of the organization. In a true sense the value of land in the Middle Ages was the value of social association, and the places of residence and occupation, coextensive in handicraft technology, were located close to those of other members of the same gild.[19]

The distribution of these occupational zones had no rationale in terms of intra-urban locational economics. They were located by 'occupational accident rather than by rent-paying ability'.[20] Within them, because house, workshop, shop and store rooms were situated in the same building, because burgage plots were narrow, the better to spread precious street frontage, and because the master, his family, journeymen, apprentices and servants lived under the same roof, 'the residential structure of the medieval town was chiefly vertical', with the shops on the ground floor, the master's family quarters on the floor above, and, higher still, the rooms of the journeymen, apprentices and servants and the store rooms.[21] The result was occupational zoning and social class mixing; the city was 'many centred' in distinct craft quarters, each with its own shops, workplaces and full social spectrum.[22] 'Class organization of city space was not so obvious as it is in urban areas today.'[23]

These social geographical patterns can all be deduced from the existence of a social order in which status was not based on wealth; where the means of production were owned by, and the selling was done by, the producers; and where the producers were organized

17. Ibid., p. 101.
18. Ibid., p. 105.
19. Ibid., p. 103.
20. Ibid., p. 105.
21. Ibid., p. 105.
22. Ibid., p. 105.
23. Ibid., p. 106.

into institutions which regulated trade and through which the city was governed, with no social distinctions within and between the gilds, in which each apprentice and journeyman had the opportunity of becoming a master and all masters, of whatever gild, were freemen, participating equally in the civic control of 'a popular rather than patrician society'.[24] But Vance introduced an incompatible element into this urban society in a few statements scattered through his argument. He stated that 'for the most part . . . towns were crowned . . . by some form of patriciate created from the leading citizens of the place itself'.[25] This patriciate was recruited, unlike that of the pre-industrial city, from the merchant gild, and the members of this gild occupied the city centre for economic reasons: 'admittedly, the borders of the square might hold higher business potential than the back streets . . . for the gild merchant'.[26] Thus a small group, which was pre-eminent in status and wealth, lived in the centre of the city, and responded to economic criteria in the choice of its place of residence, expressing its preference, presumably, by bidding high rents for central locations. This situation is completely unconformable with the basic model of a 'one-man-one-vote' pre-capitalist city where there were no differences in wealth and status between gilds and where occupational zones were not based on economic criteria. This 'merchant city' really represents the germ of a completely different model of social order and economic geography from that of the pre-capitalist city.

The treatment of the poor is even more cursory than the treatment of the merchants. They have little place in the pre-capitalist city of craft gildsmen. Only one reference is made to them: 'outside [the ordered existence of the medieval town] lurked the proletariat subject to riot and contention'.[27] Engels's 'reserve army' must, of course, exist in any city. But it can be surmised that it would be larger in a city dominated by a merchant patriciate than in an egalitarian gild city. Where a group which was economically and socially dominant based its power on wealth, and where conspicuous consumption would thus be *de rigueur*, and where seasonal and extreme climatic factors would profoundly affect the business activity of the patriciate and the employment it provided – where, that is, menial and intermittent occupations were relatively common – conditions were more propitious for the emergence of a large 'reserve army' than in a craft gild city serving a local hinterland. Whereas such a social stratum formed an integral part of Sjoberg's pre-industrial urban social structure, and that of the 'merchant city', it

24. Ibid., p. 101.
25. Ibid., p. 106.
26. Ibid., p. 105.
27. Ibid., p. 106.

falls, as Vance admits, outside the social order from which his main deductions about the social geography of the pre-capitalist city are made. As to how numerous they were, or where they lived within the city, in the vertically zoned areas or elsewhere, his basic model makes no suggestions since the poor, like the merchants, are mentioned only in *ad hoc* references.

THE CAPITALIST CITY

The demise of the pre-capitalist city occurred in the sixteenth century. Thenceforth, men owned rather than held property. Ownership became divorced from use, and 'a class of capitalists arose that had little to do directly with the production and trading activities of the town, or with the conduct of its government'.[28] The new dominant group was not, then, the equivalent or lineal successor of the patriciate of the pre-capitalist merchant city, and its existence contrasted even more markedly, of course, with the social order on which the pure form of pre-capitalist city was based.

As the accumulation of capital by individuals became not only morally acceptable, but the criterion of social status and power, so did competition for urban land plots grow, and their evaluation was now in terms of their yield as capital. These factors, in turn, entailed the occupation of land plots by that use which could yield the highest rent. The gilds, embodiments of protectionism, communalism and permanent structural order, were anachronistic to the new social ethos, and they declined. 'Once the basis upon which medieval social life was anchored had been modified, it was totally abandoned',[29] and with it went any influence which tended towards the evaluation of urban land plots in terms of their social ascription. Housing and workplaces became separate as the cement of craft organization dissolved because each use had different rent-paying propensities on particular plots. Within the residential districts, zoned by occupation whilst craft organization and its social accoutrements prevailed, class zoning became newly apparent, with rent-paying ability forming the index and arbiter of class ascription. Because house size was positively linked with price and price with builders' profits, the provision of housing through the market occasioned a shortage of cheap newly built small houses. At the same time, fashions were changing and these changes were reflected in new house styles. With the outward incremental growth of the built-up area, the currently most fashionable houses were inevitably concentrated on the periphery of the city. As a result, the wealthy

28. Ibid., p. 107.
29. Ibid., p. 113.

moved out and the poor occupied the old-central area housing stock that they vacated. Thus evolved a social geographical pattern which was radically different from Vance's gild city of socially mixed occupational zones, and the inverse of his merchant city and Sjoberg's pre-industrial city: wealth was concentrated on the periphery, poverty in the centre.

CHANGE AND THE CITY

The statements of both Sjoberg and Vance are basically 'ideal type' models in which a sequence of economic development is predicated as the determinant of social structure and the nature of social change. Sets of archetypal social functional relationships are ascribed to stages in the sequence, and these entail certain kinds of residential distribution patterns, which change as the economic structure and attitudes of society change. Their models differ fundamentally simply because they abstracted different aspects from the complex matrix of economic relationships to act as the prime movers of their causal sequences, and this, in turn, led them to focus attention upon different aspects of the sociology of the pre-nineteenth-century urban world. After his definition of technology as the primal economic variable, Sjoberg could recognize only one major economic discontinuity of sufficient magnitude to engender fundamental social change, and that social discontinuity which seemed most commensurate in scale and correlative in time was the destruction of feudalism and the emergence of industrial-urban society. The stability and nature of the pre-industrial city is, then, analytically dependent upon the economic categorization used in the model.

But the way that production was organized did change before the Industrial Revolution, so that, given the economic variable upon which it was based, Vance's pre-nineteenth-century city must change before the late eighteenth century. However, the fact that this aspect of economic life was continuously, if gradually, changing in the towns of Western Europe from late medieval times made the calibration of stages in the sequence difficult. The pre-capitalist city presented relatively few problems in this respect because a social institution which was clearly linked with economic production and which had clearly recognizable geographical ramifications could be recognized in the gild. But the stage produced by the emergence of capitalism is much more difficult to handle. Capitalist organization and attitudes cannot be encapsulated in an archetypal social structure. Their impact on urban social geography is, as a result, less amenable to rigorous codification than either pre-industrial technology, with its correlatives of a rigid social dichotomy and immutable and absolute social values, or pre-capitalist production, with its gilds. Because there is no possibility of hypothesizing an archetypal social order from which to make ecological deductions, the links between the economic variable and residential patterns are more difficult to distinguish, and Vance was, in fact, forced to treat the capitalist city in terms of reflections upon how the geographical consequences of the development and general espousal of this new morality could be observed in a rather biased sample of passages from George's description of seventeenth-century London.[30]

None the less, although the incorporation of changes in the mode of production involved analytical difficulties, it does seem to accord with other influential theories on the links between economic activity and the structure and mores of society.[31] Moreover, the social changes of Vance's capitalist period represent what sociologists have defined as a fundamental element of social modernization, the transition from *Gemeinschaft* to *Gesellschaft*,[32] and he is not alone in recognizing such changes in European urban society of this period. According to Wrigley, many of those characteristics ascribed to the influence of industrialization by Sjoberg were already becoming evident well before the Industrial Revolution, and he proposes a distinction between modernization and industrialization, in social terms, as a result.[33] But whether these social changes had any recognizable impact on urban residential patterns, or whether they affected, in any really marked way, those sociological parameters which specifically influence residential choice, are questions which sociologists and historians had never addressed before Vance's rather idiosyncratic interpretation of a discursive account of seventeenth-century London.[34]

---

30. George, M. D. (1925) *London life in the eighteenth century* (London).
31. Most notably those of Marx.
32. These concepts were formulated by F. Toennies. They are polar types representing, on the one hand, relationships which are formulated on the basis of historical experience and cultural norms, and on the other, relationships which spring from the exercise of the 'rational will' on the basis of its desires for the future. The derivation of the concepts, and the illustration of their sociological significance, requires argument of an intricacy which would be out of place here, where it is sufficient to state that the change from one to the other in ordinary life represents the fundamental attribute of social modernization. See Mann, P. H. (1970) *An approach to urban sociology*, pp. 190–8 (London).
33. Wrigley, E. A. (1972) 'The process of modernization and the Industrial Revolution in England', *J. interdisciplin. Hist.* 3, 225–59.
34. What Vance interprets as an outward movement of the wealthy from central London was mainly a westward and outward shift of the court, government and 'society'. Those who derived their wealth from work in the city itself continued

It is quite clear, then, that there is considerable room for fundamental disagreement about the nature of the pre-nineteenth-century city, in Western Europe at least: a firm foundation does not exist from which to launch generalizations about an ecological transition. It is equally clear that these disagreements cannot be completely resolved by 'testing' the two models against empirical evidence. They are 'ideal types' in the sense given to the term by Weber, and such simplifications are meant to convey the quintessential characteristics of a theoretically polar situation, not to replicate reality. Nevertheless, it is possible to probe empirically the questions that the differences raise. These are not simply about where the rich and poor members of society lived and whether there was a change in the spatial distribution of wealth and poverty before the nineteenth century. The more fundamental questions with which both models seek to grapple concern the structure of urban society, the links between this structure and the economic base of cities, and the way that it was reflected in patterns of residential choice. A search for empirical answers to these questions will not only help to evaluate the models of Sjoberg and Vance as representations and explanations of pre-nineteenth-century patterns of urban social geography but also, and perhaps more important, it will provide some soundly based factual information to supplement knowledge which has to date been mainly based upon deduction about why people chose particular kinds of neighbours in pre-nineteenth-century cities.

SOME EMPIRICAL EVIDENCE

THE DISTRIBUTION OF WEALTH

The earliest British taxation assessments which have been analysed on the ward, parish or street level at which they were collected are the Hearth Tax Assessments of 1662–66 and 1669–74, and the Survey of London's inhabitants within the walls made under an Act of 1694. There are thus, as yet, no studies of the distribution of wealth in British towns which fall definitely within Vance's pre-capitalist category, and which can be referred directly to his statements about

to live centrally there until at least the late eighteenth century. Rudé maintained that 'there had long been a tendency for poorer tradesmen to move toward the *periphery*' (my italics); Saunders Welch stated in 1753 that the trade in old and ruinous houses was on the outskirts of the city, and Glass concluded that the wealthy central area and poor periphery were 'still visible in the 1830s'. See Rudé, G. (1971) *Hanoverian London* (London); George, op. cit., and Glass, D. V. (1968) 'Notes on the demography of London at the end of the seventeenth century', *Daedalus* 97, 581–92.

the social geography of such towns. Even the seventeenth-century studies are by no means perfectly suited for the purpose in hand. Only Glass's work on London[35] contains a map which can be related to the hypotheses of Vance and Sjoberg, but this can be supplemented by the work of Hoskins on Exeter,[36] Butlin on Dublin,[37] and an analysis of the transcription of the Newcastle upon Tyne Hearth Tax Assessment Return of 1665 made by Welford.[38]

These tax returns provide information on the number of hearths and stoves in each household whose owner was liable to the tax, and sometimes, too, of the exempted poor.[39] It is generally accepted that these data provide a reasonable reflection of the size of the houses of a town and of the wealth of their occupants,[40] although inns and tenemented buildings had large numbers of hearths which did not reflect their occupants' wealth, and the possibility of their existence must be borne in mind when interpreting the information.[41] The households were usually listed by ward, parish or street, which were quite numerous in the large towns.

From these lists a number of indexes of the wealth of the households in the various wards of a city can be devised. First, the percentage of the households in each ward which was liable to the tax provides an indication of the degree of poverty there; second, the average number of hearths in the households of the taxed population reflects the wealth of the non-poor of a ward; and third, the proportion of exceptionally large houses, say those with more than six hearths, indicates the prevalence of the houses of the wealthiest citizens of all in a ward. The second of these measures has been mapped for Dublin, Exeter and Newcastle in Figure 1A–1C.[42] But this index reflects only one facet of the wealth of wards

35. Glass, D. V. (1966) 'London's inhabitants within the walls,' *Lond. Rec. Soc. Publs 2,* p. xxiii.
36. Hoskins, W. G. (1935) *Industry, trade and people in Exeter 1688–1700* (Manchester).
37. Butlin, R. A. (1965) 'The population of Dublin in the late seventeenth century', *Ir. Geogr.* 5, 51–66
38. Welford, R. (1911) 'Newcastle householders in 1665: assessment of hearth or chimney tax', *Archaeol. Aeliana,* Ser. 3, 7, 49–76.
39. For a recent review of the value and uses of the assessments, see Patten, J. A. (1971) 'The hearth taxes, 1622–89', *Local Popul. Stud.* 7, 14–27.
40. Glass used tax liabilities as an index of social status in London, and Hoskins considered that a close correlation existed between the number of hearths in a household and the status, wealth and occupation of its inhabitant. Glass (1966) and (1968) op. cit. and Hoskins, op. cit.
41. Hoskins, W. G. (1957) 'Exeter in the seventeenth century: tax and rate assessments, 1602–1670', *Devon and Cornwall Rec. Soc.,* N.S. 2. p. xvii.
42. The ward map of Exeter has been taken from Hoskins (1935) op. cit., p. 113, and the map of Dublin parishes from C. Brooking's map of Dublin, drawn in 1728. The Newcastle ward map was prepared by the author from a verbal description of the boundaries of wards given in Welford op. cit.; the map 'Newe Castle'

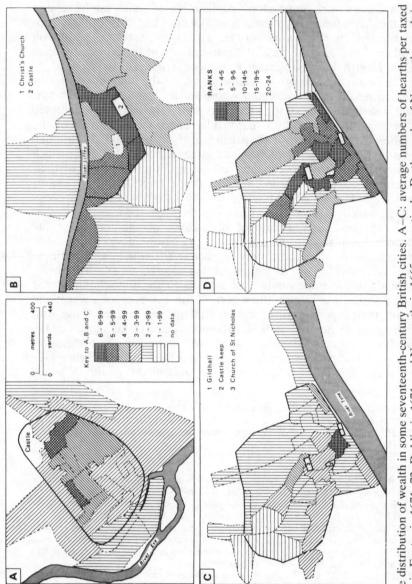

Fig. 1 The distribution of wealth in some seventeenth-century British cities. A–C: average numbers of hearths per taxed household in Exeter in 1671–72; Dublin in 1671; and Newcastle in 1665, respectively. D: the ranks of Newcastle wards in 1665 on an index combining the average number of hearths per house, the percentage of tax payers in each ward, and the percentage of houses with six or more hearths.

and is not obviously superior to the other two, and although the coefficients of concordance between the three variables are high at 0.80 for Exeter and 0.89 for Newcastle, there is not perfect correlation, so that information is present in the other two data series which is not contained on Figures 1A–1C. Consequently, an attempt was made to derive a compound index of the wealth of the households of wards by ranking the sums of the ranks scored by each ward on each of the three variables.[43] These ranks of the summed ranks for Newcastle wards are plotted in Figure 1D. Because it includes more information which is descriptive of the indicated variable, and because the procedure of ranking obliterates some exceptionally large differences at the top and bottom of the interval scales, this map provides a much clearer general pattern of variations in the wealth of wards than that which portrays only the average numbers of hearths per taxed household.

But all four maps display strikingly similar patterns. In all cases houses of various sizes were unevenly distributed, and quite marked peaks existed in each city. In all three, these peaks were located in proximity to the castle, either between the castle and the main place of worship, as in Exeter and Dublin, or, as in Newcastle, between the castle keep and the gildhall. This location did not correspond with the main 'market square', or place of business. Indeed, such topographical 'centres' did not always exist in pre-nineteenth-century cities. In Exeter there was none, different commodity markets being located in different parts of the town;[44] in Newcastle there were nine markets, and six of them were located, like the twice-yearly fairs, in a single central market place of overwhelming predominance (see Figure 2).[45] But this main market area, which comprised Mordon Tower ward, was filled with relatively small, poor households, and

inset on Speed's map of Northumberland (1610); 'A plan of Newcastle' inset on the map of Northumberland by A. Armstrong and Son (1769), and a 'Town Plan of Newcastle upon Tyne' (1745), ref. MPF 267 in the Public Record Office. The extra-mural boundaries of wards in Newcastle were estimated from the plan of 1745, and for Exeter from a plan of 1744, which is reproduced in Hoskins (1935) op. cit. The extramural parish boundaries of Dublin continued beyond the edge of Brooking's map, which omitted some of the very poorest areas of the city.

43. This procedure for deriving a set of 'true scores' from a number of highly correlated but different series of scores was suggested by Kendall. See Siegel, S. (1956) *Nonparametric statistics for the behavioural sciences*, p. 238 (New York).
44. Hoskins (1935) op. cit., pp. 23–5.
45. Nine markets are depicted on the plan of 1745, and these have been plotted on Figure 2. A topographical description of 1649 mentioned six markets: that in Sandhill for 'fish and other commodities'; that in Pilgrim Street for wheat and rye; that in the Side for 'milk, eggs, butter &c', and, in the large triangular space to the north west of St Nicholas' church, partially filled with rows of shambles, there were the oatmeal, flesh, bigg (barley) and oat markets. W. G., 'Chorographia: or a description of Newcastle upon Tine' (1649), reprinted in *The Harleian Miscellany* 3 (1809), 267–84.

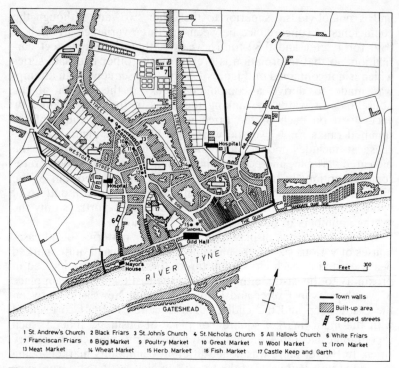

Fig. 2 Newcastle in 1745, showing the built-up area, streets, main buildings and markets. Although there had been growth since 1665, the basic lineaments of the town and the locations of the markets and major buildings were substantially the same then.

ranked twentieth out of the 24 wards on the index of wealth. Although two wards which fringed this central market area, Newgate and Stank Tower (see Figure 3 for the locations of wards), ranked 2.5 and 4.5 on the compound index of wealth, other market-edge wards were of low rank, and generally the wards with the largest houses and least poverty were not in this economically central part of the city but well to the south of it on the high bank across which the castle was linked to the riverfront and bridge-head by steep narrow lanes, some of which were stepped (see Figure 2).[46] Figure 1D demonstrates how wealthy areas radiated out from this core towards

46. 'This town (a great part of it) placed upon the highest and the steepest hills that I have found in any great town; these so steep as horses cannot stand upon the pavements – therefore the daintiest flagged channels are in every street that I

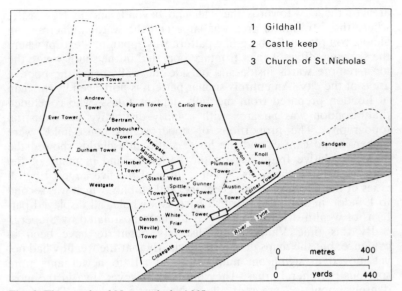

1 Gildhall
2 Castle keep
3 Church of St.Nicholas

Fig. 3 The wards of Newcastle in 1665.

the main gates, especially in the south, along the main thoroughfares of the city.[47]

In Newcastle, then, it seems to have been a combination of main road frontage and the 'strategic facilities' of castle, parish church, gildhall and riverfront which fixed the location of the highest status areas. In Exeter and Dublin, which were not so important as ports, the riverfront did not have the same influence, and there it was where the castle, cathedral/parish church and main road frontage combined that the highest status areas were found.

These patterns ostensibly go a considerable way to corroborate Sjoberg's hypotheses. So, too, does the prevalence of a sharp decline in wealth away from the peaks towards the walls or the outskirts of the cities. Because of the short circumference of the walls in relation to the built-up area of the city, the whole of intra-mural Dublin was characterized by relatively large houses, but the wall marked a sharp break between areas of high and less high status except in the case of St Audon's parish, which straddled it. In those parts of Exeter where the wards were small enough to allow a pattern to emerge, the size of houses decreased away from the core

have seen: hereupon may horses go without sliding', Hawkins, E. (ed.) (1844) 'Travels in Holland, the United Provinces, England, Scotland and Ireland, 1634–35, by Sir William Brereton, Bart.', *Chetham Soc.* 1, p. 86.
47. The major inns were located on Newgate and Pilgrim Streets on the plan of 1745.

area of the city towards the wall and beyond, and in Newcastle, where the intra-mural area was large and the wards numerous, an almost completely Sjoberg-like pattern was apparent – except where the skewing effect of river frontage operated in the south – with the most remote wards inside and outside the walls being the poorest areas of the city. An entirely similar pattern is portrayed by the map of London prepared from the 1695 data by Glass, who concluded that 'London was an area with a fairly distinctive pre-industrial topography. The proportions of upper status house-holds were higher in the centre, and the lower status households showed the greatest relative frequency on the periphery and in many of the parishes without the walls'.[48] Thus, three of the five largest English cities of the late seventeenth century, and Dublin, which was second to London in size in the British Isles as a whole, all displayed patterns of wealth distribution similar to those postulated by Sjoberg.

By this time Vance's capitalist city ought to have been in evidence, but the maps demonstrate clearly that the wealthy had not yet moved in significant numbers, if at all, to newer and more spacious peripheral areas. They did not, however, live in the most densely populated areas of all, in Newcastle at least. There, the Spearman rank correlation coefficient between the density of households and the compound index of wealth of wards was +0.03, so that high status was correlated with neither high nor low densities, and the spatial patterns of wealth and population density were equally regular, but completely different (compare Figures 1D and 4).

Just as there was no indication of the existence of the capitalist city in late seventeenth-century Newcastle, neither was there any sign of the pre-capitalist city. With wealth and status spread within occupational groups which were spatially segregated and located willy-nilly over the city, a randomly variegated, rather than spatially concentrated, pattern of wealth distribution would have occurred. In the mercantile variant, the patrician group was concentrated around the market area. Neither of these patterns existed. Clearly Sjoberg's pre-industrial city model provides a much better approximation of the patterns of wealth distribution which actually existed in four of the largest British cities in the late seventeenth century.

THE STRUCTURE OF SOCIETY

Was the sociological order which underlay these patterns congruent with that of Sjoberg's model? Did an élite which was largely

48. Glass (1968) op. cit., p. 583.

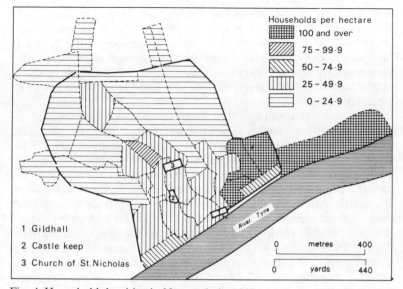

Fig. 4 Household densities in Newcastle in 1665.

divorced from the economic functioning of the city dominate its government and occupy the high status core, surrounded by occupationally specialized gild areas and, beyond them, the 'outcasts' and 'poor' – non-gildsmen in unincorporated or malodorous occupations?

Because of the complex and voluminous nature of the Freemen's and Company rolls of seventeenth-century cities, and the labour involved in processing them, these questions will be pursued through an analysis of Newcastle only.

Information on the distribution of power within this urban society can be derived from lists of mayors,[49] accounts of inter-gild strife[50] and descriptions of the functions and composition of the Companies of Hostmen[51] and Merchant Adventurers.[52] Occupational data can be gathered from a number of sources. The ad-

49. Hunter Blair, C. H. (ed.) (1940) 'The mayors and lord mayors of Newcastle upon Tyne, 1216–1940, and the Sheriffs of the county of Newcastle upon Tyne, 1399–1940', *Archaeol. Aeliana*, Ser. 4, 18.
50. Dendy, F. W. (1911) 'The Struggle Between the Merchant and Craft Gilds of Newcastle in 1515', *Archaeol. Aeliana*, Ser. 3, 7, 77–101.
51. Dendy, F. W. (ed.) (1901) 'Extracts from the Records of the Company of Hostmen of Newcastle upon Tyne', *Surtees Soc.* 105.
52. Dendy, F. W. (ed.) (1894, 1899) 'Extracts from the Records of the Merchant Adventurers of Newcastle upon Tyne', *Surtees Soc.* 93 and 101.

missions lists of the Merchant Adventurers.[53] record whether a member was a mercer, draper, or boothman – the three constituent 'mysteries' of the Company [54] – and/or a member of the Eastland Company. The members listed in the admissions lists of the Hostmen's Company[55] were also almost invariably Merchant Adventurers, but they dealt largely in coal and had the additional right to 'host' strangers.[56]

There were thus apparently four or five distinct occupational associations within the merchant community. But by the late seventeenth century these were not all functionally distinct. The three constituent mysteries of the Merchant Adventurer's Company had little significance except as avenues of access to the larger association, and the activities of members of the separate sub-groups apparently differed little. Moreover, after *c.* 1630 almost all Merchant Adventurers were members of the Eastland Company, so that it is not possible to distinguish from the surviving records between those who traded nationally and those who traded internationally. Consequently, the single occupational group of 'merchant' must be used to accommodate all Merchant Adventurers except hostmen, whose control of the coal trade still remained current.

The occupations of those who were not merchants (as well as those who were) can be identified in the lists of admissions of freemen.[57] These lists comprise two kinds of record, the Gild Books

53. Given in Dendy (1899) op. cit.
54. The company had for long been coextensive with the Merchant Gild. Theoretically, drapers dealt in cloth, the boothmen in corn, and the mercers in 'mercery' – precious goods brought over long distances.
55. Given in Dendy (1901) op. cit.
56. In Newcastle, as in many English cities, there existed the custom of 'foreign bought and foreign sold'. 'Strangers' or 'foreigners', those who were not freemen of the city, could not sell goods there except to a freeman, and they could only buy from freemen. Linked with this custom was that of 'hosting' – a group of freemen, the 'hostmen', had the duty of entertaining strangers and acting as their business agents whilst they stayed in the city in return for a percentage of the proceeds of any transactions made. To facilitate the easy collection of custom duties, a statute of 1529 enacted that no person could ship, load or unload any goods anywhere within the tidal limits of the Tyne except at Newcastle. As a result, all coal owners must ship their coal from Newcastle, and this could only be done through the agency of the hostmen, who thereby gained a monopoly of the Tyne coal trade. This hitherto loosely articulated group within the merchant community was given separate company status by Elizabeth I in return for a grant of £80 and a tax of 1/- per chaldron on all coal shipped from the Tyne.
57. Hope Dodds, M. (ed.) (1923) 'The Register of Freemen of Newcastle upon Tyne', *Newcastle upon Tyne Rec.* Ser. 3. A few additional occupations were obtained from Welford, op. cit. (mainly doctors of medicine and ministers of religion) and from Hodgson, J. L. (1914 and 1919) *Archaeol. Aeliana*, Ser 3, 11, 65–118 and 16, 151–4.

and the Register. The former have survived only for the period 1645–53. They record the proceedings at the three Gild Days held each year, when an apprentice who had served his time and entered his name had it called through his gild. If no objections were made to the name of an apprentice called on three consecutive Gild Days, then he became a freeman and and could have his name inscribed on the Register of Freemen. Not all suitors at the Gild Days were made freemen as objections were quite numerous, and not all new freemen had their names immediately recorded in the Register, so that the latter provides a less complete and less chronologically exact record of the mercantile and craft affiliations of the inhabitants than the Gild Books. However, the original Register, or nearly contemporary transcriptions of it, survive for almost every year from the 1580s, giving comparable records over the whole period during which the inhabitants of the town in 1665 would have been admitted to practise their trades there. Of course, these registers do not provide full details of the occupations of all the inhabitants, but only of those belonging to gilds, and not even all gildsmen were necessarily entered. On the other hand, they do not merely record gild affiliations, because 63 different occupations were recorded by an average of 73 people per year, so that the Register does provide a reasonably full, if not perfectly accurate, record of the occupations practised by those who belonged to neither the lowest nor the very highest strata of society, and who alone had the right to be involved in the government of the town.

The occupations given in the registers were classified according to the scheme given in detail in the Appendix. There are three main categories: merchants and those giving personal services (category A), those in shipping and service trades (category B), and manufacturers (category C). These categories are split into nine sub-groups which contain the more than 50 recorded occupations or combinations of associated occupations, and those who became mayor. The percentages of the total registered entries in each category and sub-group for each five-year period 1635–64 are given in Table 1, which shows that there was relatively little change in the proportions employed in each group of occupations over this period and provides a reasonably unbiased sample of the occupational structure of the gild membership of the town in the mid seventeenth century.

The admissions list of the Merchant Adventurers and the Register were searched from 1634–70 for the occupations of those who were taxed in 1665, and therefore named on Welford's list. Of these 1472 inhabitants the occupations of 41 per cent can be established with reasonable certainty, and a further 10 per cent can be placed in an 'uncertain' class, where the occupation may have been one of a num-

TABLE 1 A comparison of the occupational structure of the Freemen's Rolls, 1635–64 and the sample of occupations derived from the Rolls via the Hearth Tax Assessment Returns of 1665

Years	Total freeman admissions[a]	Percentage of total per occupational group											
		A1	A2	A	B1	B2	B3	B	C1	C2	C3	C4	C
1635–39	320	19	4	23	14	12	15	41	6	4	18	10	35
1640–44	172	14	4	18	24	13	10	47	8	3	11	14	35
1645–49	374	18	4	22	19	13	8	40	8	5	11	14	38
1650–54	300	17	2	19	24	14	10	48	9	6	10	8	33
1655–59	386	20	6	26	20	10	8	39	8	5	10	12	35
1660–64	350	21	5	26	22	9	10	41	7	7	11	9	33
1635–64 (a)	2202	18	4	22	21	12	10	43	8	5	12	11	35
In taxed sample (b)	627	36	7	43	11	10	6	27	7	4	9	10	30
$\frac{b}{a}$	0.29	2.00	1.83	1.95	0.52	0.83	0.60	0.63	0.88	0.80	0.75	0.91	0.86

[a] Excludes the two or three per year whose occupations were not entered, mainly the recipients of personal freedom.

ber in the same sub-group or category.[58] This is a large sample of occupations, representing 25 or 30 per cent of the total taxed and untaxed working population in 1665. But it must be used with especial caution, because it is biased in two ways.

First, it does not truly replicate the occupational structure of the town as delineated in the Register of Freemen. A rough comparison between the occupational structure of the Register and that of the taxed population of 1665 whose occupations are traceable is provided in Table 1 which gives the ratios of the percentages in each occupational category and sub-group in the two sets of data. The table shows that the merchant and personal service groups are both considerably over-represented in the taxed sample; a result, presumably, of the non-registration of merchant freemen, the non-admission of those in personal service occupations, which did not all have gilds, and the relatively high proportion of these groups who were wealthy enough to be liable to tax, and who are therefore

---

58. Where a name appeared only once on both the hearth tax list and an admissions list, it was assumed that the occupation given in the latter was followed in the ward indicated in the former in 1665. This involves two presumptions. First, that the person whose name was given in the heath tax return lived in the property in question and was not an owner who rented the house out. In general, the occupier was liable to the tax, but in the second Revising Act of 1664 it was stipulated that the tax on hearths in the houses of leaseholders who were exempt was to be paid by their landlords. It may be, therefore, that some persons who were listed with two hearths or less in a ward did not live in that ward, although the number of leasehold properties was not necessarily large, and it is not known how far this provision of the Act was actually put into practice. The second presumption is that there was little occupational mobility. Again, little is known about this, but it was probably not common; there were ordinances in Newcastle against changing craft, which could only be done by transferring to the appropriate gild and paying the required fine. It seems reasonable to suppose that the occupations and places of residence in 1665 of those persons who were mentioned only once on each list are, generally, known accurately from a matching of the lists.

However, such reasonable certainty, appropriate for 41 per cent of the taxed population, cannot be achieved for a further 10 per cent whose names appear more than once on one or on both lists. Such names need not necessarily be rejected completely, because it sometimes occurred that the different occupations which could be ascribed to a household were in the same occupational sub-group or category. These names were therefore classified as of uncertain occupation, and used in appropriate calculations. Some householders in 1665 were widows. If the widow's surname appeared only once in the admissions list, the entry has been assumed to be that of her husband and, as widows often continued their husband's occupation after his death, as Laslett has shown, his occupation has been ascribed to her household in 1665. If the widow's surname appeared more than once on the admissions list, then that household has been placed in the 'uncertain' category, and used in calculations for aggregate occupational groups where appropriate. See Meekings, C. A. F. (1940) 'The Surrey hearth tax, 1664', *Surrey Rec. Soc.* 17; Patten, op. cit., and Laslett, P. (1971) *The world we have lost*, p. 8 (London).

named on Welford's list. The shipping sub-group is least well represented in the taxed sample, the low figure for the sub-group as a
whole being almost entirely due to the massive under-representation
of the master mariners, for whom the ratio between the percentage
of entries on the Register 1635–64 and the percentage in the taxed
sample of 1665 was only 0.48. The second kind of bias in the taxed
sample is the variation in the proportions of the taxed populations
of wards whose occupations are known, ranging from over 90 per
cent in Pink Tower ward to only 32 per cent in Herber Tower ward.

Both of these kinds of bias in the sample of 1665 will affect the
significance of correlations between occupations and wealth on a
ward basis, and they mean that maps of occupational distributions
by ward must be interpreted with some caution. None the less, even
when treated with the appropriate reservations, these data can still
yield information on the questions posed earlier about the social and
occupational structure of the town and the ways in which they were
related to the geography of wealth.

A wealthy urban residential group which was not directly connected with the economic functioning of the city undoubtedly
existed, but its members lived in Westgate and the northern part of
Denton Tower wards, peripheral to the wealthy core of the city
(compare Figures 1D and 3).[59] All the indications are, too, that this
group did not exert much influence in the government of the city:
the merchant community was clearly dominant in both wealth and
municipal power.

The wealth of the merchants is clearly demonstrable. The Spearman rank correlation coefficient between scores on the compound
index of wealth and the proportions of the taxed populations of
wards that were merchants was +0.87, whilst the correlation between wealth and the proportions of ward populations who were
freemen of any kind was only +0.56. These statistics suggest that
the merchants formed a wealthy élite within the community of
freemen, and this suggestion is fully corroborated by the relative size
of the merchants' houses compared with those of other occupational
groups (see Table 2). The merchants had, too, a tight grip on the
government offices of the city. Of the 31 mayors who held office
between 1637 and 1684, four lived outside the town – two seem to
have had no city residence – and only four were not members of at
least one of the merchant companies. This pre-eminent municipal
position of the merchants was guaranteed by charter; only they were
allowed to buy and sell purely for profit in the town, and their gild
had firm control over the election of all the town officers, a control

59. W. G. op. cit., p. 278.

TABLE 2   The average number of hearths per house of those in the occupational sub-groups in 1665

Occupational sub-group[a]	Size of sample	Average hearths per house
A1	228	5.0
A2	42	3.9
B1	70	2.6
B2	62	2.9
B3	37	1.8
C1	44	1.5
C2	23	2.6
C3	59	2.2
C4	62	2.1

[a] The composition of these sub-groups is given in the Appendix.

which it maintained in the face of intermittent craft-gild opposition until well into the eighteenth century.[60]

There was, then, neither a non-economically active urban élite nor a one-man-one-vote system of government. Moreover, distinctions in wealth and power were not limited to this simple dichotomy between the merchants and the rest. The merchant community was

60. Those who were not members of the merchant gild could only buy what they needed for the practice of their craft or for the sustenance of their household, and they could only sell what they themselves had made. Only the merchants, then, could trade on a large scale as middlemen. This was the basis of their wealth. Their control of municipal government stretched back to the fourteenth century and survived a number of assaults from the craft gilds. A Royal Decree of 1515 entrenched them in an unassailable position. It reaffirmed the exclusive right of the merchants to act as middlemen, ordered that more than one trade could not be practised simultaneously, and that a change of craft required goods to the value of £10 and the payment of a fine. Thus were the craftsmen kept in their economically inferior position. The election of town officials was ostensibly liberalized in 1515. Twelve 'felawshippes or crafts' (the drapers, mercers, booth-men, tanners, skinners, taylors, saddlers, bakers, cordwainers, butchers, smiths and fullers) out of the thirty which then existed were each to present two 'moost proued men and moost discrete of theymself' to form a committee of 24. This committee·was, in its turn, to 'electe, chose and name' four burgesses who were then to choose eight other burgesses. These twelve were then to choose a further twelve, and this group of 24 was then to elect the city officials. However, the nucleus of four selected by the original 24 must be 'Burgesses as hath been both Maires and Aldermen of the said Towne' already, and so must the eight elected by them. The erstwhile dominance of the merchants was thus perpetuated by this apparent liberalization of the franchise, which was again only slightly eroded in a later revision in the reign of James 1. See Dendy (1911) op. cit.; Dendy, F. W. (1921) 'Gilds and their survival', in Dendy, F. W., *Three lectures on old Newcastle, its suburbs and gilds*, pp. 46–7 (Newcastle), and Gross, C. (1890) *The gild merchant*, Vol. II, pp. 382–5 (Oxford).

TABLE 3 The average number of hearths per house of members of occupations with more than ten representatives in the sample of 1665

Occupation	Sub-group	Size of sample	Average hearths per house
Mayors	A1	26	8.4
Hostmen	A1	53	5.7
Other merchants	A1	149	4.3
Bakers	B2	25	3.2
Master mariners	B1	14	3.1
Mariners	B1	23	3.0
Barber-surgeons	A2	27	2.5
Joiners	C2	12	2.5
Cordwainers	C4	27	2.4
Weavers	C3	11	2.2
Shipwrights	B1	30	2.0
Butchers	B2	22	2.0
Coopers	C2	11	2.0
Tailors	C3	26	2.0
Tanners	C4	20	2.0
House-carpenters	B3	13	1.6
Blacksmiths	C1	28	1.4

a large one, comprising about 20 per cent of the total freeman community, and sharp stratification developed within it. By the seventeenth century the members of the Company of Hostmen had attained dominance. They were wealthier than the remainder of the merchant group, with an average of 5.7 hearths per house compared with 4.3, and it was within this small clique, which never provided more than 4 per cent of the total freemen's registrations in any five-year period from 1635–64, that municipal control resided. Of the 31 mayors who held office between 1637 and 1684, 22 were Hostmen. Thirteen were governors of the Hostmen's Company, and only three men who held this office between 1637 and 1684 did not also hold the mayoralty within that period. This supreme status of the leading Hostmen was also reflected in the size of their houses, with the mayors/governors averaging 8.4 hearths per house (see Table 3).

Below the merchant community, the craft gilds were similarly differentiated in wealth and power. The only gilds recognized by the Merchant Adventurers, during a period of theoretical leniency, for the purpose of qualifying for admission to their company, were the 'twelve principal mysteries of the town' which had existed as corporate groups since 1342.[61] This status classification still had

61. Dendy (1901) op. cit., p. 41.

meaning in 1665. The nine non-mercantile trades of the twelve had the right to limited participation in elections and had a meeting place in the same building, 'called now Bannet Chessy Friars', whilst the fifteen 'by-crafts' had even more circumscribed municipal rights and 'every one of them hath their meeting-houses in the towers of the wall'.[62]

These inter-craft differences are also reflected in the house size data (see Tables 2 and 3). The victualling trades (B2) were the wealthiest non-merchant group on the evidence of hearth figures, followed by the shipping (B1) and woodworking (C2) trades. At the bottom came the building (B3) and metalworking (C1) trades, whose practitioners had, on average, less than two hearths in their houses. These sub-group averages conceal some quite large house sizes in particular occupations which have been grouped with poorer ones; the master mariners, bakers and mariners averaged more hearths per house than the barber-surgeons, who were placed in the wealthy A2 sub-group (see Table 3), and so did the fullers, feltmakers and skinners, who do not appear on Table 3 because there were less than ten of them in the 1665 sample.

Other inhabitants, unpossessed of the freedom of the city, formed a much larger social stratum below these taxed craftsmen. Those untaxed in 1665 made up 43 per cent of the population of the city. The vast majority had one hearth in their houses, the rest only two.[63] Some of their number were undoubtedly poorer members of the ancient mysteries and by-crafts.[64] A much larger proportion was probably composed of members of incorporated crafts such as cook, collier, carrier, porter and keelman who seem rarely to have been admitted to the freedom of the city. Certainly, it is likely that the massive 79 per cent of the inhabitants of Sandgate ward who were untaxed, comprising 510 heads of households, were keelmen and seamen, for 'without this gate [are] many houses, and populous, all along the waterside; where ship-wrights, seamen, and keelmen most live, that are employed about the ships and keels'.[65] A further proportion of the 'poor', and the one to which this assignation is most appropriate, would be composed of Engels's 'reserve army of city labour', an army about which little information has survived.

---

62. W. G. op. cit., p. 278.
63. Welford, op. cit., p. 56.
64. This was certainly the case in Wigan, where a number of officers of craft com-panies appeared in the exempt list in the hearth tax assessment returns of 1664. (This situation was revealed by matching data on occupations and company office holders given in the Court Leet Rolls with the tax returns.)
65. W. G. op. cit., p. 272.

THE RELATIONSHIP BETWEEN SOCIAL STRUCTURE
AND THE DISTRIBUTION OF WEALTH

Such a finely structured hierarchical society could have been related to the well-patterned distribution of wealth in a number of ways. Two possible extremes exist: either marked occupational concentrations could have occurred, as suggested by Sjoberg and Vance, with the spatial pattern of wealth reflecting the marked differences in the wealth of the various occupational groups; or a more 'modern', 'class-zoned' structure could have existed, with those of equal wealth and status living in close proximity irrespective of their occupations. This situation is in many ways similar to that envisaged by Vance for the capitalist city, although its grounding in a merchant-dominated society and its spatial expression in a wealthy central area are not, of course, congruent with that, or any other, stage of his model.

The location quotients of the occupational categories and sub-groups were calculated in an attempt to discover the extent to which the first of these possible extremes existed. A location quotient, according to whether it is greater or less than 1.0, indicates whether a ward contained more or fewer in a particular occupational group that would be expected on the basis of its population[66] and the number in the occupational group in the city as a whole. The quotients for wards in which there were less than five in an occupational group were ignored and, after an examination of the frequency distribution of the quotients for all the wards for all the occupations, values of 1.3 and 2.0 were used to indicate the existence of 'significant' and 'marked' occupational specialization in wards. The quotients for the three occupational categories are plotted in Figure 5A, which demonstrates the existence of two quite separate occupational sectors, separated by an almost continuous belt of wards with lower quotients in all three occupational categories, and therefore mixed occupational structures. These mercantile and manufacturing sectors correspond with those described in a topography of Newcastle written in 1649. The first, centred in the south-west, contained other mercantile 'strategic facilities' besides the gildhall,[67] and the second,

66. In the calculation of these and later statistics, the 'populations' of the wards were taken to constitute those persons on the tax list whose occupations are known.
67. The gildhall was built on the river-ward side of 'the Sand-hill, a market for fish, and other commodities; very convenient for merchant adventurers, merchants of coals, and all those that have their living by shipping. There is . . . a long key or wharf, where ships may . . . unload their commodities and wares . . . [on] it, are two cranes for heavy commodities, very convenient for carrying of corn, wines, deals etc., from the key . . . In this market place are many shops and stately houses for merchants, with great convenience of water, bridge, garners, lofts, cellars and houses . . . In this Sand-hill standeth the town-court, or

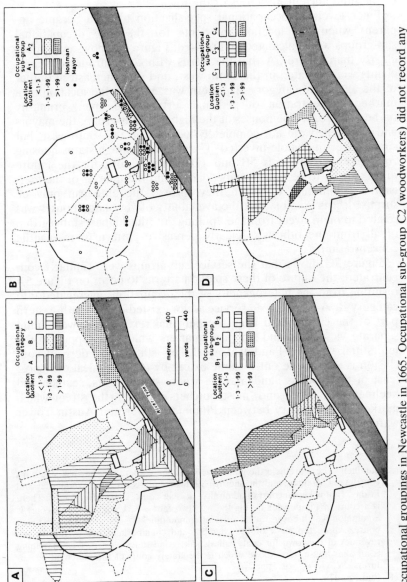

Fig. 5 Occupational groupings in Newcastle in 1665. Occupational sub-group C2 (woodworkers) did not record any location quotients greater than 1.29.

centred on Mordon Tower ward, contained the main market, 'where all sorts of artificers have shops and houses', and the meeting house of the nine ancient mysteries of the town.[68]

Finer levels of occupational specialization by area became apparent when the location quotients for the nine occupational sub-groups were calculated and plotted. Figure 5B shows even more clearly than Figure 5A that the wards with concentrations of merchants were situated in the south-west, and that the eastern outlier of the aggregate category A pattern was, in fact, the location of a marked concentration of personal service tradesmen, primarily barber-surgeons. The houses of the highest status group, the mayors and hostmen, were not completely localized in the south-west, but spread over the whole inverted 'T' shape of the high status housing zone (compare Figures 5B and 1D). The reasons for the failure of this group to be tightly embedded within the quarter of the mercantile community of which they formed the élite can only be surmised: it is possible that the availability of very large houses was related to main street frontage, 'pulling out' this highest status group of all from the otherwise clearly pervasive pattern of mercantile concentration.[69]

Figure 5C shows that the service sub-groups were similarly concentrated, the failure of these spatial patterns to occur on Figure 5A resulting from the heterogeneity of the occupations aggregated into category B. A pronounced service sector existed in the south-eastern part of the city. Inland from the personal service area were quite separate victualling and shipping quarters which overlapped in the interstitial ward of Pandon Tower. This statistically derived conclusion is also borne out to some extent by topographical evidence: 'east of the town is Sandgate . . . where ship-wrights, seamen and keelmen most live', and 'most butchers dwell' in the street which marked the boundary between Plummer Tower and Austin Tower wards.[70]

---

guildhall, where are held the guilds every year . . . where the mayor keepeth his court every Monday, and the sheriff hath his county-court upon Wednesday and Friday. In it is kept a court of admiralty, or river-court, every Monday . . . There is a court of Pie-powder during the . . . two fairs . . . Under the town-court is a common weigh-house for all sorts of commodities . . . Near this is the town-house, where the clerk of the chamber and chamberlains are to receive the revenues of the town for coal, ballast, salt, grindstones etc . . . Next adjoining is an alms-house . . . Above which is the stately court of the merchant adventurers. W. G., op. cit., pp. 276–7.

68. Ibid., p. 278.
69. In 1649, Pilgrim Street was described as 'the longest and fairest street in the town' and Westgate Street as 'a broad street and private', although the areas surrounding them were of much lower status. Ibid., p. 277.
70. Ibid., pp. 272 and 277.

The tendency for occupational sub-groups to be concentrated and segregated was apparent also in the manufacturing trades, although in this case the contiguity of wards which contained concentrations of particular sub-groups of occupations, representing the existence of craft 'quarters', was not so pronounced as in the service trades. The degree of segregation was quite high; only Mordon Tower ward contained marked concentrations of more than one occupational sub-group, and only Pilgrim Tower ward contained significant concentrations of different manufacturing sub-groups. Loosely articulated metalworking and leatherworking quarters existed, but the woodworkers were 'over-represented' in no ward, and the wards which contained concentrations of textiles and clothing manufactures were widely separated and located in the merchant and service sectors of the city.

It is difficult to determine the degree to which this concentration and segregation of economic activities percolated down to the level of individual crafts because the populations of some wards were very small and those of others very large relative to the numbers involved in any one trade, and ward boundaries frequently followed or cut streets, so that it was possible for actual concentrations to be 'dispersed' between a number of wards. Table 4 shows those crafts in which 40 per cent or more of the practitioners were localized in three or fewer neighbouring wards and in which numbers were sufficiently large to render percentage statements meaningful. Only

TABLE 4   The localized crafts of Newcastle in 1665

Craft	Total membership	Wards	% of total in named wards
Slater and bricklayer	8	Carliol Tower	75
Baker	25	Austin Tower and Pandon Tower	52
Butcher	22	Plummer Tower, Gunner Tower and Austin Tower	50
Shipwright	30	Sandgate	50
Barber-surgeon	27	Corner Tower, Wall Knoll Tower, and Austin Tower	48
Blacksmith	28	Mordon Tower, Pilgrim Tower and Carliol Tower	48 46
Master mariner and mariner	37	Wall Knoll Tower, Sandgate and Pandon Tower	43

eight of the crafts appear on the table. Although the reason for the absence of some of the remainder is that they had too few members, in other cases, particularly in leatherworking, woodworking and clothing and textiles, it is that the practitioners were dispersed through non-contiguous wards. Table 4 shows with great clarity that it was the service trades which tended to be most localized, corroborating the results of the statistical analysis of the sub-group data: all the service crafts in which numbers were reasonably large were strongly concentrated in the victualling and shipping quarters of the city.

An analysis of the sample of 1665 demonstrates quite clearly, then, that occupational groups were concentrated and segregated to a significant extent in Newcastle, finer distinctions existing within broad mercantile, victualling, shipping and manufacturing quarters. Each of these quarters contained its own particular 'strategic facilities' and, where relevant, specialized retail outlets. If it was not, perhaps, 'many centred', Newcastle was definitely 'four sectored': certainly, there was not a single 'centre' around which all activities were organized as they are around a central business district. This tendency towards the spatial grouping of craft activities must not be exaggerated. Some trades were scattered through many wards, some through a few widely separated ones, and some wards contained concentrations of a few trades which were in no ways affinitive. Moreover, in no case was there absolute concentration and in all trades there were 'stragglers', scattered willy-nilly across the city.

None the less, even though these qualifications are necessary, strong tendencies towards occupational grouping did exist. What is more, these groupings were quite clearly related to the distribution pattern of house sizes. The wealthiest wards, in the south-west, scored high location quotients for the wealthiest trades, whilst the poorest wards were characterized by high location quotients for the poorest trades or low quotients for all trades and therefore a greater than 'expected' preponderance of non-freemen. It can be concluded, then, that there was some tendency towards the first of the possible extreme relationships between social structure and the geography of wealth that was defined earlier.

But, as the location pattern of mayors' and hostmen's houses hinted, the situation was not quite so simple as these correlations between the residential status of areas and the wealth of occupational groupings suggest. Newgate, Gunner Tower and Bertram Monboucher Tower wards, for example, ranked 2.5, 4.5 and 6.5 on the compound index of wealth, but did not score high location quotients in any sub-group of trades, whilst Stank Tower ward, in which only the relatively poor leatherworkers were over-represented, ranked 4.5 in wealth. The results of a two-way analysis of variance of the average size of houses classified by wards and the nine occupational sub-groups further demonstrates this complexity.[71] Although there was significant variation, at the 0.1 level of probability, of hearth size classified by occupational sub-group independent of variation in the ward means; there was also significant variation in the ward means independent of variation in the occupational means at the same level of probability. Clearly, in addition to the tendency for the wealth of wards to vary according to the wealth of localized occupational groups, there was also a tendency for other wards to be wealthy of otherwise irrespective of their occupational make-up.

The degree and disposition of this 'class-zoning' is portrayed in Figures 6A–D. These show the number of standard deviations that the average numbers of hearths in the houses of members of each occupational sub-group in each ward lay from the over-all average numbers of hearths for the members of the occupational sub-groups. They thus show where the houses of practitioners of each trade were larger and smaller than the average for their trade. Of course, one would not expect each occupational sub-group to have the same average house-size in each ward. Some random variation must occur, especially between sample means such as these, and perhaps little can be read into the differences which lay between, say, −1.00 and +1.00. Nevertheless, the differences between the averages for certain wards and the city-wide averages were so great, and the wards which recorded high positive and negative deviations were so consistent across occupational sub-groups, that a certain degree of 'class-zoning' is strongly indicated.

The pattern of positive and negative deviations from the mean house-size of occupational category A corresponded with the pattern of location quotients for that group. Generally, although there were detailed exceptions, the wards where merchants were 'over-represented' were also those where their houses were larger than average, and vice versa (see Figure 6A). The service trades displayed a similar tendency. The wealthiest members of this category, the victuallers, had houses which were larger than their sub-group average in the area where their houses were most concentrated, and away from this core area their houses became smaller with an almost regular progression. But in the wards where the shipping and building trades were concentrated the houses of the members of these generally poorer trades were on the whole smaller than the sub-group means, with a transition zone in Pandon Tower ward where the victualling and shipping quarters overlapped.

71. The empty 'boxes' in the matrix were filled in by a computer routine devised by Mr N. Wrigley of the Department of Geography, Southampton University, who kindly ran the program for me.

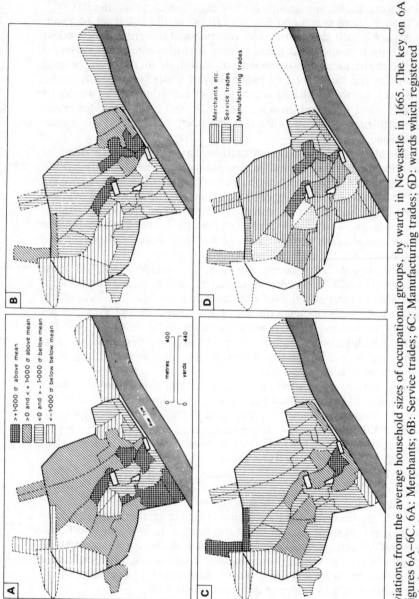

Fig. 6 Deviations from the average household sizes of occupational groups, by ward, in Newcastle in 1665. The key on 6A refers to Figures 6A–6C. 6A: Merchants; 6B: Service trades; 6C: Manufacturing trades; 6D: wards which registered positive deviations from the mean number of hearths per house for the three occupational categories. There were no service tradesmen in Pink Tower ward.

This reversal, with areas of the greatest concentration of a trade containing members with houses smaller than the average for their trade, was even more marked in the manufacturing crafts (see Figure 6C). Some of the manufacturing wards of the city, such as Mordon Tower, Pilgrim Tower, Denton Tower and Pandon Tower, registered negative deviations from the average house-size of manufacturing tradesmen, and the positive deviations in these trades occurred in the southern, mercantile, area of the city. The patterns for the three occupational categories are mapped together on Figure 6D, which shows that the areas of highest residential status were as closely correlated with areas where the houses of the members of various occupational sub-groups were consistently wealthier than the average for their craft as they were with areas where wealthier occupational sub-groups were concentrated.

It seems, then, that the core areas of the wealthier trades contained the wealthier members of those trades and, in addition, 'creamed off' the wealthiest practitioners of crafts whose members were generally poorer.[72] Furthermore, the core areas of poorer trades contained only the less wealthy members of those trades and the poorest practitioners of crafts which were generally wealthier. However, this reinforcement of patterns based on occupational zoning was not the only way in which 'class zoning' operated. Certain wards existed, notably Newgate, near the market, which contained larger-than-average houses in all three occupational categories but high location quotients in none of them (compare Figures 6D and 5A–D), and others, notably Ever Tower in the north-west, had smaller-than-average houses in all three craft categories and no concentration of any poorer trade. In these wards, perhaps, true 'class-zoning', rather than the hybridized form which prevailed in other wards, occurred. But, in diametrical opposition to Vance's

---

72. The major exceptions were the relatively large houses of the manufacturing and service tradesmen in Fickett Tower and Durham Tower wards in the north-west; the relatively large houses of the merchant group in the two large wards of the north-east, and the relatively small houses of the merchants in White Friar Tower ward in the south-west. In the first case, the wards concerned were on main roads to gates, and the numbers of tradesmen who lived in them were small, so that one or two exceptionally large houses in an occupational group (a weaver with 8 hearths in Fickett Tower Ward, for example) could markedly affect the averages. In the second case, the two wards flanking Pilgrim Street contained, along that thoroughfare, relatively large numbers of mayors and hostmen (see Figure 5B). The small positive deviations registered by these wards resulted from a combination of these large houses with the generally smaller than average houses of the other merchant adventurers who lived in what was, relative to the main concentration of merchants' houses, a peripheral area. The smaller than average houses of the merchants of White Friar Tower Ward might (but need not necessarily) indicate that the residential status pattern of the merchant core was itself sorted around the wealthy nucleus of Pink Tower ward.

class-zoned capitalist city, the poorer wards were peripheral and the wealthier ones central.

DISCUSSION AND CONCLUSION

Conclusions about the general applicability of the models of Sjoberg and Vance obviously cannot be drawn from evidence about the society and economy of one city and about the distribution of wealth in three others. At its widest, the scope of the following conclusions will comprise the larger British cities of the seventeenth century. Indeed, Newcastle was in some ways distinct even within this small set. The lucrative control of London's coal supply provided a stronger base for the power of its merchant oligarchy than existed elsewhere, and the intimacy of its influence on London's welfare, plus its importance as a military strong-point, prompted more-than-usual interference from central government in its internal affairs. None the less, like most of the other larger British cities of the period, Newcastle was a port, governed by a small oligarchy, with an occupational structure reflecting the dominance of trade and craft industry in its economic base. In the context of residential patterns, these congruencies are sufficiently fundamental to ensure that conclusions based upon Newcastle data will have more than purely local significance. But a definition of the exact scope of these conclusions is not of great importance to the main objective of this study, which is simply to examine how far the models of Sjoberg and Vance are representative of the conditions which actually obtained in a particular city to which they should be applicable. A specification of the full set of cities to which any discrepancies that are found here are relevant must obviously await detailed work on cities of different sizes in different places at different times.

Predictably, the social geography of Newcastle in the mid seventeenth century was more complicated than any of the archetypes of Sjoberg or Vance. But it was not just more complicated: it was fundamentally different. Newcastle was not a feudal pre-industrial city, nor was it a pre-capitalist or a capitalist city. A merchant clique was pre-eminent in wealth and municipal power. Its social dominance was expressed geographically in the existence of a mercantile quarter in that part of the city where its economic purposes were best served and where the institutions through which it dominated the city were located. In addition, the city possessed other regularly patterned occupational districts which were in some areas reinforced by 'class zoning', and in others countervailed by it. If the city must be fitted into the schemes of Vance and Sjoberg, then it could be said to represent some hybrid of the mercantile pre-capitalist and the capitalist cities. Vance's stress upon the importance of economic power and relationships as ecological determinants within the city undoubtedly gets nearer to the truth of the matter than Sjoberg's feudal social order, in which the dominance of an élite group was derived from non-economic and extra-urban sources.[73]

Indeed, it might seem possible to read the evidence in ways which go much further towards corroborating Vance's ideas about the emergence of capitalist cities – an expectation which is also produced by the changes, spear-headed in the cities, which were demonstrably occurring in English society in general at that time. It could, for example, be hypothesized that the occupational-cum-wealth spatial groupings of Newcastle really reflected affinities based upon wealth and 'class' rather than the occupational congruencies which underlay them. Or, it could be hypothesized that the partial scattering of occupational groups into areas of similarities in wealth represented the beginnings of 'class-based' residential zones and the break-up of craft areas.

Neither of these hypotheses can be sustained. They require the existence of analytical chimera and ignore social and economic reality. Whether or not 'capitalism' had developed in Newcastle and engendered the crystallization of 'class' affinities cannot be demonstrated because these terms cannot be defined in ways which make their empirical existence demonstrable. Moreover, it is at least arguable that the first does not necessarily entail the second,[74] and that 'social class' is an intellectual device which has little relevance to seventeenth-century English society.[75] But it can be unequivocally demonstrated that economically and socially functional groups based on occupations still existed. The craft gilds and the companies of

73. This kind of social structure was probably common in British towns. The largest were ports before the Industrial Revolution, and, generally, 'the organization of [trade] was so closely connected with the earliest form of municipal constitution as to have made it possible to argue that constitution and the Gild Merchant were one and the same thing'. In medieval Southampton this merchant dominance was expressed in an exclusive residential area in that part of the town most convenient for them, just as it was in seventeenth-century Newcastle. Unwin, G. (1904) *Industrial organization in the sixteenth and seventeenth centuries*, pp. 16–17 (Oxford) and Platt, C. (1973) *Medieval Southampton*, pp. 264–6 (London).
74. Laslett, op. cit., pp. 18–20.
75. Ibid., pp. 23–6; Woolrich, A. (1968) 'The English revolution: an introduction' in Ives, E. W. (ed.) *The English revolution 1600–1660*, 1–34, (London) and Supple, B. W. 'Class and social tension: the case of the merchant', ibid., 131–44. Supple argues that the merchants formed the only true 'class' group in seventeenth-century English society. It is difficult to see how this situation can be made conformable with theories which suggest that class affiliations were produced by the rise of capitalism, which also destroyed the merchant hegemony.

Hostmen and Merchant Adventurers had not yet become functionally hollow avenues of access into an urban society of equal opportunity and an urban economy of free competition. The gilds and companies had power over their members in seventeenth-century Newcastle; their members still acted in concert through them, and still had their municipal rights defined by their affiliations with them.[76] It would be unreasonable to suggest, in the face of this, and given the congruence of workplace and home in a craft economy, that the spatial groupings of people following the same occupations did not have their rationale in the practice of those occupations.

It is true that the evidence shows that these occupational groupings were neither absolutely firm in outline nor all-embracing in membership. It is also true that persons of dissimilar occupations lived mixed up together in certain parts of the city. But this situation may merely signify that the numbers practising particular trades had grown beyond the capacities of the areas in which their members were mainly concentrated. Certainly, the economy of the city was growing after the Civil War according to the evidence of admissions to freedom (see Table 1), and the occupational concentrations were all located in crowded and completely built-up parts of the city (compare Figures 2 and 5). If this was so, the additional craftsmen would have to find houses wherever they were available. Little is known of the seventeenth-century housing market, but it can be surmised that the options would not be legion, and that the customer would have to base his choice, or the specification of his commission to the builder, on the size of his particular household-cum-workforce. The degree of 'class-zoning' that was apparent might signify no more than this – that the economy of the city was growing. It is certainly not necessary to postulate the existence of 'class' affiliations based upon wealth to explain it. Indeed, it is as reasonable to argue that the growth in the numbers of craftsmen caused dispersal and a consequent weakening of occupational group ties, and that it was therefore a precursor and not a result of the development of other kinds of social associations.

One is left with the conclusions that pre-industrial cities did not necessarily exist before the Industrial Revolution, and that pre-capitalist cities could flourish in a capitalist era. They indicate the inadequacy of the models of Vance and Sjoberg. Sjoberg ignored the social and economic changes which occurred in Western Europe, and particularly in its cities, between medieval times and the In-

76. See Dendy (1901, 1921) op. cit. and Rowe, D. J. (1966) 'The records of the company of shipwrights of Newcastle-upon-Tyne 1622–1967', *Surtees Soc.* 181, Vol. 1, which give extracts from the proceedings and ordinances of some of the gilds in the mid seventeenth-century.

dustrial Revolution. Vance accommodated them, but his model is inadequate in its mediation of the development of capitalism through a change in the attitude towards land holding to affect the social geography of cities. More proximate determinants of land plot assignment practices existed. The relationships between workplace and home, in functional and spatial terms,[77] the size and composition of households, and the nature of the housing and land markets are all more intimately related to the structure of society and the reasons why residential choices are made. The first two are vitally important components of the *Gemeinschaft* social structural relationships of pre-modern urban society: in a large part they were what made it pre-modern.[78] The third is the only possible mechanism for transmitting social changes into changed residential patterns. Questions about these aspects of pre-nineteenth-century cities and about how they changed in response to economic changes must be addressed and answered before the distinctiveness of these cities can be understood. Only after such understanding has been gained will it be possible to formulate a reasonable and reliable set of generalizations about the social geography of cities before the 'ecological transition', and to comprehend what, exactly, that transition comprised.

ACKNOWLEDGEMENT

Thanks are due to the University of Liverpool for a contribution towards the cost of illustrations.

APPENDIX

The production of generalized maps and tables required the classification of occupations into groups within which strong affinities of some kind existed. Unfortunately, no single criterion could be ap-

77. Vance, J. (1967) has dealt with this relationship in a stimulating paper in *Econ. Geogr.* 43, 95–127.
78. The role of these institutions in maintaining social and economic functioning in English cities in the seventeenth century, when plagues reduced the populations of some towns by up to 50 per cent, resulting in a vast influx of migrants and when the Civil War caused short-term economic and longer term political and religious upheaval, would repay study.

plied to produce a classification of pre-industrial urban occupations which was suitable for this particular analysis. The classification given below resulted from a set of compromises: other compromises could have been applied to produce different classifications, but the groupings which have been devised are at least as appropriate to the needs of this study as any other set of categories.

Historians have usually classified pre-industrial urban occupations according to the raw materials used or handled in them. This procedure is inappropriate here because it cuts across the fundamental distinction between merchants and manufacturing craftsmen. Classes A and C reflect this distinction. Class A contains, besides the merchants, those who provided personal services which were largely outside the remit of the Merchant Adventurers monopoly, and who were not, therefore, disabled from achieving similar wealth and influence. Within Class C, the manufacturing craftsmen were classified according to the raw materials they worked on except for the shipbuilders, who were not classified under 'manufacturing wood' because they operated on a scale which was completely different from that of the joiners and coopers, and they were influenced by locational requirements which were different from those of the main body of manufacturing craftsmen. The latter characteristic, at least, suggested that the shipwrights were more appropriately classified with the other shipping occupations.

Those occupations which were neither mercantile nor manufacturing posed considerable problems of classification. They comprise the shipping, victualling and building crafts, which have been lumped together in category B as 'shipping and services'. This group thus contains, basically, the residuals which could not be appropriately fitted into the other two major categories. There were, obviously, few functional links between these three kinds of activity (this is illustrated by the patternless nature of the location quotients of this group, mapped on Figure 5A). Because the data for the sub-groups were treated individually, it mattered little whether these three kinds of occupation were grouped into one category or classified as three quite separate ones. So that the summary maps and tables could be produced in a standard format, the former procedure was adopted.

The occupations which are bracketed in column 3 are those with which the preceding craft was linked in a gild. If such crafts were given alone as occupations in the admissions list, they have also been listed separately below.

1 Category	2 Sub-group	3 Occupation
A. Merchants and personal service	1. Merchants	Mayor; hostman who was not a mayor, merchant who was neither a mayor nor a hostman
	2. Personal Service	Goldsmith and scrivenor; recorder; minister of religion; doctor; apothecary; physician and barber-surgeon (and wax and tallow chandler)
B. Shipping and services	1. Shipping	Shipwright; master mariner; mariner; and carrier and carriageman
	2. Victualling	Baker (and beer brewer); butcher; brewer; miller, and confectioner
	3. Building	Mason; slater; waller (and bricklayer and plasterer); pavior; house carpenter; plasterer; plumber, and glazier (and painter)
C. Manufacturing	1. Metal	Blacksmith; anchorsmith; spurrier and lorimer; cutler; armourer; whitesmith; pewterer; locksmith; pulleymaker, and coiner
	2. Wood	Joiner, and cooper
	3. Clothing and Textiles	Weaver; fuller (and dyer); feltmaker; sailmaker; upholsterer; ropemaker, and tailor
	4. Leather	Tanner; skinner (and glover); currier; saddler, and cordwainer

Editorial suggestions for further reading

N. Alldridge, 'House and household in Restoration Chester', *Urban History Yearbook* (1983), pp. 39–52.

E. Jones, 'London in the early seventeenth century: An ecological approach', *London Journal*, 6 (1980), pp. 123–33.

D. Keene, 'A new study of London before the Great Fire', *Urban History Yearbook* (1984), pp. 11–21.

Chapter 8

CIVIC MENTALITY AND THE ENVIRONMENT IN TUDOR YORK

D. M. Palliser

[*Northern History*, 18 (1982)]

As the author admits, attempts to understand the 'collective mentality' of townspeople will always be based on fragmentary evidence and lack the firmness or agreed criteria for proof found in economic or political history. Here David Palliser collects material from his study of Tudor York, a conservative city in politics, religion and arguably in its economic basis, to argue the case for a continuity of medieval 'assumptions, relationships and physical surroundings' amidst great changes. As he shows, what persisted were the efforts of townspeople to cope with the fluctuations and crises of urban life through the ordering of time and space, provision for health and education and so on. Within his period, moreover, he sees significant shifts, for example in housing and language. These changes cannot be understood without considering the national picture, and York's experience may not be typical of other large towns, let alone of smaller places with a less dominating medieval heritage. Compared to pre-Reformation and Stuart towns, Tudor towns still lack systematic analysis of this kind, despite the assumption, repeated here, that the Reformation was a cultural watershed.

One of the most daunting aspects of studying a Tudor or Stuart community is the realization that one's picture of it must remain forever fragmentary and incomplete. Certainly many communities are abundantly documented, and Macfarlane has recently concluded that 'in some respects, the records are better for the late sixteenth and seventeenth centuries than for any subsequent period'. By correlating all the surviving types of document for one Essex parish, he concludes that 'the belief that little can be found out about ordinary people in the past is a myth' and that virtually all the villagers appear in the records.[1] Nevertheless, there is a great difference between assembling and analysing the factual data on a Tudor population – numbers, relationships, occupations, wealth, and so on – and understanding what they thought, hoped, believed, and feared. Several excellent recent studies, one or two of which have been described as the 'total history' of their communities (by the publishers rather than their authors), have provided excellent portraits of some aspects of the towns or villages concerned while leaving others in shadow for lack of information.

For this reason my own study of sixteenth-century York concentrated on the better recorded aspects of the city, and it could not be pretended that a 'total history' was possible.[2] Yet enough fragmentary hints remain in the records to suggest a little, at least, of the everyday lives and preoccupations of the citizens and while a rounded picture is not possible, the attempt is worth making. York was a large city of between 8000 and 12 000 people, with an occupational structure and a story of economic decay and recovery which seem to have been much more typical of large Tudor towns and cities than has sometimes been allowed, and an attempt to understand the collective mentality of its citizens will, it is hoped, contribute to our growing understanding of sixteenth-century life.

I

Sixteenth-century Englishmen experienced a perceptible increase in the precision with which they measured time and space and located themselves within those dimensions. Developments in printing, chronology, navigation, astronomy, and cartography all played a part, as well as a less easily definable shift from a medieval cosmological frame of reference towards a more secular and measurable framework. The process was, however, gradual and far from uniform, and one must not exaggerate the change accomplished on mental habits already many centuries old.

The pre-Reformation concept of time was at once more rigid and more flexible than that of a later age. Men thought of themselves

---

1. A. Macfarlane, *Reconstructing Historical Communities* (Cambridge, 1977), pp. 32, 131.
2. D. M. Palliser, *Tudor York* (Oxford, 1979). Since this article was completed, an interesting study of another area of popular mentality, based partly on York city evidence, has been published: J. A. Sharpe, *Defamation and Sexual Slander in Early Modern England: the Church Courts at York*, Borthwick Papers, no. 58 (York, 1980).

as living between the two great fixed points of Creation and Doomsday, the latter an event expected in the relatively near future. The mental framework of York citizens is embodied in the Corpus Christi plays, which started with the Creation and ended with a vividly-depicted Last Judgement. The plays were performed – and were popular – until the fifteen-seventies, and though they had been composed much earlier, there is no reason to think that their cosmology was thought antiquated in conservative York. Several arbitrations between quarrelling citizens in the reigns of Henry VII and VIII arranged an end to disputes 'from the beginning of the world until this time', and testators commonly arranged, without any sense of incongruity, for prayers or doles 'evermore' or 'so long as the world shall endure'.

Medieval tradition had played its part by fitting the city's history quite precisely into the Biblical chronology. The citizens possessed not only a dim but real memory of the city's Roman greatness, but a firm belief in a pre-Roman history which they derived from Geoffrey of Monmouth. King Ebrauk, Geoffrey had said, had founded the city, 'which city he called Kaerebrauc after himself', about 1000 B.C. or so, at the time 'King David was reigning in Judea'. Ebrauk was the first figure to greet Henry VII at his entry to the city in 1486, and a stone statue of the legendary king was much venerated, being moved in 1501 from its ancient position on a street corner to a place of honour in the Common Hall chapel.[3] There is no record of the citizens' reaction to Polydore Vergil and William Camden, who attacked Geoffrey's veracity, but their retention of the Ebrauk statue after the Reformation suggests that they were slow to abandon their legends, like the Londoners, who cherished Brutus of Troy as their founder.

Yet, if the citizens could give dates with assurance to events like the Creation or the foundation of York, they were often vague about the immediate past. No parish registers are known to have been kept in York before 1538, and as late as 1570 a woman's age could be established only by the well-tried method of oral testimony about her date of baptism. Witnesses in court were often vague about their ages, a warning to historians that the precision often required by the Crown – men to come of age at twenty-one; or to serve in the militia between sixteen and sixty – was simply unattainable. An exception was the epitaph of Canon John Reynald, recording that he died in 1506 in his seventy-fourth year, about five in the afternoon on Christmas Eve. Some other early Tudor churchmen, such as Archbishop Lee, have their ages recorded on

3. *Y(ork), C(ivic) R(ecords)*, ed. A. Raine, Yorkshire Archaeological Society Record Series (8 vols. 1939–53), I, 156; II, 171; A. Raine, *Mediaeval York* (1955), pp. 59–60.

epitaphs; but such precision came later for laymen, and no alderman before 1597 is known to have had his age recorded on his tomb.[4]

Measurements of time were used very subjectively: a city custom could become 'ancient' after twenty or thirty years, presumably measured against the memory of those alive at that time, yet a church rebuilt two or three generations previously could be described as 'newe', probably in contrast to the assumed age of other church fabrics. The widespread reliance on memory was inevitably risky: Leland was given a completely garbled account of the building of Walmgate Bar, although the alleged event had happened only fifty years before. Yet preference for living rather than written testimony was deep-rooted. It was typical that the Corporation, investigating common rights in Tang Hall Field in 1524, should have drawn on the memory of eight witnesses aged between sixty-four and eighty-six. In 1541 the Corporation, awaiting the first royal visit for fifty-four years, searched their records for 'precydents' of earlier visits, but this was done, it would seem, only for lack of surviving witnesses. The next royal visit did not take place until sixty-two years after that, in 1603, yet on that occasion a crucial point of processional etiquette was settled purely 'by report of ancient men' about the precedent set in 1541. The episode, even if it relates to testimony at second-hand as one phrase suggests, testifies to increased longevity as well as to a stubborn preference for eye-witness evidence.[5]

Even annual reckoning was no simple task. Alongside the dating of years from 25 March or from the anniversary of the sovereign's accession, there were three alternative civic years, reckoned respectively from 3 February (the mayoral year), 29 September (the shrieval year) and 15 January (the chamberlains' year, used for financial accounts and lists of freemen). The normal conversational dating in York was, apparently, by mayoralty, and it was possible for a midwife to recall correctly the succession of mayors for the previous thirteen years at least, though not all citizens reckoning by this method were reliable. The Corporation minutes are fortunately free of ambiguity, for the clerks invariably dated meetings by the regnal year, except for a few days in July 1553 when the method would have involved a choice between two rival queens. Even so, the Corporation minutes are not entirely unambiguous about dating. Orders were often given for action on 'Wednesday next' or such other days, and in some cases (as with troop movements) the time allowed was too short. Dr Hanham has reasonably suggested that

4. Y. C. R., VII, 16; F. Drake, *Eboracum* (1736), pp. 298, 452, 504, 521.
5. *The Itinerary of John Leland*, ed. L. T. Smith (5 vols, 1907–10), I, 54; *Y(ork) C(ity) A(rchives)*, MS B9, fols 103–05; *Y. C .R.,* IV, 56; T. Widdrington, *Analecta Eboracensia*, ed. C. Caine (1897), p. 265; Drake, *Eboracum*, App., p. li.

'Wednesday next', as in Scotland today, meant the Wednesday *after* next.[6]

Years were also divided more irregularly into seasons, and punctuated more unevenly by festivals and ceremonies, than can easily be appreciated. Half of the year, from Advent Sunday to Midsummer Day (the Nativity of St John the Baptist), was dominated by church feasts and fasts, with an underlying rhythm of periods of fast and preparation (Advent and Lent) alternating with seasons of feast and rejoicing (Christmas and Easter/Whitsun). The late medieval calendar, with its moveable feasts and numerous saints' days, was complicated even for the clergy to follow, and the 'pie' for calculating feasts and lessons was an essential handbook. A single consignment of printed books into York about 1510 included no fewer than 570 French pies.[7] Even these did not cover all eventualities, for the province of York had its own 'York use' which differed slightly from the predominant Sarum rite, and many clergy also possessed printed copies of that. The number of church festivals was, of course, drastically reduced at the Reformation, but the seasons of abstinence and feasting were not greatly affected.

There was no clear separation between ecclesiastical and secular calendars. Christmas, for example, was a blend of devout churchgoing, civic ceremony, and popular bawdy. It was ushered in on St Thomas's Day (21 December), when the sheriffs, having heard mass at All Saints', Pavement, proclaimed the 'Yoole girthol': 'all manner of whores, thieves, dice-players, and all other unthrifty folk be welcome to the towne . . . at the reverence of the high feast of Yoole'. On the same day it was the custom that 'two disguised persons called Yule and Yules wief should ryde thorow the citie vere undecentlie and uncomelie drawing great concourse of people after them to gaise, often times committinge other enormities'. Such, at least, was the description of the riding given by the purse-lipped Ecclesiastical Commissioners when they abolished the ceremony in 1572, calling it 'a very rude and barbarouse custome mainteyned in this Citie and in no other citie or town of this realme to our knowledge'. One would have welcomed a more detailed account of what seems to have been a fascinating pagan survival.[8]

Christmas Eve was celebrated with music, again linked with the old pagan names. James Ryther recorded in 1589 that in many parts of Yorkshire, and especially in York, 'they crie Yule Yule . . . against their principall feaste', adding in explanation, 'they call

6. Borthwick (Institute), (York), MSS. R VII G32, C1037; *Y. C. R.*, V, 89; A. Hanham, *Richard III and his Early Historians 1483–1535* (Oxford, 1975), p. 36fn.
7. E. Brunskill, 'Missals, portifers and pyes', in *The Ben Johnson Papers*, II, ed. B. P. Johnson (privately pr., York, 1974), separately paginated 1–36.
8. Drake, *Eboracum*, p. 197; J. S. Purvis, *Tudor Parish Documents of the Diocese of York* (Cambridge, 1948), pp. 172–73; *Y.C.R.*, VII, 55.

Christmas Yule and use yt after carrolls, but most on the even at their doors'. It was an 'ancient' custom by 1524 that the city waits played at the mayor's house on Christmas Eve and the feast itself, transferring on St Stephen's Day to the 'eldest' alderman and then working through the bench in order of seniority. The feast itself was of course honoured with special church services, and even after the Reformation 25 and 26 December remained the only two consecutive days in the year when the Corporation attended services in full regalia. Even in the Minster, however, pagan survivals and the 'misrule' of the festive season were present. Mistletoe was placed on the high altar on Christmas Eve, and the custom of electing a boy bishop from among the choristers continued until 1537. Twelfth Night was doubtless observed as a popular festival, and the rural custom of feasting on Plough Monday, the Monday after Twelfth Night, was certainly kept up in the city's satellite villages as a prelude to winter ploughing.[9]

The Christmas season ended with Candlemas (2 February) which was shortly followed by Shrove Tuesday. The universal custom of a celebration on the eve of Lent was so much accepted that there is little record except of practices which, like the Yule Riding, were under attack. The custom banned in the seventeenth century, by which apprentices and journeymen had climbed one of the Minster towers every Shrove Tuesday to ring the 'Pancake Bell', suggests a relic of an ancient carnival and was paralleled in many towns and villages. Lent itself remained a time of austerity both before and after the Reformation, at least to the extent that meat-eating was forbidden and offenders punished; and in the fifteen-thirties the Lenten demand for fish was such that Suffolk fishermen found it worthwhile to rent shops in York for the season. In the fifteen-eighties however, Fr Mush alleged that the well-to-do were generally eating meat in Lent under the pretence of fish dishes, and it may be that the traditional prohibition was being increasingly flouted.[10]

The other major festivals of the Christian year, such as Easter, Whitsunday, and Trinity Sunday, were of course occasions for special services; and all the major local feasts fell into the same period. John Wilson recorded the special days celebrated at York before the Reformation as the Translation and Deposition of St William (8 January and 8 June), the Elevation and Deposition of St

9. British Library, Lansdowne MSS 119, fol. 112v; Y.C.A., MSS B10, fols 109–10; B30, fol. 303r; T.W.B., 'York boy bishops', *Y(orkshire) A(rchaeological) J(ournal)*, XII, 400; F. R. Fairbank, 'York boy bishops', *Y.A.J.*, XII, 497–88; *Y. C. R.*, IV, 117; A. R. Wright, *British Calendar Customs,* e.d. T. E. Lones, Folk-Lore Society (3 vols, 1936–40), III, 93–103, 194–97, 225.

10. Wright, *British Calendar Customs*, I, 13–15; *Y.C.R.*, IV, 4; Y.C.A., MS C3, 1535–36 book, pp. 99, 105; 1538–39 book, fol. 21r; *The Troubles of Our Catholic Forefathers*, ed. J. Morris (3 vols, 1872–77), III, 435.

Oswald (15 April and 28 February), St Bosa's Day (9 March) and the Deposition of St Sewall (18 May), but he mentioned no similar feasts in the second half of the year. The ritualistic half-year concluded with several feasts in which, as at Christmas, liturgy, civic ceremonial, and popular merry-making were combined. St George's Day was celebrated by a play, procession and sermon held on St George's field; Rogationtide was observed at York under the name of 'Cross Week', with special processions until they were banned at the Reformation; and the city parishes, like their rural neighbours, beat the parish bounds on Ascension Day. On Corpus Christi Day the craft gilds between them performed the fifty-two plays of the great York cycle of miracle plays. On the morrow of the feast the consecrated elements, housed in a jewelled silver-gilt shrine, were carried in procession from Holy Trinity Priory to the Minster and St Leonard's Hospital. The procession was led by the clergy of the Corpus Christi Gild, but the mayor, city councillors, and craft gilds also took part, and the householders along the route were expected to decorate their house fronts with bed-coverings and to strew rushes and flowers before their doors. Finally the Eve and Feast of St John the Baptist (23 and 24 June) were celebrated as Midsummer Eve and Day, with services, bonfires, and the annual feast of the drapers' and tailors' gild, of which the Baptist was the patron saint.[11]

The only regular day of rest was Sunday. Corporation and gilds had for long combined to prohibit normal working on Sundays: Sabbatarianism was of course not a Protestant innovation. The major difference was in the observance of festivals, which were reduced after the fifteen-thirties. The average working year in Europe before the Reformation has been estimated at 200 days, though William Harrison's figure for England seems to come to 255, a figure which had increased by Elizabeth's reign to 280. The Corporation gradually changed their attitude to festal holidays as their religion became more Protestant. In 1561 they performed the Corpus Christi plays as usual, though dressing 'in semely sadd apparell and not in skarlet' since the feast was no longer 'kept holy day'. By 1587 they had abandoned all such Catholic festivals, and they even agreed to prevent begging on surviving red-letter days 'bycause it soundeth of popery'. As a small compensation for the loss of Catholic feasts, a number of consciously Protestant celebrations were substituted, but the only one introduced in Elizabeth's reign was the anniversary of her accession, celebrated on the 'Queen's day' at York from the

11. J. Wilson, *The English Martyrologe* (1608, repr. Amsterdam & New York, 1970), pp. 7–8, 55–56, 64–65, 97–98, 130–31, 151–52; *Y.C.R.*, III, 14; IV, 109, 150; V, 105–06, 120, 182; Wright, *British Calendar Customs*, I. 137; R. Davies, *Extracts from the Municipal Records of the City of York* (1843), pp. 245–49; B. P. Johnson, *The Acts and Ordinances of the Company of Merchant Taylors in the City of York* (York, 1949), pp. 18–33, 53.

fifteen-seventies. It was important to be quite clear what feasts were observed, for the city fathers were not alone in keeping special clothes to wear. Many an ordinary citizen, as his or her will shows, possessed two sets of clothes, one for workdays and one for holy days.[12]

The Corporation kept their own seasonal observances, often associated with sacred or popular feasts. The civic year may be said to have begun during the Christmas season, when on St. Maurus's Day (15 January) a new mayor, chamberlains, and bridge-masters were elected in the Common Hall. On St Blaise's Day (3rd February) the council and commons again met in the hall, when the mayor-elect took his oath of office, and the councillors, officers and commons took their oath to him. After his installation, the new mayor gave a venison feast for the councillors and some of the commons. The summer was a quieter period, with no major civic ceremonies except for an obscure custom called the Fishing Day, held variously in June, July, or August, and probably an assertion of the Corporation's powers as conservators of the river Ouse. The river was ceremonially fished in one or more civic barges, and the catch was made the occasion for a special dinner. Then came the election of the city's two sheriffs on St Matthew's Day (21 September), followed by their installation at Michaelmas, on which day the retiring sheriffs gave a feast for the councillors. In the autumn, usually in October or early November, the mayor and aldermen were expected to lead a contingent on horseback to ride the city's bounds. This ritual could be omitted because of flooding, but otherwise its regular observance was considered an important safeguard in demonstrating the city's territorial rights. In 1566 the citizens requested, and obtained, a revival of the practice 'for that we may know our lybertyes and loose no part of our ryght'. This ceremonial demarcation of the bounds was followed by a demonstration of the city's rights within those bounds, known as the sheriffs' riding. A few days after Martinmas (11 November) the sheriffs, with the city waits playing before them and a following of citizens and gentry, rode through the main streets, making an ancient proclamation about law and order, and concluding with a feast. A month later it was again the sheriffs who proclaimed the feast of Yule and so ushered in another year.

Not enough studies of urban calendars have been made to show how typical York's may have been. At Coventry, Mr Phythian-Adams has persuasively argued, the year was divided between a ritualistic and a secular half, the former (24 December–24 June) containing almost all the major civic events as well as major religious

---

12. W. Harrison, *Description of England in Shakespere's Youth*, ed. F. J. Furnivall, New Shakespere Society (2 vols, 1908), I, 32; *Y.C.R.*, VI, 17; VIII, 159.

observances, the latter being marked only by the elections of officers not representing the whole community, such as gild masters, and by ceremonies linking town and country like riding the bounds.[13] At York the distinction seems less clear-cut at the secular level. If most civic officials were elected in the winter, the sheriffs were chosen in September; if the rural riding of the bounds was an autumn ceremony as at Coventry, so too was the sheriffs' riding through the streets. Moreover, craft gild ordinances drawn up before 1550 stipulate elections of officers at various dates between 7 January and 18 October, with no preponderance in any one season. It is true, however, that after the Reformation the Corporation and the gilds did begin to concentrate such activities in the summer. Of twenty sets of gild ordinances drawn up between 1551 and 1600, fourteen stipulated that the annual election meeting should be held either on St James's Day (25 July) or on the Monday before or after.

By Elizabeth's reign measurement of time was becoming more systematic. Parish registers were accustoming the citizens to precision with life-spans, and printing and the impact of the Reformation were popularizing the more regular division of years into months and days. Furthermore, an increase in the number and precision of clocks was allowing the hours of the day to be measured more carefully. The innovation was gradual and scarcely perceptible. Already in 1479 there were chiming clocks at the civic chapel on Ouse Bridge and at All Saints Church, Pavement, and the opening times for the city gates were expressed in hours by 1482. Clockmakers were, however, few and far between, and normally combined their occupation with other part-time work. After John Rypplay in the mid-fifteenth century, who apparently made church clocks over a wide area, no freeman was admitted as a clockmaker until Robert Platters in 1591–92. John Newsome, who repaired the Ouse Bridge clock in 1593, had taken up freedom as a locksmith, while the clocksmith John Wilson who died in the plague of 1604 does not appear in the freemen's register as such. Furthermore the early clocks were not true striking clocks, but were attached to bells rung by hand. In 1576 William Greneup was paid to keep the Ouse Bridge clock and to ring a bell daily, 'at fyve of the cloke in wynter and foure of the clocke in summer by the space of a quarter of an hower'. Knowledge of the time, especially at night, probably still depended on the occasional round of the bellman or the city waits; one of the waits possessed in 1558 a 'lowde trible pipe' that he 'plaide the morne watches withe'. Church bells remained, however, the normal means of marking service-times and other special events. A parish meeting, even an illegal one like a gathering of resisters

---

13. C. Phythian-Adams, 'Ceremony and the citizen', in *Crisis and Order in English Towns 1500–1700*, ed. P. Clarke and P. Slack (1972), pp. 57–85.

to the poor rate, would be summoned by a church bell, while a ceremonial occasion like a royal visit was marked by a peal from all the churches together: 'it was grett melodie for to here the bells rynge thorough the cite', as an officer attending Princess Margaret recorded in 1503.[14]

The existence of clocks, however, allowed an increasing precision in organizing the working day, by what Jacques le Goff has called 'merchant's time'. In 1585 the city fathers agreed to 'keepe their houre in this House at eight of the clocke in the morninge', paying a 2*d.* fine if they arrived by 8.30 a.m. and 4*d.* if later still. The hour of rising was naturally early in summer when daylight was so important. In the fifteen-forties a mass on Foss Bridge chapel was advanced from 11 a.m. to 4 a.m. 'by the advice of the parishioners there, as well as for their commodity as travelling people', and in 1581 a wedding was held in St Michael-le-Belfrey just after 5 a.m. 'then and ther beinge a sufficyent congregation'. The defensive wording suggests that weddings were rarely held so early, but the citizens would certainly be up by that time, as at Coventry, where the day-bell was rung at 4 a.m. daily. The normal times of opening and closing the city gates, winter and summer, were 5 a.m. and 9 p.m. (the comparable hours at Coventry were 4 a.m. and 9 p.m.) and in legal theory wage-earners were at work from 5 a.m. to 7 or 8 p.m. between March and September. There is little evidence of the actual hours worked in York, but water-carriers were in 1578 forbidden to work between 10 p.m. on Saturdays and 5 a.m. on Mondays, which certainly suggests a long day as well as growing Sabbatarianism.[15]

II

Consciousness of the passage of time was closely bound up with consideration of diet and health. The day was regulated by meal-times as much as by church services or clock time, and the year by seasons of feasting and fasting closely related to the availability of food.

14. *York Memorandum Book*, ed. M. Sellers, Surtees Society, cxx and cxxv (2 vols, 1912–15), I, 171–72, 223; *Y.C.R.*, I, 65; VII, 138; VIII, 37; Borthwick, MS Y/HEL 1, entry dated 28 Aug. 1604; Borthwick, prob. reg. 15. pt. 2, fol. 291r; *Drake, Eboracum*, app., p. xix.
15. Y.C.R., I, 65; V, 48; VIII, 93; *Y.C.A.*, MSB27, fol. 70v: *Registers of St. Michael le Belfrey, York*, I, ed. F. Collins, Yorkshire Parish Register Society (1899), p. 35; *Certificates of the Commissioners appointed to Survey the Chantries . . . in the County of York*, ed. W. Page, Surtees Society, XCI and XCII (2 vols, 1894–95), 61; C. Phythian-Adams, *Desolation of a City* (Cambridge, 1979), pp. 74–76.

Death and sickness were all too common, whether produced by disease or by malnutrition or both, and many of the epidemic diseases had a seasonal incidence which added its own grim rhythm to the cycle of ceremonies and festivals.

Food supplies were always uncertain in a large Tudor city, incapable of feeding itself from its own common fields and smallholdings. In normal times supplies from York's rural hinterland, with its varied arable, pasture, marsh, and fen, were adequate, but a bad harvest could leave the farmers with no surplus to sell, while an epidemic in York would frighten them away from its markets, as the plagues of 1550 and 1604 undoubtedly did. Supplies became chronically uncertain towards the end of Elizabeth's reign, as the effects of population pressure and inflation made food more expensive in real terms, and almost unobtainable after a bad harvest, when the local countryside had no grain to spare for the hungry city. In 1586–87, and again in 1596–97, famine followed disastrous harvests, and during the latter crisis York was importing grain from Nottinghamshire, Leicestershire, and even from overseas.

The townsmen nearest to self-sufficiency in food were the owner and lessees of closes outside the walls, and the freemen as a whole. The freemen enjoyed permanent pasture rights over some common land, notably Knavesmire and Hob Moor, and rights of average over more extensive areas, allowing them to graze animals after the harvest, usually from Michaelmas to Lady Day. In 1547 sixty-four citizens petitioned against restrictions on their rights, arguing that they 'and the moste parte of the power [poor] comminalitie of the said Citie ar not habill to mayntayn there famelie and household unlesse that they may have there said common'. The point was apparently taken, and thereafter the Corporation made fewer attempts to enclose the commons. The pasturage enabled freemen to keep cattle both for meat and milk: a tanner bequeathed to his grandchildren 'my cowe to gyve them mylke with all'. Non-freemen could occasionally be granted pasture rights as a privilege, like the vicar of All Saints, North Street, who was too poor to buy the franchise but was permitted to keep two cows on Knavesmire to maintain his family. The freemen usually herded their cattle back from the commons each evening, driving them through the narrow streets, as James Ryther complained in 1589; and the inventory of James Taylour's Walmgate tenement mentions a 'kowe house' attached. Few non-freemen could keep cattle, but pigs were apparently an alternative for many; they were kept in sties even in the city centre, and allowed to roam the streets scavenging, despite repeated prohibitions. The townsmen could also, if they possessed backyards, enjoy their own poultry, eggs, and honey. One vicar of St Maurice's owned six bee-hives, and Taylour's house included, besides the cowshed, a cock and seven hens – listed among the goods in the kitchen, which was probably a detached structure at the rear.[16]

A list of foods and drinks available in York could readily be compiled, but what is almost entirely lacking is any indication of normal diets. The menus for the dining-hall of the Minster vicars choral do exist for the last eleven years that they ate together in hall (1563–74), but of course they were a small well-to-do and untypical group. Meat, fish, wheat (for bread), and malt (for ale or beer) were bought in large quantities, and the general impression of their diet, like that of contemporary aristocratic households, is of 'huge quantities of meat and bread washed down in oceans of beer and wine'.[17] As this was typical of the servants' diet as well as their masters', it could well be that servants in the richer citizens' homes also enjoyed plenty of meat, though the poor as a whole probably had little, and that largely rabbit or pigeon, judging from the frequent references to coneysellers and dovecotes.

Bread-grain was certainly an index of wealth and social rank: the prosperous ate wheaten bread, but rye was the staple breadcorn of the vale of York, and as late as 1677 ordinary household bread was 'made of rye, and . . . coarse and black'. At the other extreme, York bakers produced a special wheaten loaf, highly prized and often given to distinguished visitors. Thomas Coghan, writing in 1584, thought that 'we have as good wheate in Englande . . . as may be founde in any countrie in all Europe, and as good bread is made thereof, especially that of Yorke, which they call maine bread'. It is therefore surprising that by 1595 mayne bread had been almost displaced by a new fashion for spiced cakes. The Corporation, mindful that mayne bread was not baked 'in any other city or place' and was 'one of the antientest matters of novelty to present men of honour, and others repairing to this city', ordered ten shillings' worth to be baked weekly, and promised to buy it themselves for lack of other customers. Fashions are, however, rarely prevented by sumptuary laws, and in the early seventeenth century mayne bread gave way to spiced cakes despite its patronage by James I.[18]

Pulses, peas, and beans were all grown in Yorkshire in sufficient quantity to be shipped outwards from Hull, but diets remained generally deficient in fresh fruit and vegetables, and vitamin

16. *Y.C.R.*, I, 38; IV, 89, 161–63; V, 23, 25, 129; Y.C.A., MS. B32, fol. 18r; Borthwick original probate inventories of J. Taylour 1574, A. Adam 1578; Borthwick, probate reg. 14, fol. 51r; D. M. Palliser, 'A hostile view of Elizabethan York', *York Historian*, I (1976), p. 21.
17. Y(ork) M(inster) L(ibrary), Vicars Choral Kitchen Book; L. Stone, *The Crisis of the Aristocracy 1558–1641* (Oxford, 1965), p. 559.
18. *York as they Saw It*, ed. D. and M. Palliser (York, 1979), p. 25; T. Coghan, *The Haven of Health* (1584), p. 23; R. Davies, *Walks through the City of York* (1880), pp. 253–57.

deficiency diseases like scurvy and pellagra must have been common. However there were always some gardens with apple and pear trees, and a group of obscure 'sellars of apples' in the streets, while in 1601–02 the first 'costerdmonger' was admitted to the franchise, a sign of a slow improvement in eating habits. Indeed, York is considered by the historian of early gardening to be the 'earliest important centre of nursery gardening' in England, not excluding Oxford. A Corporation lease of 1541, requiring the tenant 'to graft and set fruyt treys . . . and to leyff them growing of the sayd grownd' at the expiry of the lease, he considers especially significant, and there is some evidence that the market gardening of fruit and vegetables, for which Stuart York was noted, originated directly from the orchards of dissolved religious houses like the Blackfriars. Seed vegetables were certainly being bought at York by local villagers as early as the fifteen-nineties.[19]

Drink, like breadcorn, was partly a measure of social status. Presents to visiting dignitaries often included a tun or hogshead of imported wine, but the normal drink for most citizens was ale or beer. Complaints about excessive maltmaking and brewing after 1540, and the existence of 83 brewers and 122 alehousekeepers by the fifteen-nineties, suggest a high consumption of both drinks; and it must be remembered that the figures probably understate their popularity, for much brewing, as with baking, was done in the home. Some 'crab mills' in Jubbergate probably served for cider-making as a cheaper alternative to ale. For the very poor there was of course water, though only the wealthy had private wells, and the rivers were polluted; many citizens relied on water-carriers for their supplies.[20]

The diet of the poor was not only monotonous but uncertain; and inadequate food produced malnutrition, disease, or even death from starvation. Death-rates often exceeded birth-rates in any event, but superimposed on this unhealthy pattern were the major epidemics, which so often followed a run of bad harvests, as in 1520–22, 1550–52 and 1558–58. It is true that the nationwide famines of 1587 and 1597–98 did not produce a heavy rise in mortality, but even then York was certainly suffering shortage of grain, and a few inhabitants did die of starvation, while many others may have suffered great privations. The poor were at all times more vulnerable to illness, whether through lack of food or through the lower resistance to disease produced by malnutrition or by crowded and unhygienic living conditions; and the gap may have widened in Elizabeth's reign as the rich improved their standards of housing and diet. The epidemics

---

19. J. Harvey, *Early Nurserymen* (1974), p. 63; *Y.C.R.*, IV, 72; *The Victoria History of the County of York East Riding*, ed. K. J. Allison, III (1976), 195.
20. Palliser, *Tudor York*, p. 167; Raine, *Mediaeval York*, p. 164.

of the early Tudor period, and the terrible 'new ague' of 1558–59, struck rich and poor alike, carrying off city councillors and senior clergy as well as lesser folk, despite the attempts of some councillors to save themselves by flight. It is noteworthy, however, that the bubonic plague of 1604 no longer had such a levelling effect. Whereas twenty-four city councillors died in the decade 1501– 10, many apparently of epidemic disease, and twelve in the disastrous year of 1558, only two, Alderman Trew and Councillor William Wood, died in 1604, a year that saw 30 per cent of the population die; and even of those Trew's can be dismissed as not an epidemic death. He, and Alderman Brooke's widow, were significantly among the handful of parishioners of All Saints, Pavement, not described as 'infectid' in the list of burials for 1604–05.

Epidemics can easily distract attention from the high death-rate even in plague-free times. Numerous diseases and infections which killed, crippled or at least impaired health and working efficiency must have been constantly present, though the parish burial registers are not helpful in identifying them. Only the illnesses of city councillors and officials were recorded systematically, and even then the cause was rarely noted, except for two cases of severe gout and frequent mention of infirmity through old age. The Elizabethan Corporation's poor relief measures did, however, include frequent financial or medical help for the sick or crippled, and this source furnishes examples of the common afflictions of the time. Apart from several cases of lameness and unspecified 'impotency', there was a poor man 'having the Frensh pocke' (syphilis), 'a poore wenshe which hath hir fete allmoste rotted of', and two men with sore legs; one was to have his leg cut by surgeons, and another to be paid to travel to the hot baths at Buxton.[21]

Medical care was rudimentary, and most townsmen must have relied on herbs, traditional remedies, orthodox prayer, the unorthodox consulting of 'cunning men', or simply on Nature's healing power. Elementary treatment like bleeding could be carried out by the barber surgeons: ninety-three barbers, surgeons or barber-surgeons (the terms were almost interchangeable) were admitted to the franchise in the sixteenth century, together with sixteen apothecaries, who made up prescriptions for doctors. The doctors of medicine, or physicians, scarcely figure in the freemen's register; only four were admitted, the last being Dr Stephen Thomson (1528– 29), physician to the sixth Earl of Northumberland. The doctors were certainly a select group whose small number and high fees

---

21 Y.C.A., MS B9, fol. 63V, B13, fol. 115V; *Y.C.R.*, VII, 147; VIII, 2; M. C. Barnet, 'The barber-surgeons of York', *Medical History*, XII (1968), 24–25.

would have put their services beyond the reach of most townsfolk, but they were not so few as the register implies, for most lived in St Peter's Liberty out of the city jurisdiction, and practised among the clergy, lawyers and visiting gentry. They included Dr Stephen Tuble, a city chamberlain in 1556–67, Dr Thomas Vavasour of Ogleforth, a recusant who appears to have exercised a mission among women frequenting his 'maternity clinic', as Mr Aveling calls it, and Dr Roger Lee, another recusant. Both Vavasour and Lee are naturally better recorded for their religious than their professional activities, but Lee is also known for his common sense in sending sickly patients out of the city to recover in better air. Another was 'Mr Lister', whom Sir Thomas and Lady Hoby of Hackness consulted regularly on their visits to York in 1599 and 1600. He was a family confidant as well as doctor, prescribing 'phesicke' and bloodletting, and listening while Lady Margaret talked 'of some of my greves'.[22]

A more surprising choice of medical adviser was Robert Maskew, alderman and grocer, who was frequently commissioned by the Corporation. He was, however, an apothecary as well as a grocer (the two trades often went together), and his colleagues may have preferred one of their own number to supervise cases in which they were involved. In 1578 he was instructed to examine an alleged case of French pox in collaboration with three surgeons, but later he often acted alone. In 1584 he was paid by his colleagues for curing three sick women, one of them, 'Katherine Myers otherwise called Fond Kate', being perhaps deranged. In 1585 he was commissioned to treat one Johnson's wife of an unspecified dangerous disease, and later was paid 30s. for 'curing' and housing her, though she was now said to have died.[23]

Medical knowledge was especially inadequate when faced by mental illness, and drastic remedies were tried in an almost experimental spirit. Henry Relfe, being 'distracted', was in 1593 to be kept and relieved at the city's expense, but also to be whipped 'to se if by that means he will be brought to be more quiet'. Like several other 'distracted' men and women, he was kept at the 'Bean Hills', a prison in the disused Fishergate Bar which specialized in housing lunatics. Another 'distrect' woman was kept at the city's charge in St Thomas's Hospital, while in 1598 two men were paid

---

22. *Y.C.R.*,V, 122 ('Tuble' misprinted 'Turle'); VII, 132; J. C. H. Aveling, *Catholic Recusancy in the City of York 1558–1791*, Catholic Record Society (1970), entries indexed under Lee, Vavasour; *The Topographer and Genealogist*, II, pp. 407–08; *Diary of Lady Margaret Hoby 1599–1605*, ed. D. M. Meads (1930), pp. 73, 113–15, 146–47.

23. *Y.C.R.*, VII, 182; Y.C.A., MS B28, fols 143r. 175r; B29, fols, 29r, 63r.

by the Corporation 'for watching Roberte Morton, being sick and distracted, and for keeping of him in his house, and from doing himself harme . . . till it was known what his sicknesse was'.[24]

It was not always possible to prevent the insane from doing themselves harm, though suicide was apparently rare. The only recorded case in a councillor's family was that of Katherine, widow of Councillor Thomas Dawson. Thomas had died in the autumn of 1539, and in the following March Katherine 'of a devyllisshe mynde and entent dyd . . . wilfully and felonsly slay and murder herself'. Her share of Thomas's estate was thereby forfeit to the Corporation, though the children were allowed to keep their portions. A sample of every tenth year's ancient indictments in the court of King's Bench, which should include all deaths by violence, produced only two cases of suicide, both in 1584. Such a number for the whole of York over ten years sampled would imply a suicide rate of only about 2 per 100 000, but plainly the sample is much too small for reliability, and one suspects that other suicides were charitably concealed as accidental deaths.[25]

The King's Bench sample may not have statistical validity, but it does yield examples of the risk of sudden death to which the men of a crowded and unhygienic city, with swords and daggers freely available, were exposed. The five inquests of 1532–33 all involved sudden deaths of prisoners in the castle gaol, which must have been especially unhealthy that year: two died of agues, one of a 'frauncye', and one female prisoner of 'the woman's felon'. Accidental deaths were of two men drowned in the Ouse and Foss while washing themselves, a labourer overcome by foul air while scouring a well for Christopher Harbert, and a girl servant scalded by falling into a vat while brewing. Verdicts were also returned on three men killed in affrays and brawls in the streets of the city, and an illegitimate baby suffocated and strangled by its mother. The Star Chamber records for Henry VIII's reign include several cases of manslaughter or attempted manslaughter in affrays, like the servant or servants killed in a fight in Aldwark between the retainers of rival gentry, or the lawyer attacked without warning at his inn in Micklegate who was saved because his cries brought help from the adjacent house – an incidental testimony to the thinness of partition walls. One may make allowance for exaggeration in accusations of attempted murder, but the general picture is of an armed citizenry where woundings or deaths were ever-present threats. Fewer such

---

24. *Y.C.R.*, VIII, 51; Y.C.A., MS B31, fols 40r, 388V; Raine, *Mediaeval York*, p. 299.
25. *Y.C.R.*, IV, 39, 52; P(ublic) R(ecord) O(ffice), KB9/661, fols 72–73.

cases are known for Elizabeth's reign, but that may reflect only the availability of sources for the earlier period.[26]

The usual form of violence or threatened violence was of wounding with the nearest available weapon, but another fairly common threat was to burn down one's enemy's house, an easy enough task with a timber-framed structure. No actual case of successful arson is recorded, but the Corporation had to impose numerous recognizances binding enemies not to do so. The earliest such recognizances noted were imposed in 1532 and 1545 on six citizens, four of them aldermen or future aldermen; and once the surviving quarter sessions books begin in 1560 larger numbers are recorded. Two samples have yielded 265 pairs of such recognizances in the quinquennium 1571–75, and 198 in 1591–95.[27]

Policing was inadequate, but it seems to have been sufficient to prevent a breakdown of law and order except when faced by large numbers of rioters or rebels. Besides the parish constables, there were the serjeants of the mayor and sheriffs on hand to impose the peace or to make summary arrests. Those accused of crimes would be prosecuted before the sheriffs' court, the city petty or quarter sessions, or the city or county assizes, and if convicted of capital offences were liable to be hanged at Tyburn on Knavesmire, the gallows for both city and county. Those in exempt jurisdictions, however, had the dubious pleasure of separate gallows, a privilege zealously maintained by the medieval religious houses and their successors. St Mary's gallows in Burton Stone Lane, and St Leonard's at Garrow Hill, were both in use even after the dissolutions, while two men were hanged in Marygate in 1594–95 'for killing of Mr Farley', presumably on another gallows of St Mary's Liberty.[28]

For those awaiting trial, or convicted of non-capital offences, there was again a parallel system of prisons. Tenants of the extensive liberty of the Minster chapter could be imprisoned in Peter Prison, while until about 1580 the archbishop maintained a separate prison for criminous clergy. Another prison for clergy was housed in St Leonard's Hospital until the dissolution. Most convicted laymen, however, were committed to the royal prisons. The principal one, housed in the Castle, was for offenders from the whole county and could be so crowded as to be extremely unhealthy. In 1581 'gaol fever' or typhus killed nineteen prisoners, and in 1606 the total

26. PRO. KB9/490, fol. 60;/523, fols 41, 76;/585, fol. 216;/607, fols 104–05;/636, fol. 201;/660, fol. 89;/661, fols 70–71; *Yorkshire Star Chamber Proceedings*, ed. W. Brown *et al.*, Yorks. Arch. Soc. Record Series (4 vols, 1909–27), II, 67–73; III, 128–31.

27. Y.C.A., MS B11, fol. 116v; B17, fols 84v, 89r; F2, F3 and F6 *passim*.

28. R. B. Pugh, 'Prisons and gallows', in *The Victoria History of the County of York: the City of York*, ed. P. M. Tillott (1961), pp. 497–98; Bodleian Library, Oxford, MS Gough 8, p. 119.

prison population exceeded 140. Perhaps it was overcrowding at the Castle which persuaded the Council in the North to commit some prisoners to Davy Hall instead, as they did after the exposure of the Wakefield Plot in 1541. The Corporation's main prisons, nicknamed the Kidcotes, were housed on Ouse Bridge: the sheriffs' kidcotes (one for men and one for women) were mainly for felons, and the mayor's (again one for each sex) for debtors. Many recusants were also imprisoned in the kidcotes, and some have left descriptions of the terrible conditions there; but as in all Tudor prisons money could buy relative comfort. The prisoners in the chambers over the Exchequer on Ouse Bridge were allowed as a privilege to retain those chambers on payment of 3s. 4d. a year 'during their naturall liefs, if they be not delyvered or discharged of their imprisonment'. The pressure on space became acute, however, partly because of the number of imprisoned recusants, and from the fifteen-seventies and 'eighties several smaller civic prisons were established within two of the city bars and elsewhere. Like many other cities, York found its stone gates and towers too useful to be kept exclusively for military defence; the use of town gates as prisons can be paralleled at London, Chester, Durham, Newcastle, and Oxford.[29]

Whatever the risks to life and health from crime, they must have been much greater from the squalid and insanitary conditions in which most citizens lived. The point should not, perhaps, be over-laboured. Contemporary travellers did not complain of the squalor of York, indicating at least that it was not significantly worse than that of London or other large cities; and the frequent references to rubbish-dumping occur almost entirely in repeated corporation by-laws forbidding such offences. Certainly the very repetitions are a warning against equating legislation with enforcement; but equally they indicate a city council far from complacent about sanitary conditions. The city fathers were well aware of the connection between dirt and disease. When plague struck in 1550 their first thought was to punish those keeping swine within the walls, and in the spring of 1600 they expressed concern that many parishioners were refusing to 'sweep their doors weekly', fearing 'that if the same be no better cleansed when warm wether comes inne then yt hath bene this winter tyme, that infeccon may growe therby'.[30]

Street-cleansing and street-lighting services remained minimal throughout the Tudor period, though there is evidence of gradual and hesitant improvements. Water supply, despite schemes for piped

29. Pugh in *VCH York*, pp. 492–93, 496–97; *Y.C.R.*, IV. 8; VII, 99; VIII, 90, 130, 135; Y.C.A., MS B31, fol. 372; B32, fol. 218V; *Letters and Papers, Henry VIII*, XVI, no. 875; *Belfrey Registers*, ed. Collins, I, 25; H(istorical) M(anuscripts) C(ommission), *Ormonde Manuscripts*, p. 117; *Miscellanea: Resusant Records*, ed. C. Talbot, Catholic Record Society (1961), p. 277.
30. *Y.C.R.*, V, 28; Y.C.A., MS B32, fol. 78br.

water, continued to depend on carriage from wells and the rivers. There were, it is true, a number of public conveniences – 'houses of ease' or 'necessary houses' – at the bars, on Ouse Bridge and elsewhere, but they were scarcely adequate for a city averaging perhaps 10 000 people. The lack of refinement in public can be glimpsed in a mason's artless explanation of how he had been robbed while playing at dice in the 'Dragon' in Lop Lane: 'when he had played asmoch as he wolde, he . . . layd oon pece of golde upon the borde . . . and went to the dore to make watre . . . and at his commyng ayen from the dore his pece of gold was gone'. The passage of a century, however, witnessed a growing demand for privacy and modesty; in 1600 the Corporation were demanding 'that a portall of wainscott shalbe mayd in the inner howse at the common hall before the pissinge hole ther'.[31]

III

By the end of the century, also, growing wealth and demand for comfort had led to better standards of housing, at least for the wealthier and middling citizens. The combined evidence of documentary references and of surviving buildings indicates one active period of house-building in the latter half of the fifteenth century, and another beginning in the last quarter of the sixteenth, separated by seventy years or so in which very little took place. The survey of Micklegate and its side-streets by the Royal Commission on Historical Monuments records four groups of houses datable to the late fifteenth century and the row 85–89 Micklegate, probably erected by Holy Trinity Priory about 1500. It also lists numerous houses of the late sixteenth and early seventeenth centuries (the two are not always distinguishable) beginning with the Plumbers' Arms, Skeldergate, of about 1575. In between these two periods of activity, however, there is nothing recorded except for two houses in Micklegate, one of about 1530 and one of mid-century date. Documentary sources tell the same story. Numerous houses were rebuilt in the fifteenth century, but record has been found of only ten rebuilt between 1500 and 1570, chiefly by aldermen and other wealthy citizens. After that, such records become more numerous, and over 30 new houses are mentioned between 1571 and 1600.[32]

---

31. *Y.C.R.*, I, 106, misprinting 'watre' as 'ware'; Y.C.A, MS B32, fol. 77r.
32. Royal Commission on Historical Monuments, *An Inventory of the Historical Monuments of the City of York*, III (1972), passim; D. M. Palliser, 'Some aspects of the social and economic history of York in the sixteenth century' (unpub. D. Phil. thesis, Oxford Univ. 1968). pp. 349–50, 394A–C.

A time-lag has frequently been observed between getting and spending, and the almost complete absence of new domestic building between about 1500 and 1570 is readily explicable in terms of York's early Tudor decay. It would explain the preference in many cases for minimal alterations rather than rebuilding, as when in 1574 a lease provided that the tenant 'should build the forefront a newe'. It was during Elizabeth's reign that towns like Shrewsbury and Exeter were building ostentatiously, while York was not only leaving the monastic sites vacant but was failing to maintain its existing stock of property. In 1587, in accordance with an act of 1540, the city council made proclamation on twenty-seven decayed houses or waste sites: they would confiscate the land unless the owners rebuilt. Yet only in five cases was the clerk able subsequently to add 'builded' in the margin of the list.[33]

The cost of a new house is given only occasionally, but it must have been considered expensive in relation to other forms of investment, since even the aldermen built little. Scraps of evidence suggest, however, that substantial repairs were very expensive in relation to the cost of a house. Around 1500 Thomas Darby sent a bill to the merchants' gild, whose tenant he had just ceased to be after thirty-eight years, saying that he had paid £76 rent for those years and £46 of his own money for repairs. He had also left behind in the house improvements worth £23 6s. 8d. The grand total of his expenses was £145 6s. 8d., he concluded forcibly, 'gwylk sum wolde by vj hals guds howssis als ytt ys'. In 1558 Alderman North, in his will, stated a ratio of repairs to value lower than Darby's but still very high. His dwelling house, he said, was worth 33s. 4d. a year, and his wife was to spend 20s. every two years on its repair.[34]

The high cost was partly accounted for by the almost universal use of oak as a building material. Some medieval stone houses remained in use, but almost all known Tudor housing was timber-framed, despite the fact that the more durable brick was spreading from Hull and the East Riding. Timber needed renewing more often, and it was also becoming scarcer as the Vale of York became denuded of its woodland. Margaret Walton was only prudent when she bequeathed a house to Suzanna Acklame together with 'tymber to maynteyne the same'. Stone was probably too costly a material for most citizens, and its only common use was for plinths ('ground soles') to protect the timber uprights from rotting, such as St Mary's Abbey planned for a new house in Bootham. Even after the Reformation, when the religious houses were being demolished and treated as quarries, no citizens' houses are known to have been built

33. Y.M.L., MS Acc. 1966/2, 19, fol. 24r; Y.C.A., MS B29, fols 207–08.
34. York Merchant Adventurers' Archives, MS D62; Borthwick, prob. reg. 15, pt. 2, fol. 289.

of re-used monastic stone, though the stone additions to the King's Manor, and the major town house which George Young built about 1600, probably used this source. At the other extreme of the social scale, there were perhaps still a few houses of cob or beaten mud. One house in Coney Street, described in 1491–92, had a stone wall to the Ouse but also plaster walls and 'mudde wallez'.[35]

Yet if most houses remained of traditional timber-framed type, they were often made more comfortable within through structural improvements and extra furnishings. Chimneys of bricks or stone, for example, allowed safe heating on each floor in houses of more than one storey, and landlords and neighbours were concerned to ensure their installation if there was a fire risk. Thus in 1578 a tenant of the merchants' gild was enjoined 'to take downe the mudd chymney . . . and to make it upp agayne with stone', while in the same year a Bootham man was presented by his neighbours 'for kepinge a fyer in his house without a chymney'.[36]

Another spreading improvement was the use of domestic window glass. The admissions of freemen glaziers imply an interval between the demand for church glass and a new demand for domestic windows; with one exception, no glazier was admitted between 1536 and 1552. Early references to domestic glazing show that it was scarce and moveable. A mayor's widow had taken glass windows from St Leonard's Hospital, and at her death in 1513 ordered them to be returned; a merchants' tenant, about 1550, was proud to have improved his house with 'a greatt baye wyndow of xiij[th] stanshons glasenedd' and 'a lesse windowe glasenede'. Even the Common Hall was only partly glazed in 1556, the other windows having wooden shutters; while some citizens at that period had only 'window cloths', and one Minster canon covered his principal windows with 'windewe clothes' and 'a carpit for a wyndewe'. Some freemen did without glasse windows at all until late in the century; the house of John Harper in Stonegate can have had no glazing in 1583 when he was disfranchised and ordered to shut up his shop windows, for he was told that 'if he will have any light then he to make a glass windowe'. Gradually, however, the more prosperous citizens of Elizabethan York patronized the glaziers, just as they replaced the painted 'haulyngs' or wall-hangings of their ancestors with wainscot panelling.[37]

35. Borthwick, prob. reg. 23, fol. 340; *Y.C.R.*, II, 150; Y.C.A., MS B7, fols 51v, 56v.
36. York Merchant Archives, MS D82; Y.C.A., MS E31, pt. 1, fol. 85r.
37. *Test(amenta) Ebor(acensia)*, ed. J Raine *et al.*, Surtees Society (6 vols, 1836–1902), V, 38; Raine, *Mediaeval York*, p. 142; York Merchants' Archives, MS D75; Borthwick, original probate inventories of T. Marser 1547, R. Hewton 1553, J. Tessimonde 1558 Y.C.A., Ms B28, fol. 99v.

Such improvements in housing standards for the richer citizens may well be not unconnected with their health. The fact that bubonic plague in 1604 largely spared the wealthy may be linked at least in part to better living conditions. On the other hand, the very heavy death-rate among the poor in that year could well reflect worsening housing standards. The population of York may have nearly doubled in Elizabeth's reign, and yet – as in the parallel cases of Worcester and Norwich – there was too little new housing to match the increase. Many poor were crammed into overcrowded tenements, or into rows of mean cottages and hovels in the backyards of the larger properties. Byelaws for York itself (1578) and for the satellite manor of Acomb (1581) aimed to reduce the problems caused by subtenants or 'undersettles' crowding into the 'fire houses' or dwellings of more substantial householders.[38]

IV

Yet the mass of the citizens remain, inevitably, shadowy creatures. The surviving archives, and visitors' accounts, have much to say of their physical and political environment, but the commonplaces of the human life that passed within them were naturally not a subject for comment, although court cases and wills may occasionally afford a glimpse as an incidental detail. The only description of the citizens on which southern visitors to York frequently ventured to comment was on their dialect. William of Malmesbury had complained in the twelfth century that York speech was 'so crude and discordant that we southerners cannot understand it', and although the differences narrowed in the later middle ages, the Corporation minutes for Henry VII's reign were still written in a gritty Northern speech. It is full of dialect words such as 'kirk' for church or 'lig' for lie, of expressions obsolete in the south like 'ilkan' for 'every one', and of consistent spellings reflecting a different pronunciation, such as 'hard' for heard.

By the reign of Elizabeth the language was approaching the norm of court and capital, though the accent spoken in the streets probably remained strong. As late as 1736 the York surgeon and historian Drake could complain that 'the common people speak English very ill; and have a strange affected pronunciation of some words, as *hoose, moose, coo*, for *house, mouse, cow* and so on'. The written records of Tudor York also represent a more conscious-

---

38. Palliser, *Tudor York*, pp. 133, 285; *Court Rolls of the Manor of Acomb*, I, ed. H. Richardson, Yorks. Arch. Soc. Rec. Series. CXXXI (1969), p. 72.

ly literary language than would have been spoken in conversation, and it is only in the occasional reporting of direct speech – especially of slander, insults and insubordination, where the exact wording was important – that something of the blunt and often earthy language of every day was allowed to intrude into the official records. Typical of many was the outburst of George Horsley, apparently on being brought before the sheriffs' court, 'that my lord mayor, his bredren and shyrryffs were more mete to dryve pyggs to the feyld than to be Justics of Peace, and saying if I had knowen this, they shuld have kyssed me of the hole of the arse or they shuld have broght me hydder'.[39]

The citizens' life-cycle, from cradle to grave, was punctuated by ceremonies and rituals, and marked by the acquisition and loss of family and kindred, and something of its reality can be glimpsed from the records. The new-born child's first *rite de passage* was the christening, performed as soon as possible after birth for fear of an early death. The christening provided the boy or girl with god-parents, or 'sponsors' as they were called after the Reformation, whom it is clear often became as close to them as blood-relatives; and it also furnished him or her with a name. Surnames were now almost always hereditary, though a few men bore alternative surnames, and one or two still followed the medieval practice of naming themselves from their father's Christian name. Councillor Thomas Dawson (c. 1482–1539) was also called Thomas Bartram after his father Alderman Bartram Dawson (d. 1516), while the stationer Thomas Newell was apparently the son of Newell or Neville Mores.

At the same time, Christian names were becoming more varied, partly perhaps to make individual identity clear as surnames became fixed. Of those ninety-five males admitted to the franchise in the decade 1500–10 (and therefore born about 1480–90), over two-thirds shared the three standard late-medieval names of William, John, and Thomas. The same three names were still the most popular among the 264 admitted between 1590 and 1600, but the proportion had dropped from 68 to 44 per cent, and names like James, Christopher, and Edward were becoming popular for the first time. Women's names similarly became more varied, the predominant Janes or Joans, Margarets and Isabels of early Tudor times sharing the field with a greater number of alternatives.[40] York was a large enough

39. *York as they Saw It*, ed. Pallisers, pp. 5, 38; Y.C.A., MS B18, fol. 9v. Characteristically, Raine's printed edition of the last entry (*Y.C.R.*, IV, 137) omits the second clause.

40. Parish registers have not been drawn on here, as they begin only c. 1540 and take account only of baptisms of natives. Male names were counted from the *Register of Freemen*, women's names from recorded wives of aldermen. Both sources are socially biased, but random mentions of poorer townsmen suggest that precisely the same names were popular among them.

city for a man to be difficult to identify without knowing both names, as the Council in the North discovered in 1596. The Privy Council had ordered them to search for 'one Greene, a tall black man, dwelling in the city of York', and a harbourer of Jesuits and priests. As they supplied no Christian name, the President's men searched the houses of all the Greens they could trace – four in all – only to find them all 'very conformable to her Majesty's laws'.[41]

The high level of infant mortality was accepted, like epidemics, as an inevitable fact of life, and only occasionally did an expression of grief or resignation find record. One man reminded his wife in his will of 'some children she knowethe I had by hir, I thanke the Lord my God for them, and He hayth also taiken them from us againe, I geve Hym lyke hartie thankes'. Conversely, many children who survived were orphaned, and brought up either by guardians or by a surviving parent who had remarried. The Corporation occasionally had to take action against a heartless stepfather, like Thomas Phillipson 'who hath his wyves sonnes porcon in his hands and suffreth the boy to go abegging and to lye forth a dores under the shop stalls by night', and relations with stepchildren could be as bitter as folk-belief has it. William Atkyrk, an alderman's son whose mother had remarried, called her 'hor and bawde' within his stepfather's house, and said openly 'that he was mynded to have shot at his father in lawe [stepfather] with a crosbowe'.[42]

York, like other cities, had its own court of orphans which safeguarded the estates of children of freemen, and it must have been its work which was alluded to in tax remissions when Queen Elizabeth spoke of the Corporation's great charge in educating fatherless children. The records of the court have vanished, but one may guess that York had similar arrangements to those at Norwich, where the Corporation paid 'selecte women' to teach crafts and letters to children without parents who could pay for their education.[43]

The schooling of children generally, and not only of orphans, is very obscure. The educational historian A. F. Leach devoted all his attention to the grammar schools of the city, but they were very much secondary schools catering for a wealthy or fortunate minority who wished to add a classical training to a basis of elementary education in English. The degree to which the latter was available can be inferred from the fragmentary but invaluable records of the extent of literacy. The most frequent evidence at York consists of lists of signatures and marks attesting documents, from which the proportions signing their names can be calculated; but the results do

41. *HMC, Salisbury*, VI, 339
42. Borthwick, prob. reg. 22, fol, 68; Y.C.A., MS B31, fol, 306v; *Y.C.R.*, III, 73.
43. *Y.C.R.*, VI, 67; VIII, 56; *The Records of the City of Norwich*, ed. W. Hudson and J. C. Tingey (2 vols, 1906–10), II, 352; Palliser, *Tudor York*, p. 79, n.1.

not necessarily reflect the extent of literacy. Nevertheless there is a certain consistency in the records consulted for the latter part of Elizabeth's reign, when attested documents became common. Most suggest a literacy rate among adult males between two-fifths and two-thirds, of the same order as the 48 per cent rate at Chester in 1642, the only urban Protestation Return of that year to provide evidence of literacy. By contrast, there is almost no evidence at all for female literacy at York, which was probably much lower. Even Margaret Clitherow, the daughter and wife of prosperous citizens who held the civic chamberlainship, 'learned to read English and written hand' only when imprisoned, and four women out of five who subscribed to a schedule of St Denys's parishioners in 1594 made marks, though nearly half the men signed their names.[44]

Archbishop Lee, in his injunctions of 1538 to the Dean and Chapter of York Minster, ordered the clergy within their jurisdiction to charge their parishioners to have the Ten Commandments, Lord's Prayer, and Ave Maria in English 'in there howsses written or inprented and themselves to learne them and cause their childerne and servauntes to learne them'. Plainly this was a counsel of perfection; a butcher claimed that Mayor Hogeson in 1531 had tricked him over an acquittance, he 'haveyng no perseverance in wryttyng nor yett redyng but alonly his owne name'; another freeman, who received a letter in 1551, immediately gave it to one of the mayor's sergeants 'that his boye myght reade it'; and another in the 1550s professed himself unable to distribute a collection of deeds to their owners as he was 'smallye lettered', though the meaning there seems to have been illiterate of Latin. It may be that literacy increased during the century, for more and more proclamations about everyday affairs were posted up in public instead of being left to word of mouth and the 'bellman' or town crier. In 1562 the Corporation ordered the innholders' regulations to be 'fayre wrytten and sett up on postes where they might best be seen and redd of all men'; and in 1574 the charges for hiring labourers were to be written on 'tables' at three public places so that the labourers could not profess ignorance of them.[45]

Such widespread literacy indicates widely-available education, though not necessarily a large number of schools, for there were other ways of acquiring the basic skills of reading, writing, and – for merchants and craftsmen – accounting. Some nobles, clergy, and officials employed private tutors; a 'learned and godly schoolmaster'

44. Palliser, *Tudor York*, pp. 173–74; *Troubles of our Catholic Forefathers*, ed. Morris, III, 375; D. Cressy, *Literacy and the Social Order* (Cambridge, 1980), pp. 73, 191.
45. Y.M.L., original printed injunctions of Abp, Lee 23 Sep. 1538; PRO, C1/772/54, C1/1429/82; *Y.C.R.*, V, 67; VI, 45; VII, 91.

taught Huntingdon's great-nephew and probably others of the numerous children at the Manor in 1594–96, and the sons of Vice-President Osborne were similarly tutored privately in the sixteen-thirties. Other children were taught at home by their own parents or guardians. Canon Atkinson, dying in 1571, made the draper William Allen guardian to his son and asked him 'to lerne hyme to write and to use hyme as hys owne'. Apprentices might be instructed by their masters *in loco parentis*, and not only in their craft; one apprentice made it a ground of complaint that he had served his master for more than three years 'without any lernyinge instruction or techinge clothinge or aparell to him given'.[46]

Another source of teaching, particularly geared to business training, was the city scriveners. One, Edward Richardson, was in 1587 licensed by the city council 'to teach scholers within this cittie to reed, wryt and cast accompt'. Ten years later Richardson was vexed to find a rival in practice. Thomas Fowler, another scrivener, 'set up at the corners of diverse strets in this cittie certeyne printed notes or papers declaring his faculty trade and conynge towching instructing of children to write, cast accompts, cipher and such like'. Richardson stuck a mocking Latin couplet at the foot of the posters – an indication that sufficient passers-by would appreciate the joke – and was promptly imprisoned by the Corporation.[47]

Nevertheless, many children must have acquired elementary education in schools of one kind or another. There are no systematic records of petty, unendowed schools as there are for the grammar schools, but casual references have been located to a dozen such schools, mostly in the second half of the sixteenth century. Several were clearly parish schools, like that of St Michael-le-Belfrey, where 'seats for children and scollers' were installed in 1592 in the church, but where in the following year a parish assembly agreed 'that there shalbe no scollers taught in the church, and that the scole master shall have warnyng given hym to provide other wise'. Grindal's injunctions to his clergy in 1571, in obedience to the canons just promulgated, ordered that 'if ye cannot preach, ye shall teach children to read, to write, and to know their duties towards God, their prince, parents and all others'.[48]

46. *Calendar of State Papers Domestic*, 1595–97, p. 164; C. Cross, *The Puritan Earl* (1966), p. 54; J. Hunter, *South Yorkshire*, I (1828), 143n; Borthwick, Dean & Chapter prob. reg. 5, fols 65, 113; PRO, C1/324/12.
47. Y.C.A., MSS B29, fol. 184r; B31, fol. 272r.
48. Y.M.L., Acc. 1966/2, 19, fols 25–28; *Visitation Articles and Injunctions of the Period of the Reformation*, ed. W. H. Frere and W. M. Kennedy, Alcuin Club Collections (3 vols, 1910), III, 281. For other parish and elementary schools, see Palliser, *Tudor York*, p. 175, and J. H. Moran, *Education and Learning in the City of York 1300–1560*, Borthwick Papers, no. 55 (York, 1979).

If the education of most children remains obscure, other aspects of their lives are even more shadowy. Mr Laslett points out that about a quarter of the English population at any one time were under the age of ten, but that 'these crowds and crowds of little children are strangely absent from the written record'. Their games and customs are almost totally unrecorded, apart from cryptic references to 'children's lights' in churches and to a 'children's hill' in one churchyard, or to the occasional brutal custom such as the schoolboys' right to whip dogs seen in the streets on St Luke's day. Otherwise children tended to be taken for granted unless they became antisocial. A Corporation order of 1520 that 'no man from hensfurth . . . shall suffre ther chyldren to go with clapers uppon Shere [Maundy] Thursday and Good Friday' must have reflected an intolerable noise to find its way into the minutes. Vandalism was as familiar then as now, James Warton being prosecuted in 1613 for leaving piles of cobbles against Holy Trinity, King's Court 'by [which] means divers children have climbed up and broken the glasse windows of the church with stones'. Equally familiar were the complaints of the elderly against the young; the grammarian Whittinton said that in 'great cytees' like London and York 'the chyldre be so nysely and wantonly brought up, that (comenly) they can lytle good', and the epitaph on one York alderman asserted that his sixteen children were 'not bad as children are now, but all good'.[49]

Only one record of an individual childhood has survived. Marmaduke Rawdon (1610–70), the son of a merchant living on the Pavement, furnished some details of his early life to his biographer, affording precious glimpses of a prosperous childhood under James I. When very young, he was asked by a gentlewoman visiting his father 'why he did nott come to thir howse to play with hir little boy'. At nine, he broke an arm while 'playinge amongst other boyes in a yarde amongst the timbers of an old howse'. At twelve, he was playing with a York physician's children in their father's garden and orchards, and he burned his face when he and '3 or 4 boyes more of his consorts' improvised a firework there. Up to the age of sixteen, the games he was allowed 'on play dayes' were archery and bowls, but he also swam and rode horses without his parents' knowledge.[50]

49. P. Laslett, *The World We Have Lost* (2nd edn 1971), pp. 108–10; Raine, *Mediaeval York*, pp. 160–61, 250; *Y.C.R.*, III, 70; J. Addy, *The Archdeacon and Ecclesiastical Discipline in Yorkshire 1598–1714*, Borthwick Papers, no. 24 (York, 1963), p. 22; *The Vulgaria of John Stanbridge and the Vulgaria of Robert Whittinton*, ed. B. White, Early English Text Society, orig. ser. CLXXXVII (1932), p. 116; Drake, *Eboracum*, pp. 219, 295 (translated).
50. *The Life of Marmaduke Rawdon*, ed. R. Davies, Camden Society, LXXXV (1863), 1–3.

Rawdon was 'brought-up with all manner of learning that the city of York could afford', which has been taken to mean that he was one of the fortunate minority who attended one of the city's grammar schools. The lack of surviving registers prevents any analysis of their pupils, but a number of aldermen and leading citizens left large bequests, some of £10 a year or more, to 'find' their children at school, presumably at one of the grammar schools. York possessed two such schools until the Reformation, when certainly one and probably both were closed; but they were replaced by the new foundations of Holgate's school in 1546 and St Peter's in 1557; and they seem to have catered for city boys from prosperous homes as well as the sons of leading Northern gentry, clergy, and officials. A very few York boys, chiefly the sons of aldermen, can be traced as having gone on to higher education at the University of Cambridge or at the Inns of Court.[51]

These youths, prolonging their education until the age of twenty or more, were a fortunate minority. Most boys and girls would have taken employment or service at a much younger age. Many of the York boys were apprenticed, and after the completion of their term they would, if fortunate, become masters themselves, or if not, would remain in service as journeymen. The normal age of apprenticeship is not known; a boy could be fully trained for a craft by sixteen, though the glovers' gild insisted that apprenticeship could not end until the age of 24. Traditionally, during the period between childhood and marriage, the youths or young unmarried men would have formed themselves into youth groups of the kind described for sixteenth-century France by Professor Davis, with a social, critical, and satirical function. The cordwainers' servants formed their own socio-religious gild quite distinct from that of their masters, though this need not have been an especially youthful organization. Some, if not all, parishes had an association of 'yonge men' who kept up a 'young men's light' in the church, and their groups may have been identical with those who maintained 'summer games lights' in the churches. All the mentions of such groups are pre-Reformation, and it may well be that they disappeared, together with so many other ceremonial and corporate bodies, during the troubled years of dissolutions and religious revolution.[52]

51. Palliser, *Tudor York*, pp. 175–76, 222–23, 264, 274.
52. D. M. Palliser, 'The trade gilds of Tudor York', in *Crisis and Order in English Towns*, ed. Clark and Slack, pp. 99, 104, 115; Raine, *Mediaeval York*, pp. 160–61; Y.M.L., Dean & Chapter prob. reg. 3, fol. 34; Borthwick, prob. reg. 9, fol. 469. cf. N. Z. Davis, 'The reasons of misrule: youth groups and charivaris in sixteenth-century France', *Past & Present*, 50 (1971), 41–75.

V

There is little evidence that sexual relations before marriage were general, though about one bride in five was pregnant. Presentments for immoral sexual behaviour of any kind were few in number; thus at the archdeacon's visitation of 1598, covering most of the city parishes, only nine or ten couples were presented for fornication (and four for adultery), and four unmarried women were alleged to have borne children; and not all were found guilty. At the same period, however, the Corporation were implying that premarital sexual relations were increasing; they may have been counting all cases of relations begun before the church ceremony, even if the couple were already espoused and considered themselves virtually married. There was, complained the city fathers, a general report in the city that in recent years many maidservants and unmarried women had become pregnant. Some of the men responsible, thinking to mitigate their offence, had afterwards married the women, while others of the fathers had left the city, to the great charge of the parishes where the bastards were born:

> And yet that notwith standinge the marriags of such of theme as have so offended have been graced asmuch by bryde beddes and offerands as though they had bene honest women, wherbye it is thought that others have bene and wilbe the rather imboldened to comyt suche wickedness. In regard whereof, and for that it semeth that such bridebeddes and offerands weare at the begynnynge thereof brought in use for the better gracinge and butyfyinge of honest maydes marriages and for ther advancements in that behalf and not for fornicatours or adulterers,

bride beds and offerings were forbidden for any woman whose child was known to be conceived outside marriage. The date was 1599, and it would be tempting to link such strictures with the growing Puritan spirit among the aldermen. Yet the Corporation, like that of Exeter, another city where Puritanism came late to dominance, had long taken a hard line on sexual offences, and it seems that moral offenders were perceived as dangers to society just like vagabonds.[53]

Altogether, sexual relations whether inside or outside marriage are understandably not well recorded. The existence of prostitution is clear, the prostitutes being occasionally banished from the walled area to the suburbs, but their numbers, location, and organization (if any) remain obscure. It is also unclear whether or how prostitutes, or women in general for that matter, were able to prevent

---

53. Palliser, *Tudor York*, p. 119; Borthwick, RVIE 1a, fols 1–10; Y.C.A., MS B32, fol. 54v; W. T. MacCaffrey, *Exeter 1540–1640* (Cambridge, Mass., 1958), p. 97.

conception. Layton, writing from York in 1536, told Cromwell of great corruption among the York religious, including the use of *coitus interruptus* and abortifacients. He was a hostile witness, but there are hints that various contraceptive practices were known in the sixteenth-century North.[54]

The Church, of course, had a jurisdiction over sexual morals which it interpreted widely. Archbishops Neville (1464–76) and Wolsey (in 1518) both followed Peckham of Canterbury in interpreting the seventh commandment to cover fornication and every sexual relation not permitted by the right use of marriage. Cases of incontinence as well as adultery were therefore dealt with by the archiepiscopal courts. Even cases of earthy slander were solemnly investigated rather than overlooked. In 1525 the Commissary General had to rule on an action brought by a widow of St Mary Castlegate parish against two neighbours, one of them her parish priest. The rector was said to have exclaimed – though the allegation was held not proven – 'The fowle divele taike that cuntte, that swyvys so oppynly that all Yorke . . . wonderis apon'. The Corporation, however, were not prepared to leave such matters exclusively to the Church, and especially after the Reformation they acted against individual sexual offenders, usually punishing the women more severely than the men.[55]

Espousal or 'handfasting' was the simple ceremony by which a couple pledged marriage, and it was recognized as valid by the church courts provided that it was conducted in the presence of witnesses and in the absence of legal impediments. Typical of many was the ceremony described by a witness in 1581 'that it is the common voce of the pariching of Belfra and in Sancte Lowrance pariche that tha [the couple in question] be handfast to gether'. He deposed 'that Thomas Stabill said to Janet Leke, "I am content to have youe to my wyfe and al other to for saik for the lowe of youe, and ther to plight I the my truyth"'. Janet made a similar reply, 'and so tha drew hands'. Other such reported handfastings took place in a wine cellar of the abbot of St Mary's, and in a house in Petergate. On the latter occasion the couple followed their declarations by taking hands, kissing and drinking together. Such contracts could not be set aside, though an angry parent might put restraints on the offender. In 1582 William Tattersall confessed that he had 'contracted matrimony with Mary Bell, daughter of Richard Bell, gentleman, without his consent or knowledge, in a house door over against Mr Paler's house in Coney Street upon Saturday then next before about

54. *Three Chapters of Letters relating to the Suppression of Monasteries*, ed. T. Wright, Camden Soc., 1st ser. XXVI (1843), 97; E. A. Wrigley, *Population and History* (1969), p. 127.
55. Borthwick, RVII C132, G178; *Y.C.R.*, VI, 12, 13, 157; VII, 52; VIII, 58.

eight o'clock in the evening', in the presence of four witnesses. For this the Ecclesiastical Commission imprisoned him, and on his release they put restrictions upon his communication with Mary and upon his demand for a dowry, but there seems to have been no question of stopping the marriage altogether.[56]

Many marriages, however, were based on parental choice and on sufficient dowries, rather than on romantic love and parental disapproval. The frequent bequests of money 'for the marriage of poor maidens' show how necessary a dowry could be; and two York sisters petitioned the Lord Chancellor that they had had their 'portions' of £35 kept from them after their father's death, and that they had no wealth or friends to help them to marriage apart from their legacies. Weddings were, of course, unlike espousals, public ceremonies performed in church; but they were also the occasions for rejoicings as new family groupings and alliances were created, and were often followed by a lavish feast accompanied by music. Finally, the couple were put to bed in the 'bridebed' ceremony already mentioned. There is no clear description of such an event at York, but the household regulations of the neighbouring Earl of Northumberland describe the aristocratic equivalent. After a banquet and dancing, the bride is led to the groom's chamber and put to bed with him. Then an usher summons 'the parsonne that shall doo the seremonyes forthe hallowing of the bedd'. After the hallowing, wine is served to the assembled company, who then leave the couple alone and lock the door.[57]

It was taken for granted that a husband had authority over wife as well as children. When Mayor Dyneley was humiliated by having to answer publicly for his wife's recusancy, Archbishop Sandys told him bluntly 'that he is unmete to governe a cittie that can not governe his owne howsehold'. The married woman's sphere was the work of the home, or the supervision of it if she had servants. When Dr Lee's wife was placed under arrest for recusancy, she was still permitted to go home daily 'for thre or foure houres . . . for ordering of hir husbands house'. Some of the richer wives, Fr Mush alleged, disdained domestic tasks; he praised Margaret Clitherow because 'she would not disdain, as many do . . . to make the fire, to sweep the house, to wash the dishes, and more gross matters also, choosing rather to do them herself, and to set her maids about sweeter business'. The subordination of married women was shown,

56. Borthwick, R VII G27, 130, 173, 175, 2031; P. Tyler, 'The administrative character of the Ecclesiastical Commission for the Province of York, 1561–1585' (unpub. B. Litt. thesis, Oxford Univ. 1960), p. 100: I am grateful to Dr Tyler for permission to quote from his thesis.
57. PRO, C1/35/351/56 Bodleian Library, MS Eng. Hist. b 208, fol. 30v.

for example, by the fact that the mayor and aldermen were not accompanied by their wives in watching the Corpus Christi plays; instead, the wives formed a separate party.[58]

Marriage added to a man's kin by bringing him into a new circle of relatives; this could mean more obligations, but also more alliances. Alderman Peter Jakson was described as 'greatly alyed' in York 'by marriage of hys wifes daughters', and certainly one of them married Peter, son and heir of the wealthy Sir John Gilliot. Kinship, whether by blood or marriage, involved mutual obligations, and the intricacies of family genealogies had a practical importance. James Blaids testified in court that he was related to Ralf Symson, the future alderman, in the fourth degree, showing that the 'degrees' calculated by ecclesiastical law were well understood by laymen. An even more remarkable example concerns the Herberts or Harberts. Richard, a Monmouthshire gentleman who settled in Yorkshire, was a second cousin of the William Herbert who became first Earl of Pembroke (d. 1570). Richard's family settled in York as merchants, his son Christopher (d. 1590) and grandson Thomas (d. 1614) being in turn aldermen and mayors of the city. Thomas's grandson Thomas Herbert (1606–82) left York for London, achieving fame as groom of the bedchamber to Charles I and author of the best account of his last days. The two branches of the family had by then been separated for a century; yet in 1640 one of the Monmouthshire Herberts acknowledged Thomas as his kinsman, and in 1649 the fourth earl called him 'my cousin Tom Herbert', though they were only fourth cousins twice removed. As Laslett remarks, 'It is astonishing how distant a connection qualified for the title "cozen"'.[59]

Feelings within the immediate family were naturally unrecorded as a rule; the chief exceptions were a few last wills where strong feelings of love or dislike broke through the conventional phraseology of bequests. A family quarrel was evident in the case of Robert Johnson, who left 13s. 4d. to his daughter

> so that she never maike my wiff no besynes for, and [if] she doo, I will shoo have nothing, and I doo har noo wrong as my curate shall recorde the trewght, for she knowis well enewht that she is furth with hir part with the better.

58. Borthwick, R VIII, H.C.A.B. 9, fol. 9iv; H.C.A.B. 11, fol. 265v; *Troubles of our Catholic Forefathers*, ed. Morris, III, p. 375; A. J. Mill, 'The Stations of the York Corpus Christi Play', YAJ. XXXVIII, 496–97.
59. Yorks. *Star Chamber Proceedings*, I, 31–32; Borthwick, MS RVII G204; R. Davies, 'A memoir of Sir Thomas Herbert', *YAJ*, I, 182, 214; R. H. Skaife, 'Civic Officials' (MSS, 3 vols, York City Library), II, fol. 361v; Sir T. Herbert *Memoirs* (1702 edn), p. 120; Laslett, *World We Have Lost*, p. 192.

Or a testator might take the opportunity to declare a strong affection, as did Alderman Robert Brooke:

> I have found in my wife great love to me and to all my friends and careful alwaies for me and my affaires and of our children, so that I have found her alwaies wise and discrete, and alwaies the feare of God before her eyes.[60]

Perhaps the feelings of living men are best captured in the dramatic reported speech of the occasional nuncupative will in the probate registers. When a dying man had no time left to dictate a normal will, his intentions were copied down exactly as he gave them, in dialogue with his neighbours. On 3 June 1562 Tristram Litster, innholder, 'beyng verie seike', was urged by four friends to make his will,

> and beyng verye desyrous to answere, with moche payne said, 'My wyf shall have all' . . . Then beinge further examined by Oswald Wilkinson yf his meanynge were that his wyf shall have the occupyinge of his house and goods, and lyke a naturall mother to bring up her children withe the same and to dispose the same emongst them at her discrecion, answered, 'Yea, what els? for my wyf is all my care'.

Similarly Rowland Wilkinson (1572),

> being askid . . . to whom he wolde all that he had . . . maid answeare and said, 'Who sholde have that which is myne but my mother? For all that I have came through her'.

Rather different was the scene at the bedside of the maltster Thomas Walton in 1573:

> he did saie, 'Dame, be not angrie withe me. Youe gave me a house that you saide coste xx^li, and I give Margaret youre daughter it againe, as frelie as you gave yt me. Ye thinke I will put somethinge from youe, but I will putt nothinge from youe'.[61]

The solemn moment of making a will was often almost the last act in a citizen's life; a comparison of dates of will, death, and probate, where known, shows that the will must often have been dictated from the deathbed. Swinburne testified to a widespread superstition in the North that a man who made his will while in good health 'should not live long after', a belief still held in the York area within living memory. A few citizens' wills indicate that the document was drawn up by a notary or by the testator himself, but normally the parish clerk or priest seems to have been sent for to write it. The clearest picture of such a deathbed scene was given by

---

60. *Test. Ebor*, V, 165; Borthwick, reg. 27, fol. 596.
61. Borthwick, prob. reg. 17, fol, 94; prob. reg. 19, fols 515, 883.

a priest and parish clerk who in 1559 visited Richard Wattersonne in Bootham, finding him lying 'in a ynner parlour upon a trundell bed by the fire side'. They ministered extreme unction and were witnesses to a codicil which Richard added to his will, though in this case it was not a priest who actually wrote it down. The testator would in any case bear in mind that the Church had jurisdiction over probate, and the choice of a cleric might seem only sensible. He would also ensure performance of his will, under the oversight of the church courts, by appointing executors to carry out its provisions, and perhaps also 'supervisors' to ensure that the executors acted as he wished.[62]

Professor Thrupp has suggested for London that friends were chosen as executors and patrons as supervisors, but a sample of 126 York wills does not suggest such a clear distinction. One hundred and ten of the testators named close relatives, usually wives and children, as executors, and where they did not do so there is a strong presumption that no close relatives survived. Only half the testators (62) named one or more supervisors, and these were sometimes relatives, and in other cases priests or fellow-craftsmen. Only a very few named obvious patrons, one of them being the notary and merchant John Chapman, who nominated the Dean of York and Archdeacon Magnus. Despite all these precautions, it was all too easy for a testator's wishes to be ignored after his death, and numerous complaints survive by heirs allegedly unable to inherit or by executors or supervisors hampered in trying to administer an estate.[63]

Burials, like weddings, were public acts of solidarity by relatives, colleagues and friends. The cordwainers, carpenters, and bakers, and doubtless other gilds, required all their members to attend each other's weddings and funerals, and there were to be gild contributions to the funeral expenses if the estate of the deceased was insufficient. The well-to-do were buried in coffins, but this was expensive; one widow gave five 'towells' to St Michael-le-Belfrey 'to carry the poore of this parishe to the churche to be buried'. Funeral doles remained popular despite the disapproval of the post-Reformation ecclesiastical authorities, drawing many beggars to attend. The Corporation in 1615 forbade doles to be distributed at funerals, as it was 'the chief cause which doth not onely drawe the poore of this cittie but also of the countrie from their dwellings wherby they neglect ther labor and so continewe in great multituds begging in this cittie'. The friends and relatives accompanying the coffin held a wake or feast, and some testators specified the fare in

---

62. H. Swinburne, *A Briefe Treatise of Testaments and Last Willes* (1590), p. 24; Borthwick, MS RVII G763.
63. S. Thrupp, *The Merchant Class of Medieval London* (Ann Arbor, 1962), p. 261; sample of all citizens' wills for 1521–30 in Borth. Inst. probate registers.

detail. A baker wanted the mourners to have bread, ale, and cakes at his house; while a rich widow in 1509 prescribed a lavish wake for poor as well as rich.

> I will have my *derege* in my house, and yerto be had comfettes, sugir plattes, and suckittes, and I will my nebours from Stanegait ende to Bothome bar be at my *derige* and at dener; . . . and at tharbe sceallapis of mayne breid, and at the poore be well and honestly served as the richar to the valour of xs. ; and at xxs. worth of farding breid be delt to poore pepell.[64]

VI

Professor Dickens has justly spoken of 'the harsh lot of the average townsman' of Tudor York, with diminishing holidays, falling real wages, long hours of labour, and few domestic comforts, and has warned that 'the social historian would be unwise to dwell too exclusively upon the picturesque aspects of life'. It cannot be too strongly stressed that the lives of the well-to-do were much better recorded than those of the poor, and that if many aspects of life were hard and drab, the position must have been far worse for labourers and paupers.[65]

It has, for instance, been customary to pay homage to the cultural life of the city, but books were available only to the literate, and even those, in conservative York, were not primarily readers of the humanists and dramatists. Miles Coverdale, author of the first English translation of the whole Bible, was born in York but left it early in life, and suffered the proverbial fate of the prophet in his own country. The stock of a city bookseller in 1538 was confined entirely to legal and liturgical works, with no books by the leading humanists. The archbishops of York included Wolsey, patron of scholars, and Lee, a distinguished humanist writer, while the most distinguished canons included John Colet, William Turner the naturalist, and Lawrence Nowell, a pioneer of Anglo-Saxon studies, but the list is misleading, as none of them spent much time in York except Lee. Even the fact that York was one of the earliest provincial centres of printing and publishing is misleading; all the books printed and published there between 1493 and 1533 were liturgical or grammatical.

64. Y.M.L., MS Y I di; Y.C.A., MS E55A, fol. 15r; E22, fol. 230v; B34, fol. 64av; *Belfrey Registers*, ed. Collins, I, 238; Borthwick, prob. reg. 22, fol. 58; *Test. Ebor.*, V, 5.
65. A. G. Dickens, 'Tudor York' in *VCH York*, p. 159.

Before the Reformation, indeed, book-reading was almost wholly confined to churchmen and lawyers, and the only large collections of books recorded belonged to senior ecclesiastics. A rector of All Saints, North Street, who died in 1535 owned the most modern Latin and Greek dictionary, works by Cicero, and the *Adages* of Erasmus, though he was exceptional even among the clergy. Later in the century, laymen other than lawyers did begin to mention books in their wills, though where titles were given the extent of their collection was usually a Bible or a copy of Cooper's *Dictionary*. Thomas Colthurst (1588) was exceptional in owning a Bible, Plutarch's *Lives*, and the *Chronicles* of Guicciardini and Holinshed, though it is fair to remember that books listed in wills would not necessarily represent all those owned. Furthermore, very few inventories survive for laymen, and it is inventories that allow a picture of book ownership in other Tudor towns like Exeter, Manchester, and Worcester. Music-making, outside the Church and the professional gild of minstrels, may likewise have been a minority activity, though from the fifteen-thirties onwards a number of laymen began to record instruments among their possessions.[66]

A more popular use of music was probably, then as now, as an aid to hard and monotonous labour. The Corporation on occasion paid musicians to play at 'common works', when labourers were conscripted for unpopular tasks. It would, however, be more realistic to think of leisure activities for most townsmen, in so far as hard work allowed leisure, in terms not of music or the arts but of cards, dice, and bull-baiting. Bulls were regularly baited on the Pavement, and the sport was so popular that butchers were not allowed to slaughter bulls before they had been baited. There are frequent references to card and dice games and to such games as 'shovegroat', nearly always in connection with taverns and alehouses, and often in connection with restrictive by-laws imposed on labourers by the Corporation. There were frank status limits on some games: bowls, which was popular among city councillors, obviously attracted those lower down the social scale, and in 1579 the Corporation ruled that no artificers could henceforth play at games like bowls, or even bet on them, 'but such as shalbe assessed in the subsidie books at x^{li} or above, excepte such as haith borne office of worship within this cyttie'. The theatre likewise attracted the suspicions of the city fathers. Companies of players frequently visited York, but when in James I's reign a group of citizens started a local theatre, it was

---

66. *Test. Ebor.*, IV, 279–82; V, 258–59; D. M. Palliser and D. G. Selwyn, 'The stock of a York stationer, 1538', *The Library*, 5th ser. XXVII (1972), pp. 207–19; C. Cross, 'York clerical piety and St Peter's school on the eve of the Reformation', *York Historian*, 2 (1978), p. 18; Borthwick, prob. reg. 23, fol. 799.

quickly suppressed for encouraging manual workers to turn actors 'and fall to an idle course of life'.[67]

Even drinking, perhaps the chief pleasure of the poor, was restricted. In 1530 the Corporation were troubled by 'myche unthrifty rewle and demeanour that is nightly used by power laborers . . . the whyche usys common tayverns [and] ayle houses, and theyre playes at dyes, cards and oder unlaufull games', and ordered them to return to their homes by 8 p.m. on work days. Similarly, in 1588, they ordered labourers to be 'restrained from the alehowse' to prevent them from drinking away 'all that should maynteine their poore wifes and children at home'. No doubt there was well-intentioned concern here, but one suspects that many labourers were driven to drink by a squalid environment, a pattern that was still evident to Rowntree three centuries later. The York Corporation, like that of Nuremberg, seems to have based its attitudes on a deeply pessimistic view of human nature which required constant vigilance and control of the citizens, and especially the poor, if they were not to go astray.[68]

VII

Leisure was in any case very limited for most sixteenth-century townsmen and townswomen, except for the frequent enforced leisure of unemployment or underemployment. 'The *minutiae* of life in preReformation society were determined in a manner more akin to that of a school or the forces in the modern world – not least, perhaps, because the waking hours of the week were so continuously occupied that . . . there were few occasions when malcontents could regularly congregate in any number and so threaten the social order'.[69]

It is very difficult to appraise the quality of Tudor urban life, even for an unusually well-documented city. Modern judgements are apt to fall into the opposite traps of romanticism or of patronizing pity. All that can be said unequivocally is that the basic inherited framework of urban life was little changed during the century, despite the external pressures of political change, religious revol-

---

67. *Y.C.R.*, IV, 53; VI, 149; VII, 19; *Y.C.A.*, MS B27, fol. 183r; M. Sellers, 'York in the sixteenth and seventeenth centuries', *English Historical Review*, XII (1897), 446.
68. *Y.C.A.*, MS B11, fol. 101V; *Y.C.R.*, III, 134 (misreading 'dyes', i.e. dice, as 'dyverse'); *Y.C.R.*, VIII, 158; G. Strauss, 'Protestant dogma and city government: the case of Nuremburg', *Past & Present*, 36 (1967), 38–58.
69. Phythian-Adams, *Desolation of a City*, p. 79.

ution and severe inflation. Most citizens of York in 1603, as in 1485, lived in a world of assumptions, relationships, and physical surroundings which could have been very little different from those of their ancestors in 1400 or even earlier, but which is so alien to our modern experience of urban life as to be very difficult to penetrate. It was a similar perception which persuaded MacCaffrey that 'probably the most important aspect of Exeter's history in the sixteenth century was the continuity of medieval custom'. Dyer's study of Tudor Worcester, a perhaps more dynamic community with a textile boom as well as a population boom, still concludes that economic change coexisted with 'a large measure of administrative and social conservatism'. The changes often seen as dividing 'medieval' from 'modern' England – printing, Renaissance culture, new attitudes to government, and so on – bulk much less large at the local, municipal level.[70]

The one major exception is perhaps the religious revolution which we conveniently summarize as the Reformation. It meant not only changes in doctrine and church government, to which many townsmen may have been indifferent, but great and often violent alterations to the physical context of worship, the confiscation of lands and ornaments given for pious uses, the destruction of chantries and of a whole way of popular Catholic life centred on ceremonies, ritual, and pageants. It was this shattering of medieval mirrors, to use Phythian-Adams's graphic phrase, which so clearly changed the mental and physical context of the Tudor citizen's world. If the evidence for York and some other large towns is not as clear as for Coventry, there is nevertheless little reason to doubt that many towns 'lost many of the advantages of medieval community life', even if the new urban society which emerged during the seventeenth century 'also cast off its shackles'.[71]

Editorial suggestions for further reading

C. Phythian-Adams, *Desolation of a City: Coventry and the Urban Crisis of the Late Middle Ages* (Cambridge, 1979).
B. Reay (ed.), *Popular Culture in Seventeenth-Century England (1985)*.

70. MacCaffrey, *Exeter 1540–1640*, p. 281; A. D. Dyer, *The City of Worcester in the Sixteenth Century* (Leicester, 1973), p. 256.
71. Phythian-Adams, *Desolation of a City*, p. 278; cf. Palliser, *Tudor York*, p. 226–59.

Chapter 9

'THE RAMOTH-GILEAD OF THE GOOD': URBAN CHANGE AND POLITICAL RADICALISM AT GLOUCESTER 1540–1640

Peter Clark

[in P. Clark et al. (eds) *The English Commonwealth 1547–1640* (Leicester, 1982)]

This ambitious essay attempts, through a study of Gloucester, to link two controversial arguments: that most middle-sized towns suffered considerable economic and social dislocation during the century before the Civil War and that many towns became Parliamentary strongholds during that war. Neither proposition holds true for all towns, as Clark admits, nor did the latter neccessarily follow from the former. Clark sees the necessary connecting factor in the emergence of a puritan magistracy eager to use religious reform to strengthen social order. This was a conservative aim in the local setting, but led to radicalism in the national context due to the destablizing actions of the early Stuart kings and Archbishop Laua. This final suggestion has received considerable confirmation in recent work. It is less clear that the urge to create a 'godly commonwealth' can helpfully be called 'puritan', or that it was confined to towns suffering a socio-economic crisis. Nor does Clark entirely explain the loyalty of ordinary Gloucester people to the lead shown by his oligarchic group; here factors such as fear of Welsh and Irish catholics and broader civic feeling might be considered.

Few provincial towns more amply justified Edward Hyde's attack on 'that factious humour, which possessed most corporations' during

1. Research for this paper has been generously supported by the Social Science Research Council and the Open University Research Board. I am indebted to Dr P. Morgan and Dr A. Foster for their research help and to Dr P. Corfield for her comments on an early version of this paper. The scriptural parallel in the title first appeared in verses by the city puritan Samuel Kenrick which prefaced J. Dorney's *Certain Speeches Made upon the day of the Yearly Election Of Officers in the City of Gloucester* (1653).

the Civil War than the county town of Gloucester. From the late 1620s the city was increasingly at odds with the Crown over political and religious issues and in 1640 returned as a burgess to the Long Parliament, Thomas Pury, one of the leading supporters of the Root and Branch bill.[2] In 1643 Gloucester held out valiantly against a lengthy royalist siege and the defenders' success was, to quote Bishop Goodman, 'indeed the turning of the wheel, for ever after the parliament-forces prevailed . . .' Despite the vicissitudes of war and political settlement, the city remained loyal to successive parliamentary régimes. After the Restoration it was duly and harshly punished by the Crown.[3]

To understand Gloucester's development as a leading radical stronghold we shall need to examine not only the short-term influences of the decade or so before 1640, but also the major secular problems and pressures affecting all aspects of the community from the mid-sixteenth century. Many of these problems – demographic, economic, social, political, and cultural – were not unique to Gloucester but exemplified the general dislocation which has recently been seen as widespread among English county towns during the Tudor and early Stuart periods.[4] On the other hand, it will be argued here that the very intensity of Gloucester's problems helped forge a particularist strategy of civic survival – a vision of an embattled godly commonwealth, of a city on the hill. It was this perception of the community which in the rapidly changing religious and political climate of the late 1620s and 1630s played a vital part in the progressively bitter conflict between the city and the Crown.

1

Gloucester was fairly typical of the hundred or so second-rank towns in Tudor England. A Roman settlement, it owed much of its early importance to its location at the first easy crossing place above the mouth of the Severn and at the centre of a communication network stretching north-south along the Severn valley and east-west towards London and Wales. By 1483 it had acquired an impressive array of

2. Clarendon, Edward, Earl of, *The History of the Rebellion and Civil Wars in England* (ed. W. D. Macray, 1888), II, 470; *Mr Thomas Pury Alderman of Glocester his speech* (1641); for Pury see M. F. Keeler, *The Long Parliament 1640–41* (Philadelphia, 1954), 316–17.
3. F. A. Hyett, *Gloucester in National History* (1896), 100–24; S. Rudder, *The History and Antiquities of Gloucester* (1781), 120–1; Gloucestershire RO (hereafter GRO), GBR 1470, fos. 4–19.
4. P. Clark and P. Slack, *English Towns in Transition* (1976), esp.158–9.

corporate privileges including an extensive jurisdiction over two hundreds of the county, the so-called inshire. John Leland noted in the 1530s: 'the town of Gloucester is ancient, well builded of timber and large and strongly defended with walls'.[5] At this time it had a population approaching 4,000 and held second place (after Bristol) in a county hierarchy of nearly 30 urban centres, most of them small market towns.[6]

In the century before 1640 Gloucester's population grew substantially to just over 5000. Part of the increase resulted from natural growth, but the major share came from immigration. While parish register evidence indicates there may have been a surplus of baptisms over burials in better-off inner parishes like Holy Trinity, this was almost certainly cancelled out by deficits in poorer outer parishes such as St Aldate's. With plague increasingly an urban phenomenon, there were serious outbreaks at Gloucester in 1573, 1578, 1593–4, 1603–4, 1625–6 and 1637–8.[7] In critical decades like the 1590s even respectable parishes incurred net losses of population and had to recruit new inhabitants from outside the community. Gloucester witnesses appearing before the diocesan courts between 1595 and 1640 provide substantial biographical data to confirm that migration was a dominant feature in the city's demographic growth (see Table 1).[8]

Less than a quarter of the witnesses had failed to move at some time in their lives, nearly a half had previously resided outside the city limits, while about 25 per cent had come to Gloucester from outside the county – from adjoining areas like Herefordshire and Worcestershire as well as from further afield. Though our sample is too small to make any positive correlation between migrational patterns and occupational groupings, a significant number of the incomers were what we might call *betterment* migrants, respectable men and women travelling fairly short distances in the hope of economic improvement. Many of them became urban apprentices. Thus of 1643 apprentices whose indentures were enrolled at Gloucester between 1595 and 1640 31 per cent were city-born, 44

5. M. D. Lobel (ed.), *Historic Towns*: I (1969), pt iv, 1–2; W. H. Stevenson, *Calendar of the Records of the Corporation of Gloucester* (1893), 16–19; L. T. Smith (ed.), *The Itinerary of John Leland 1535–1543: Parts IV and V* (1908), 57–8.
6. A. Everitt, 'The market town' in J. Thirsk (ed.), *The Agrarian History of England and Wales: IV* (1967), 471.
7. P. Ripley, 'Parish register evidence for the population of Gloucester 1562–1641', *Bristol and Gloucester Archaeological Society Transactions* (hereafter BGAS), XCI (1972), 203–4; GRO, GBR 137/1451, fos. 58v and 143v; PRO, St Ch 8/4/9; HMC, 12th Report App. IX, 476, 490.
8. Ripley, op. cit., 203. The data is derived from diocesan deposition books, GRO, GDR 79 *et passim*; for some of the problems in exploiting this kind of material see P. Clark, 'The migrant in Kentish towns 1500–1640', in P. Clark and P. Slack (eds.), *Crisis and Order in English Towns 1500–1700* (1972), 119–21.

TABLE 1   Physical mobility among Gloucester witnesses 1595–1640

	Male %	Female %
Stationary	27.2	19.0
Unspecified move	16.2	23.0
Move within city	7.6	10.0
Move from county	23.8	22.0
Extra county move	25.2	26.0
Sample	210	100

per cent had come from the county, whereas only 16 per cent had travelled from outside Gloucestershire. Again over 40 per cent were the offspring of gentlemen, yeomen, or substantial distributive traders.[9]

A very different and, in magisterial eyes, far less acceptable kind of physical mobility before 1640 involved *subsistence* migrants – poor servants, labourers, and petty craftsmen who had been driven on to the road by dire necessity and who poured into Gloucester, particularly during periods of major difficulty like the 1620s. Of the many vagrant poor arrested in the city in the early seventeenth century, a substantial number had tramped over 100 miles, mostly travelling across western England.[10] Others, however, came from nearer home. Rural over-population was a severe problem in Elizabethan Gloucesteshire, especially in the poorer pastoral areas of the Vale of Tewkesbury and the Cotswold slopes where the situation was aggravated by enclosure.[11] Some poor labourers migrated into local market towns or squatted in the Forest of Dean; others flocked to Gloucester hoping for work, relief, or a few scraps from the bustling markets. Swelling the ranks of the city's many indigenous poor they posed a serious threat to social order and civic government.[12] In this way demographic pressure was a key variable affecting city fortunes and the mentality of the ruling classes before the Civil War.

9. Ibid., 134 *et seq*. The apprenticeship evidence is taken from GRO, GBR 1458. I intend to discuss the general limitations of apprenticeship data on another occasion.
10. For pauper immigration to other towns see P. Slack, 'Vagrants and vagrancy in England 1598–1664', *EcHR*, n.s XXVII (1974), 360–79 GRO, GBR 1453/1542, fos. 34, 117; 1453–4/1542–3, *passim*.
11. PRO, SP 12/114/32; J. Thirsk, 'Projects for gentlemen, jobs for the poor: mutual aid in the Vale of Tewkesbury 1600–1630', in P. McGrath and J. Cannon (eds), *Essays in Bristol and Gloucestershire History* (1976), 148–9; GRO, GDR 89 (Robertes v. Darston).
12. Gloucester City Reference Library (hereafter GCL), MS. 16,526, f.99; W. B. Willcox, *Gloucestershire: A Study in Local Government 1590–1640* (New Haven, 1940), 156, 157n.

The crucial difficulty with Gloucester's population growth, both native and immigrant, was that it coincided almost exactly with a period of profound and in certain respects brutal change for the city's economic structure. During the late Middle Ages Gloucester had a strongly pluralistic economy, its markets servicing the neighbouring countryside, its port trafficking in coastal and foreign commerce, its religious houses attracting pilgrims and other visitors, its industries employing many citizens. In the fifteenth century Gloucester's leading industry was still the manufacture of woollen cloth, though the making of metalware ran it close, with capping not far behind. The overall picture both before and after 1500 seems to have been one of moderate prosperity.[13] In 1487–8 it is true the city fathers complained to the king of 'the great ruin and decay of the habitations, mansions and tenements of the said town. . .', but such complaints were part of the conventional rhetoric of petitioning the Crown. When, in 1536, the city secured its inclusion in a general statute for the repair of towns one suspects that Gloucester was jumping on a bandwagon set in motion by other centres. Certainly there is little hard evidence that the city was undergoing that deep-seated economic crisis which we are told was affecting many established towns, particularly in eastern England, during the first half of the sixteenth century. Judging from the freemen's lists clothing and capping were still prospering,[14] while Gloucester merchants built ships to trade with France and the Mediterranean and expanded ties with Bristol, which was also enjoying fairly buoyant trading conditions until mid-century. Even the economic loss of the old religious houses in Gloucester was more than offset by the accession of a large episcopal household and church courts as a result of the creation of the new diocese in 1541.[15]

13. Lobel, op. cit., 9–10; R. Perry, 'The Gloucestershire woollen industry 1100–1690', *BGAS*, LXVI (1945), 58–9; J. Langton, 'Late medieval Gloucester: some data from a rental of 1455', *Transactions of Institute of British Geographers*, n.s. II (1977), 272–5.
14. *HMC*, 12th Report App. IX, 406–7. The complaint prefaced a petition for a reduction in the city fee-farm; there is no evidence the Crown granted this *Statutes of the Realm* (ed. A. Luders, T. E. Tomlins *et al.*, 1810–28), III, 531 (Gloucester was not included in subsequent Henrician legislation for towns); C. Phythian-Adams, 'Urban decay in late medieval England', in P. Abrams and E. A. Wrigley (eds.), *Towns in Societies* (1978), 159–85; GRO, GBR 1300/1355; see also Perry, op. cit., 112.
15. PRO, E 134/25 Elizabeth/H3; J. Vanes (ed.), *The Ledger of John Smythe 1538–1550* (1974) 7, 36, 49 *et passim; idem*, 'The overseas trade of Bristol in the sixteenth century' (unpublished Ph. D. thesis, University of London, 1975), 390; *VCH*, Gloucestershire, II, 26.

TABLE 2   Occupational structure of Tudor and Stuart Gloucester
(expressed as % of period sample)

		1535–54	1608	1653–72
1	Gentlemen	1.7	9.4	7.5
2	Professional	0.2	0.3	0.5
3	Distributive	8.3	16.9	7.7
4	Service workers	2.9	2.6	3.9
5	Agricultural	10.5	5.4	1.4
6	Food processors	15.2	14.9	18.1
7	Metal processors	5.2	8.2	12.3
8	Wood workers	3.8	3.4	6.3
9	Textile workers	15.4	12.2	5.8
10	Leather crafts	12.9	12.2	18.8
11	Clothing workers	17.1	8.2	11.3
12	Building workers	2.8	3.8	1.3
13	Misc. skilled	1.2	2.5	4.9
14	Marine	2.8	0.0	0.2
	Sample	421	390	586

Severe difficulty in Gloucester's economy mainly occurred after 1550. At root was the contraction of the city's textile industries. In the early 1580s the magistrates asked: 'whether the trade of cappers and clothiers be not much decayed in Gloucester within twenty or thirty years past?' To some extent the answer can be discerned from the changing occupational structure outlined in Table 2.[16]

Even making allowance for the difficulties in comparing sets of data, there seems to be little doubt that the textile and allied clothing trades registered a major fall in importance. From their leading position in the occupational order in the early Tudor period, they had fallen by the seventeenth century to secondary status, out-paced by a number of other trades. As one weaver declared about 1635:

16. GRO, GBR 1375/1450, f.103v. The first and third sets of data are taken from freemen registrations in GRO, GRB 1300/1450, f.1300/1355. 1466B. The 1608 material is derived from the fairly comprehensive muster returns printed in *Men and Armour for Gloucestershire in 1608* (1902), 1–10. To assist comparison of data those persons engaged in unskilled or semi-skilled work (particularly numerous in the 1608 listing) have been omitted from the analysis, as also those whose occupations are unspecified. The freemen evidence is probably biased towards respectable trades; the muster return is (nominally) limited to men aged 16–60. The 1653–72 data may also be affected by the growing fluidity of occupational styles at that time. For a general discussion of the problems of occupational classification in this period see J. Patten, 'Urban occupations in pre-industrial England', *Transactions of Institute of British Geographers*, n.s. II (1977), 296–311.

'whereas there were heretofore above a hundred looms going, now there are not above six or seven looms constantly wrought in all the city'. Those clothiers and weavers who remained employed only a few workers. The collapse of capping was no less striking. In 1583 it was said that 'before Sir Thomas Bell and one Mr Falkoner kept great numbers of people at work spinning and knitting of caps . . . [but] now there are very few set to work in that trade'.[17] Clothing suffered from stiff rural competition encouraged by the exemption of the city's main rivals, the Stroudwater clothiers, from the 1557 Act which sought to confine clothing to towns.[18] But Gloucester's plight was further exacerbated by the growing dominance of London merchants in the marketing of cloth which destroyed the city's chances of serving as an outlet for rural textiles. In the case of capping, the principal culprit seems to have been a growing fashion for more fanciful headgear, probably imported from London.[19]

We know less about metal-working in the city. If the data tabulated in Table 2 is any guide, the period before 1640 was one of modest growth, but from a lower base than in the fifteenth century –perhaps due to the decline of the important specialist craft of bell-founding after the Reformation. Pin-making, introduced in the 1620s, was mainly a late Stuart success story. One of the few industries which obviously continued to flourish in our period was leather-working, notably tanning. As in other towns, this undoubtedly reflected strong demand for leather products, especially from better-off rural consumers. On other hand, most of Gloucester's tanners were small men (few bore civic office) and there was little growth of secondary industries. Tanning was unable to lead the city economy out of its industrial decline.[20]

With its industrial sector in disarray Gloucester came to depend heavily on its marketing role. By 1608 distributive trades formed the largest specific occupational grouping in the city (see Table 2), while mercers held nearly a quarter of the common council seats between 1580 and 1600. Gloucester, like other towns, did increasingly well

17. PRO, E 134/11 Charles I/M45; 25 Elizabeth/H3.
18. For the general trend: Clark and Slack (eds.), op. cit., 11; *Statutes of the Realm*, IV, 323–6. Worcester's textile industry which continued to flourish into the late sixteenth century had special legislative protection from rural competition after 1533: A. D. Dyer, *The City of Worcester in the Sixteenth Century* (1973), 117
19. G. D. Ramsay, *The Wiltshire Woollen Industry in the Sixteenth and Seventeenth Centuries* (1943), 131 *et seq.*; G. Unwin, *Industrial Organization in the Sixteenth and Seventeenth Centuries* (2nd edn, 1957), 71–2; for attempts to establish substitute industries see: GRO, GBR 1394/1500, f.241 *et seq*; VCH, Gloucestershire, II, 190; Willcox, op. cit., 256n.
20. H. B. Walters, 'The church bells of Gloucestershire', *BGAS*, XVIII (1893–4), 238, 243; Willcox, op. cit., 254–5; C. Phythian-Adams, 'Urban crisis or urban change?', in *The Traditional Community under Stress* (Open University course A 322, 1977), 20; PRO, E 134/4 Charles I/E3.

catering for the new prosperity of rural society.[21] From their large shops near the High Cross mercers and haberdashers sold luxury or semi-luxury wares to visiting gentry and yeomen farmers as well as supplying the small part-time stores which started to appear in the countryside. By the 1610s we find nearly a dozen country carriers coming from up to 15 miles away to collect goods.[22] Some of the wares in Gloucester shops had been imported via Bristol like the large quantities of oranges, wines, oils, and raisins listed in 1583; others, particularly the latest fashions in dress, came overland from London. 'Returning' money to pay for purchases from the metropolis was a well-established practice by 1600, and at least two carriers operated weekly between Gloucester and London in the 1630s. At the same time, the city did not have everything its own way in the marketing field. There was strenuous competition from the multitude of smaller market towns in the county, particularly in the provision of more basic commodities, while Bristol to the south took some of the cream of gentle custom with its more sophisticated range of high quality goods.[23]

Gloucester's main strength in inland trade derived from its role as a marketing centre for cereals. As Bristol's magistrates remarked jealously about 1583: 'Gloucester stands not upon any trade of merchandise but of corn and grain'. In the Elizabethan period the Vales of Berkeley, Gloucester and Tewkesbury were fertile corn-growing areas selling their grain principally through Gloucester. Leading city merchants like Thomas Rich, John Taylor and Thomas Machin shipped vast amounts of wheat and malt down-river to Bristol, the West Country, Wales and southern Ireland. They benefited especially from the recovery of Bristol's long-distance commerce in the 1580s and 1590s, supplying much of the grain which Bristol ships carried into the Mediterranean and further afield.[24]

21. For data on other towns see Clark and Slack, op. cit., 102–3; in 1605 the city acquired a third fair (Stevenson, op. cit., 39).

22. PRO, E 134/22 James I/M13; Bodl., MS. Engl. Misc. E.6, f.39v *et passim*; GRO, GDR 114 (Dorney *v.* Haselton); GBR 1422/1544.

23. PRO, E 134/25 Elizabeth/H3; 22 James I/M 31; REQ 2/275/13. In 1609 William Woodwall condemned the 'flaunting in fashions . . . nowadays used of many' in the area south of the city: *A Sermon Vpon the xii, xiii and xiiii verses* . . . (1609), 22. J. Taylor, *The Carriers Cosmographie* (1637), sig. B 2v; Bodl., MS. Engl. Misc. E.6, *passim*; P. McGrath (ed.), *Merchants and merchandise in seventeenth century Bristol* (Bristol Rec. Soc., XIX, 1955).

24. GRO, GBR 1375/1450, f.91v; E. Kerridge, *The Agricultural Revolution* (1967), 113–4, 126–7; eg. PRO, St Ch 8/220/1; E 134/25 Elizabeth/H3; E 190/1241/1, 3, 5–6 *et passim*; Vanes, thesis, 46, 391–2. For more on the active trade with Camarthen and other Welsh ports see E. A. Lewis (ed.), *The Welsh Port Books (1550–1603)* (Cymmrodorion Rec. Series, XII, 1927), xxxii, xxxv. Gloucester was also a major transhipment centre up the Severn: e.g. PRO, E 134/4 Charles I/E3, T9.

Another growth point in the city economy was its service sector. 'Gloucester', we hear in the 1580s, 'is a great thoroughfare . . . and a great market situated in the heart of the country where great concourse of people is'. Justices, jurors, witnesses, and litigants flocked to the city: to the church courts in the cathedral; to county quarter sessions, the main political and administrative forum of the nascent county community, held at the castle or a city inn; to the assizes sitting twice a year in the Boothall; occasionally to the Council of the Marches meeting (as in 1592) in the cathedral close.[25] Prosperous visitors lodged in the 12 great inns along the main streets (often packed to capacity at peak times); other lesser folk made do with the city taverns or numerous alehouses. Despite civic ordinances the larger victualling establishments not only lodged merchants and traders but increasingly provided the venue for business deals and negotiations, away from the inclement hurlyburly of the open market.[26]

Professional men also exploited the town's growing importance as a social centre. None did better than the lawyers who served the great tide of litigation encouraged by landed prosperity: by the turn of the century there were about 20 Gloucester-based practitioners – counsellors, attorneys and proctors. But well-heeled country clients also lined the pockets of physicians, surgeons, scriveners, and schoolmasters. The cathedral school in particular taught the children of gentry families from a wide area of western England. Some country gentry began to reside in the city for part of the year, renting perhaps a house in the cathedral close. Lesser landowners moved there permanently like Richard Pope of the Leigh, concerned 'for the education of [his] divers small children', or Henry Gilbert of Whaddon living there 'for his better service of God and for recovery of his wife's health by physic'.[27]

25. GRO, GBR 1375/1450, f.86; cf. F. S. Hockaday 'The Consistory Court of the diocese of Gloucester', *BGAS*, XLVI (1924), 195–287; BL, Harleian MS. 4131, fos. 478–569v; for the growing importance of county quarter sessions in this period see J. Hurstfield, 'County Government *c*. 1530–c. 1660', in *VCH*, Wiltshire, V, esp. 92 *et seq.*; GRO, GBR 1889B, f.63.
26. GRO, 1696/1885; GDR 114 (Boyle *v*. Messenger); GBR 1376/1451, f.449. For a valuable account of the growing socio-economic importance of inns see A. Everitt, 'The English urban inn', in *idem* (ed.), *Perspectives in English Urban History* (1973), 91–137; for the splendid Gloucester New Inn see W. A. Pantin, 'Medieval inns', in E. M. Jope (ed.), *Studies in Building History* (1961), 169–73.
27. Number of lawyers based on examination of GRO, GBR and GDR records; for Gloucester doctors see J. H. Raach, *A Directory of English Country Physicians* (1962), 103; also GDR 79 (White *v*. Thair); J. Bruce (ed.), *Letters and Papers of the Verney Family* (Camden Soc., 1st ser. LVI, 1853), 156, 160; Rudder, op. cit., 396; GDR 159 (Blomer *v*. Estcourt); PRO, SP 14/181/35 (I); see also A. Everitt, *Change in the Provinces: the Seventeenth Century* (Dept. of English Local History, University of Leicester, Occasional Papers in English Local History, 2nd ser. I, 1972), 44–5.

The expansion of the tertiary sector undoubtedly took up some of the slack in urban economic activity, but it worked no miracles for local prosperity. Indeed in some ways this expansion aggravated the instability of the economy. With its greater reliance on rural demand the city's economic performance was now highly vulnerable to those sharp oscillations of the agrarian economy which recurred in the late sixteenth and early seventeenth centuries. Too often problems caused by harvest difficulty were compounded by plague epidemics which caused the isolation of the city from its hinterland. Naturally in times of dearth Gloucester's grain trade still yielded lucrative returns for leading merchants shipping corn, but this merely underlined the falling level of general demand among ordinary citizens faced with soaring food prices. Increased coastal traffic had other drawbacks for the urban economy, encouraging a desertion of the old longer-distance trades and leaving city commerce at the mercy of the erratic fortunes of Bristol and other West Country ports. Last but not least, Gloucester's economy was vulnerable in one further way. The growth of the city as a social centre depended to a large extent on the fickle patronage of county gentry. This custom might easily transfer itself to a rival town if the city fathers failed to play up to the gentry's political sensitivities.

In the mid-1620s all the problem birds came home to roost and there was a full-scale crisis. Foreign war dealt a mortal blow at the fading cloth industry; harvest failure created food shortage and widespread poverty; plague brought inland trade to a standstill (for a while); coastal shipping was disrupted by a commercial crisis at Bristol and difficulties in the North Atlantic fishery; county patronage was seriously alienated by the city's bitter opposition to gentry demands for concessions over the inshire (discussed below). Gloucester's economy remained badly depressed into the 1640s. As we shall see, these years of crisis, the culmination of a prolonged period of economic instability, had a considerable influence on the growing radical outlook of city leaders prior to the summoning of the Long Parliament.[28]

28. GRO, GBR 1377/1452, f.105; PRO, REQ 2/163/90; *APC*, 1586–7, 71–2; GBR 1375/1450, f.92; 1420/1540, fos. 131–2; *HMC*, 12th Report App. IX, 476–7; W. B. Stephens, 'Trade trends at Bristol, 1600–1700', *BGAS*, XCIII (1974), 157; *idem*, 'The West-Country ports and the struggle for the Newfoundland fisheries in the seventeenth century', *Transactions of the Devon Ass.*, LXXXVIII (1956), 91–3.

3

Another vital factor helping to engender a radical mentality in the years before 1640 was the growth of social polarization and tension. Already by the 1520s the subsidy rolls suggest that over 40 per cent of those taxed were assessed at the lowest rate, while only 6 per cent were rated at more than £40. By the mid-seventeenth century the wealth pyramid may have been more steeply tapered. Though the hearth tax returns are not directly comparable with the earlier subsidy rolls they do shed some crude light on the pattern of wealth: thus of those taxed in 1664, only 5 per cent paid at the highest rates of nine hearths or above, whereas 54 per cent were assessed at the minimum rate of one or two hearths. If there was a trend towards increased economic inequality, it probably reflected the industrial malaise from the mid-sixteenth century with the resultant decline in the number of substantial clothiers, as well as the way that medium-rank traders were discouraged from staying in Gloucester by the heavy burdens of civic office-holding. No less important, it also mirrored the high prosperity of leading Stuart merchants, their fortunes based on the large profits of inland and coastal trade.[29]

Not only were the Gloucester *potentiores* increasingly wealthy compared to ordinary freemen and poorer inhabitants, but they displayed their wealth in more conspicuous forms – in new and better buildings in the centre of town, in household furnishings, books, plate, and dress. Though statistical data is lacking for Gloucester, we do have evidence for Canterbury, a similar county centre. There a sample of probate inventories 1560–1640 demonstrates that distributive traders spent three times as much on their apparel as building craftsmen. In the late sixteenth century they invested about twice as much in luxury furnishings as building craftsmen; in the next 40 years it was nearly four times as much. At Gloucester city magnates aped the manners and fashions of the landed gentry, styling themselves gentlemen and procuring coats of arms. They even began to acquire rural residences: in 1624 we know that at least half the aldermanic bench had houses in the adjoining country-side.[30]

While the urban elite began to develop its own class consciousness and identity, at the bottom end of the social spectrum there was massive, escalating poverty as the urban economy proved unable to adjust to rising demographic pressure. In St Aldate's parish, for in-

---

29. PRO, E 179/113/189; GRO, D383, part ii.
30. Eg., GRO, 1376/1451, f.27; PRO, E 134/40 Elizabeth/H9. The inventories used in this analysis are in Kent AO, PRC: 10/1–72; 11/1–7; 27/1–8; 28/1–20. J. Mac-Lean and W. C. Heane (eds.), *Visitation of the County of Gloucester . . . 1623* (Harleian Soc., XXI, 1885), 96, 100–1, 106–7; GRO, City Map of 1624.

stance, the number of poor receiving relief trebled between the late 1570s and the 1630s and in the crisis years of the 1620s nearly 40 per cent of the parish was probably destitute. As in other provincial centres the hard core of traditional impotent poor was now steadily overshadowed by a looming mass of labouring poor, unable to secure work or afford rising food prices; many had been forced into tramping and vagrancy as a last resort. In addition, years of prolonged depression forced even marginal poor, the semi-skilled or small craftsmen, on to the poverty line.[31]

Along with the growth of poverty went increased social segregation. Just as the city magnates tended to live in great houses near the main market at the Tolsey, or by the wharves in St Nicholas's parish, the poor were crowded into squalid housing in outer parishes like St Aldate's and St Mary de Lode, the latter in unhealthy marshlands. Though never ghettos in the modern sense, such areas developed their own fairly distinctive social physiognomy. They were afflicted by a high incidence of morbidity and mortality: plague made its first appearance at Gloucester in 1638 in St Mary de Lode, while St Aldate's had the heaviest known mortality of city parishes during the 1630s.[32] Such areas were also prone to high levels of crime and disorder. Taking offenders indicted before city quarter sessions 1639–43 we find the largest contingents came from St Mary de Lode and Barton Street, both impoverished districts. Among the offenders from these areas were numerous alehouse keepers, often running unlicensed establishments in back alleys. Such houses not only victualled and lodged the countless incoming poor, but also offered a meeting-place for local paupers; there they might forget their misery with cheap alcohol and illicit sex. In addition, poor tippling houses often had a communal or neighbourhood role, serving as the centre for more traditional folk rituals and attracting the lower orders away from church services. Poor alehouses, in fact, seemed to many wealthier tradesmen the mainspring of an underground world of immoral, irreligious poor which threatened the mores, power and institutions of established society.[33]

31. GRO, P 154/6, OV 1/1–14; in 1624 the magistrates noted the 'great want and misery' of the city poor; GBR, 1376/1451, f.496v; 1453/1542, f.62v *et passim*; PRO, SP 16/194/11 (I). See the acute situation elsewhere in J. F. Pound (ed.), *The Norwich Census of the Poor 1570* (Norfolk Rec Soc., XL, 1971), 7–21; P. Clark, *English Provincial Society from the Reformation to the Revolution: Religion, Politics and Society in Kent 1500–1640* (1977), 239–41.
32. The physical polarization was mirrored in the pattern of rental values: P. Ripley, 'The trade and social structure of Gloucester 1600–1640', *BGAS*, XCIV (1976), 119–20. GRO, GBR 1444/1566, fos. 147v–8; Ripley, 'Parish register evidence', 203.
33. GRO, GBR: 1450/1572; 1376/1451, fos. 529–31; 1453/1542, f.113; 1450/1572, fos. 483 and 484; for more on alehouses see P. Clark, 'The alehouse and the alternative society', in D. Pennington and K. Thomas (eds), *Puritans and*

Increased social polarization spawned tension and sometimes conflict. There was recurrent criticism of the ruling elite and during 1586 clothworkers rioted in and about the city over shipments of grain and malt out of Gloucester at a time of acute local shortage. Again in 1604 at the height of the plague epidemic 'disorder and unruliness of the people' was widespread, with a particularly serious disturbance over magisterial directives for the burial of the dead. Fresh disorder broke out in St Mary de Lode parish during the epidemic of 1638.[34]

The poverty problem and the associated order issue dominated the debates and decisions of the ruling elite in the decades before 1640. In response the city established, mostly piecemeal, an intricate system of poor relief. By comparison with eastern towns Gloucester introduced only a handful of limited measures during the early sixteenth century. Concerted action came from the 1560s as the city economy deteriorated. Parishes levied statutory poor rates, a house of correction was opened, and the city experimented with various schemes to set the poor on work.[35] The critical decade of the 1590s provoked the usual flurry of expedients: beadles to whip vagrants out of town; the isolation and relief of plague victims; and the establishment of coal and grain stocks for the poor. In the years of worst difficulty city officials imported grain from Bristol, Shrewsbury, London, and the Continent to provision the destitute.[36] As well as instituting these general measures the city fathers sought to alleviate the special plight of the local poor through revamping hospitals and almshouses. St Bartholomew's, a major almshouse, was reorganized and extended in 1569; during the 1590s the city secured control of St Mary Magdaken Hospital which was refounded in 1617 with an annual pension from the Crown; finally all the main hospitals were brought under centralized aldermanic control in the 1630s. In addition there was a high level of magisterial charity, mostly directed at founding work stocks and encouraging small or young tradesmen with interest-free loans. Overall, Gloucester's relief measures lacked the grand complexity of the schemes found in certain other puritan cities like Salisbury or Norwich, but they seem to have been im-

Revolutionaries (1978), 47–72. The Gloucester puritan William Loe complained that 'the rude people . . . seldom or never think of' Christ: *The Blisse of Brightest Beavtie* (1614), 15.

34. Eg., GRO, GBR: 1444/1566, f.72v; 1454/1543, f.13; 1376/1451, fos. 17v, 18v, 84, 98v; HMC, 12th Report App. IX, 458–9; PRO, SP12/188/47; St Ch 8/4/9; GBR, 1444/1566, f.162v.
35. Cf. E. M. Leonard, *The Early History of English Poor Relief* (1900), 23–45; one of the few early measures at Gloucester was the registration of local beggars (*HMC*, 12th Report App. IX, 436–8). GRO, GBR 1349–61/1403–15; 1375/1450, f.79; 1375/1451, f.69; 1453/1542, f.125; 1394/1500, f.241 *et seq.*
36. GRO, GBR 1394/1500, f.269 *et seq*; 1376/1451, fos. 122v, 143v, 144v, 167; BL Lansdowne MS. 76, f.101; *HMC*, 12th Report App. IX, 459; APC, 1597, 119.

plemented with drive and relative efficiency, particulary after the turn of the century.[37]

On top of these relief measures Gloucester magistrates endeavoured to combat the dual menace of poverty and disorder through a progressive tightening up of the administrative machinery. Exploiting to the full their power as justices of the peace, small groups of aldermen met several times a week to deal summarily with vagrants and other suspected persons, and to keep a close eye on parish officials. From the mid-Tudor period the city council had issued a series of ordinances against disorderly alehouses and these were strictly enforced from the 1620s. As well as clamping down on unlicensed alehouses the magistrates sought to compel all victuallers to buy supplies from a small group of common brewers under magisterial control.[38] In 1635 the new orders for the city hospitals excluded those poor who had previously kept alehouses. The same regulations also appointed an 'overseer of the manners of the poor'. Concerned with the large numbers of poor who never went to church, the magistracy inaugurated (in September 1632) a special lectureship to preach godly obedience to the poor in St Mary de Lode church and St Bartholomew's, while their puritan betters heard their own sermons at St Nicholas. Godly preaching was as important an instrument of social control as statutory relief and endowed charity.[39]

Thus the city fathers mobilized a battery of measures to overcome the massive social problems and pressures which menaced the city before 1640. Up to a point their tactics were successful. There was no breakdown of public order. Yet the measures themselves did little to resolve the underlying problems; at best they were palliatives. In the 1620s and for much of the 1630s, when the city faced severe economic recession, the situation was tense and difficult.

37. GRO, GBR 1324/1378; *VCH*, Gloucestershire, II, 121–22; *Civitas, Glouc. Ordinances statutes and rules made . . . for the good government of the several hospitals . . .* (n.d.); GRO, GBR 1701, f.82 *et seq.*; P. Slack, 'Poverty and politics in Salisbury 1597–1666', in Clark and Slack (eds.), op. cit., 180–94; Leonard, op. cit., 311–15.
38. GRO, GBR 1453–4/1542–3: *HMC*, 12th Report App. IX, 445–7; GRO, GBR 1376/1451, fos. 39–40, 529–31; in 1639–43 the largest number of indictments at city quarter sessions involved alehouse-keeping. For action in other puritan towns see: Colchester, Assembly Book 1576–99, f. 149 *et seq.*; J. C. Cox (ed.), *The Records of the Borough of Northampton: II* (1898), 304–5.
39. *Civitas, Glouc.*, op. cit., 16, 18–20, 26–7; GRO, GBR 1376/1451, fos. 560–2.

4

Civic attempts to preserve social order and stability had powerful repercussions so far as the political structure was concerned. Rising expenditure on various forms of poor relief contributed to the growing insolvency of city government. In the early 1550s there was still a regular surplus on the stewards' accounts, but from the 1560s the deficits mounted inexorably – by the 1580s the average was £45 a year and still rising. The problem was that while expenditure increased (boosted by price inflation) traditional sources of revenue (rents, tolls) stagnated. In consequence, members of the corporation had to dip into their own pockets in order to keep the city afloat. By the 1570s the convention was established that the four incoming stewards would lend the chamber cash to clear the current deficit; they in turn would be reimbursed by their successors the following year. In 1579 the new stewards refused to pay up and precipitated a financial crisis, though they eventually submitted. Six years later steward John Brooke held out obdurately and financial collapse was only averted by the outgoing steward accepting payment a year late. Likewise, the sheriffs and mayor frequently incurred expenditure on the city's behalf which proved difficult to recover. In 1604 townspeople witnessed the unseemly spectacle of the sheriffs distraining and carting away the shop goods of the mayor, Thomas Rich, because they claimed they had received insufficient revenue to pay the city fee-farm at the Exchequer.[40]

The financial burdens imposed by office-holding had wide-ranging consequences for civic politics, accelerating the trend towards oligarchy. The political situation at Gloucester was similar to that in most corporate towns with basic political privileges confined to a minority of inhabitants – the freemen. By the early seventeenth century there were about 500 freemen, between 30 and 40 per cent of the adult male population. From their ranks were recruited the members of the main civic assembly, the 40-strong common council, which in turn supplied the mayor and aldermen. The growing cost of office-holding made this step-ladder to power, always awkward to climb, appear downright dangerous. Once elected, councillors had to run the costly official gauntlet of serving two years as steward and then twice as sheriff. Predictably a rising number of freemen refused to accept election to the council and those who did tended to be well-established merchants and traders. Even so, a significant

40. GRO, GBR: 1394/1500, *passim*; 1376/1451, fos. 67v *et seq.*, 86v *et seq.*; PRO: St Ch 8/4/8; E 134/3 James I/M3. Civic insolvency was increasingly common at this time; for more examples see A. B. Rosen, 'Economic and social aspects of the history of Winchester 1520–1670' (unpublished D. Phil. thesis, University of Oxford, 1975), 99, 101; *VCH*, Warwickshire, VIII, 266 (Coventry).

proportion found the financial strain too much and dropped out of the council after one or more spells of official service.[41]

Almost by definition members of the aldermanic bench were wealthy citizens able to survive the gruelling exigencies of office. After serving an extended period as ordinary councillors most entered the inner circle when they were at the peak of their business careers, usually aged about 50. From the subsidy records for the 1590s we can see that the bench comprised many of the wealthiest inhabitants. A few were mini-tycoons with over £3000 in real and personal possessions, but the average estate was probably somewhat under £1000. A large part of aldermanic wealth was invested in property, a growing amount outside the city walls.[42] Group identity was fostered by joint business enterprises and credit connections as well as by the ubiquitous ties of kinship. Aldermanic power was also buttressed in two other ways. Firstly there was the authority of age and long service. Many aldermen served 20 years or more: the average age of members of the bench in 1580s and 1590s was nearly 60. Secondly, the decades before 1640 saw the bench monopolize almost all the principal non-conciliar offices in the city. They were masters of the main craft gilds, governors of the numerous city hospitals, and justices of the peace *ex officio*, while two-thirds of the city's burgesses in Parliament 1601–40 were likewise alderman.[43]

The growth of oligarchic government was the most obvious political development in Gloucester in the decades before 1640. At the heart of civic politics there was a steady shift of power away from the ordinary councillors towards an inner cabinet of mayor and aldermen. The royal charter 1483 placed the election of the mayor in the hands not of the council as a whole but of the aldermen and

41. GRO, GBR: 1878; 1376/1451, fos. 187v–8, 251v, 506v; PRO, E 134/3 James I/M3. The average age at entry to the council in the last part of Elizabeth's reign was 39.

42. Of the 20 wealthiest inhabitants assessed in 1594 13 were acting or future aldermen and two more connected to the bench by high legal office (PRO, E 179/115/430). J. Browne senior, a mercer, died worth about £2000 in goods in 1593; Thomas Machin, another mercer, died in 1614 with an estate in lands, sheep and goods estimated at £5–6,000 (PRO, REQ 2/118/59; St Ch 8/4./9). See also Ripley, 'Trade and social structure', 122. Comparative data on urban wealth is detailed in R. Grassby, 'The personal wealth of the business community in seventeenth-century England', *EcHR*, n.s. XXIII (1970), 230–3. For the property holdings of the Norwich aldermanic bench see B. H. Allen, 'The administrative and social history of the Norwich merchant class 1485–1660' (unpublished Ph. D. thesis, Harvard University, 1951), 340, 351, 356.

43. PRO: St Ch 8/220/1; E 134/30, 31 Elizabeth/M4; C3/324/55; for the gerontocratic bias in society as a whole see K. Thomas, 'Age and Authority in Early Modern England', *Proceedings of the British Academy*, LXII (1976), 5–10; GRO, GBR 1416/1535 (reversed): *HMC*, 12th Report App. IX, 523; Stevenson, op. cit., 38; W. R. Williams, *The Parliamentary History of the County of Gloucester . . . 1213–1898* (1898), 190–4.

twelve 'more lawful and discreet' members of the council; in 1605 James I's charter limited the electoral college to the aldermanic bench alone, though the rights of senior councillors were restored in 1627. Aldermen themselves were co-opted on to the bench in our period and while other elections to civic office were made by the council as a whole, there was a large measure of aldermanic influence. By the seventeenth century this influence was brought to bear through a pre-election day meeting of the mayor and aldermen which nominated candidates for the various offices. Even more crucial, given the many pressing problems of the city, was the way that members of the bench took charge of day-to-day administration through the Friday court of aldermen at the Tolsey and through more informal meetings during the week. Again as justices the same men presided over city quarter sessions which by 1600 wielded many new administrative powers, particularly in the field of social order. Controlling sessions the aldermen also had at their beck and call a bevy of new officials – overseers of the poor, highway surveyors and the like. Finally, the increasingly powerful office of town clerk was largely filled by clients of the bench.[44]

Meantime, the common council as a whole suffered a marked diminution in its political importance. Despite the major expansion of local administrative business, the number of council meetings remained static with an average of only ten a year, while meetings were often rigged to the oligarchy's advantage. In 1603–4, for instance, it was said that mayor Rich summoned meetings at short notice when he 'well knew divers of the council to be forth of the city'. Even when a crisis compelled action by the whole council – as over conflict with the inshire gentry in 1624 – the bench ensured that authority was delegated to a committee dominated by aldermen. Oligarchic power made itself felt outside the council chamber too. At parliamentary elections, one of the few occasions when ordinary freemen could make their views heard, aldermanic gerrymandering was the order of the day. In the 1597 election the veteran populist candidate Thomas Atkins claimed that members of the bench had rushed proceedings and ignored the voices of nearly 100 freemen. In 1604 there was another magisterial campaign to railroad their candidate through the election meeting though this time they were foiled by a dissident alderman. But thereafter at elections the bench seems to have had its own way.[45]

44. Stevenson, op. cit., 18, 37, 41; GRO, GBR: 1396/1501, f.424 *et seq*; 1376/1451, f.188; PRO, St Ch8/A 20/11; A1/15. The more open, consensus politics in the late medieval town is discussed by S. Reynolds, *An Introduction to the History of English Medieval Towns* (1977), ch. 6.
45. GRO, GBR: 1376/1451; 1878; PRO, St Ch: 8/4/9; 5/A 20/11; 8/228/30; J. E. Neale offers a useful account of the city's Tudor elections in *The Elizabethan House of Commons* (1949), 260–9.

Civic ritual in the medieval city had brought together in formal unity all the members of the body politic in quasi-religious drinking and processions, as at Midsummer and St Peter's eve. But by the late sixteenth century ceremonies served primarily to demonstrate oligarchic power and control. Most civic ritual was focussed on the bench and chief officials with formal progresses to sermon or court in scarlet or puce ritual dress and with ever more elaborate civic regalia. By the mid-seventeenth century the high point in the civic calendar was an elaborate dinner on Nomination Day when, as we have seen, the city leaders effectively fixed the names of incoming officers.[46]

As we shall discover this growing concentration of civic power and initiative in the hands of a small group of magnates was to have major political implications for the city, particularly in the years before 1640. At the same time it is important to see this development in the context of the critical problems and difficulties which Gloucester faced from the mid-sixteenth century: the decay of its staple industries; the problems of civic finance; the high cost of office-holding and the reluctance of many citizens to serve. All these factors undoubtedly contributed to the oligarchic trend, as did the expansion of civic administration due to rising poverty and other internal problems, which dictated the need for a semi-permanent committee of leading townsmen. Of course external pressures were also significant. Not only did the mounting demands of central government increase the work-load of town governors but the Crown showed a clear preference for local cliques of reliable men. As well as wanting active local agents to implement royal policies, the government was increasingly concerned at the severe social pressures in towns and the danger that non-oligarchic rule might open the door to social and political anarchy. Such concern was also shared by leading townspeople. As the Gloucester magistrates declared in 1584, 'experience has taught us what a difficult thing it has always been to deal in any matter where the multitude of burgesses have voice'.[47]

Oligarchic rule led to constant complaints of corruption and abuse. Some were clearly justified. In the 1590s there was a series of frauds involving the corn stock for the poor: Alderman Garnons was said to have profited by up to £160. But most abuse was less glaring, at least after the turn of the century when the ruling elite with its increasingly puritan complexion dealt harshly with serious offenders. On the other hand, low-key abuse was undoubtedly

---

46. *HMC*, 12th Report App. IX, 431, 529; GRO, GBR; 1394/1500, f.19 *et seq.*, 1376/1451, f.188; 1396/1501, f.464v.
47. *HMC*, 12th Report App. IX, 457; for an analysis of the general growth of urban oligarchy at this time see Clark and Slack, op. cit., 128–32.

widespread before 1640. Leases of city lands at beneficial rates were hurried, huggermugger, through council for aldermanic clients; town offices were sold; aldermen under-assessed each other for the subsidy; city contracts had a habit of going to members of the bench (in 1604 plague victims were buried in civic shrouds bought from the mayor's shop). Structural abuse of this kind was probably inevitable given the need to compensate town governors for the oppressive burdens of office-holding. But it was also a mechanism by which the ruling elite managed to secure friends and clients and consolidate their control over the common council and burgesses generally.[48]

Resentment over increased oligarchic power and abuse sometimes chimed in with wider social discontent to produce serious agitation – as in 1604. But communal conflict never became as threatening and large-scale as in other provincial towns: the ruling elite never lost command. One reason for this may have been the growing effectiveness of the magisterial apparatus of social and political control. Another may have been the responsibility and cohesiveness of the ruling group particularly after 1600, with its progressively puritan identity. In addition most respectable members of the body politic probably recognized the need to avoid rocking the boat at a time when the city was faced by massive internal problems as well as by mounting opposition to its corporate privileges from outside.[49]

Prior to the Reformation the city had clashed repeatedly with the abbey of St Peter's over their respective common land rights. Some of this rivalry continued after the abbey's refoundation as a cathedral, but the last major dispute occurred in 1583–4 and ended firmly in the city's favour. Thereafter relations with the close were good, much better than in most cathedral cities.[50] More worrying for the oligarchy was growing friction with the inshire, the county hundreds controlled by the city. Crucial here was the magisterial policy of weighting taxes and other royal levies against the country areas, thereby lessening the burden on the economically depressed city, while at the same time consistently refusing inshire inhabitants any say in civic government or the election of MPs. A number of clashes occurred in the late Elizabethan period, but the real crisis came in the 1620s. Then a group of inshire gentry organized petitions to Parliament calling for the right to representation and secured from the Crown a commission of association which enabled

48. PRO, St Ch 8/254/23; 8/4/9; GRO, GBR: 1376/1451, f.174v; 1453/1542, f.16; PRO, St Ch 8/4/8–9; 228/30; GRO, GBR 1376/1451, f.92–v.
49. PRO, St Ch 8/228/30; 207/25; eg. Clark, *English Provincial Society*, 340–1; *HMC*, 13th Report App. IV, 164 (Winchilsea).
50. GRO, GBR: 1375/1450, fos. 115v and 116; 1376/1451, f.86; PRO, SP 12/171/24; the city continued to dominate the close liberties after the Restoration: R. Beddard, 'The Privileges of Christchurch, Canterbury: Archbishop Sheldon's Enquiries of 1671', *Archaeologia Cantiana*, LXXXVII (1972), 93–100.

them to sit as justices at city quarter sessions. The magistracy protested vehemently against this innovation, 'whereby an ill example will be given for knights and gentlemen to infringe and invade the liberties of all cities of England'. The next two years were spent in the frantic re-assertion of corporate rights, ending in the costly acquisition of a new charter in 1627. Resistance continued, however, and eventually triumphed at the Restoration when the inshire was returned to county jurisdiction.[51]

City control over the inshire provoked further trouble with the county authorities. In the last part of the sixteenth century the lords lieutenant tried to force the city to pay more than its customary share of royal levies because of the prosperity of the inshire. Relations between the corporation and the county justices became equally strained. In 1595, for example, the justices kept the mayor and aldermen kicking their heels waiting for a meeting to discuss grain exports only to leave town without telling them. Mutual suspicion continued to overshadow dealings between the county and city right up to 1640.[52]

The Council in the Marches of Wales was another source of anxiety for city rulers. There were several nasty collisions and in 1597 the mayor was fined and imprisoned. But in general the Council was too far away to pose a real threat, while conciliar process could sometimes be used to overawe outsiders.[53]

Ambivalence also coloured relations with the Crown. On the one hand the central government could be an invaluable patron, granting new economic privileges such as the customs house in 1580, supporting the magistracy against popular agitation, helping to ward off gentry attacks. On the other hand, the expansion of Tudor government led to mounting interference in the urban community, most notably during the crisis of the 1590s. In addition, Court magnates, eager to extend their party patronage networks, sought to nominate their clients as recorders, town clerks and MPs. The Earl of Leicester, for instance, managed to secure the reversion of the Gloucester recordership for Richard Davies in 1587. Three years before, however, he had been sharply rebuffed when he had demanded the right to appoint one of the burgesses in Parliament.[54]

---

51. GRO, GBR 1889B, f.16; PRO, St Ch 5/A 20/11; GBR 1878; PRO, PC 2/45, p. 209; Lobel, op. cit., 13.
52. GRO, GBR: 1452/1574, f.59 *et seq*; 1889B, fos. 3 and 79v; for another dispute with the county justices: ibid., f.56.
53. GRO, GBR, 1376/1451, fos. 167v, 170, 172v, 203v *et seq*. Interestingly, the city never took a prominent part in the onslaught on Council jurisdiction from the 1590s (Willcox, op. cit., 26–7).
54. Eg., *APC*, 1595–6, 327–8; 1596–7, 154, 277–8; parallel developments in other towns are noted by J. W. F. Hill, *Tudor and Stuart Lincoln* (1956), 77–n; GRO, GBR 1376/1451, f.108; *HMC*, 12th Report App. IX, 457–8.

In fact for most of the period Gloucester managed to retain royal favour without making too many concessions. Here it was helped by the fragmented nature of Court politics in the Elizabethan and Jacobean periods. From the 1570s the city enjoyed the patronage of William Cecil, Lord Burghley and later his son the Earl of Salisbury. Their support was invaluable in winning royal grants and in frightening off predatory courtiers and their country clients. In grateful return the city granted annuities and promised its political loyalty.[55]

From the 1620 relations with the Crown began to deteriorate. One obvious reason was the high level of royal demands during a period of acute economic and social difficulty for the city. Thus the Forced Loan met growing resistance from local lawyers, members of the elite, and ordinary burgesses, while there was widespread opposition to billeting in 1627 and 1628. The city was incensed at the high and uncustomary level of military burdens imposed upon it and frightened at the disorders which the troops caused. Despite protests to the government the magistrates could obtain no redress.[56] Fundamental was the growing limitation on provincial access to the Court evident by Charles I's accession. Already in 1624 Gloucester had experienced great difficulty in getting its views on the inshire dispute heard at Court; by the late 1620s the communication problem had become almost insuperable. It was not just that the Court was less open than in the past, but it was increasingly antipathetic to provincial opinions with a puritan intonation. Unable to secure any satisfaction at Court the city demonstrated its resentment in increasingly forthright and principled terms. Not only was Parliament's Remonstrance against Tunnage and Poundage entered in the city records, but in February 1629 John Browne junior, a leading alderman and one of the city's burgesses, declared in the Commons: 'The strength of the king is in the hearts of his subjects. They do the king the greatest disservice that persuade' him to levy customs 'against the good will of the subjects . . . A curse upon all such as shall infringe the liberty of the subject'. Though Browne was probably a moderate puritan, it seems likely that there was by now a core of leading citizens committed to more radical religious beliefs.[57]

55. GRO, GBR, 1889B, f.3; PRO, SP 14/63/45, 68; *HMC, Salisbury* MSS., XVII, 353; XXIII, 125; GRO, GBR 1376.1451, f.66v.
56. PRO, SP 16/56/8; 77/30, 30(I); 94/57; *HMC*, 12th Report App. IX, 478–9, 482, 486; GRO, GBR 1413/1542, f.117v.
57. GRO, GBR: 1878; 1452/1574 (at end); W. Notestein and F. H. Relf (eds), *Commons Debates for 1629* (Minneapolis, 1921), 201, 231.

At this juncture we need to look in detail at urban ideology, one of the most vital and combustible elements in the interaction of urban change and political radicalism. Religion undoubtedly continued to be the dominant force in the city's cultural matrix after the Reformation. Gloucester had an early reputation as a centre of religious reform. During the 1530s there was an active protestant following in the city and within a decade or so most of the traditional religious superstructure had been demolished.[58] From the 1580s we have clear signs of a growing puritan bias: godly preachers, civic lectureships, attacks on catholics, private annotation of sermons, bans on players, conventicles in inns. In 1617 when Laud as dean of Gloucester sought to reform cathedral services it was said of the city opposition: 'Assuredly these zealous people are our precisians, the number whereof is great in this place'.[59]

How do we explain the growing tide of puritan activity? A major factor was the appalling state of the established ministry. In 1603 two-thirds of the city parishes were too impoverished to have resident ministers and for most of our period had to make do with poor, unlearned curates. Nor did the cathedral generally offer much in the form of godly enlightenment. For most of Elizabeth's reign it was beset by internecine feuding, corruption, and episcopal conservatism, while the following period was dominated by chronic non-residence.[60] Disenchantment with the established religious order was compounded by wider changes in the cultural life of substantial citizens. Most important was the expansion of educational facilities. By 1600 there were probably upwards of a dozen petty schools in Gloucester, plus the two endowed grammar schools – the municipal

---

58. *LP*, X, 463; XII(1), 139–40, 313; XII(2), 484; also K. G. Powell, 'The social background to the Reformation in Gloucestershire', *BGAS*, XCII (1973), 115–117.

59. GCL, MS. 29, 334; GRO, GBR 1376/1451, fos. 176v–7; *HMC*, Salisbury MSS., V, 207; R. *Willis, Mount Tabor or Private Exercises of a Penitent Sinner* (1639), 105; GRO: GBR 1376/1451, fos. 71v and 72; GDR 89 (at front); B. Taylor, 'William Laud dean of Gloucester 1616–21', *BGAS*, LXXVII (1958), 89.

60. W. J. Sheils (ed.), 'A survey of the diocese of Gloucester 1603', in *An Ecclesiastical Miscellany* (Bristol and Gloucestershire Archaeological Soc., Records Section, XI, 1976), 68–9. In 1583–4 we hear: 'all the townsmen clergy [are] very poor' (Lambeth Palace Library, Cartae Misc. XII/7); in 1641 there was a petition against 'the promoting of many lewd, worthless and ignorant persons into the ministry, especially in the city, where singing men of the cathedral are made ministers, and set over most of the parishes in the city, being known to be grossly ignorant and very scandalous for their lives' (GCL, MS. JF.4.13). F. D. Price, 'Bishop Bullingham and Chancellor Blackleech: a diocese divided', *BGAS*, XCI (1972), 175–98; PRO, REQ 2/165/182; *DNB*, Bullingham, John; P. Heylyn, *Cyprianus Anglicus* (Dublin, 1719), pt i, 44.

TABLE 3   Overall literacy of Gloucester witnesses 1595–1640

	Per cent literate	n
Male	64.4	205
Female	4.1	100

TABLE 4   Male literacy at Gloucester according to occupational groupings 1595–1640 (expressed as % of sample)

Occupational group	Signatures
1 Gentlemen	91.2
2 Professional	100.0
3 Clothing trades	63.6
4 Leather trades	61.5
5 Food and drink	69.6
6 Textile	74.2
7 Household goods	0.0[a]
8 Distributive	100.0
9 Building trades	62.5[a]
10 Yeomen	73.3
11 Husbandmen	8.3
12 Labourers	0.0[a]
13 Rural miscellaneous	0.0[a]
14 Service industries	18.2
15 Servants	40.0[a]
16 Miscellaneous	16.6[a]
17 Unspecified	55.5[a]

[a] = small sample

Crypt school and the cathedral school.[61] One result was a high level of male literacy. This can be seen from the subscriptions of witnesses before the church courts (see Table 3), though it has to be remembered that the data is possibly biased towards upper social groups.[62]

The incidence of literacy was particularly high in those occupational categories associated with marketing and internal trade (see Table 4).

Enhanced literacy was almost certainly accompanied by increased reading and ownership of books. Though the city library proposed by Bishop Goodman in 1629 did not materialize until the late 1640s, citizens had access to small parish libraries and many probably

61. Eg., GRO, GDR: 55 (unfol.); 89 (Hallowes *v.* Trotman); D 326, ZI; R. Austin, *The Crypt School, Gloucester* (1939), 47 *et seq.*; *VCH*, Gloucestershire, II, 321–6; the city not only financed the Crypt School, but from the 1620s augmented the stipend of the cathedral schoolmaster (GRO, GBR 1376/1451, f.521).
62. Data in Tables 3–4 derived from deposition books, GRO, GDR 79 *et passim*.

bought books from the two or three stationers operating in early Stuart Gloucester. Such developments permitted and possibly encouraged a greater stress on the reading of the scriptures and other religious works and a more critical attitude towards the established Church. By the 1620s John Deighton, a city surgeon, who owned a number of medical and religious books (including Foxe), was busy supplementing Foxe's account of the Marian martyrdoms in Gloucestershire by talking with parishioners and descendants.[63]

Puritan activity in Gloucester was also promoted by some of the major social and economic developments affecting the community before 1640. The city's expanding coasting trade brought it into close contact with puritan Bristol and those other godly towns of the South-West, Barnstaple and Bridgewater, while many city mercers and drapers doubtless imbibed the radical truths of metropolitan Puritanism. A growing number of the Gloucestershire gentry who patronized city shops and services also had a staunchly puritan outlook. Even the cathedral, which was plagued by non-residence and abuse, housed a handful of puritan luminaries from the 1580s to the 1620s, men with a following in the city and its vicinity. Among these were Dean Anthony Rudd, Bishop Miles Smith and Thomas Prior, who was both sub-dean and a city lecturer.[64]

Yet there can be little question that the key to the puritan advance in the community lay in the role of the urban elite. As we have already seen, Gloucester's economic and social structure in this period was dominated by a narrow group of merchants and traders who through their position on the magisterial bench also kept a tight rein on city government. It was this group which took the lead in the spread of puritanism in the city. By the 1590s if not before we know that a number of aldermen and senior councillors were actively sympathetic. In 1598 they secured the appointments of William Groves, a local puritan, to a weekly lectureship in the elite parish of St Michael's, with the city chamber making up any shortfall in voluntary donations. From 1611 the magistrates established a

63. BL, Sloan MS. 1199, fos. 92v and 93; S. M. Eward (ed.), *A Catalogue of Gloucester Cathedral Library* (1972), vii–viii; GRO: P154/6, CW 1/10a; P154/14, C1/41; Ripley, 'Trade and social structure', 118; for more urban evidence see P. Clark, 'The ownership of books in England, 1560–1640: the example of some Kentish townsfolk', in L. Stone (ed.), *Schooling and Society* (1976), 95–109; BL, Harleian MS.425, f.121; Deighton's books are listed in GRO, D381.
64. J. Latimer, *Annals of Bristol: Seventeenth Century* (1900), 58, 145, 148–9; J. R. Chanter and T. Wainwright, *Reprint of the Barnstaple Records* (1900), II, 13, 100; D. Underdown, *Somerset in the Civil War and Interregnum* (1973), 22; G. Davies (ed.), *Autobiography of Thomas Raymond and Memoirs of the Family of Guise* . . . (Camden Soc., 3rd ser. XXVIII, 1917), 113; G. A. Harrison, 'Royalist organization in Gloucestershire and Bristol 1642–5' (unpublished M. A. thesis, University of Manchester, 1961), 16; DNB, Rudd, Anthony; BL, Stowe MS. 76, f.249; Heylyn, op. cit., 44; Rudder, op. cit., 351.

twice-weekly lectureship which was served in succession by two committed Calvinists, Thomas Prior and John Workman. In 1617 the
agitation against Laud's erection of an altar in the cathedral was
largely orchestrated by puritan aldermen.[65] During the first part of
James' reign the puritan caucus faced opposition from a faction led
by Alderman John Jones, the diocesan registrar, with support from
the close and lesser freemen. But by the late 1610s the puritan group
was dominant. In·1618, despite the king's recent Declaration of
Sports, the maypole in St Nicholas parish was pulled down and a
country conservative, Christopher Windle, blamed puritan ministers
aided and abetted by the magistrates and mayor. During the 1620s
and 1630s the city fathers patronized distinguished puritan schoolmasters and apparently tried to remodel the city hospitals on more
puritan lines.[66]

Influential in the progressively puritan bias of Gloucester's rulers
were some of the general variables noted earlier. Almost all were
educated men; quite a number were distributive traders with close
ties with London or Bristol; one or two also had family connections
with the cathedral godly. The son of Alderman Christopher Caple,
Richard, was a distinguished puritan preacher in the county who
suffered suspension during the 1630s. Having said this, we also need
to take into account other pressures directly or indirectly related to
the host of structural problems which assailed the city in the century
before 1640. To civic leaders trying to govern a community beset by
rising population, economic instability, widespread poverty, and
other social and political difficulties, puritanism, with its emphasis
on public control and godly discipline, had a powerful appeal. Puritan
ideology served to buttress and justify measures concerning the poor
and lower classes. It further served to consolidate oligarchic authority
and to unite the ruling elite during a period of sustained communal
stress.

A further aspect of the ruling elite's growing commitment to
puritan ideology also needs to be considered here. In a critical
period when the city was menaced not just by internal difficulties
but by external threats, from the county and the Crown, the concept
of a godly civic commonwealth led by committed puritan magistrates
offered a vehicle for resurrecting in a modified form some of the
communal cohesion and particularist cultural identity of the older,
medieval city. Gloucester was to be a sober, orderly city on the hill,
its preachers and almshouses, schools and citizenry a godly beacon
to the villages and market towns of the shire. And in part the vision
was realized. Thus after a visit in 1642 Richard Baxter declared

65. GRO, GBR 1376/1451, fos. 176v–7, 236, 466–7; Taylor, op. cit., 89.
66. PRO, St Ch 8/4/8; 207/25; Taylor, op. cit., 89; BL, Royal MS. 12. A.LXX, f.9v
    et seq.

(with some understandable exaggeration), that he had found 'a civil, courteous and religious people as different from those at Worcester as if they had lived under another government'.[67]

6

We have argued then that the long-term changes and stresses in the urban community from the mid-sixteenth century created acute fears of social breakdown and, equally important, accelerated the trend towards oligarchic government. We have also analysed how the new all-powerful ruling elite increasingly patronized puritan tenets and values. Yet if all this helps us to understand why Gloucester became an important puritan centre in the early Stuart period, it does not by itself provide a sufficient explanation of the city's growing commitment of radical politics before and after 1640. How did the puritan county town of the first part of the century, with its concern for social order and communal survival, turn into the embattled radical citadel of the 1640s ready to risk almost everything for the parliamentary cause?

A vital factor in the growing political and religious radicalism of the city was the sharp deterioration in Gloucester's economic fortunes during the 1620s and 1630s. We noted earlier how a conjunction of long- and short-term economic problems caused a major recession in the mid-1620s. This depression persisted through the next decade: industry continued to decay and trade on the Severn stagnated.[68] In consequence poverty was endemic, reaching crisis proportions with the dearth of 1630 and the massive outbreak of plague in 1638. On the political front civic finance tottered on the verge of bankruptcy (the cumulative deficit had reached nearly £700 by 1640), and there was open conflict with the county gentry (thus in 1638 the county refused to come to the aid of the plague-stricken city).[69]

In this grave situation, with magistrates almost overwhelmed by difficulty, the policies and actions of the Caroline régime seemed to

67. *HMC*, Salisbury MSS., XIV, 149; XV, 47–8; *CSPD*, 1635, xli; T. Fuller, *The Worthies of England* (ed. P. A. Nuttall, 1840), I, 563–4; Hyett, op. cit., 98. The idea of the godly citadel was a recurrent theme in the addresses of John Dorney, the town clerk, to the magistrates in the 1640s. (Dorney, op. cit.).

68. See above, p. 173; Willcox, op. cit., 177n; PRO, E 134/11 Charles I/M45; J. Taylor, 'John Taylors last Voyage (1641)' in *Works: II* (Spenser Soc., 1873), 3, 25, 29–30.

69. GRO, GBR 1420/1540, fos. 166–7,231; *Privy Council Registers,* IV, 423–4; GRO, P 154/6, OV 1/14; GBR 1396/150l, f.141; 1454/1543, f.13.

pose a direct threat to civic survival. As we know, the Crown's repeated financial and military exactions during the late 1620s provoked considerable opposition in Gloucester; after 1634 there was growing discontent over ship money. Not only did the successive levies weigh heavily on a badly depressed community, but they opened the door to further acrimonious conflict with the gentry of the inshire and the county.[70]

Equally disturbing was the Crown's new religious strategy with its emphasis on more ritualistic services, its devaluation of puritan concern with the godly discipline of the lower orders, and its rejection of the long-standing Calvinist consensus over Church theology. Though Arminian tenets were never apparently enunciated from city pulpits at this time, puritan worthies had only to look at the new-found confidence of city recusants (including the new diocesan registrar Henry Jones) to suspect that the Caroline hierarchy was already well on the way to Rome. On the other hand, it would be wrong to exaggerate the city's alarm at this theological turnaround. At the local level, the magistrates remained on good terms with their maverick conservative bishop, Godfrey Goodman. Even the Laudian innovations in church worship (including the railing of altars) caused no serious trouble: many city parishes apparently ignored the diocesan directives with impunity.[71]

Where serious conflict with the hierarchy did occur was in regard to those central pillars of the godly commonwealth – the city's preachers, hospitals and schools. In the mid-1620s there may have been a dispute with cathedral conservatives over a projected lectureship there. In 1633 major trouble erupted when John Workman, the city's leading puritan divine and principal lecturer for more than a decade, used the occasion of an assize sermon to condemn continuing abuses in the Church, superstitious images and, that bane of public order, popular dancing. The attack on dancing was interpreted (rightly) as a counter-blast to the recently re-issued Declaration of Sports which encouraged popular activities of that sort, and Workman was summoned before the High Commission. Strongly supporting their preacher, the city magistracy voted Workman his stipend indefinitely. At this point Archbishop Laud, who doubtless recalled how city puritans had crossed him in 1617, determined to humiliate Gloucester's governors: a number were hauled up to London and eventually fined (the total cost in fines and expenses

70. GRO, GBR 1377/1452, p. 86; *Privy Council Registers*, V, 205; *CSPD* 1635, 470; 1636–7, 109; PRO, PC 2/44, pp 265–6; PC 2/45, pp. 169, 209.
71. For a general discussion see N. Tyacke, 'Puritanism, Arminianism and counter-revolution' in C. Russell (ed.), *The Origins of the English Civil War* (1973), 132–43; GRO, GDR 190; PRO, SP 16/308/22; H. C. Dancey, 'The high cross at Gloucester', *BGAS*, XXIV (1901) 299, 302; GRO, GBR 1377/1452, p. 76; GDR 201 (Sept. 1639).

was later estimated at £200). Workman himself was hounded out of the diocese.[72]

Nor was this the end of Laud's onslaught. In 1635 he authorized a rigorous inquest into the recent magisterial reorganization of the city hospitals and the supposed appointment of a nonconformist to a hospital living. Once again the city fathers had to appear before High Commission and produce the city council books in their defence: the proceedings lasted until 1638. Within two years the archbishop was intervening again, this time to prevent the corporation dismissing the Laudian John Bird as master of the Crypt school. According to the magistrates, Bird had so neglected the school 'that very few able scholars have been sent thence to the university'. In place of Bird they wanted to appoint the eminent puritan John Langley who had recently been removed by Laud's visitors from successful charge of the cathedral school. With Laud's support Bird managed to stave off removal until 1641. Overall, in this attack on the city's schools, hospitals and preachers, in the determined attempt to disgrace the city's magistrates, the hierarchy, with royal support, appeared hell bent on demolishing the bulwarks of the godly commonwealth, on opening the doors wide to social anarchy.[73]

By the mid-1630s if not before the city's attitude towards the Crown was one of sullen hostility. Under concerted royal attack the former preoccupation with puritan stability and order was transmuted into a new strategy of radical resistance. Early in 1640 the city fathers may have had some hand in the planned voyage from Gloucester of 100 colonists to the puritan safety of New England. But salvation was near at hand. During 1639 one of the city's radical curates went to Scotland, quite probably with magisterial connivance, and made contact with presbyterian opponents of the régime. Once the Long Parliament met, the city lobbied hard for radical religious reform and, when war broke out Gloucester determined, in the words of John Corbet, 'not to stand neutral in action but to adhere unto one party with which they resolved to stand or fall'.[74]

72. GRO, GBR 1376/I451, f.508; J. N. Langston, 'J. Workman, Puritan Lecturer in Gloucester', *BGAS*, LXVI (1945), 219–31; *HMC*, House of Lords MSS., n.s. XI, 4I8–19; GRO, GBR 1377/1452, pp. 18, 23, 121.
73. *CSPD*, 1637–8, 285–7; PRO, SP 16/379/88; GRO, GBR 1377/1452, p. 132; J. Bird, *Grounds of Grammer Penned and Published* (1639), sig. A2v–3; *CSPD*, 1635, xl.
74. *Privy Council Registers*, VII, 629; VIII, 46; X, 509; *CSPD*, 1639, 519–21; J. Washbourn, *Bibliotheca Gloucestrensis* (1825), 6–7.

To sum up, we need to see the growth of radical politics at
Gloucester in a wider urban perspective, to ask how far Gloucester's
experience was shared by other English towns in the run-up to the
Civil War. Though we know less about political developments in
towns than about changes at the county level, all the signs are that
Gloucester's route march to militancy was fairly atypical. Several
towns, like Winchester or Chester, became supporters of the king
during the early 1640s,[75] while of those centres which eventually ad-
hered to the parliamentary cause, many were clearly unenthusiastic
and intermittently expressed a strong preference for neutralism.
Quite often urban rulers had been pushed into opposing the king –
both before and after 1640 – by communal agitation. In such towns,
like Canterbury, Chichester, Norwich, Hull, Leicester, and Newcastle, there was frequently a long record of civic division and
factionalism, with town oligarchies unable to maintain effective control; as often as not these divisions were exacerbated by gentry interference and religious sectarianism. This was in striking contrast
to the situation at Gloucester where, as we know, the puritan
magistracy exercised firm control before 1640. The socio-economic
background also differed. While many provincial towns undoubtedly
suffered some economic and social dislocation in the century before
1640, most appear to have escaped those intense pressures which
Gloucester suffered, particularly in the 1620s and 1630s, pressures
which helped forge the powerful political cohesion and radical
mentality of that city and its leaders.[76]

At the same time, Gloucester's radical experience was probably
not unique. A number of corporate towns like Northampton, Salisbury, Barnstaple, Taunton, Colchester and possibly Coventry,[77] as

75. A. M. Johnson, 'Politics in Chester during the Civil War and the Interregnum
  1640–62', in Clark and Slack (eds), op. cit., 204 et seq.; Rosen, op. cit., 237–44.
76. Clark, English Provincial Society, 340–1, 381–2 et passim; idem, 'Thomas Scott
  and the growth of urban opposition to the early Stuart regime', Historical Journal, XXI (1978), 1–26; A. Fletcher, A County Community in Peace and War:
  Sussex 1600–1660 (1975), 234–9 et passim; P. Zagorin, The Court and the Country
  (1970), 149–54; VCH, Leicestershire, IV, 66–8, 74–5; D. Hirst, The Representative of the People? Voters and Voting in England under the Early Stuarts
  (1975), 46–64. There is virtually no evidence of sectarianism in Gloucester before
  1640; for activity after 1640 and concerted magisterial opposition see R. Bacon,
  The Spirit of Prelacie Yet Working . . . (1646),1–5.
77. Northampton: Northamptonshire RO, Northampton Assembly Book, 1547–1627,
  fos. 422, 426; 1627–1744, fos. 14, 42, 45, 62; see also Cox, op. cit., 179–80 et
  passim. Salisbury: P. Slack, 'Religious protest and urban authority: the case of
  Henry Sherfield iconoclast, 1633' in D. Baker (ed.), Studies in Church History:
  IX (1972), 295–302; Clark and Slack (eds.), op. cit., 164–94; P. Slack, 'An election to the Short Parliament', BIHR, XLVI (1973), 108–114 (Salisbury's puritan

well as unincorporated centres like Birmingham and Manchester, distinguished themselves by a similar staunch opposition to the king and his armies.[78] Like Gloucester they were bastions of the parliamentary cause, rallying points for the provincial godly. Though we lack detailed information on some of these communities, all or most of them seem to have had two features in common with radical Gloucester: firstly, they were dominated, on a formal or informal basis, by thoroughgoing puritan *potentiores*; secondly, they may well have suffered acute economic and social instability in the years before 1640. If the declining gentry have now been exorcised from the putative ranks of the parliamentary party, we must not ignore the major contribution to the Revolution of declining or economically unstable towns.

Editorial suggestions for further reading

P. Collinson, *The Birthpangs of Protestant England* (1988), pp. 28–59.
J. T. Evans, *Seventeenth-century Norwich: Politics, Religion and Government 1620–90* (Oxford, 1979).
R. Howell, 'Neutralism, conservatism and political alignment: The case of the towns 1642–9', in J. Morrill (ed.), *Reactions to the English Civil War* (1982), pp. 67–98.

magnates, on the defensive in the 1630s, had recovered power by 1640). Barnstaple: R. W. Cotton, *Barnstaple and the Northern Part of Devonshire during the Great Civil War 1642–6* (1889), 13 *et passim*; Chanter and Wainwright, op. cit., 65 *et passim*; Stephens, 'West Country ports', 92–3. Taunton: Underdown, op. cit., 22, 41, 80; J. Toulmin and J. Savage, *The History of Taunton* (1822), 410 *et seq.*; *CSPD*, 1634–5, 32. Colchester: T. Cromwell, *History and Description of the Ancient Town and Borough of Colchester* (1825), I, 88 *et seq.*; *APC*, 1626, 103–4; 1630–1, 358–9. Coventry: *VCH*, Warwickshire, VIII, 163, 218–19, 265–6.
78. Birmingham: C. Gill, *History of Birmingham: I* (1952), esp. 48–54; S. C. Ratcliff and H. C. Johnson (eds.), *Warwick County Records: II* (1936), 3, 4, 6 *et passim*. Manchester: J. P. Earwaker (ed.), *The Court Leet Records of the Manor of Manchester: II* (1885), 239–40, 288–9; *III* (1886), 122, 163, 268; F. A. Bruton, *A Short History of Manchester and Salford* (1924), 111–14, 118–20; A. P. Wadsworth and J. De Lacy Mann, *The Cotton Trade and Industrial Lancashire* (1931), 33–5, 42–3, 68.

Chapter 10

NEWCASTLE AND THE NATION: THE SEVENTEENTH-CENTURY EXPERIENCE

Roger Howell, Jr.

[*Archaelogia Aeliana*, 8 (1980)]

Tudor and Stuart Newcastle expanded rapidly due to the booming coal trade with London. This made its relations with the court and capital particularly important, especially as an inner ring of coal merchants sought to control city government. Here Roger Howell explores the political effects of this relationship, tracing a continuous struggle for power in the city which led to a complex and ever-shifting pattern of alliances with outside parties. But when outside parties threatened to exercise control over local affairs, rather than merely supporting local groupings, even former allies would object. The essay brings out the artificiality of dividing local from national issues in a period when such topics as monopoly, church policy and the correct balance of liberty and authority had both a local and a national meaning. The crisis points on which Howell concentrates saw such local and national perspectives come together, though not always in predictable ways. Not all towns were as polarized into two factions as Newcastle, nor as concerned with events in the capital, but his observations on local–central relations are broadly applicable.

The interaction of local community and central government is one of the pervasive themes of the history of early modern England; it is also, from the standpoint of historical analysis one of the most perplexing. While never wholly neglected, even by those historians whose focus was on broad national issues of constitutional or religious conflict, local history and the sense of local perspective have increasingly drawn the attention of those investigating the development of politics and political structures in Stuart England. The results have been stimulating and refreshing, and yet some key problems of interpretation remain. From a view of historical development that stressed the centrality of the court and parliament, there has been a marked shift of interest to the local political perspective, to the realization of the importance of local issues for the vast bulk of the political nation, and towards the view that political attitudes and actions were shaped more by local perceptions of developments than they were by abstract and general concerns with issues of economic, political, or religious liberty so beloved by an earlier generation of historians.[1] The change of emphasis has no doubt served as a healthy corrective, but what has not yet emerged is a satisfactory working model of the interaction of the two perspectives. If a history of seventeenth-century England written from the vantage point of Westminster distorts and exaggerates the picture, the replacement of it by a history written solely from the vantage point of the parish pump does little better. What one needs to know is the manner in which the local issues, local perceptions, and local problems shaped and informed the national perspective as they were expressed and generalized, for example, in parliament, and conversely how that sense of generality, which is so integral a part of the national perspective, was transferred and perhaps translated back into the framework and language of local politics.[2] That the flow of influence was not unidirectional seems obvious enough; conflict, for example, over a particular local clergyman influenced in major ways the locality's view of national religious policy, but in equally significant fashion a sense of national religious policy informed the locality's interpretation of its own particular situation.[3]

Newcastle in the seventeenth century provides a useful case study of the interaction of local community aspirations and perceptions with the broader issues agitating state and church throughout the century. The pattern of interaction was far from tidy or clear-cut; there were times when the interests of Newcastle coincided closely enough with the intentions of central policy to make a close working partnership seem appropriate and orderly, but equally there were occasions when the divergence became so marked as to raise questions not only about the specific application of policy to Newcastle, but also about the general nature of the policy itself. If there are threads to be found that run consistently through the whole story,

1. For a general discussion of this tendency with respect to the years of the English Revolution, see R. C. Richardson, *The Debate on the English Revolution* (London, 1977), chap. 7. R. Howell, *Newcastle upon Tyne and the Puritan Revolution* (Oxford 1967), was an early attempt to apply this perspective. J. S. Morill, *The Revolt of the Provinces* (London, 1976), is an excellent recent study informed by this perspective.

2. This critical point is raised, briefly discussed, but not wholly resolved in R. Ashton, *The English Civil War: Conservatism and Revolution 1603–1649* (London, 1978), chap. 3, esp. pp. 67–70.

3. This situation is amply reflected in the case of Newcastle in the period of the English Revolution. See Howell, *Newcastle and the Puritan Revolution*, chaps. 3 and 6.

they can perhaps be reduced to two. On the one hand, Newcastle, given its sizeable population and its obvious political, economic, and strategic importance, was always a natural area of concern for the central government, whether that government were king and parliament, king acting alone, parliament acting alone, or parliament and lord protector. On the other hand, the Newcastle reactions to such forms of solicitous attention were highly likely to be conditioned by local perceptions of the extent to which they reinforced or diminished the town's cherished sense of liberty and local authority. The stronger the impression of diminution of local liberty and authority, the greater was the possibility that specific local grievance would be translated into a generalized rejection of governmental policy, or, put in another way, the more likely it was that discussion of issues would rise above exclusively local concerns and begin to embrace the characteristics of the 'national' issues that dominate histories written from the perspective of the central government. While the consecutive history of the interaction of local and national affairs is beyond the scope of a single paper, a series of case studies drawn from one of the areas where the potential for conflict was high, namely the structure and functioning of local government including the election of members of parliament, can illustrate well the general nature of these relationships for the period between the accession of James I and the Glorious Revolution.[4]

The latter part of the sixteenth century had witnessed an intense struggle in Newcastle over issues related to the structure of local government. That struggle was basically the result of the increasing dominance in local affairs exercised by a small and exclusive clique of powerful merchants. Almost entirely composed of mercers and coal traders, the inner ring, or 'lords of coal'[5] as they were dubbed at the time, were already in a dominating position by the mid-Elizabethan period, well before their control was legitimated and firmly established by charters from the crown; in the period between 1581 and 1591, each of the major coal traders served a term as mayor of the town, eight of those so serving being directly involved in the management of the Grand Lease.[6] This process, by which

---

4. The interaction of local and national perspectives was hardly confined, of course, to the political sphere, and given the relations of political, religious, and social factors, the isolation of the political element for study here has some aspects of artificiality. This paper is not intended to minimize the importance of the other forms of interaction but rather to offer some suggestions about the manner in which the process of interaction worked by examining its specific manifestation within the political sphere.

5. B. L. Lansdowne MSS 66, no. 86.

6. Welford, *History of Newcastle and Gateshead* (Newcastle, 1884–7), 3: 420. C. H. Hunter Blair, *The Mayors of Newcastle upon Tyne 1216–1940 and the Sheriffs of the County of Newcastle upon Tyne 1399–1940* (Newcastle, 1940). pp. 44–6. The

power in the world of trade was extended directly to the political sphere, was not unresisted, and there was something in the way of a reform group in the 1590s which sought to preserve the rights of the general body of freemen in town government and to rescue what was conceived as the burgesses' share in the Grand Lease from the private interests of the grand lessees. Though the reform movement succeeded in capturing the mayoralty in 1593, its success was neither impressive nor sustained.[7]

Two factors account, in the main, for the limited success of the reform group, and each has a bearing on the complex interaction of central and local government. On the one hand, the reformers were themselves in an ambiguous position. Hardly classifiable among the economically disinherited of Newcastle, they did not seek the destruction of a system of privilege and monopoly; their aim was the far more limited one of widening the inner ring to a slight degree to include others from the upper levels of town life. Yet as allies they could only expect aid from interests which sought a wider destruction of the privileges of the town; the Bishop of Durham and the Lord Mayor and chief traders of London were allies of precisely this stamp. It is not unreasonable to conclude that support of this kind probably did as much to curtail the activities and enthusiasm of the reformers as any overt opposition on the part of the inner ring itself.[8] On the other hand, the reform movement was also faced by a powerful coalition of interests in support of the growing stranglehold of the inner ring on Newcastle politics, for the aspirations of the lords of coal meshed closely with the drift of national policy. Generally speaking, both the Tudor and Stuart monarchs sought to obtain control of the governing bodies of the boroughs, and the most obvious way in which to pursue this policy was to remove the choice of those governing bodies as far as possible from the hands of the whole community of citizens.[9] Thus, at the start of

---

grand lessees holding office were William Johnson, William Riddell, Henry Anderson, Henry Mitford, Henry Chapman, Roger Nicholson, William Selby, and George Farnaby.

7. Lionel Maddison was the mayor in 1593; he was said to be in sympathy with the reformers and to have 'proved the Townes interest in the grannde lease'. B. L. Lansdowne MSS 81, no. 41.
8. 'The Lord Mayor of London noted in January 1596 that the prominent reformer Henry Sanderson refused to act in any way to the prejudice of the Newcastle corporation and would only testify on behalf of London if the suit were directed solely against the co-partners of the Grand Lease. J. U. Nef, *The Rise of the British Coal Industry* (London, 1932), 2: 124. The general difficulties of the reform group over this point are usefully discussed ibid., 2: 121–25.
9. For a brief discussion of this point, see J. H. Sacret, 'The Restoration Government and Municipal Corporations', *EHR*, Vol. 14 (1930), pp. 232–59 and B. L. K. Henderson, 'The Commonwealth Charters', *TRHS*, 3rd Series, vi (1912), pp. 129–62.

the seventeenth century, crown policy and the desires of the dominant political group in Newcastle were in apparently total agreement. Local circumstances had led to the increasingly powerful position of a ring of related families with interests in the coal trade. They provided exactly the sort of tight and potentially dependent oligarchy that the crown was seeking, a dependency moreover that could be intensified by royal action to support the monopoly position of the Hostmen. The result of this close community of interest is to be found in the charters of Elizabeth I and James I to the town and to the Hostmen.[10]

The pattern of government thus established was to remain the political framework for seventeenth-century Newcastle, and political debate was to revolve around its preservation from change, either as the result of local initiatives to widen the base of power or as the result of royal desires to tighten the element of control even further. To forestall the first threat, the inner ring could call on royal support, since the crown had as substantial an interest in maintaining the tight monopoly control as the town oligarchs did; the problem was that recourse to such support from the central government raised the potential for increased royal interference in town affairs. What was, in its origins, a nice conjunction of interests could under stress become something quite different, and that realization obviously influenced in profound ways the interaction of Newcastle government with central government throughout the seventeenth century.

That the stranglehold of the inner ring on town government was the norm for the seventeenth century is graphically revealed by an analysis of town office holding. Such an analysis also reveals clearly that the key to the inner ring was a simultaneous position of strength in both the Merchant Adventurers (particularly the Mercers) and the Hostmen, rather than a base in the Hostmen alone.[11] The latter company, it should be remembered, was accessible to any free burgess 'of any free mystery' by the charter of James I; the very fact that entry was 'open' in this manner meant that the company could not, by itself, serve as the screen that filtered membership into the inner ring.[12] On the other hand, the combination of membership in

10. On the charters and the nature of town government, see Howell, *Newcastle and the Puritan Revolution*, pp. 42 ff.
11. For a more detailed discussion of this point, see ibid., pp. 46–7. In any case it is clear that the Hostmen did not exactly usurp power from the older merchant gilds as some have asserted. For an example of this sort of view, see *A Short View of the Rights of the Freemen of Newcastle upon Tyne in the Town Moor* (Newcastle, 1962).
12. F. W. Dendy, ed., *Extracts from the Records of the Company of Hostmen of Newcastle upon Tyne* (Durham, 1901), Surtees Soc., vol. 105, p. xli; J. F. Gibson, *The Newcastle upon Tyne Improvement Acts. . . . with an Introductory Historical Sketch* (London, 1881), p. xxxvi. While the Hostmen argued that this

the Merchant Adventurers and the Hostmen was a striking feature of those who ruled the town throughout the seventeenth century.[13] Between 1600 and 1640, 28 different people held the office of mayor; of these 18 were both Mercers and Hostmen, and 8 others were members of other branches of the Merchant Adventurers and the Hostmen. The remaining two holders of the office were both Merchant Adventurers. Between the Restoration and the Glorious Revolution, 29 different men held the office of mayor; of these 27 were definitely members of the Merchant Adventurers, and at least 20 and probably 22 were also members of the Hostmen at the same time. The same sort of preponderance is seen in other aspects of office-holding as well; those who became sheriffs, both before the Civil War and after the Restoration, reflect the same affiliations, as do members of parliament for the town. It is striking, for example, that of the 8 different men who served Newcastle as a member of parliament from 1600 to the summoning of the Long Parliament, all were both Merchant Adventurers and Hostmen, and only one was not a Mercer.[14]

The omission of the years 1640–60 from the above analysis was both deliberate and significant. In the confused years of the Civil War and Interregnum, the pattern of inner ring dominance was profoundly challenged. But if the overall nature of the interaction of central government and local government is to be appreciated fully, it must be recognized that there were other occasions outside those chaotic decades when challenges were raised in equally clear fashion. It should not be thought, for example, that the chartered establishment of inner ring control shut off the sort of protest that had characterized town politics in the 1590s; instead it tended to intensify the cleavages that had marked that decade by making the successors of the reform group of the 1590s a dissident element within the corporation.

The Shrove Tuesday riot of apprentices in the town in 1633 reveals this clearly and also casts some useful light on the central problem under investigation, the interaction of the locality and the

---

provision did not include the 15 bye-trades, this point was not consistently enforced; for example, Thomas Turner, a barber surgeon, was admitted on 17th January 1604. Dendy, *Records of the Hostmen*, p. 267

13. Statistics on the mayors and sheriffs are compiled from Blair, *Mayors and Sheriffs of Newcastle;* M. H. Dodds, ed., *The Register of Freemen of Newcastle upon Tyne* (Newcastle, 1923): and the records of the Hostmen and Merchant Adventurers.

14. Statistics on MPs are compiled from C. H. Hunter Blair, 'Members of Parliament for Northumberland and Newcastle upon Tyne 1559–1831', *Archaelogia Aeliana* 4th Series, xxiii (1945); Dodds, *Register of Freemen;* and the records of the Hostmen and Merchant Adventurers.

central government.[15] Ostensibly the riot had been caused by the construction of a lime kiln on the town drying ground by one Christopher Reasley, a non-freeman who had connections with the inner ring. It is clear, however, that Reasley was the pretext rather than the cause of the troubles, and it is striking that the representatives of the central government suspected this before the town authorities were willing to admit it was the case. Secretary Coke was already referring to the events as 'the late seditious riot' before the true circumstances surfaced.[16] What was actually at stake, as Coke shrewdly surmised, was the monopoly of the inner ring and the continuing desire of a reform element in the town to modify it. The surviving evidence suggests that the town authorities felt themselves to be in a somewhat ambiguous position with respect to the central government's interest in the affair. While they welcomed support of their position, they were reluctant to see that support extended to too close an enquiry into their affairs, and the mayor, at least, was clearly less than happy with Coke's suggestions that he should have taken more forceful immediate action; if nothing else, such reprimands appear to have suggested to those in Newcastle a lack of understanding on the part of governmental authorities of the nuances of the local situation.[17] When the real issues surfaced in June 1633 in the form of a petition from 700 or more burgesses to the King,[18] the inner ring was no doubt grateful for the support it received for its position from the royal government, although it seems that, from the perspective of the central government, the events looked rather more sinister than they did from the local perspective. In retrospect, it appears that the petitioners were well within the reform tradition that had been established in the 1590s. In that sense, they were, of course, of considerable concern to the inner ring. But crown authorities saw a deeper significance in the events, drawing attention to a growing population of mariners, colliers, keelmen, watermen and those of mean condition 'who are apt to turn everye pretence and colour of grievance into uproare and seditious mutinye'.[19]

Although the evidence is by no means unambiguous on this point, it appears that the town authorities, while desirous of royal support

15. For a detailed discussion of the riot, see Howell, *Newcastle and the Puritan Revolution*, pp. 53 ff.
16. *Cal. S. P. Dom., 1625–49 Addenda*, p. 453.
17. For Coke's criticisms see ibid. For the mayor's despondent response see *Cal. S. P. Dom., 1631–33*, p. 585.
18. PRO SP/16/240/27. The text of the grievances is printed in Welford, *History of Newcastle*, 3: 313–15.
19. PRO SP 16/245/32. The Council of the North noted that it had decided to look more fully into the matter because they realized the significance of the town to the King. Ibid.

for their position, were concerned about the form that support might take in the deteriorating political conditions of the 1630s. The reform group was limited in their manoeuvring by essentially the same concern, for they too had no interest in lessening the independent privileges of the town, yet this is precisely what increasing reliance on the support of the central government might be thought to lead to. What was happening was that the politics of the town were increasingly complicated by the development of national politics as it became clear that opposition to the inner ring and opposition to the policies of Charles I did not always go hand in hand. This point can be illustrated by a number of circumstances. Opposition to the imposition of ship money, for example, tended to pull inner ring and reformers together; resistance appears to have been widespread, with the general body of burgesses rallying behind the inner ring in a determined effort to avoid payment after the first two levies.[20] Attempts by the crown to influence local elections were likewise sternly resisted. In 1639 the King expressly warned the town 'that they should be very careful in choosing the mayor for this next succeeding year and by no means admit any factious or seditiously affected person to that place'.[21] It is clear that his message was intended to forestall the election of Robert Bewick, a Puritan against whom he had been specifically warned.[22] Yet Bewick was elected and no trace of local discontent about the choice is to be found. That he did not owe his election exclusively to his Puritan opposition to the crown is obvious enough; he was a Hostman and Mercer, a previous holder of the mayoralty, and a member of the inner ring, but that he was elected against the express wishes of the crown is an equally obvious indication of the limits of inner ring subservience to the crown, even at a time of apparently increased agitation over their position.

The municipal and parliamentary elections held within a short time of each other in 1640 provide further examples of the extent to which national politics and local political traditions interacted.[23] The swing in the municipal elections against Puritanism can be attributed to external factors, but not to the machinations of the crown, however helpful the results were for the crown's purposes.

20. M. H. Dodds, 'Ship Money', *Newcastle Citizen*, Vol. 1 (1930), pp. 68–70. Cf. also *Cal. S. P. Dom., 1638–9*, pp. 4–5, 80, 105, 321, 325; *Cal. S. P. Dom, 1639–40*, p. 460; *Cal. S. P. Dom., 1640*, p. 133.
21. *Cal. S. P. Dom.*, 1639, p. 480.
22. Ibid., pp. 450–51; the informant was Sir John Marley.
23. For a detailed discussion of these elections, see Howell, *Newcastle and the Puritan Revolution*, pp. 124 ff. The discussion of the elections to the Long Parliament should be supplemented by R. Howell, 'The Elections to the Long Parliament in Newcastle: Some New Evidence', *Archaelogia Aeliana* 4th Series, xlvi (1968), pp. 225–7.

The Scottish invasion and occupation had been the critical factor, and the feeling had clearly grown up that Puritan religious sympathies with the Scots had been at least partially responsible for the occupation of the town.[24] The elections to the Long Parliament remain somewhat obscure, but one clear fact does emerge, and that is the widespread support for men of local connection. Of the three candidates who stood in the election, only one was thoroughly typical of inner ring politics, Sir Henry Anderson, and he was returned unopposed. The other seat was contested between John Blakiston, whose close local connections were counterbalanced by the fact that he was not a powerful and wealthy Hostman and the knowledge that he was prominently identified with the Puritan movement, and Sir John Melton, a total outsider to town politics, Secretary to the Council of the North, and a pronounced Straffordian. If powerful external backing was sufficient for Melton to be elected on one return, it should be remembered that the proceedings in the election were under investigation for corrupt practices by the Committee for Privileges when Melton died and that it was subsequently decided simply to amend the return in Blakiston's favour, rather than hold a new election, a strong indication of the popularity of his candidacy in the original election. That an outsider to the inner ring and a Puritan to boot could achieve this level of support in a climate that was clearly anti-Puritan, while a court backer with powerful connections could not attract more significant support, even though aided by the fear that parliamentary reformers would assault the privileged position of the Hostmen, is a telling illustration of the power of local identification and independence in the politics of the period.

The years of the civil wars and Interregnum were to see the pattern of Newcastle politics altered, at times by the application of external pressures.[25] On two occasions in those years, the rights of election of mayor were over-ridden by outside authority. In October 1642 Sir John Marley was elected by mandamus from the king; in 1645 he was removed from office by an ordinance of parliament and Henry Warmouth substituted in his place.[26] There were, in addition to these actions, various purgings of the town corporation reflecting the shifting fortunes of the war. In April 1643 Henry Warmouth was

24. For an example of the reaction against the Scots, see *A Letre from an Alderman of Newcastle Shewing in Part the Grievances There* in M. A. Richardson, ed., *Reprints of Rare Tracts* (Newcastle, 1847), vol.1. This letter appears to have been circulated in manuscript form. There are copies in PRO SP 16/466/89; Bodleian Library Tanner MSS 65, ff. 110–11v; B. L. Harleian MSS 1576, ff. 312–13v; William Trumbull MSS, xx, f. 48 (Berkshire Record Office).

25. For a detailed discussion of political life in Newcastle in this period, see Howell, *Newcastle and the Puritan Revolution,* chaps. 4 and 5.

26. A. M. Oliver, *The Mayoralty of Newcastle upon Tyne* (Newcastle, 1910), pp, 21–2.

removed from his aldermancy for neglect of duty,[27] while the following September 35 freemen were disfranchised.[28] Following the reduction of the town to parliament, the chief royalists such as Marley and Sir Nicholas Cole were ordered to be purged by parliament.[29] Such interference in the normal life of the corporation is hardly surprising, given the conditions of the time, but it is not easy to come by evidence concerning the town's reactions to such exterior pressures, which they clearly would have resented and resisted under normal circumstances. What evidence there is, however, suggests that the existing structures of the town showed remarkable resiliency in the face of such pressures, and that, where changes did occur, they were at least in part the result of anticipatory changes stemming from town initiative rather than wholly imposed alterations from outside.[30]

The existence of a substantial and important core of town office holders who not only survived all changes in government but cooperated with each in turn is a case in point. Men whose roots were firmly fixed in the pre-Civil War corporate exclusiveness of the town continued to serve as active members of the corporation while Newcastle was held for the King, reduced by the Scots, subjected to parliamentary control and ultimately the control of the Lord Protector, and then returned to what was essentially its pre-war political condition at the Restoration.[31] The loyalties of such men might well seem baffling, both to the more zealous partisans of their own age and to subsequent generations of historians because, in a real sense, they had no fixed loyalties with respect to the large and complex questions that were agitating national politics. At the worst, they can be pictured as secular vicars of Bray; looked at in a more positive light, they are men whose concerns for the stability and smooth functioning of traditional local arrangements were paramount.

An analysis of the changes which actually were made during the period reinforces the impression of the persistence of local structures

---

27. M. H. Dodds, ed., *Extracts from the Newcastle upon Tyne Council Minute Book 1639–1656* (Newcastle, 1920), p. 24.

28. Ibid., pp. 27–8. The order was confirmed at the beginning of October, ibid., pp. 29–30.

29. They were named in an act of 24th March 1644/5. Newcastle Common Council Book 1645–50, Tyne and Wear County Archives, f. 25. They were also named in the ordinance for the government of Newcastle, 26th May 1645. *Lords Journal* 7: 395.

30. The pattern is not unusual to Newcastle. I have discussed this point in more general terms in R. Howell, 'The Structure of Politics in the English Civil War', *Albion,* vol. 11, no. 2 (1979), pp. 111–27.

31. Examples among the aldermen would include Robert Shafto, Mark Milbank, and John Emerson. Again, the existence of this middle group, which successfully sought accommodation with successive and conflicting regimes, would seem to be a general feature of urban politics in the period rather than a peculiar Newcastle feature. Cf. Howell, 'Structure of Urban Politics', pp.116–19, 122–3.

and rivalries, even in the face of intense pressures from outside, a persistence that is frequently disguised at first glance because of the patterns by which the labels of the 'national' struggle – royalist versus parliamentarian, presbyterian versus independent – were taken up by the participants themselves and superimposed on the 'local' struggle. One certain result of the reduction of Newcastle to parliament was an alteration, extending throughout the Interregnum, in the old inner ring control of town government. The new governing clique, led by Thomas Bonner and the Dawson family, appears to have established an impressive hold on the mayoralty;[32] in 1656 it was alleged that the Dawsons in collusion with Bonner had managed the election for mayor as they pleased for some years past,[33] and the results of elections seem to validate the allegation. But while the Dawsons had, in effect, ridden to power on the back of the parliamentary victory, they did not represent a totally new impulse in the politics of the town. They could trace their roots to the reform movement of the 1630s, and their behaviour in office was completely consistent with that line of descent. They had no interest in destroying the privileges of the town; their concern was to broaden the base of monopoly control only slightly to include themselves and their most immediate supporters. In practice they proved as uncompromising in their opposition to genuine reformers and as staunchly defensive of the charter rights and independence of the town as any of the older oligarchs they had for the moment displaced.[34]

Between the establishment of the parliamentary corporation in 1645 and the reshaping of town government in the aftermath of the Restoration, two aldermen were removed from office, and the circumstances surrounding their removals can be taken as further evidence for the persistence of local issues disguised in the terminology of national issues. The first to be removed was John Cosins in 1647;[35] although there is some ambiguity about the circumstances of his removal, the chief issue seems to have been the newly created ascendancy of the Dawson group. If Cosins was not a member of

---

32. For a detailed discussion of the Bonner-Dawson clique, see Howell, *Newcastle and the Puritan Revolution*, chap. 5.

33. Newcastle Common Council Book 1650–9, Tyne and Wear County Archives, f. 406.

34. This was revealed clearly, for example, in their struggle with Ralph Gardner. If anything, Gardner seems to have fared less well under the parliamentary corporation than he had when the inner ring predominated. See R. Howell, *Monopoly on the Tyne 1650–58: Papers Relating to Ralph Gardner* (Newcastle, 1978).

35. The effective order for his removal was dated 24th March 1647. Dodds, *Council Minute Book*, pp. 68–9. An order to remove him had been signed as early as 18th February. Newcastle Common Council Book 1645–50, Tyne and Wear County Archives, Cf. 110. It is interesting to note that Cosins invoked both a 'local' and

the inner ring, his repeated recourse to the town charter as the core of his attack on the Dawsons suggests that he was arguing the case of the inner ring or at least a case with which they could readily identify. Following Cosins' removal, his affairs became much entangled with broader national issues. Cosins himself was a conservative Presbyterian parliamentarian and in the context of a growing split between the Presbyterians and the Independents, exacerbated by disturbances in the army, his report that there was danger the town might be secured against the present government received excited attention in London.[36] But it should not be thought that the issues thus raised were the ones which had led to his expulsion, for it was not until the beginning of July, more than three months after his expulsion, that the Newcastle authorities raised the argument that Cosins intended to bring the Scots back into England, embroiling the nation once more in civil strife.[37] The impression that the root of the trouble was local and connected with inner ring resistance to the Bonner–Dawson clique is further heightened by the minor riot following Bonner's election as mayor the next year; it was triggered off by the actions of Edmond Marshall, a servant and apprentice of Cosins, and appears to have had no connection with broader issues of national politics.[38]

The second alderman removed was Leonard Carr, and his case even more clearly reflects the general pattern which has been suggested. Carr was an established figure in the town and in most ways, other than his origins in Yorkshire, a person typical of inner ring politics; he had become an alderman by 1642, had served as steward and governor of the Hostmen before the Civil War, and had been assistant and governor of the Merchant Adventurers in addition.[39] He had admittedly participated in the defence of the town in 1644,[40] but it is striking that no question of his loyalty appears to have been raised on the occasions of royalist scares in 1648, 1651, and 1655. But in 1657 articles accusing him of royalist sympathies were pre-

a 'national' argument against his removal. On the one hand, he relied on the charter for his position; on the other, he argued he could not be removed since he was brought in by parliamentary ordinance. Ibid., ff. 124–6.

36. *Commons Journal.*, 5: 208. Cosins was not alone in commenting on this subject. Cf. the two letters from Skippon, the parliamentary governor of Newcastle, printed in H. Cary, *Memorials of the Great Civil War 1642–1652* (London, 1842), 1: 229–32.

37. *Commons Journal.*, 5: 229.

38. Dodds, *Council Minute Book*, pp. 102–4.

39. Ibid., p. 21; MSS Hostmen, Old Book, ff. 185, 187, 188; MSS Merchant Adventurers, Order Book, ff. 1, 18, 26.

40. Cf. E33 (17), *A True Relation of the Late Proceedings of the Scottish Army* (London, 1644), pp. 11–13; *Kingdomes Weekly Intelligencer*, no. 69, 21–7 August 1644, pp. 556–7; E16 (5), *A Particular Relation of the Taking of Newcastle* (London, 1644), pp. 12–13, 9 (2nd pagination).

sented to the Council of State.[41] On close examination, the charges now appear to have been fabrications,[42] but they were sufficient to convince the Council of State; that body directed the mayor and Common Council to remove Carr, which was done on 28th December 1657.[43] The spurious nature of the charges against him and the fact that he was an ill man over 80 years old at the time of his removal suggest that this is something other than the case of an active and loyal corporation reporting on and with the help of the Council of State removing a dangerous royalist. When one realizes that Carr had been an outspoken opponent of the Bonner–Dawson clique,[44] questioning their management of elections and accusing them of extensive abuses of power, all the while continuing to hold an aldermancy and preventing the election to it of one of their own supporters, the whole episode assumes a quite different character and becomes an excuse to eliminate a person who was a problem in local affairs and to the Dawsons rather than in national affairs and to Cromwell. The election of a close supporter of the Bonner–Dawson clique, Ambrose Barnes, to fill the vacancy would seem to complete the picture.[45]

One final observation about the politics of Newcastle in the aftermath of the parliamentary victory needs to be made: despite a clear recognition on the part of parliament that the town corporation should be reshaped to serve new purposes and new loyalties, the overall form which that reshaping took appears to have been generated as much from below as from above. It is suggestive, for example, that there was a sizable time lag between parliament's naming of delinquents to be removed in March 1645 and the local enactment of their disfranchisement in late September 1645.[46] What is even more telling is the evidence which suggests that the parliamentary ordinance for settling the government of Newcastle confirmed an existing situation rather than created a new one. Details of how the town government functioned between the reduc-

---

41. *Cal. S. P. Dom., 1656–7*, p. 272.
42. On the falsity of the charges, see Howell, *Newcastle and the Puritan Revolution*, pp. 180–81.
43. *Cal. S. P. Dom., 1656–7*, pp. 226–7; Newcastle Common Council Book 1656–1722, Tyne and Wear County Archives, f. 12v.
44. Cf. Newcastle Common Council Book 1650–9. Tyne and Wear County Archives, f. 406.
45. It is perhaps suggestive that George Blakiston, a younger generation member of an old-style Newcastle political family, resigned from the Common Council in protest at the election. Ibid. f. 467. But it may be that the objection was simply to Barnes's youth. Cf. W. H. D. Longstaffe, ed., *Memoirs of the Life of Mr Ambrose Barnes* (Durham, 1867), Surtees Soc., vol. 50, p. 99.
46. Newcastle Common Council Book 1645–50. Tyne and Wear County Archives, f. 25.

tion of the town and the parliamentary ordinance are scanty.[47] Part of the resulting obscurity concerns the critical entry into aldermanic office of Henry Dawson and Thomas Bonner, but there is no doubt that they were occupying such places a month or more before parliament named them.[48] Likewise, one of the aldermen named in the parliamentary ordinance does not appear in the first list of the new corporation, nor for that matter in any subsequent list of town office holders, and it is surely more than coincidence that his place was assumed by a relative of Henry Dawson.[49] Bulstrode Whitelocke was later to assert that the House of Commons took order for settling the magistrates of Newcastle in violation of their charter;[50] on one level that observation was valid, but on another it was misleading. If the breaking of inner ring control and the rise of the Bonner–Dawson clique constituted something in the way of a civic revolution, it was a revolution which in key ways had been engineered from within Newcastle itself and the parliamentary role can more accurately be described as a confirmation of a situation already existing in the town.

The restoration of the monarchy in 1660 and the consequent purging of the corporation in 1662 allowed for the re-establishment of inner ring control. But again, the process by which that control was established must be observed carefully if the delicate interaction of town affairs and central government actions is to be rightly understood. The task of investigation is complicated by the fact that no complete list of members of the town government exists for 1660–61 and thus tracing the changes in membership between 1659 and 1662 is difficult. But the only signed order for the mayoral year of John Emerson shows that at least one of the old inner ring oligarchs, Sir John Marley, who had been purged in the 1640s, had re-established himself in the town government before the actual purging under the terms of the Corporation Act,[51] and there is some additional

---

47. No records of meetings of the Common Council were kept until 28th March 1645. Dodds, *Council Minute Book*, p. 25. The financial machinery of the town appears to have been reestablished more quickly. Receipts were kept from 22nd November 1644 and payments from the fourth week of October. Newcastle Chamberlains' Accounts 1642–5, Tyne and Wear County Archives, ff. 58, 190v.

48. They are among the signatories of a letter to Speaker Lenthall a month before the first official notice of their appointment. *Commons Journal* 3: 714.

49. The alderman so named was Henry Lawson, the fifth senior member of the Common Council. Dodds, *Council Minute Book*. p. 21. William Dawson appears in his place in the earliest list of the parliamentary corporation which dates from the audit of accounts, 4th October 1645. Newcastle Chamberlains' Accounts 1642–5, Tyne and Wear County Archives, f. 167.

50. B. Whitelocke, *Memorials of the English Affairs from the Beginning of the Reign of Charles I to the Happy Restoration of King Charles II* (Oxford, 1853), 1: 348.

51. Newcastle Common Council Book 1656–1722, Tyne and Wear County Archives, f. 43.

evidence to suggest that others in this category, Sir Nicholas Cole and Sir Francis Bowes among them, had done the same.[52] The actual purge of 1662 was a relatively limited affair, and again there must be a sizable suspicion that the impetus for the precise changes made came from within the town rather than from without. Five aldermen were removed, all clearly associated with the Bonner-Dawson group; five members of the old inner ring of pre-Civil War days replaced them.[53] Those whose early careers and family connections had cut them out for inner ring politics survived, their activity in the Commonwealth and Protectorate corporation notwithstanding.

The Restoration, then, returned Newcastle politics to its normal seventeenth-century stance. The inner ring dominated, grateful no doubt for the general support of the monarchy, but anxious, as before, that this solicitous concern should not interfere in local rights and privileges under the guise of solidifying that support. The increasingly aggressive stance of the later Stuart monarchs towards the issue of royal control of boroughs made that sort of partnership in the long run impossible. The fine line between support and control had always made such conflict a potentiality; the policies of Charles II and James II made it a reality.

For the initial part of the reign of Charles II, the political situation in Newcastle appears to have been relatively settled, even though the activities and agitation of dissenters became a prominent part of the scene and inevitably had political overtones.[54] The town had been quick to make a loyal address to the restored monarch, expressing the hope that he would be the instrument to unite a divided church, compose a distracted kingdom, and ease an oppressed people.[55] In the heady atmosphere of the Restoration itself, aggressively overt royalism became the order of the day; at the parliamentary elections a health was drunk to the King and confusion

52. Ibid, f. 44.
53. Those removed were George Dawson, Christopher Nicholson, Henry Rawlings, William Johnson, and Peter Sanderson. Seated in their stead were Sir James Clavering, Sir Francis Anderson, Sir Francis Liddell, Henry Maddison, and Cuthbert Carr. Predictably, the middle group represented by Robert Shafto, Mark Milbank, and John Emerson survived.
54. Concern about the dissenters is widely reflected in the literature emanating from the Newcastle clergy in the later Stuart period. Cf. for example, J. March, *The False Prophet Unmaskt* (London, 1683); J. March, *A Sermon Preached before the Right Worshipful the Mayor, Recorder, Aldermen, Sheriff &c of . . . Newcastle* (London, 1677); J. Rawlet, *A Dialogue betwixt Two Protestants* (London, 1685); and J. Shaw, *No Reformation of the Established Reformation* (London, 1685). When Thomas Story visited a conventicle at Newcastle he was most impressed by the political overtones. 'Expecting to hear something like Doctrine from so noted a Man among them', he was disappointed that the message was substantially 'suggestions of Jealousy and Dislike against the Government'. *A Journal of the Life of Thomas Story* (Newcastle, 1747), p. 3.
55. *Cal. S. P. Dom., 1660–1*, p. 4.

to Zion,[56] while a number of tracts were locally published to stress the deep and continuing loyalty of the town.[57] For his part, the King in February 1664 by a charter of inspeximus confirmed the charters of Elizabeth I and James I with their ancient privileges.[58] As late as 1682, John March, the vicar of Newcastle, could express in a sermon the confident feeling that the magistrates of Newcastle and the monarchy were still working in a pattern of close co-operation, despite the many distractions that plagued national affairs:[59]

> This famous Town, over which you preside, has always been esteemed a place of very great importance . . . Now a Town of this importance, as it well deserves, so in such times of distraction as we live in, it may justly challenge the greatest care and vigilance of those that are intrusted with the Government of it, And I do heartily rejoice, that I need not fear the least imputation of flattery, whilest I proclaim to the world that as there is not any Town which can equal it for Trade, Populousness, and wealth, so there is none that doe Surpass it, and but very few that equal it in point of Loyalty and Conformity.
> This Happiness and Glory we owe in great measure to that Loyalty and Conformity which shine forth in your own Examples; partly also to that great encouragement you give unto the Loyal and Orthodox Clergy of the place, but chiefly to the due exercise of your Authority, in surpressing Conventicles, those notorious Seminaries of Popery, Schism, and Rebellion.

Despite these hopeful comments, a crisis was at hand in the relations between Newcastle and the central government. In the last years of his reign, as he sought to rule without parliament, Charles II escalated the pressure exerted by the monarchy on the boroughs, and Newcastle was one of the targets of that pressure. The precise nature of the intrigue and in-fighting that ensued escapes us at some key points, but the general outcome of the pressure was clear enough. The attempt to enforce confusing and ultimately unpopular royal policies through the manipulation of the corporation in defiance of its chartered rights led to a repudiation of the Stuart monarchy which the corporation had long claimed to support.

The first act in the unfolding crisis appears to have passed off with surprisingly little overt negative reaction. Early in 1684, Charles II signified to the corporation that he expected a surrender of their

---

56. E1038 (8) *The Lords Loud Call to England* (London, 1660), p. 19.
57. R. Astell, *Vota Non Bella* (Gateshead, 1660); R. Hooke, *The Bishops' Appeale or an Address to the Brethren of the Preshyteriall Judgement* (Newcastle, 1661); R. Thompson, *The Loyall Subject* (Newcastle, 1660 and 1662).
58. J. Brand, *The History and Antiquities of the Town and County of Newcastle upon Tyne* (London, 1789), 2: 193.
59. J. March, *Th' Encaenia of St. Ann's Chappel in Sandgate* (London, 1682), sig. A3–A3v.

charter, 'which was to be renewed on condition that the mayor, recorder, sheriff, and town clerk might always be in the King's power to appoint or confirm'.[60] While the surrender was not enrolled, the King granted a new charter in 1685, in it constituting several new aldermen and reserving to himself the power to displace the mayor and aldermen at his pleasure.[61] The charter itself did not reach Newcastle until after the death of the King; the proclamation of James II and the arrival of the charter fell within two days of each other. A contemporary tract recalled the two events as being the cause of great celebration;[62]

> Bells rang, Minstrills play'd, and Cannon did Thunder . . .
> Pikes, Muskets and Drums, and mony gay Fellowes
> The King's Health was Drunk at ilk Tavern and Ale-house
> Instead of fair water their Fountains sprang Clarret.

The tract labelled the new King 'the justest Man on Earth',[63] and referred to the charter as 'their Rule, their Light, and their Guide'.[64]

As the unhappy mayoralty of Sir Henry Brabant revealed, the actual situation was far from as stable as these observations might suggest.[65] Brabant himself was a confirmed loyalist, one who, as Richardson observed in the nineteenth century, 'carried his attachment to the sovereign to an extent bordering on monomaniacism'.[66] His administration appears to have been the source of contention from the very beginning, though it is unclear whether his attitude towards the crown or his rivalry with other town political figures, especially Sir William Blackett, was the root cause of the difficulty. In any case, the clash led to efforts by both sides to the controversy to invoke the aid of the crown in support of their position. The election of the sheriff and Common Council had been suspended by Brabant because of an effort to elect his opponents; he wrote to the Earl of Sunderland to seek royal support and appears to have received it, for he summoned the electors, told them he had the King's support, and asked if they had any reason why the Common Council as named by him should not be sworn. He recalled that Sir

60. Brand, *History of Newcastle*, 2: 194.
61. Longstaffe, *Memoirs of Barnes*, p. 176n.
62. G. Stuart, *A Joco-Serious Discourse in Two Dialogues* (London and Newcastle, 1686), pp. 1–2.
63. Ibid. sig. A4.
64. Ibid. p. 3.
65. The following account of events in the mayoralty of Brabant is drawn substantially from *The Eve of the Revolution in Newcastle upon Tyne* in M. A. Richardson, ed., *Reprints of Rare Tracts* (Newcastle, 1847), vol. iv.
66. Ibid. p. 15. The biographer of Barnes recorded that Brabant once declared 'if the king should command him to kill a man in cold blood, he took himself bound in conscience and duty to execute his command'. Longstaffe, *Memoirs of Barnes*, p. 193.

William Blackett, speaking for the dissident group, 'dissatisfiedly said they had nothing to do, since your Majesty took the power from them, and so departed before the said Common Council could be all sworn'.[67]

In an apparent attempt to solidify his position, Brabant called a meeting of all the freemen of the town to explain the nature of the King's interference. According to his account, the meeting was awkward since his opponents 'did most wickedly disperse and spread abroad that the Mayor called a Gill [sic] in order to give up their Charter, which made the Mobile much more numerous at and about the Town Court that day than ever was seen before'.[68] This uneasiness about the charter suggests that the picture of happy acceptance of Charles II's new charter may be somewhat overdrawn. Despite the obstruction of a significant number of aldermen, Brabant was able to calm the crowd by assuring them there was no further action contemplated with respect to the charter. 'They unanimously gave a great shout of "God bless the King" and were dismissed without any disorder. All things', he noted, 'looked very serene and peaceable amongst the Commons, of which the far greater number are very loyall, but of late years much disheartened by the overawe of the Magistrates, who make a great many act against their inclinations'.[69]

The next stage in the crisis came by an unexpected route. Sir William Blackett, utilizing his position as a member of parliament, appears to have been able to persuade the crown to purge the corporation under the terms of Charles II's charter, in order to reduce Brabant's forces to a minority. Given the fervent loyalty of Brabant himself, the action of the crown at this juncture is difficult to explain, unless it is assumed that Blackett's true intentions and feelings were deliberately misrepresented, as Brabant claimed.[70] Even more puzzling is the failure of the crown to make any reply to Brabant's impassioned petition that the situation be rectified and the ascendancy of the Blackett group curtailed by a royal order continuing Brabant in his mayoralty for an additional year.[71]

The tenseness of the situation and the interaction of local rivalries with national issues was well illustrated in the celebrated struggle during Brabant's mayoralty to erect in Newcastle a statue of James II.[72] It is clear that Brabant himself was the moving force behind

67. *Eve of the Revolution in Newcastle*, p. 8.
68. Ibid. p. 9.
69. Ibid. pp. 9–10.
70. Ibid. p. 10.
71. Ibid. pp. 13–14.
72. On the statue see M. R. Toynbee, 'Fresh Light on William Larson's Statue of James II at Newcastle upon Tyne', *Archaelogia Aeliana* 4th Series, xxix (1951), pp. 108–17; M. R. Toynbee, 'A Further Note on William Larson's Statue of

the decision to erect the statue, but the Blackett group entered strong objection to the scheme and refused to sign an order for it until Brabant threatened to send a list of those who would not sign directly to the King. At this point, he noted, they agreed, 'more out of fear than love'.[73] If the opposition to Brabant had its origins in local rivalries, it was by now clearly intertwined with national concerns as well. Blackett may not have hesitated to use the King to purge the corporation, but when it came to erecting a statue to him, his supporters were not slow to declare publicly that 'the erecting of the said statue looked like Popery'.[74]

In the succeeding municipal elections, the Blackett group had its way. Brabant was not continued in office, and the Blackett-backed candidate Nicholas Cole was elected mayor. Although Cole's mayoralty passed without undue intensification of the growing rift between crown and community, two events falling within it were disturbing pointers to the continuation of crisis. At the end of May the King sent a mandate to the corporation instructing them to admit Sir William Creagh, a notorious papist, to his freedom and he was duly admitted a month later.[75] In September, an address, signed by Cole as mayor, was sent to the King; though couched in terms of formal loyalty, it clearly expressed deep concern about a growing pattern of interference with civic privileges and overt support of Catholics in the process. It thanked the King for his 'repeated acts of grace and bounty vouchsafed to this your ancient corporation' but then added the significant qualification that the thanks were being extended for those acts 'not only in the free enjoyment of our liberties and privileges, but more especially in the full exercise of the professed religion of the Church of England, whereof we are true members, true loyalty being inseparable from the principles of that church'.[76]

In the months that followed, the intertwining of local grievance with general national policy was intensified. There is every reason to suspect that Newcastle's antagonism towards the King would have markedly increased even had they conceived the interference with local conditions to be directed against the corporation alone; when they could see it as part of a broader policy, their sense of grievance in like manner broadened. Newcastle's experience in the last years of James II was far from unique; that unhappy monarch was busily unravelling the complex web of support for the monarchy that his brother had so patiently created, and his hand fell clumsily on many

James II at Newcastle upon Tyne', *Archaelogia Aeliana* 4th Series, xxxiv (1956), p. 91.
73. *Eve of the Revolution in Newcastle*, p. 13.
74. Ibid.
75. Longstaffe, *Memoirs of Barnes*, p. 176n.
76. Ibid.

corporations and institutions.[77] In Newcastle the net result of his machinations was the alienation of the older governing elite by his interference with the charter, the alienation of the nonconformists by his papist policy, and the eventual restoration of inner ring control in reaction to both these developments.

In 1687 John Squire was elected mayor in succession to Nicholas Cole; as a Merchant Adventurer and Hostman, he was a typical inner ring candidate. At the end of December, James II, acting under the terms of the new charter, moved to reconstruct the corporation into a more pliant instrument of his will. By mandate he displaced the mayor, six aldermen, the sheriff, the deputy recorder, and fifteen of the Common Council. In addition he commanded the electors to choose the recently intruded Sir William Creagh as mayor, along with a carefully selected new set of officials to replace those he had removed.[78] Apparently the electors refused to elect them on the grounds that they were 'papists and persons not qualified' but this action had no effect, for Creagh and his colleagues assumed office notwithstanding.[79] Within a month the new corporation had drafted what was described as 'a remarkably fulsome address'[80] to the King, but it was not sent, a majority of the Common Council over-ruling it. Despite that setback, the adherents of royal policy appear to have believed that they had succeeded in controlling the corporation for James II. In a sermon preached before the mayor on 29th January 1688, a Jesuit Philip Metcalfe remarked that on the basis of 'universal applause' he could only conclude that Creagh 'commanded the hearts of all'.[81] If Metcalfe was apparently blind to the tension created by royal interference in the town's politics, he did sense that Creagh's religion was a source of contention: 'our Prince is pleased with your constant Loyalty; the famous Town of Newcastle with your prudent Government; good Christians with your exemplary life; I wish your Religion were in the same esteem with many as your Person is'.[82] Given the consistently anti-Catholic stance of the Newcastle clergy in the years preceeding 1688, the latter point was hardly surprising.[83] Even Vicar March, who

---

77. M. Ashley, *James II* (Minneapolis, 1977) and J. Miller, *James II: A study in Kingship* (London, 1977), *passim*.
78. Longstaffe, *Memoirs of Barnes*, p. 176n.
79. Ibid.
80. Ibid.
81. P. Metcalfe, *A Sermon Preached before the Right Worshipful the Mayor of the Town & County of Newcastle upon Tyne* (London, 1688), sig. A2.
82. Ibid. sig. A2v.
83. For examples of this anti-Catholicism, cf. J. March, *A Sermon Preached before the Mayor*; J. March, *Sermons Preach'd on Several Occasions* (London, 1699); J. Rawlet, *A Dialogue betwixt Two Protestants*; J. Rawlet, *An Explication of the Creed, the Ten Commandments, and the Lords Prayer* (London, 1679); J. Shaw, *No Reformation of the Established Reformation*; J. Shaw, *Origo Protestantium*

could not accept the Glorious Revolution in good conscience, had never been able to tolerate the slightest sympathy for the religion of his royal master.

In fact, both religious and political concerns were present. If the traditional elite had been disturbed by the issue of a new charter and the use made of it to date, their concern must have been immeasurably heightened by a further breach of the privileges carried out with the connivance of Creagh and his subservient colleagues.[84] In February a *quo warranto* was served on the mayor; the closeness of the date to that of the failure to carry the loyal address to the King is suggestive. At the beginning of March Creagh and his colleagues surrendered the charter of Charles II, although once again the surrender was not enrolled. Sometime after 9th June and before 22nd September James II granted a further new charter to the town 'whereby the ancient custom of electing the mayor &c and burgesses for parliament were changed and the same in great measure put into the power of the mayor and aldermen', a power being 'reserved in the King to place or displace'.[85] The most plausible reconstruction that can be made of the ensuing municipal elections is that a combination of dissenters who opposed the Catholicism of Creagh and his colleagues and traditional Newcastle political figures who were horrified by the manipulation of the town's charter combined to thwart the continuation of the Creagh group. The design of the latter was to secure the election of Catholics as both mayor and sheriff; the result was a victory for two protestants, William Hutchinson and Matthew Partis. It is certain that Ambrose Barnes played a critical role in organizing the opposition and securing the result, but it is worth remembering that his biographer was at pains to stress that this was no 'clandestine election of Dissenters' but rather that many who co-operated 'were known to be zealously affected to the Church of England'.[86]

The royal policy with respect to Newcastle was clearly in a shambles. Even a corporation already reshaped in the royal interest could not be coerced into the desired results in 1688. The last desperate gamble of reversing the policy of charter interference in October did nothing to alter the situation from the royal point of view. All it allowed was a quiet transition back to inner ring control following the repudiation of the new charters of Charles II and

or an Answer to a Popish Manuscript (London, 1679); J. Shaw, *The Pourtraicture of the Primitive Saints* (Newcastle, 1652). For the importance of anti-Catholicism in the period, see J. Miller, *Popery and Politics in England 1660–1688* (Cambridge, 1973).

84. Longstaffe, *Memoirs of Barnes*, p. 176 n.
85. Ibid. Oliver gives the date of 24th July for the new charter. Oliver, *Mayoralty of Newcastle*, p. 25.
86. Longstaffe, *Memoirs of Barnes*, pp. 176 n. 177–8.

James II.[87] On 5th November Hutchinson and Partis relinquished their offices, to be replaced by Nicholas Ridley, the sheriff of 1682, and Matthew White, both typical inner ring figures; as James Clephan put it, 'corporate life had flowed back to its old channels'.[88] It was coincidental but appropriate that the soon-to-be William III landed on the same day.

To use the terminology of modern political discussion, one could argue that the political consciousness of Newcastle had been considerably, if perhaps temporarily, raised in the events that culminated in the Glorious Revolution. It has been raised in that familiar progression by which specific grievance was generalized and then elevated to the level of ideological opposition. In describing these events with specific reference to Newcastle in the following year, James Welwood noted, 'The Accession of a Popish Prince to the throne, the barefac'd Invasion of Liberty and Property, the palpable Incroachments on Laws and Fundamental Constitutions . . . were Events too great and important not to awaken England out of a Lethargy the reiterated Promises of preserving the Protestant Religion as by Law establish'd had cast her into'.[89] His analysis is substantially correct. A corporation whose general stance was in favour of the crown because of the support the crown could give to its own peculiar forms of monopoly was turned to opposition when support was replaced by control; a dissenting element excluded from town political life was not long deceived about the true import of James II's interest in toleration and not willing to continue their support at the price demanded. In December 1688 Lord Lumley entered Newcastle declaring 'for the protestant religion and a free parliament'[90] and in May of the following year the statue of James II was pulled down by an unruly mob incited to action by the garrison soldiers.[91]

Not everyone in Newcastle accepted the Glorious Revolution without question. A sermon by Thomas Knaggs preached in June 1689 struck a strongly protestant and loyal note and asked for a blessing on the forces of William and Mary in the war against the French; in his preface to the printed version, Knaggs noted 'A few

87. Blair, *Mayors and Sheriffs of Newcastle*, p. 79.
88. J. Clephan, 'William Hutchinson Merchant Adventurer', off-print from *Archaelogia Aeliana* 4th Series, 1880, p. 16.
89. *Vindication of the Present Great Revolution in England in Five Letters Pass'd betwixt James Welwood M. D. and Mr. John March* (London, 1689), sig. A2.
90. *Universal Intelligencer*, no. 1, 11 Dec., 1688, quoted in *Destruction of the Statue of James the Second at Newcastle* in M. A. Richardson, ed., *Reprints of Rare Tracts* (Newcastle, 1847), vol. iv. p. 8.
91. Ibid, pp. 9–17. The frequently repeated statement of Bourne that the statue was torn down in 1688 is clearly erroneous. H. Bourne. *The History of Newcastle upon Tyne* (Newcastle, 1736), p. 131.

hot, inconsiderable men among us were very angry after I preach'd it'.[92] Vicar March, though remaining strong in his denunciation of papacy, could not reconcile his view of monarchy with the events of 1688; in July 1690 he was warned by the Common Council that his salary would be stopped unless he would pray for William and Mary by name.[93] But for the bulk of the population, the outcome of these stirring events meant the return to life as normal, at least so far as political life was concerned. At various points throughout the century local and national politics had intersected in ways that intensified the nature of political debate. Local grievances became the medium through which many national concerns were perceived, while the issues and labels of national debate were used to clothe the continuing local political struggles. The two perspectives were deeply intertwined. If local issues or the local interpretation of issues continued to be predominant and concern for the town's chartered privileges remained to the fore, both were touched, influenced, and informed by the constant concern of the national government for the secure allegiance and peaceful governance of such a populous and economically important town.

Editorial suggestions for further reading

J. Barry, 'Politics and religion in Restoration Bristol', in M. Goldie *et al* (eds), *The Politics of Religion in Restoration England* (Oxford, 1990), pp. 163–90.

J. T. Evans, *Seventeenth-Century Norwich: Politics, Religion and Government 1620–90* (Oxford, 1979).

J. Miller, 'The Crown and borough charters in the reign of Charles II' *English Historical Review*, 100 (1985), pp. 53–84.

92. Longstaffe, *Memoirs of Barnes*, p. 436.
93. Ibid. p. 438. *Vindication of the Present Great Rebellion in England*, p. 25 accuses March of labelling the actions of the Prince of Orange 'with the infamous Names of Rebellion, Damnation and the like'. March himself asserted that passive obedience was 'a Principle founded in the Word of God'. Ibid., p. 5.

Chapter 11

THE CORPORATE TOWN AND THE ENGLISH STATE: BRISTOL'S 'LITTLE BUSINESSES' 1625–1641[1]

David Harris Sacks

[*Past and Present*, 110 (1986)]

This article argues even more strongly for the interpenetration of the local and national in urban politics. Like Newcastle, Bristol had a mercantile oligarchy at odds with a wider middling group, but, unlike Howell, David Sacks looks chiefly at the regular routine of town–state relations, emphasizing the fusion of economic and political interests, above all through the legal framework of franchises and urban government. These, Sacks insists, render meaningless any attempt to identify a localist perspective, and he illustrates how the constitutional controversies of early Stuart England became embedded in local politics well before the crisis of 1640. An obvious gap in this account is any consideration of religion, where, as Clark and Howell both show, the local and the national often found their most explosive connections. But Sacks is not seeking to offer a rounded account of urban politics leading to Civil War, but challenging the localist interpretation on its strongest ground, the supposed primacy of localism in the petty affairs of the economy and administration. Recent work on the mid-Tudor period and such topics as poverty and market regulation suggests that this model is applicable to smaller towns.

1. Earlier versions of this paper were presented to the Cambridge Seminar on Early Modern History (Cambridge, Mass., April 1981), to the Middle Atlantic Section of the North American Conference of British Studies (New Haven, March 1982) and to the Anglo-American Historical Conference (London, July 1983). I wish to thank the following scholars for helpful comments and advice: Samuel H. Beer, Jay Boggis, John Brewer, John Clive, Sigmund Diamond, Stephen Diamond, James Henretta, Roger Howell, Norman Jones, Wallace MacCaffrey, Nathan Miller, Stephen Poppel, Conrad Russell, Simon Schama, Kevin Sharpe, Arthur J. Slavin, Lawrence Stone, David Underdown, Stephen White and James Wilkinson.

In the introduction to his *Parliaments and English Politics*, Conrad Russell refers us to the large 'body of local studies' that has appeared in the last twenty years. These works, he says, present findings 'incompatible with many of the traditions' of English political history, which usually stress the existence of a national polity unified by a single regime of governing institutions and a common understanding of political issues. Instead, these local studies suggest a different political world where 'obstructive localism' often prevailed 'above any concept of national interest'. In this same opening chapter Russell also discusses what he calls 'little businesses'. Little businesses are largely local businesses, primarily of a petty economic or administrative nature. These, Russell reminds us, represent the majority of the work of a parliament, and, as he says, often 'may have concerned members and their constituents more than some of the great matters which are more familiar to us'.[2] We might add that such little businesses also represent the majority of the work of the privy council and other arms of royal government.

But are these little businesses also evidence of localism? On their face they might seem to be, for the repair of bridges or the maintenance of lighthouses – to use Russell's examples – hardly appear the stuff of grand politics. Such a conclusion depends, however, upon what story we are telling. If we are interested in the more traditional forms of political history, they should be thought of as Russell does. Local issues had been the stock-in-trade of royal government from the Conquest, if not before. Do not Thames river fish weirs appear in Magna Carta? The issues seem of significance only to those in the local communities affected by them. But what if we are interested in the history of the state? When looked at in this context, little businesses suggest the local community's inability to accomplish its goals or resolve its difficulties with its own political resources. From one viewpoint, then, little businesses indicate not localism but the need of the local community to call upon the state to help it perform necessary services or cope with its own internal problems, including perhaps social rifts and political divisions. And here there may be much more of a story to tell.

In what follows, I shall explore this issue more fully as it applies to the history of Bristol in the reign of Charles I and particularly in the 1630s. These years were especially problematic for the provincial town, but far from contributing to localism they enhanced the

2. Conrad Russell, *Parliaments and English Politics, 1621–1629* (Oxford, 1977), pp. 4, 8, 37. See also Conrad Russell, 'Parliamentary history in perspective, 1604–1629', *History*, lxi (1976), pp. 25–6. The phrase 'little businesses' was used originally by Edward Conway the younger in a letter to Sir Dudley Carleton, dated 18 Apr. 1624: Public Record Office, London (hereafter P.R.O.), S.P. 14/163/1, quoted by Russell, *Parliaments and English Politics*, p. 37.

penetration of national into local politics and thus heightened the interrelation between the community and the state. But before we can proceed, we must take a somewhat closer look at the idea of localism.

I
LOCALISM IN PERSPECTIVE

Localism is a theory of *mentalité*, although probably most of its proponents would shudder at the word. It defines the mental horizons that supposedly bounded the social and political world of most inhabitants of Tudor and early Stuart England. According to Alan Everitt, the leading spokesman for the school, each town and county was a 'self-conscious and coherent community with a distinct life of its own . . . in which politics played merely an intermittent part'. Although a sense of identification with the national community was also growing in the sixteenth and seventeenth centuries, the local community 'gradually gained ground at the expense of other local groups and of the state', and normally called forth the stronger allegiance. As a result, the 'recurring problem' of the period was not any rivalry between king and parliament, and still less between a feudal aristocracy and a bourgeoisie, but 'conflict between loyalty to the local community and loyalty to the state'. 'Implicit in the social development of the sixteenth and seventeenth centuries', Everitt says, was 'the inevitable collision between local and national loyalties'.[3]

As a consequence of this paradigm, England's seventeenth-century crisis, long considered a great revolution by Whig and Marxist alike, has begun to lose its revered status among many historians. Where scholars once happily thought of this period as the seed-time of English liberty or the birth-day of British capitalism, many have come to treat it as no more than an era of political dislocation that altered little and settled nothing. Everitt, for example, argues that in most places the Civil War itself was really a matter

---

3. Alan Everitt, 'The County Community', in E. W. Ives (ed.), *The English Revolution, 1600–1660* (New York, 1971 edn), p. 49; Alan Everitt, *Suffolk and the Great Rebellion, 1640–1660* (Suffolk Rec. Soc. iii, Ipswich, 1960), pp. 33–4; Alan Everitt, *Change in the Provinces: The Seventeenth Century* (Univ. of Leicester, Dept. of English Local Hist., Occasional Papers, 2nd ser. i. 1969), p. 10; Alan Everitt, 'The Local Community and the Great Rebellion', repr. in K. H. D. Haley (ed.), *The Historical Association Book of the Stuarts* (London, 1973), pp. 76–7, 79.

of local feuds in which factions drawing membership from the same social class contested for control of the local community, often under the banner of national party labels, but without true commitment to the party programmes.[4] Recently Roger Howell has argued that 'local issues or national issues seen in local terms' also dominated politics in the towns. Rather than serving as 'the natural recruiting ground' for revolutionaries, these places sought internal peace, local accommodation and, when war came, neutrality, not impassioned engagement in the great ideological battles of the day. Thus he warns us that a provincial centre like Newcastle or Bristol was 'sub-political', that is, a society 'in which the conduct of local affairs received the main emphasis, interest in national affairs a secondary one'.[5]

The attractiveness of this interpretation is not hard to see. With one swift thrust the localist has sought to impale both the Whig and the Marxist on the sword of anachronism. Both these viewpoints presuppose the existence of a national arena for political action. But if in truth Tudor and Stuart England was organized primarily by township and county – with local factional rivalries, not great con-stitutional principles or broad class interests, determining the divisions – it would have been incapable of having a transforming social or political revolution. The main problem of the period, then, would be the shifting relations between the localities and the central authorities – or, as Trevor-Roper has said, 'the relations between society and the State'.[6]

This argument turns on the localists' use of the concept of 'community'. In everyday language the word can mean no more than a collectivity of people having common interests and sharing common activities. The localists, however, consider the community more narrowly, as a bounded social system of a particular type, or, in Everitt's words, 'a little self-centred kingdom on its own'.[7] The type is what sociologists sometimes call a '*Gemeinschaft*', a small community characterized by multi-faceted, face-to-face and per-manent social relationships in contrast to the partial, impersonal and transitory relationships found in the larger society. These are qualities that enable such communities to be studied as complete

4. Everitt, *Suffolk and the Great Rebellion*, pp. 11–36; Alan Everitt, *The Community of Kent and Great Rebellion, 1640–1660*, 2nd edn. (Leicester, 1973); Everitt, 'Local Community', pp. 76–99.
5. Roger Howell, 'The Structure of Urban Politics in the English Civil War', *Albion*, xi (1979), pp. 115, 126 and *passim*; Roger Howell, *Newcastle-upon-Tyne in the Puritan Revolution* (Oxford, 1966), p. 336 and in general pp. 334–49 *passim*. Cf. Mrs J. R. Green, *Town Life in the Fifteenth Century*, 2 vols. (New York, 1894), i, pp. 1–2.
6. H. R. Trevor-Roper, 'The General Crisis of the Seventeenth Century', in Trevor Aston (ed.), *Crisis in Europe, 1560–1660* (Garden City, N.Y. 1967), p. 72.
7. Everitt, 'County Community', p. 48.

social organisms having their own interlocking systems of social relations. There is, in other words, a strong functionalist character to this work, which assumes the existence of autonomous communities.[8]

A theory of the state and of politics follows logically from this understanding. Students of *Gemeinschaft* assume that political activity based on broad ideologies and universal political principles is not a widely diffused mode of behaviour before modern times. If it appears at all, it is concentrated among an élite at the centre. In local communities politics has not as yet become an autonomous field of action in which rival parties single-mindedly contest for control of government agencies and public policy. Instead the pursuit of power remains entangled in the web of undifferentiated social relations exemplified by kinship groupings and patronage networks. The state, then, symbolizes the realm of politics as we know it in modern society, while the community represents the sub-political realm of faction typical of the pre-modern world. The two can coexist, but not permanently. In the long run the former will overwhelm the latter.[9]

For the localist historians, the seventeenth century represents a clash between these two modes of political organization and political behaviour. The story they tell is one of crisis in which the poor integration of local communities into the national polity is only one among many symptoms of the existence of a weak state. The principal characters of the narrative are the justices of the peace and town magistrates, who found themselves caught between their obligations to their neighbours and their duties to the nation, making their positions, in Conrad Russell's words, 'inherently self-

8. The classic account of *Gemeinschaft* is to be found in Fernand Tönnies' seminal work of 1887, *Community and Society*, ed. and trans. Charles P. Loomis (New York, 1963). See also Max Weber, *The Theory of Social and Economic Organization*, trans. A. M. Henderson and Talcott Parsons, ed. Talcott Parsons (New York, 1964 edn), pp. 136–9; and Emile Durkheim, *The Division of Labor in Society*, trans. George Simpson (New York, 1933). By the Second World War the idea of community as a special kind of social form had received general currency in English usage: Raymond Williams, *Keywords: A Vocabulary of Culture and Society* (New York, 1976), pp. 65–6. Cf. H. P. R. Finberg, *The Local Historian and his Theme* (Univ. of Leicester, Dept. of English Local Hist., Occasional Papers, i, 1952), pp. 5–8; Everitt, 'Local Community', p. 76; Alan Everitt, *New Avenues in English Local History* (Leicester, 1970), p. 6; Alan Everitt; *Ways and Means in Local History* (London, 1971), p. 6.
9. See Robert A. Nisbet, *The Quest for Community* (New York, 1970 edn), pp. 98–120; Max Weber, 'Politics as a Vocation', in his *From Max Weber: Essays in Sociology*, ed. and trans. H. H. Gerth and C. Wright Mills (New York, 1946), pp. 77–128, esp. pp. 77–87; Max Weber, 'Class, Status, Party', ibid., pp. 180–95, esp. pp. 194–5; Edward Shils, 'Center and Periphery', in his *The Constitution of Society* (Chicago, 1982), pp. 93–109; Edward Shils, *Tradition* (Chicago, 1981), chs. 5–6, 8.

contradictory'.[10] According to this view, political upheaval comes when this weak state attempts to behave like a strong one, even though it suffers from insufficient revenues, underdeveloped national institutions and the hegemony of faction over bureaucratic tradition and political ideology. Bold state action inevitably forces local governors to choose between their dual loyalties, usually in favour of their communities and not their country.[11]

This theory of localism certainly has its merits. It has helped scholars to break new ground in social history and to reveal much that we did not know about the fabric of life in early modern England. Nevertheless, the localists may also have led us astray, for they often forget that localism is a theory of *mentalité* and thus should be grounded upon the political outlooks of those we study, rather than our own. But how is it possible, for example, to say with Russell that most seventeenth-century Englishmen 'put their county before their country',[12] unless we situate ourselves outside the historical moment of which we write and judge the national interest according to some absolute standard or from our preferred perspective? No early seventeenth-century country gentleman or town magistrate would or could have put his opposition to government policy in these terms.

By the mid-seventeenth century, of course, a number of English writers had come to see the state in opposition to society and its constituent communities. But before 1640 the theory of political organization depended on different premises that suggest a dimension of communal autonomy without also implying a rivalry with the central authorities. As regards the corporate towns, we can distinguish two different approaches.

The first I shall call the 'liberties and franchises' approach. According to Thomas Wilson – the Elizabethan civil lawyer – early modern English cities were highly independent political worlds. They make their own 'lawe and constitutions', he says, and 'they are not taxed but by their owne officers of the[ir] owne brotherhoode'; 'no other officer of the Queen nor other' possessed 'authority to entermeddle amongst them'. The queen, indeed, placed no 'governor in any towne through out the whole Realme';

10. Russell, *Parliaments and English Politics*, p. 327.
11. Conrad Russell, 'Causes of the English Civil War' (paper delivered to the annual conference of the American Historical Association, Washington, D.C. December 1980); Russell, *Parliaments and English Politics*, pp. 417–33, Conrad Russell, 'Parliament and the King's Finances', in Conrad Russell (ed.), *The Origins of the English Civil War* (London, 1973), pp. 91–116: see also Russell's introduction to this volume, pp. 1–31; Conrad Russell, *Crisis of Parliaments: English History, 1509–1660* (London, 1971), pp. 310–41.
12. Russell, *Parliaments and English Politics*, p. 121; this thought appears in slightly different phrasing a number of times in Russell's book: see, for example, pp. 8, 258, 325.

rather a city's mayor, chosen locally without reference to royal
nomination, served in the capacity of 'Queens Lieftenant'. In addition, Wilson points out, 'every citty hath a peculier jurisdiction
among themselves . . . by which jurisdiction . . . they have the
authority to Judge all matters Criminell and Cyvill'. For these
reasons, Wilson thought of cities as privileged enclaves within the
structure of government and society. 'Every citty', he says, was 'as
it were, a Comon Wealth among themselves'. Nevertheless, Wilson
recognized that at no time were English cities entirely free from the
fabric of royal rule. Their privileges, established by individual and
explicit grants from the crown, did not liberate them from the system
of royal justice nor from the obligation to pay taxes. Cities, then,
were effectively subordinated to both the will and the jurisdiction
of the crown. Although they enjoyed a great deal of self-govern-
ment, they were not completely self-contained worlds, whole unto
themselves.[13]

The second approach I shall call, despite Wilson, the 'commonwealth' approach. London's great antiquary, John Stow, does not
use the word in discussing his city. Instead he conceives of a more
encompassing commonwealth of which London was but a part. At
the conclusion of his *Survay of London*, Stow prints a long
'Apologie' for his city, written probably by the lawyer, James
Dalton.[14] It argues that:

> It is besides the purpose to dispute, whether the estate of the
> gouernement here bee a *Democratie*, or *Aristocratie*, for whatsoeuer it
> bee, being considered in it selfe, certayne it is, that in respect of the
> whole Realme, London is but a Citizen, and no Citie, a subject and
> no free estate, an obedienciarie, and no place indowed with any
> distinct or absolute power, for it is gouerned by the same law that the
> rest of the Realme is . . .[15]

If Stow could accept this view of the most highly privileged and independent city in England, he surely would have agreed that the
provincial towns were also subordinate in the same way to the
English state.

This commonwealth model offers a dual vision of urban life. For
within its boundaries a city may be said to have a community of its
own, existing for the fellowship and mutual aid and affection which
citizens give to one another. '[W]hereas commonwealthes and

---

13. Thomas Wilson, *The State of England, 1600*, ed. F. J. Fisher, in *Camden Miscellany*, xvi (Camden Soc., 3rd ser., lii, London, 1936), pp. 20–1.
14. John Stow, *A Survay of London . . . Reprinted from the Text of 1603*, 2 vols.,
ed. C. L. Kingsford (Oxford, 1908), ii, pp. 386, 387 nn.; Valerie Pearl, *London
and the Outbreak of the Puritan Revolution: City Government and National
Politics, 1625–1643* (London, 1961), p. 46.
15. Stow, *Survay of London*, ed. Kingsford, ii, pp. 206–7.

kingdomes cannot haue, next after God, any surer foundation than the loue and good will of one man towardes another', Stow's apologist says, the same is 'also closely bred and maintayned in Cities, where men by mutual societie and companying together, doe grow to alliances, comminalties and corporations'.[16] Such a community could be a democracy or aristocracy, since as a corporate body it must consist of a head to lead and members to obey, whether the head is selected by free vote, co-optation or inheritance.

Neither this view nor Wilson's leads inevitably to a localist interpretation of urban politics, since neither begins with a vision of the state as the necessary enemy of society or of the individual. But each focuses attention on different issues: the liberties and franchises approach on the relation of city government to the crown; the commonwealth approach on the relation of civic community to the state. What can we make of Bristol's little businesses using these models? Let us begin with Wilson and the franchises.

II
THE FRANCHISES AND THE CROWN 1625–1641

Any enquiry into the history of the early modern English city faces an immediate paradox. Urban society is characterized primarily by its economy: it lives by trade and manufacture. But an English city of the Tudor and early Stuart period was primarily a legal and political unit, defined by jurisdictional boundaries that offered no real barrier to economic and social change. The city stood ready to fly apart as regional, national and even international developments affected its inhabitants. What held it together, as Thomas Wilson stressed, was its corporate existence, which separated the urban community from its surroundings and granted it a unity and a capacity for collective action it otherwise would not have possessed. City franchises, then, had a significance far exceeding the important functions they permitted a municipal government to perform. In a very real sense they defined the city as a social unit. Of no place in England was this truer than Bristol.

Years ago W. K. Jordan said that he found Bristol one of the most parochial places in all England. He based this conclusion on his study of Bristol charity, which he showed to be preoccupied with the development of purely local institutions to remedy purely local ills. But he meant that Bristol's philanthropists, who typically were also its mayors, aldermen and Common Councillors, identified

16. Ibid., p. 198.

themselves primarily as burgesses of their city, not as members of the larger world of wealth and power represented by the court, the gentry, the leading lawyers and the London aldermen.[17] I cannot agree entirely with this view, because the wealthiest and most important Bristolians had business and family ties with the major financiers of London, the benchers of the Inns of Court, the west country gentry, and the officials of the exchequer, admiralty and privy council.[18] Nevertheless, Jordan's remark captures something important about the civic spirit of these leading Bristolians. If their social horizons were wide, taking them often to London and reaching beyond England to America, to the Levant and even to east Asia, their social outlook depended upon their leadership of the city's body politic. For such men the town's privileges and immunities enclosed a community of freemen, just as the town boundaries enclosed the city's territory. They distinguished its citizens from the larger body of royal subjects, without, however, separating them from the realm.

Men given to this way of thinking must have found the first fifteen years of Charles I's reign very troubling, though probably not as troubling as they would find the last nine. The reign opened with nearly half a decade of war with Bristol's main trading partners, Spain and France, which brought chaos to the city's commerce and repeated interference from royal officials.[19] The end of the war, however, yielded them only minimal relief. Throughout the 1630s Bristol was harassed by one wave of royal commissioners after another in what must have seemed an endless series of intrusions upon the tranquillity of the body politic. In 1634, for example, Alderman John Barker complained openly to Sir Edward Nicholas, one of the clerks of the privy council, of 'the molestacion which the best deserving marchants' had suffered for the past five years from:

> ungrounded informacions and pretended Bills in Starre Chamber at the Sutes of the Atturneys generall vnwonted & vexatious Comissions, false and malitious informacions of the officers of the Customs heare and insolence of his Mat[ies] messengers & Common informers . . .[20]

17. Private communication. On Bristol philanthropy, see W. K. Jordan, *The Formation of the Charities of the West of England: A Study of the Changing Patterns of Social Aspirations in Bristol, and Somerset, 1480–1660* (Trans. Amer. Phil. Soc., new ser. 1, pt. 8, 1960), pp. 5–44.
18. On the social background of the leading Bristolians, see David Harris Sacks, *Trade, Society and Politics in Bristol, 1500–1640* (New York, 1985), pp. 501, 654–711. For an argument along somewhat similar lines on the nature of the 'county community', see Clive Holmes, 'The County Community in Stuart Historiography', *Jl. Brit. Studies*, xix (1980), pp. 54–73.
19. See Section IV below.
20. P.R.O., S.P. 16/273/1.

Three years later the situation was no better. According to William Adams, the early Stuart chronicler of Bristol, merchants, brewers, soapmakers, shipowners, ministers, constables and churchwardens all suffered the repeated attentions of royal commissioners. 'From September to the month of December 1637', he says, 'our city was never free from commissions, commissioners and pursuivants of sundry sorts, which lay in several parts of our city to make inquiry not only against merchants but against tradesmen, who were examined and sent up to London, and great impositions laid on them to the grief of many'.[21] The language suggests a plague of locusts.

Locusts these crown agents probably were, set upon this fertile field to gorge themselves in lieu of taxes. Many of the commissions complained of by Barker and others had arisen directly in consequence of Bristol's dealing with the duke of Buckingham during the war years. In the 1630s, for example, Buckingham's heirs sued a large number of the city's merchants for the unpaid profits of the Lord Admiral's wartime jurisdiction.[22] Most of the other commissions also concerned settling accounts in the aftermath of the wars; they focused on concealed prizes, unpaid customs and the like.[23] That is, for Bristol the fiscal and legal effects of the wars did not end with the 1620s. Rather, peace in many respects turned out to be little more than war fought by other means, with Buckingham's ghost directing much of the action. But these matters did not violate Bristol's liberties, which neither exempted its citizens from inquiry into issues determinable at law nor denied entrance into the city to royal commissioners. Nevertheless, in the 1630s there were two challenges to the Bristolians – both threatening important franchises – that went beyond these lingering and debilitating after-effects of the wars.

Among the most important charter privileges belonging to Bristol – or to any corporate town – were its right to make by-laws to regulate the local economy and its authority to collect necessary rates to maintain vital local functions.[24] In the 1630s the point of crisis concerned the Society of Merchant Venturers, the city's most important economic organization, to which belonged the leading overseas traders, including – as we shall see – a majority of the membership of the Common Council. In 1605 the legal status of this body was

21. William Adams, *Adams' Chronicle of Bristol*, ed. F. F. Fox (Bristol 1910), p. 256.
22. See, for example, P.R.O., S.P. 16/302/109, printed in *Records Relating to the Society of Merchant Venturers of the City of Bristol in the Seventeenth Century*, ed. Patrick McGrath (Bristol Rec. Soc., xvii, Bristol, 1952), pp. 238–9.
23. See, for example, P.R.O., S.P. 16/302/109; S.P. 16/368/28; P.C. 2/45, pp. 302–3; E. 95/5319; E. 134/12 Car. I/Mich. 39; E. 134/13 Car. I/East. 132.
24. *Bristol Charters, 1378–1499*, ed. H. A. Cronne (Bristol Rec. Soc., xi, Bristol, 1945), introduction, pp. 64–5; Sacks, *Trade, Society and Politics*, pp. 24–7.

regularized by a Common Council ordinance requiring all merchant adventurers of the city to submit to orders laid down by the Council and the Society.[25] Soon thereafter the Common Council created a wharfage duty on imported goods for the maintenance of port facilities, which became the Society's principal source of revenue.[26]

From the start there was a question about the legality of this new levy, but during the early 1620s the privy council had given it support when it was needed.[27] In the mid-1630s, however, the crown's officers, searching for new sources of royal revenue, changed this policy in response to a complaint from the merchants of Barnstaple against the duties collected in Bristol's Backhall.[28] By November 1637 the matter had become the subject of a formal inquiry conducted by a commission under the leadership of the marquis of Hamilton, in which the rapacious and violent Lord Mohun, together with Robert Pawlett, Esq. and Charles Fox, Esq., acted as principal investigators. The terms of their commission were broad and included the authority to inquire under what warrant wharfage had been imposed.[29]

To the Merchant Venturers this was a frightening threat. Not only was their chief source of income under challenge, but their legal status was put in doubt as well. For inquiry into the warrant for wharfage called into question the Society's authority to enforce its own ordinances. Its royal charter of 1552 had not granted clear powers to do so and had had to be reinforced by a parliamentary statute in 1566. This act, however, had been repealed in the parliament of 1571, leaving in doubt the Merchant Venturers' ability to conduct their corporate business. Though they still possessed their charter, which allowed them to hold property and to act collectively, they seemingly lacked the power to punish those who resisted their by-laws. The Common Council ordinance of 1605 had been the

25. Bristol Archives Office (hereafter B.A.O.), *Common Council Proceedings* (hereafter *C.C.P.*), i, pp. 112–13.
26. John Latimer, *The History of the Society of Merchant Venturers of the City of Bristol* (Bristol, 1903), pp. 36–52, 64–5; B.A.O., *C.C.P.*, i, pp. 112–13, 116, 132; Society of Merchant Venturers (hereafter S.M.V.), *Book of Trade*, General Account (1610–1611), in *Records Relating*, ed. McGrath, pp. 84–8; B.A.O., *Mayor's Audit* (1606–1670 and 1610–1611); see also P. V. McGrath, *The Merchant Venturers of Bristol: A History of the Society of Merchant Venturers of the City of Bristol from its Origins to the Present Day* (Bristol, 1975), p. 71. The Society also collected duties called anchorage, cannage and plankage by virtue of an eighty-year lease granted by the city to twenty-four merchant feoffees in 1601: B.A.O., 00352(5).
27. *Records Relating*, ed. McGrath, p. 136; S.M.V., *Book of Charters*, i, pp. 95, 101; *Acts of the Privy Council* (hereafter *A.P.C.*) (1623–1625), p. 485; see also B.A.O., *C.C.P.*, i, p. 135; Latimer, *Merchant Venturers*, p. 65; McGrath, *Merchant Venturers of Bristol*, p. 71.
28. B.A.O., *C.C.P.*, iii, fo. 60[r–v].
29. P.R.O., S.P. 16/373/84.

remedy for this ambiguous legal standing, and in the 1630s only it and several subsequent Council ordinances gave effectiveness to the Society's rules and regulations.[30] The appointment of the marquis of Hamilton's commission, then, raised the possibility that the Merchant Venturers would not merely lose the wharfage duty, from which they could recover, but would be stripped of their enforcement authority and damaged beyond repair.

To guard against this prospect the Merchant Venturers and their supporters in the city government began a process of calculated delay. The commissioners' primary interest was in the merchants' account books and other records. But the Society's officers, with the aid of the town clerk, contrived by keeping these records from them to provoke the commissioners, especially Lord Mohun – whose temper was notorious – into overstepping their authority. The clerk's advice led to the arrest of the Society's Warden, while the clerk's own harsh words to the commissioners caused him to be placed under security to appear before the solicitor general. But this 'purposed opposition', as Mohun called it, spurred the commissioners into forcing entry into the Merchants' Hall to seize the account books from their locked chest. And so the pot was stirred.[31]

These proceedings resulted in a letter from the town clerk expressing outrage to Sir Edward Nicholas, by now an old and influential friend of the city. Next came a petition to the king complaining of the excesses of the commissioners, which a party of leading merchants among the aldermen and Common Councillors went to London to pursue.[32] This in turn produced a hearing in the king's presence at which Charles ordered the Bristolians and the commissioners each to present bills in Star Chamber detailing their grievances, in effect delaying further action. It was just the respite the Bristolians wanted.[33] The litigation was before Star Chamber in April 1638. At about the same time the Society decided to petition for a confirmation of its charter. Nothing is known of the negotiations, but approval came quite quickly; new letters patent were sealed on 7 January 1639. This new charter not only brought to an abrupt halt the intrusive commission on wharfage, but granted the Merchant Venturers new powers of enforcement guaranteeing their ability to impose their ordinances even on non-members. Their efforts, and according to their *Hall Book* the expenditure of £400, had

30. See Latimer, *Merchant Venturers*, pp. 36–57; *Records Relating*, ed. McGrath, introduction, pp. xii–xxi; McGrath, *Merchant Venturers*, pp. 10–23; Sacks, *Trade, Society and Politics*, pp. 596–631.
31. P.R.O., S.P. 16/373/84; S.P. 16/378/4; S.P. 16/379/1i, 2, 3, 34.
32. P.R.O., S.P. 16/373/84; S.P. 16/379/li, 34; B.A.O., *C.C.P.*, iii, fo. 81 ʳ⁻ᵛ.
33. P.R.O., S.P. 16/379/lii, 34; B.A.O., *C.C.P.*, iii, fo. 83ʳ⁻ᵛ; Adams, *Adams' Chronicle*, p. 258.

bought them an end to the uncertainty about their Society's legal position that had haunted them since 1571.[34]

Along with judicial privileges and control over local rates and local economic regulation, Bristol's important franchises also included the right to elect its officials and servants free from royal interference. Among the officials so to be chosen were several – the recorder, the town clerk and the chamberlain – whose functions made them especially responsible for co-ordinating the city's relations with the crown. Of course such men were not always chosen with complete independence. Lawrence Hyde, for example, entered the recorder's office in King James I's reign at the nomination of the earl of Salisbury, and Lawrence in turn nominated his brother Nicholas to succeed him. Even the much less prestigious position of town clerk was not free from this sort of patronage.[35] But at no time before the 1630s was the office of chamberlain subjected to the same attention from outsiders. And at no time before this fateful decade did the king intervene personally in a local election.

By letters patent of 1499, the Bristol chamberlain, with duties modelled on those of his London counterpart, was to be elected by the mayor and Common Council and to hold office during their pleasure. He was to appear on behalf of the city before the royal courts, to receive all the city's revenues, and to oversee expenditure and the enforcement of economic regulation. In consequence he served as a principal adviser to the Common Council on most matters, whether they concerned purely local issues or the city's relations with the national regime.[36] Because of his central importance to local government, the mayor and Common Council took great pains to control his activities, enforcing a corporal oath upon him, taking surety from him to meet his financial obligations and annually reviewing his accounts.[37] In practice, however, these provisions could serve as no more than deterrents against outright corruption in the management of public funds. The chamberlain's day-to-day decisions could not be monitored effectively by the Council, and only his good will and place in the community truly

34. Latimer, *Merchant Venturers*, pp. 88–97; S.M.V., *Hall Book*, i, p. 24.
35. B.A.O., *C.C.P.*, iii, ff. 23[r], 55[r–v], 96[r]; see also John Latimer, *The Annals of Bristol in the Seventeenth Century* (Bristol, 1900), pp. 23, 57; Sacks, *Trade, Society and Politics*, pp. 84, 99.
36. B.A.O., 01230 (1499), printed in *Bristol Charters, 1378–1499*, ed. Cronne, pp. 165–6, 175–7; *Bristol Charters, 1508–1899*, ed. R. C. Latham (Bristol Rec. Soc., xii, Bristol, 1947), introduction, pp. 11–13; *City Chamberlain's Accounts in the Sixteenth and Seventeenth Centuries*, ed. D. M. Livock (Bristol Rec. Soc., xxiv, Bristol, 1966), introduction, pp. xii–xiv; Sacks, *Trade, Society and Politics*, pp. 71–84.
37. B.A.O., *Old Ordinance Book*, fo. 52[r–v]; see also B.A.O., 04273(1), ff. 44[r–v], 48[r]; B.A.O., *C.C.P.*, iii, ff. 38–9; *Bristol Charters, 1508–1899*, ed. Latham, introduction, p. 12; *City Chamberlain's Accounts*, ed. Livock, introduction, p. xiv.

controlled his official behaviour. Hence the election of a new chamberlain was a major municipal event.

In 1639 the death of Nicholas Meredith, who had been Bristol's chamberlain for the previous thirty-six years, provoked a crisis with the crown. At the election of his successor in October, eight candidates presented themselves, only four of whom received votes, the winner being William Chetwyn, a well connected merchant, for whom twenty-four of the forty-one Councillors present gave their voices.[38] Among the disappointed, receiving no votes at all, was one Ralph Farmer, gent., a minor official of the chancery and an associate of the earl of Berkshire in the monopoly of the malt kilns. At the time of the election, however, Farmer, though the son of Thomas Farmer, brewer, late alderman of Bristol, had not yet sought admission to the freedom of the city, possession of which was required for the office according to the city's charters.[39] Nevertheless, before a month had passed, the Common Council received an ominous letter directly from King Charles quashing the election on the grounds that Chetwyn was a man 'out of this o[r] realm', and that his election had been for private ends, 'to the preiudice of comon libertie'. In his place the king recommended 'Ralph ffarmer a man not vnknowne vnto yo[r]selves and by many of you much desired, of whose abilities & fitness we have receaved an ample testimony and assurance'.[40] Just how the king became cognizant of the matter is unclear. The Common Councillors placed the blame on Ralph Farmer himself, whom they accused of casting 'some aspersion' on them by 'some vndue suggestions' to the king.[41] But probably Farmer's connections with the earl of Berkshire, recently sworn to the privy council, explains how he was able so quickly to obtain King Charles I's ear.

The Common Council's reaction to the king's letter shows prudence but determination. On the one hand, the members 'in

38. B.A.O., *C.C.P.*, iii, fo. 95[r–v]. The candidates were designated only by intials. The voting was as follows: 'E'=8, 'll'=7, 'T' = 2, 'C'=24. 'E' may have been Giles Elbridge, a merchant and Common Councillor; 'll' may have been Thomas Lloyd, a brewer and Common Councillor; 'T' was John Thruston, a soapmaker but not a Common Councillor; and of course 'C' was William Chetwyn, a merchant but also not a Common Councillor. William Chetwyn was the son of Thomas Chetwyn of Rudgely, Staffs., gent., and had been apprenticed to John Barker of Bristol, merchant. He became a freeman of the city on 4 July 1617 by virtue of his apprenticeship: B.A.O., *Apprentice Book (1593–1609)*, fo. 277[v]; B.A.O., *Burgess Book (1607–1651)*, fo. 93[v].
39. Farmer became a burgess by patrimony on 19 Oct. 1639, three days after this election: B.A.O., *Burgess Book (1607–1651)*, fo 283[v]. For Farmer's connection with the earl of Berkshire and subsequent career, see George Bishop, *The Throne of Blood* (London, 1656), p. 109.
40. B.A.O., *C.C.P.*, iii, fo 96[r]. The letter is dated Whitehall, 1 Nov. 1639.
41. Ibid. fo. 96[v]

obedience therevnto', immediately quashed Chetwyn's election and replaced him with Farmer, who by now had become a sworn burgess of the city. Indeed, the Councillors were willing to let Farmer hold the office even though he would not swear the required corporal oath. But at the same time, they thought it necessary to 'vindicate' themselves against Farmer. Therefore they appointed a committee to go forthwith to the court to ensure that 'the City . . . stand right in his Mat[ies] opinion'[42]. The upshot was a petition denying that the Councillors had acted in any way out of faction and reminding the king of the city's charters, confirmed by him, which 'granted the power' to the mayor and Common Council to elect one of the burgesses as chamberlain. Nevertheless, they said that, upon receiving the king's letter, they had immediately quashed the earlier election and replaced Chetwyn with Farmer. They now prayed that the king would 'ratify' the first selection, or permit them to proceed to a new election to choose between the two. This petition was quickly answered by the king giving them freedom to elect a new chamberlain and 'to swear him to that place according to their charter'.[43]

With this the Bristol Common Council proceeded to a new election between Chetwyn and Farmer. This time Farmer received eighteen votes, including those of the mayor and two sheriffs, but Chetwyn received twenty-four votes. The crisis thus was resolved and Chetwyn served until his death.[44]

These incidents, trivial though they may now seem, throw considerable light on the character of political relations between royal government and the local communities in King Charles I's reign. To begin with, they represent a fierce form of political negotiation between the parties, not unlike that practised by the crown and the City of London in the same period.[45] Each side steadfastly upheld its own position and pursued its own goals, until some suitable settlement could be achieved. In the interval politics could be highly disruptive and acrimonious. In the wharfage matter, for example, the Bristolians tried to conceal their account books, insulted crown commissioners and wilfully resisted their authority, all in hopes of provoking an intemperate man into making a fatal error in executing his charge. Royal officials were also determined to win their points without much care for the niceties. They happily summoned the

42. Ibid. ff. 96[v]–97[v].
43. B.A.O., *C.C.P.*, iii, fo. 99[r]. The king's answer is dated 20 Nov. 1639.
44. Ibid., iii, fo 98[r]. Chetwyn died in 1651: see A. B. Beaven, *Bristol Lists: Municipal and Miscellaneous* (Bristol, 1899), p. 235.
45. See, for example, Pearl, *London and the Outbreak of the Puritan Revolution*, pp. 69–106; Robert Ashton, *The Crown and the Money Market, 1603–1640* (Oxford, 1960); Robert Ashton, *The City and the Court, 1603–1643* (Cambridge, 1979), chs. 4–6.

merchants and others to London to defend themselves, 'even in the principall time of their business at home',[46] arrested the Warden of the Merchant Venturers and threatened the town clerk. According to the latter, the execution of the commissions was 'never heard to be done with such insolenc & boldnes'.[47]

But above all, these events demonstrate that the leading Bristolians – the great merchants and the mayor and Common Councillors – were thoroughly familiar with the workings of the English state and with the threats *its* little businesses might pose to their corporate tranquillity. They did not live in any sub-political, localist world, insulated from the harsh realities of politics at the centre, but one in which their most important institutions were subject to the manoeuvrings of the king and his officers and to the ambitions of the likes of Lord Mohun and the earl of Berkshire. In responding to the challenges, moreover, the Bristolians clearly knew what risks they could take, when to stand their ground and when to yield a little to save the essentials. They understood the institutions with which they dealt, the rules governing their operations, and the politics directing their actions. They knew to which officials to appeal when they had entered into difficulty and they knew their way around the court to obtain the ear of the king when it was necessary, usually relying on personal connections – most often Sir Edward Nicholas – to smooth the way. They even knew whom among the crown's agents they could provoke to a self-defeating act of temper. Thus their actions show very little of the obsequiousness or *naïveté* of the provincial seeking aid from the Great Men of the Capital. And none of the aldermen or Councillors who went to Whitehall or Westminster on one little business or another had any political illusions about what was at stake. On the whole, they were highly successful in getting what they wanted.

The liberties and franchises approach thus yields us an image of early modern English politics with two salient features. On the one hand and granted each man his due. Thus if a vital privilege needed to be defended, as it did in Bristol in the wharfage affair or the chamberlain's election, the proper course of action was to seek the wealth. In seeking favours, then, a local community or city corporation acted no differently than did Ralph Farmer seeking office or Lord Mohun seeking profit. Each participated in the same way in a national regime of politics whose code of conduct was understood by every member of the political nation. As a result, politics quite naturally became dependent upon 'bargaining and compromise',

---

46. Adams, *Adams' Chronicle*, p. 258..

47. P.R.O., S.P. 16/373/84. Dyer also says that he found the commissioners not 'fit for my societie'. Three years earlier John Barker similarly referred to the 'insolence of his Maties messengers & Common informers': P.R.O., S.P. 16/273/1.

whether within the court itself, or as the localists often remind us, 'between the centre and the localities'.[48] On the other hand, the king appears in this state as the fount of distributive as well as retributive justice, standing above such politics. The officials around him might be unfair or corrupt, given to partisan decisions on behalf of their families or clients, but he supposedly ruled with an even hand and granted each man his due. Thus if a vital privilege needed to be defended, as it did in Bristol in the wharfage affair or the chamberlain's election, the proper course of action was to seek the monarch's independent judgement. Politics then became concerned with finding a way to obtain the king's ear. There was every confidence that once he had heard the true story he would do right by all the parties.[49] This conception of the state and of monarchy is not a modern one but neither does it imply a world in which 'obstructive localism' challenged 'the national interest'.

III
THE CITY AS ORGAN AND ORGANISM

If the history of the borough franchises does not conform well to the theory of localism, what has urban history thought of according to the commonwealth approach? As we have seen, this model depends upon dualism of viewpoint. On the one hand, the city is seen as part of a larger polity – a subsidiary body of the commonwealth of England. On the other, it is said to have its own communal integrity and common purposes. From this second point of view, the very essence of urban society is the fellowship that citizens have with one another. Put in other words, from the perspective of the national polity – or more precisely of the central authorities – a city is an organization with important governmental functions to perform; from the perspective of the inhabitants it is a moral community in which head and body work together for common ends. Or, as F. W. Maitland says, it is 'both organ and organism'.[50]

This dual vision of city life raises several important issues. The members of every society are ordinarily aware of qualitative differences in their degree of personal involvement with others as

48. Russell, *Parliaments and English Politics*, p. 4.
49. See, for example, Adams, *Adams' Chronicle*, p. 258.
50. Frederick Pollock and F. W. Maitland, *The History of English Law Before the Time of Edward I*, 2 vols. 2nd edn, rev. by S. F. C. Milsom (Cambridge, 1968), i, pp. 635–6. For an interesting discussion paralleling Maitland's, see F. G. Bailey, *Morality and Expediency: The Folklore of Academic Politics* (Oxford, 1977), pp. 19–38.

regards their formal rights and obligations, and their more informal expectations, moral responsibilities and social duties. They recognize a division between Them and Us. But when a community is contained within a larger polity, as were the English towns, the lines of demarcation are often unclear. For there are overlapping levels of authority and the community's boundary is more like an open border than a guarded frontier. Men and material, ideas and influences, can pass through in either direction without passport or visa. Moreover the work of the town as an organization serving the state was performed by a much narrower group than the community as a whole. For considered in itself, a town was typically an 'aristocracy' – or rather an oligarchy – and no 'democracy', and the state's intrusions in urban life through its instruments in the town government helped define the structure of the community over which they ruled.

Bristol's history in the 1620s and 1630s can also be understood in this light. But to do so we need to establish a broader context than we used in discussing the liberties and franchises themselves.

The fundamental law governing Bristol during the seventeenth century was Henry VII's letters patent of 1499. This grant confirmed the liberties and immunities ceded in 1373, which had given Bristol its corporate status,[51] but altered the structure of the government primarily by creating a separate bench of aldermen within the corporation. Accordingly the governance of the city devolved upon a body of forty-three men – the mayor, recorder, aldermen, sheriffs and Common Councillors – selected, with the exception of the recorder, by co-optation from among the freemen of the borough, a group of about 1500 to 2000 male heads of household. This corporation formulated and enforced ordinances for the administration of the city and especially of its economy; problems involving gilds, food supplies, local trade, apprenticeship and economic relations with 'foreigners and strangers' provided the majority of its business. To aid this government in performing its tasks, the mayor and aldermen received designation as justices of the peace and of gaol delivery, which brought the city into conformity with the national system of administration then emerging in the counties. Since the mayor also served as one of the two justices of assize, the civic body was formally bound into the judicial and administrative structure of the nation. This meant that the status and power of the leading men in town government were increased, whether they were acting at a given moment as royal or purely local officials; it also meant that the crown through the mayor and aldermen now had a direct and

---

51. B.A.O., 01208, printed in *Bristol Charters, 1155–1373*, ed. N. Dermott Harding (Bristol Rec. Soc., i, Bristol, 1930), pp. 118–41; Martin Weinbaum, *The Incorporation of Boroughs* (Manchester, 1937), pp. 54–6; Sacks, *Trade, Society and Politics*, pp. 21–43.

continuous link to the city government upon which both the city and the privy council frequently relied.[52]

This tie between civic and national institutions was only reinforced when the king summoned a parliament. Bristol was alone among cities with county status in using the county franchise. But in the context of city life, the 40s. freeholder was a rare individual, since most of Bristol's property was not privately held as freehold. By the early seventeenth century, and for a good time before, the vote had come to be exercised by the mayor, aldermen and Common Councillors, who held the freehold of the borough for the commonalty, and by a small number of other men of similar social standing, who held what freehold property had fallen into private hands in Bristol at the dissolution of the monasteries. In effect, Bristol was a special type of 'corporation borough'.[53] Unlike many such places, however, the voters preferred to have MPs who were closely tied to the civic body. In the early seventeenth century, they both were almost invariably aldermen or Common Councillors; only in the parliament of 1625 and in the Short Parliament did the city revert to the sixteenth-century practice of sending the recorder as one of the two members.[54]

The men who exercised the wide powers and responsibilities of local government may have symbolized the community, but they were far from representative of its population. The acquisition of public office was a direct outgrowth of economic and social success. If a man accumulated riches (£1500 was the minimum set in 1635)[55] he was expected to accept the burdens of borough government, bearing from his own funds if necessary a portion of the financial charges.[56] Voting procedures required two candidates for each vacancy, one nominated by the mayor and one nominated at large by the remainder of the Council. But because there were only a

52. B.A.O.,01230 (1499), printed in *Bristol Charters, 1378–1499*, ed. Cronne, pp. 163–91; see also *Bristol Charters, 1508–1899*, ed. Latham, introduction, pp. 1–19; Sacks, *Trade, Society and Politics*, pp. 45–101. The basis for estimating the number of freemen is discussed ibid., pp. 468–9, 875 n. 5.

53. B.A.O., *C.C.P.*, ii, fo. 134^{r-v}; see also B.A.O., 04026(9), fo. 105^r; William Prynne, *Brevia Parliamentaria rediviva* (London, 1662), pp. 351–68; May Mac-Kisack, *The Parliamentary Representation of English Boroughs during the Middle Ages* (Oxford, 1932), pp. 32, 51–2; Derek Hirst, *The Representative of the People?: Voters and Voting and the Early Stuarts* (Cambridge, 1975), p. 195; Sacks, *Trade, Society and Politics*, pp. 56–7.

54. 'Return of the Name of Every Member of the Lower House of the Parliament of England 1213–1874', *Parliamentary Papers, 1878*, lxii, pt. 1, compared to the lists of corporation members provided in Beaven, *Bristol Lists*, pp. 185–315.

55. B.A.O., *C.C.P.*, iii, fo. 122^r.

56. B.A.O., 01230 (1499), printed in *Bristol Charters, 1378–1499*, ed. Cronne, pp. 167, 183; *Bristol Charters, 1508–1899*, ed. Latham, introduction, pp. 6–7; J. H. Thomas, *Town Government in the Sixteenth Century* (London, 1933), p. 34; Sacks, *Trade, Society and Politics*, pp. 692–708.

limited number of citizens who could afford to serve, the same candidates tended to reappear from election to election until most eventually were chosen and sworn. Not everyone willingly accepted this honour. Some preferred to pay heavy fines rather than bear the time-consuming burdens and indeterminate expenses of service. Occasionally coercion was used to force a reluctant individual into office, as when Luke Hodges, grocer, was threatened with a £200 penalty for his refusal.[57] But Common Council membership also had its rewards, since it enhanced one's status and yielded increased political power, especially in regard to economic regulation. Thus while the Councillors sought to ensure that no one who could bear office would escape, they also tended to favour kinsmen and friends, whom they could trust to support their views and interests. This joint application of economic and political standards for public office meant that the composition of the Common Council tended to reflect in a skewed fashion the distribution of wealth within the social order. Although not everyone who was eligible would necessarily be elected, the leading occupations among the citizenry were likely to be represented in some measure, with the major ones somewhat overrepresented. Hence as patterns of mobility were altered and the social hierarchy became reorganized, the structure of civic politics would also change, slowly at first but with increasing acceleration.

In the sixteenth century Bristol had experienced just such a process of social change as its commercial economy shifted to trade in luxury goods with Spain and the Mediterranean, and a new form of merchant community took shape in the city.[58] Access to the merchant leadership, once open to men of quite humble backgrounds – itinerant merchants and small shopkeepers – narrowed as a group of large-scale wholesale dealers differentiated themselves from the city's retailers and handicraftsmen. These 'mere merchants', more and more the sons of country gentry as well as of Bristol's own merchant families, habitually acted as agents, partners, creditors and brokers for one another, switching roles as circumstances required. They chartered ships together and used each other's servants as factors in overseas trade. But where merchants often appear as both creditors and debtors in their dealings with fellow overseas traders, sometimes borrowing and sometimes lending to the same individual, relations with domestic dealers were dramatically different. Clothiers, for example, tended to be the creditors of merchants, sell-

---

57. B.A.O., *C.C.P.*, iii, fo. 122¹. On refusals of office, see *Bristol Charters, 1508–1899*, ed. Latham, introduction, pp. 14–16; Latimer, *Annals of Bristol*, pp. 33, 35, 136; Sacks, *Trade, Society and Politics*, pp. 65–9.
58. The following paragraphs are based on Sacks, *Trade, Society and Politics*, chs. 6–14. The points receive further treatment in my *The Widening Gate: Bristol and the Atlantic Economy, 1450–1700* (forthcoming).

TABLE 1 Occupations of members of the Bristol Common Council
1605–1642[a]

	Number	Percentage of total known
Merchants	56	46.67
Major Retailers		
apothecary, grocer	7	5.83
draper	11	9.17
fishmonger	2	1.67
haberdasher	1	0.83
hardwareman	3	2.50
mercer	13	10.83
vintner, innkeeper	3	2.50
(Subtotal)	(40)	(33.33)
Soapmakers, Chandlers	4	3.33
Total: Leading Entrepreneurs	100	83.33
Textiles Industries		
clothier	5	4.17
Leather Industries		
pointmaker	1	0.83
Metal Industries		
cardmaker	1	0.83
wiredrawer	1	0.83
(Subtotal)	(2)	(1.67)
Food Production		
brewer	7	5.83
Gentlemen, Yeomen	5	4.17
Total Known	120	—
Unknown	3	—
TOTAL	123	

[a] Note and sources: The names of the Common Councillors were taken from
A. B. Beaven, *Bristol Lists: Municipal and Miscellaneous* (Bristol, 1899), *passim,*
confirmed against the attendance and election records in Bristol Archives Office,
Common Council Proceedings, i–iii, *passim.* The occupations of these men were
checked and corroborated using a variety of sources including B.A.O., *Apprentice
Books,* covering 1532–1658; B.A.O., *Burgess Books,* covering 1558–1599 and
1607–1651; B.A.O., *Great Orphan Book and Book of Wills,* covering 1379–1674;
B.A.O., Wills Proven before the Consistory Court, Bristol, covering 1546–1660;
and wills proven before the Prerogative Court of Canterbury in the sixteenth and
early seventeenth centuries: Public Record Office, London, Prob. 11. Evidence
also came from the State Papers, Domestic, and the records of law courts in
Westminster: P.R.O.; and from the sources printed in *Documents Illustrating the
Overseas Trade of Bristol in the Sixteenth Century,* ed. Jean Vanes (Bristol Rec.
Soc., xxxvi, Bristol, 1979); *Merchants and Merchandise in Seventeenth-Century
Bristol,* ed. Patrick McGrath (Bristol rec. Soc., xix, Bristol, 1955); and *Records
Relating to the Society of Merchant Venturers of the City of Bristol in the
Seventeenth Century,* ed. Patrick McGrath (Bristol Rec. Soc., xvii, Bristol, 1952).

ing their small quantities of fabric for 'half a year and half a year', while vintners and grocers tended to be debtors, paying back their merchant suppliers on a similar schedule.

As a result Bristol's 'mere merchants' conceived of the economy as a great chain of being with themselves at the top mediating between the domestic and international markets.[59] For them the most important aspect of trade was the importation of high-priced goods drawn largely from the Iberian Peninsula, the Mediterranean, the Canaries and Madeira. But the market for many of these commodities was highly elastic and volatile: a small oversupply could result in a large drop in prices and a severe loss of profits. Thus, according to prevailing economic theory, it was necessary for merchants to control import prices through a form of engrossing, which would keep 'commodities in reputation to maintain a trade thereby'.[60] In the mid-sixteenth century the most important overseas traders founded the Society of Merchant Venturers to give reality to this view. This body existed to co-ordinate the activities and protect the interests of these 'mere merchants', something it repeatedly attempted to do by excluding retailers and handicraftsmen from overseas trade. By necessity, moreover, the activities of these men depended upon national economic policy. To a large degree, then, the Society was a political 'pressure group', operating in the economic interest of its members, as is revealed by the streams of its petitions and letters to the king and his officers for redress of one grievance or another.[61]

What made this political role especially effective, however, was the close connection of the Merchant Venturers to the city government. Of the 123 men elected to the Council between 1605, when the Society was put on a new footing by the Council, and 1642, when Civil War events disrupted election procedures, seventy-one, or nearly 60 per cent, were associated with the Society during their careers. Sixty-two served at one time or another as its Master, Treasurer or Warden, indicating that their connections were close. Moreover, the dominance of the Merchant Venturers in Bristol's government was strengthening during the early seventeenth century. From 1605 to 1623, just over half the Council were Society members, but from 1623 to the outbreak of the Civil War the figure was 75 per cent. A similar pattern is apparent among the mayors. Be-

59. See I[ohn], B[rowne], *The Marchants Aviso,* ed. Patrick McGrath (Kress Library of Business and Economics, no. 11, 1957), p. 5.
60. Gerard Malynes, *Consuetvdo, vel, Lex Mercatoria, or The Antient Law-Merchant* (London, 1636, S.T.C. 17224), p. 152.
61. The phrase is McGrath's, in *Records Relating,* ed. McGrath, introduction, p. xxxvii; see also McGrath, *Merchant Venturers,* pp. 62–70; Sacks, *Trade, Society and Politics,* pp. 634–9.

tween 1605 and 1623 just over half were Merchant Venturers. In the following nineteen years, however, the proportion rose to more than four out of five. These changes reflect the growing importance of the 'mere merchants' in Bristol society. As Council vacancies fell open after 1605, they were filled increasingly by Merchant Venturers.[62] During the 1630s this merchant domination of the city government resulted in such a close alliance that twice in the decade the city's mayor was also Master of the Society at the same time. Moreover when parliament was summoned it was this very same merchant leadership who were sent. Alderman Humphrey Hooke, six times Master of the Society between 1630 and 1639, sat in both the Short and Long Parliaments, and Richard Longe, twice Master in the same period, sat in the Long Parliament with him. [63]

This control of the city government by the Merchant Venturers gave the Society enormous advantages both at home and in Westminster. In Bristol itself the Council regularly supported it with such boons as the ordinance of 1605 and the subsequent grant of wharfage dues. The civic body, moreover, often acted on behalf of the Merchant Venturers when favours were needed from the national authorities.[64] In 1621 and again in 1624, for example, the bench of aldermen, the vast majority of whom themselves were Merchant Venturers, and Bristol's MPs who were corporation members and Merchant Venturers as well, intervened on behalf of the Society in its effort to confirm its charter and to obtain statutory exclusion of all retailers and handicraftsmen from overseas trade.[65] And in the 1630s, as we have seen, the city government was the Society's main bulwark against the depredations of crown officials in the wharfage affair and other matters.

But as strong as this alliance was, it did not go unchallenged. The retailers and craftsmen of the city perceived the issues very differently from Merchant Venturer rivals. Rather than seeing the conduct of trade as a separate craft, they saw it as an aspect of every craft. To them the freedom to trade was a concomitant of one's

---

62. Sacks, *Trade, Society and Politics*, pp. 692–706.

63. Compiled from Beaven, *Bristol Lists*, pp. 185–315, and the 'Return of the Name of Every Member of the Lower House', pt. 1.

64 See, for example, S.M.V., *Book of Trade*, pp. 104–13; B.A.O., *C.C.P.*, ii, fo. 96^{r-v}; Miller Christy, 'Attempts towards Colonization: The Council for New England and the Merchant Venturers of Bristol', *Amer. Hist. Rev.*, iv (1899), pp. 678–702; Latimer, *Annals of Bristol*, p. 70; C. M. MacInnes, *Bristol: A Gateway to Empire* (Bristol, 1968 edn.), pp. 96–106; Sacks, *Trade, Society and Politics*, pp. 635–8.

65. S.M.V., *Book of Trade,* pp. 82–7, 146; S.M.V., *Book of Charters*, i, p. 96; S.M.V., *Treasurer's Book*, i, p. 7; all printed in *Records Relating*, ed. McGrath, pp. 9–14.

status as a burgess of Bristol, secured by the freeman's oath. The Merchant Venturers' monopoly, then, usurped the ancient rights of citizenship and those who performed this act violated the very bonds of community. Sometimes the excluded tradesmen spoke quite bitterly on the issues. 'O mercifull lorde god', some of them lamented after Thomas Chester had obtained the Society's monopoly in 1566,

> who wolde have thought that Mr Chestre being a free Citizen borne and sonne unto the naturaleste Cytizen that was in Bristol in our tyme . . . wee say who wolde have thought that Mr. Thomas Chestre by name would consent to have the cytie of bristowe made bond . . . what hath happened to thee o bristowe, bondayge bondaige and mysery for before Bristol withall for inhabitaintes were free and had theyre lybertie always to sende theyr goodes unto the sees . . .[66]

Few such protests ever were made in written form, but the issue survived right down to the Civil War. For example, opposition arose at once in 1612 after the Common Council attempted on its own to restrict overseas trade to 'mere merchants'. By 1618, if not earlier, their ordinance had come under legal challenge and had to be revised to permit some merchant retailers and manufacturers to enter the Merchant Venturers. It is for this reason that the Society began in 1621 its concerted efforts to re-establish its monopoly by statute or other means, a process that ended only with the acquisition of the new charter in 1639.[67]

Somewhat surprisingly, these controversies occasionally found their way into electoral politics in the city. Elections to high city office such as mayor or sheriff usually showed few signs of bitter division. Because the offices were costly to hold, a practice of rotation was followed by which nearly every Common Councillor was selected as he became the most senior figure who had not yet served.[68] Moreover the Council itself was so heavily dominated by the Merchant Venturers that their rivalry with the retailers and manufacturers rarely could surface. Nevertheless, this rivalry did

---

66. Letter of the Master and Company of Tuckers to William Pepwell, mayor of Bristol, 1568, printed in *Some Account of the Guild of Weavers in Bristol: Chiefly from Mss.*, ed. F. F. Fox and John Taylor (Briston, 1889), pp. 92–3.
67. B.A.O., *C.C.P.*, ii, ff. 24^v, 25^r; S.M.V., *Book of Charters* i, p. 61; S.M.V., *Treasurer's Book*, i, p. 4; all printed in *Records Relating*. ed. McGrath, pp. 6–8; Latimer, *Merchant Venturers*, pp. 67–80; McGrath, *Merchant Venturers*, pp. 39–41; Sacks, *Trade, Society and Politics*, pp. 626–31, 639–42.
68. This conclusion is based on analysis of the mayoral elections recorded in B.A.O., *C.C.P.*, i-iii. Nominations and voting were by voice until 1642 when – significantly – a secret ballot was introduced. The town clerk, or an assistant, recorded each man's vote after his name in the minute book with the initials of the party for whom he voted. Between 1599 and 1642, twenty-five mayoral elections were uncontested and a further ten show five votes or less in opposition to the successful candidate: Sacks, *Trade, Society and Politics*, pp. 708–9.

manifest itself at least twice in mayoral elections in Charles I's reign. The election of Christopher Whitson in 1626 can serve as our illustration.[69]

Whitson, sometimes identified as a sugar refiner, also earned at least part of his living as a distiller of methaglin, made from the honey which he imported from Brittany.[70] In 1612 he was among the leading protesters against the Common Council's ordinance excluding retailers and manufacturers from overseas trade; and in 1619 after the Merchant Venturers had been forced to liberalize their admissions requirements, he became one of the few redemptioners in the Society. Not surprisingly his place in the city government excited dissension from the 'mere merchants'. When he was proposed for sheriff in 1613 there were a dozen votes against him, an almost unheard-of occurrence in elections for this burdensome office. Although not all of this opposition came from Merchant Venturers, his main adversaries were a closely linked group of great Spanish and Mediterranean traders – long-time proponents of the monopolistic ideals of the Society – who were led by Alderman Robert Aldworth, perhaps the richest and best-connected Bristol merchant of his generation. By 1626 these men thought of Whitson as an overly 'puntuall' man, rigid in outlook, whom the leading Merchant Venturers could not trust to act in their best interest.[71]

Whitson's main rival for the mayoralty in 1626 was Aldworth himself, who was nominated by the outgoing mayor, John Barker, a Merchant Venturer in Aldworth's camp. Analysis of the final vote shows the leading Spanish and Mediterranean traders on the Council pitted against the retailers and manufacturers. Aldworth received

69. The only other hotly contested mayoral election in our period occurred in 1633. This election pitted Alderman Robert Aldworth, one of the main protagonists in 1626, against Mathew Warren, clothier, Christopher Whitson's brother-in-law, who in 1633 was the most senior Common Councillor who had not yet served: B.A.O., *C.C.P.*, iii, ff. 44–45.

70. Whitson was admitted to the freedom of the city of Bristol as a redemptioner in 1610, and a year later was selected to serve on the Common Council. His occupation at the time of his admission is not known, because when he was sworn to the burgessship he was listed only as a 'yeoman', a signification that in urban contexts often meant 'not a servant', or 'not a dependant': B.A.O., *Burgess Book (1607–1651)*, fo. 79[r]; Anthony Salerno, 'The Social Background of Seventeenth-Century Emigration to America', *Jl. Brit. Studies*, xix (1979), pp. 37–8.

71. B.A.O., *C.C.P.*, ii, ff. 40–41; for the Aldworth group's leadership in 1612, see ibid., ff. 24[v], 25[r], printed in *Records Relating*, ed. McGrath, p. 7. The remark about Whitson's personality appears in P.R.O., S.P. 16/41/80. If Christopher Whitson was indeed a sugar refiner, then this may have provided one point of antagonism with Aldworth, who was the founder of Bristol's first sugar house on St Peter's Back: see I.V.Hall, 'John Knight, Junior, Sugar Refiner at the Great House on St Augustine's Back (1654–1679): Bristol's Second Sugar House', *Trans. Bristol and Gloucs. Archaeol. Soc.*, lxvii (1949), pp. 110, 113–14; Sacks, *Trade, Society and Politics*, pp. 455, 458.

nineteen of the forty-two votes cast; seventeen of these came from Society members. Whitson received twenty-two votes, only eight of which were from Merchant Venturers.[72] The division among the Merchant Venturers is revealing in its own right, for the eight votes from Society members that Whitson received came from lesser members, who traded primarily in the bulky and less profitable wares of the Baltic, Normandy, Brittany and the Bay of Biscay. They were in the following of Alderman John Whitson, Christopher's powerful cousin. John Whitson's own rivalry with Aldworth and his clique went back to 1604 when Whitson was the only Spanish merchant in Bristol willing to accept the newly refounded Spanish Company's policy of admitting retailers and manufacturers to foreign trade.[73]

Curiously, the chamberlain's election of 1639 shows similar social and political cleavages. In the first vote no identifiable faction supported Chetwyn or any of his active opponents.[74] But at the second election fifteen of Farmer's eighteen votes came from leading Merchant Venturers, including four who had previously voted for Chetwyn. This made Farmer the candidate of the 'mere merchants', including the surviving members of the Aldworth clique, many of whom had been named to the Society's Court of Assistants in its new charter. Chetwyn's support consisted of a much wider range of occupations, including mercers, brewers, drapers and grocers as well as merchants. Although fourteen of his votes also came from Merchant Venturers, on the whole these were northern traders, and less influential in the Society than Farmer's supporters. Quite surprisingly the latter also were the very same men who had suffered the most serious depredations in the plague of commissions for concealed

72. B.A.O., *C.C.P.*, ii, ff. 142–3, compared to the register of Merchant Venturers' members printed in *Records Relating*, ed. McGrath, pp. 26–9.
73. The overseas trading activities of Whitson's supporters were established by comparing evidence derived from P.R.O., E. 190/1134/10 and E. 190/1135/6 to the vote registered in B.A.O., *C.C.P.*, ii, ff. 142–3. For discussion of the differences between Bristol's northern and southern trades, see *Merchants and Merchandise in Seventeenth-Century Bristol*, ed. Patrick McGrath (Bristol Rec. Soc., xix, Bristol, 1955), pp. 227–74; *Documents Illustrating the Overseas Trade of Bristol in the Sixteenth Century*, ed. Jean Vanes (Bristol Rec. Soc., xxxvi, Bristol, 1979), introduction, pp. 13–25,58–163; Jean Vanes, 'The Overseas Trade of Bristol in the Sixteenth Century' (Univ. of London Ph.D. thesis, 1975), chs. 4–6; Sacks, *Trade, Society and Politics*, chs. 7–8. Evidence of John Whitson's rivalry with Robert Aldworth can be found in *The Spanish Company*, ed. Pauline Croft (London Rec. Soc., ix, London, 1973), pp. xliii, 18, 43, 46, 101; Sacks, *Trade, Society and Politics*, pp. 619–25; B.A.O., *C.C.P.*, ii, fo. 55^{r-v}. For the relationship between Christopher and John Whitson, see B.A.O., *Great Orphan Book of Wills*, iii, fo. 250^{v}.
74. B.A.O., *C.C.P.*, iii, fo. 95^{r-v}. Alderman Humphrey Hooke, for example, voted for 'll' while Thomas Hooke, his son, voted for 'T'. In the second election both of these men voted for Farmer. It is clear that in the first election there was no consensus candidate, but there appears to have been no *systematic* effort to stop Chetwyn from obtaining the office.

prizes and unpaid customs that had descended upon Bristol in the 1630s.[75]

How can we explain this division? Unlike the Whitson case, the answer cannot be found primarily in the economic activities of the two candidates. Chetwyn himself was a well-connected merchant who had been in the Merchant Venturers since before 1618; he had been apprenticed to one of Aldworth's regular business partners. Farmer apparently did not engage in overseas trade at all. Rather, the deciding factor seems to have been the social horizons and aspirations of Farmer's party. They were politically wary and politically adept men, dependent upon the crown for their economic positions. With the granting of the Merchant Venturers' new charter in 1639, these individuals had received a great boon from Farmer's nominator, King Charles. For by confirming Edward VI's patent of 1552, the king had not only officially sanctioned the Merchant Venturers' right to act as a corporate body, but had also renewed their control over foreign trade. At the same time, he also enhanced the Society's power of enforcement, and placed its leadership under the tight control of the Court of Assistants, who were primarily Spanish and Mediterranean traders. With its new authority the Society set about drafting new by-laws excluding retailers and artificers from membership without a special Hall and forbidding Society members from participating in partnership with non-members.[76]

The acquisition of the charter and the passage of these ordinances ended an era in the history of the Merchant Venturers. Once again the Society enjoyed a secure legal footing. By June 1639 the Court of Assistants was meeting to recover outstanding debts owed the Society for wharfage and other duties. On two days twenty-nine individuals, including twelve who were not Merchant Venturers, were summoned to the Merchants' Hall to arrange for payment.[77] The new charter and new ordinances also had an immediate effect on the size of the Society's membership. For, on the one hand, it was now more difficult to trade overseas without joining, and, on the other, the Merchant Venturers' new privileges made membership more attractive. Within three years fifty-one overseas traders entered the fellowship, including five of the twelve individuals previously chastised for non-payment of wharfage. These fifty-one represent four-fifths as many members as had entered during the

75. B.A.O., *C.C.P.*, iii, fo. 98[r–v]; Latimer, *Merchant Venturers*, p. 91; see also P.R.O., E. 134/12 Car. I/East. 21; E. 134/12 Car. I/Mich. 39; E. 134/13 Car. I/East. 132; and S.P. 16/302/109: printed in *Records Relating*, ed. McGrath, pp. 238–9.
76. Latimer, *Merchant Venturers*, pp. 88–107; the names of the first Court of Assistants are given on p. 91.
77. S.M.V., *Hall Book*, i, p. 2.

entire period from 1618 to 1639. After the Merchant Venturers' hard trials of the 1630s, they seem to have won a final victory against their old local rivals.[78]

IV
LITTLE BUSINESSES AND GREAT MATTERS

Little businesses, then, reveal a political world closer to Thomas Wilson's and John Stow's than to Alan Everitt's or Conrad Russell's – one in which the members of the municipal corporations thought of themselves as king's officers performing the necessary functions of royal government in their city. They were simultaneously citizens and crown servants, city fathers and the legitimate agents of the state in their community, the one role reinforcing the other.[79] Such a structure of politics involved the complex interplay of local issues and national policies, notable citizens and crown officials, communal factions and central institutions. In this counterpoint each town offered its own variations on the major themes, though only towns with county status, especially the larger ones like Bristol, could expect to find themselves frequently caught up in the harmonies and dissonances of high policy and court intrigue. Thus if every town has its peculiar history – arising from ancient traditions and local developments – this history does not separate the town from the realm as a whole: just the reverse. For the inhabitants of such places lived out their lives in communities inevitably and inextricably bound up in the little businesses of the state.

Something of the larger significance of these little businesses can be gathered if we look to the Petition of Right. This document, justly famous in English history, has a unique place in Bristol's local history as well. In August 1628 the city's two MPs – John Doughty, an alderman, and John Barker, who had been mayor in 1625–6 – brought into the Council House 'six paper books containing the several arguments made in the Parliament house of the liberties of the subject', which the Council 'thought fit' to be 'entered into some of the register books of this city there to remain of record forever'.[80] Why were the Councillors so interested in these debates?

---

78. S.M.V., *Book of Charters*, i, pp. 63–5; *Hall Book*, i, pp. 5, 6, 7, 10, 13, 26, printed in *Records Relating*, ed. McGrath, pp. 29, 261.
79. Here I agree completely with Russell, *Parliaments and English Politics*, pp. 6–7.
80. B.A.O., *C.C.P.*, iii, fo. 6ᵛ, printed with an incorrect citation in *Merchants and Merchandise*, ed. McGrath, p. 144. The six paper books do not appear to have survived. Possibly they were a version of the so-called 'proceedings and debates', many copies of which were made and circulated after this parliament: see *Com-*

Much the best answer lies in the nature of the events that provoked the Petition in the first place. Since the wars with Spain and
France depended upon sea power, Bristol, England's second port,
inevitably found itself in the thick of the action and thus bearing what
its magistrates considered a disproportionate share of the burdens.
They were required to lay out money to supply the king's ships and
to offer him the services of their own, all without timely payment
or clear purpose. Again and again they found themselves dutifully
answering requests from the privy council for the pressing of sailors
and the staying of ships, only to be faced with countermanding orders and with seemingly inexplicable administrative confusion and
delay.[81] As merchant shipowners, deprived by the wars of their principal markets, they could do little else with their ships – their main
capital resources – except to engage in privateering, which brought
their enterprises into conflict with other naval activities and brought
themselves into all too frequent dealings with the corruption of the
Lord Admiral's agents.[82] From the inception of Charles I's reign to
the summoning of the 1628 parliament, then, wartime frustrations
had been building in Bristol, as the actions of naval commanders,
press masters, admiralty officials and the like became increasingly
intrusive. But the climax of events came in the winter of 1628, when
Captain William Buxton, under orders from the admiralty, attempted to press into royal service seven of Bristol's best ships and

mons Debates, 1628, ed. Robert C. Johnson, Mary Frear Keeler, Maija Jansson
Cole and William B, Bidwell, 4 vols. (New Haven, 1977–8), i, pp. 4–33; see
also *Commons Debates for 1629*, ed. Wallace Notestein and Frances Helen Relf
(Minneapolis, 1921), introduction, *passim*; R. M. Smuts, 'Parliament, the Petition of Right and Politics', *Jl. Mod. Hist.*, 1 (1978), pp. 714–15.

81. See, for example, P.R.O., S.P. 16/21/111; S.P. 16/23/105; S.P. 16/40/25; S.P.
16/42/84; S.P. 16/43/52; S.P. 16/47/37; S.P. 16/49/62; S.P. 16/51/31, 63, 66; S.P.
16/75/9; S.P. 16/77/10; S.P. 16/78/30, 34, 36; S.P. 16/79/6; S.P. 16/80/36,42,69;
S.P. 16/82/24; S.P. 16/94/58, 58i, 63, 63i; S.P. 16/95/43, 46; S.P. 16/96/14; S.P.
16/100/42; S.P. 16/101/39; S.P. 16/109/28; S.P. 16/113/46; S.P. 16/119/50;
A.P.C. (Mar. 1625–May 1626), pp. 38, 272; *A.P.C. (June–Dec. 1626)*, pp. 47–9,
109–10, 129–30, 209, 415–16; *A.P.C. (Jan.–Aug. 1627)*, pp. 33–4, 159–61, 398,
506, 508; *A.P.C. (Sept. 1627–June 1628)*, pp. 4, 55, 58, 75, 82–3, 105–6, 132–3;
A.P.C. (July 1628–Apr. 1629), pp. 57, 100.

82. See, for example, P.R.O., S.P. 16/1/12; S.P. 16/21/111; S.P. 16/22/22; S.P.
16/26/45; S.P. 16/29/17, 35; S.P. 16/32/33; S.P. 16/36/96; S.P. 16/37/54, 65, 86;
S.P. 16/38/77, 90; S.P. 16/41/80; S.P. 16/42/8, 14, 70, 84; S.P. 16/47/20, 37; S.P.
16/48/2, 6, 7, 28; S.P. 16/49/62; S.P. 16/51/51, 66; S.P. 16/70/48, 52; S.P.
16/72/43; S.P. 16/73/11, 11i; S.P. 16/74/20; S.P. 16/82/52, 71; S.P. 16/83/9, 23,
27; S.P. 16/87/25, 66; S.P. 16/91/75; S.P. 16/115/p. 19; S.P. 16/144/22; S.P.
16/177/12; *A.P.C. (Jan.–Aug. 1627)*, pp. 353–4; *A.P.C. (Sept.1627–June 1628)*,
pp. 86–7, 186—7, 277 , 287–8, 323–4, 342; see also J. W. Damer Powell, *Bristol
Privateers and Ships of War* (Bristol, 1930), pp. 69–85. For a general account
of admiralty regulation of privateering, see Kenneth R. Andrews, *Elizabethan
Privateering: English Privateering during the Spanish War, 1585–1603*
(Cambridge, 1964), pp. 22–31 and *passim*.

eight barques, totalling in all about 1800 tons and carrying 444 men and 106 pieces of valuable ordnance. The owners of two of the larger vessels refused to fit their ships, saying they would 'not disburse any money in setting them forth'. The 'stubbornnesse' of these men, and especially of John Barker, soon to be in parliament, Giles Elbridge, the son-in-law and partner of Robert Aldworth, and Humphrey Hooke, already a prominent Councillor and about to serve six times as Master of the Merchant Venturers, encouraged others to resist; Buxton found himself unable to complete his orders without paying 'theise stiffnecked people' for everything in advance. '[F]or if possible', he said, 'I will not be beholding to none of this towne for the smallest courtesie'.[83]

Was 1628, then, the first step for Bristol along the 'high road to civil war'? Not quite! The crisis of that year primarily agitated the city's merchants. What they wanted was relief from the heavy fiscal burdens of the war,[84] and by the summer of 1628 all those who were owed large sums by the crown had begun what can only be called a lenders' strike. 'Until repayment', the mayor wrote to the privy council on 22 August, the very same day as the six paper books were registered in Bristol, 'noe man will contribute to any further charge'.[85] But the Bristol merchants were prepared to undertake some necessary burdens, such as guarding the coasts against piracy, provided they were guaranteed in advance that their costs would be met by the crown. In June, for example, they had agreed to set forth two ships on condition that the expense would be covered by the exchequer from the proceeds of the first two subsidies recently granted in parliament. Indeed, the city's two MPs had brought this good news with them from Westminster, along with the arguments in parliament which they wished preserved in the city's records.[86] No wonder the leading Common Councillors found the issue of liberty as expressed in the Petition of Right so worthy of the special treatment they gave it.

But when the Civil War finally came to Bristol in 1642 and 1643 most of these same men, and others of similar social and economic position, sided with the king against parliament, as John Corbet,

---

83. P.R.O., S.P, 16/94/58, 58i, 63, 63i; S.P. 16/95/43; S.P. 16/96/14; S.P. 16/100/42. By the spring of 1628 the resistance of the Bristolians to the crown's demands had become focused especially on the duke of Buckingham. One reason Buxton had such difficulty in the city was that his commission came from the Lord Admiral, not the privy council. As Buxton wrote to Edward Nicholas, many Bristolians 'do think nay in a manner say that my Lords warrant will not be sufficient': P.R.O., S.P. 16/95/34.

84. See *City Chamberlain's Accounts*, ed. Livock, introduction, p. xxv.

85. P.R.O., S.P. 16/113/46

86. P.R.O., S.P. 16/108/11; S.P. 16/109/6, 28; S.P. 16/112/47, 48.

minister in the city of Gloucester in these years pointed out.[87] Even their experience in the 1630s of intrusions and usurpations by Charles and his agents does not seem to have forced them into rebellion against the king. Their long, if tumultuous, association with the crown, as its suitors and servants, culminating in their receipt of their new charter, seems to have anointed their loyalty with the chrism of self-interest.[88] As Sir Ronald Syme tells us of another era of revolution, 'liberty and the law are high-sounding words. They will often be rendered, on a cool estimate, as privilege and vested interests'.[89]

But words have political force of their own, since politics depends in part upon how the parties conceive the issues. What happened in 1628 and the period leading up to it had significantly altered this conception in Bristol as elsewhere. To secure for themselves the 'liberties of the subject', the Bristol Common Councillors adapted to their purpose a well-established procedure for registering the royal concessions and favourable judicial rulings affecting their corporate franchises.[90] By making the six paper books 'of record' they showed their intention of using them as precedents in the law courts at Bristol and Westminster against future encroachments and usurpations by the crown. In doing so they transformed the nature of the issue from one of privileges and immunities to one of individual rights. In a sense, then, they followed the framers of the Petition of Right in addressing what J.H. Hexter has identified as a general crisis of liberty. They saw their particular problems as part of a larger dilemma of fundamental law affecting everyone, not as a series of separate challenges to them alone to be met one at a time using makeshift defences.[91] Is it too much to say, therefore, that these Bristolians – for a brief moment at least – conceived that their English liberties preceded their burghal rights? And that their civic franchises alone could not protect them against the arbitrary actions

87. John Corbet, *A Historical Relation of the Military Government of Gloucester* (London, 1645), p. 14.
88. The pattern is very similar to what we find in London: see Pearl, *London and the Outbreak of the Puritan Revolution*; cf. Robert Brenner, 'The Civil War Politics of London's Merchant Community', *Past and Present*, no. 58 (Feb. 1973), pp. 53–107, and Ashton, *City and Court*, pp. 201–21.
89. Ronald Syme, *The Roman Revolution* (Oxford, 1960 edn.), p. 59.
90. For examples of the material collected in the city's register books, see *The Little Red Book of Bristol*, ed. F. B. Bickley, 2 vols. (Bristol, 1900); *The Great Red Book of Bristol,* ed. E. W. W. Veale, 5 vols. (Bristol Rec. Soc., ii, iv, viii, xvi, and xviii, Bristol, 1931–53); *The Great White Book of Bristol*, ed. Elizabeth Ralph (Bristol Rec. Soc., xxxii, Bristol, 1979).
91. See J. H. Hexter, 'Power, Parliament and Liberty in Early Stuart England', in his *Reappraisals in History: New Views on History and Society in Early Modern Europe*, 2nd edn. (Chicago, 1979), pp. 163–218.

of the crown or its officials? If most of these men saw their interests allied with the king's in 1642, this hardly diminishes the importance of this 'declassification' of liberty, in Hexter's phrase.[92] It represented a profound and irreversible shift in the conception of contemporary political problems that entered the general political culture.

Among the Bristol magistrates a sense of participation in a national economic community had developed by the early 1620s, if not before.[93] Bristol's experience of war in the later 1620s only enhanced their involvement, but the route was a somewhat surprising one. War may have thrust the Bristolians to the forefront of the battle against England's enemies, but it had not provided adequate means to pay for their efforts. For this reason, the Bristolians thought their extraordinary burdens should be shared with other Englishmen, less directly involved in military and naval operations. At first, they looked to the inhabitants of the two neighbouring counties in meeting the crown's demands for service. The cost of putting two ships to sea for the king, they said in 1626, would amount to the equivalent of eight subsidies, but 'to the counties not a half a subsidie'.[94] Since parliament in that year had not granted any subsidy at all, they seem to be arguing, why should Bristol alone bear such a heavy charge? The counties, however, refused to contribute, not only on the ground that their payment would be without precedent, but because they rejected its underlying logic. As the J.P.s of Somerset put it, we have 'noe other benifitt or p^rvilege by o^r neighbourhood wth that Cyttie, then any other countie of the kingdome'.[95] This response, self-serving though it may have been, is nonetheless a powerful one, for despite Bristol's proximity to Gloucestershire and Somerset, it formed no special community of interest with them. Why then should the counties share in a charge imposed upon Bristol?

92. J. H. Hexter, 'The Birth of Modern Freedom', *Times Lit. Suppl.*, 21 Jan. 1983, pp. 51–4.

93. See, for example, 'The Certificate of John Guy, for the Port of Bristol, 1621', Brit. Lib., Hargrave MSS. 321, ff. 103–7, printed in *Merchants and Merchandise*, ed. McGrath, pp. 140–3. For the ways in which 'grievances in trade' led to the development of generalized arguments about conditions, see Stephen D. White, *Sir Edward Coke and "The Grievances of the Commonwealth", 1621–1628* (Chapel Hill, 1979), pp. 86–141; Barry E. Supple, *Commercial Crisis and Change in England, 1600–1642* (Cambridge, 1970), pp. 197–253, Joyce O. Appleby, *Economic Thought and Ideology in Seventeenth-Century England* (Princeton, 1978), pp. 24–51.

94. P.R.O., S.P. 16/33/107. In requesting county participation the Bristolians claimed as a precedent similar payments in Queen Elizabeth's reign, but the counties denied that they had ever actually paid: P.R.O., S.P. 16/36/18; S.P. 16/60/32; see also W. B. Willcox, *Gloucestershire: A Study in Local Government, 1590–1640* (New Haven, 1940), p. 105.

95. P.R.O., S.P. 16/60/32.

But this argument can lead to two quite different visions of the English polity. On the one hand, it might seem to suggest a realm in which each county stands on its own in a loose confederation, as the localists would have it. On the other, it might imply the existence of a commonwealth in which every county participates equally in all national endeavours. By 1628 the Bristolians had come to accept this second line of reasoning and sought their relief from the newly granted parliamentary subsidies, not from the pockets of their reluctant neighbours. In doing so they followed the rationale of Somerset's Sir Robert Phelips, whose amendment to the 1624 Subsidy Act had provided that soldiers impressed in the counties would be paid directly from the subsidy rather than from local rates. This procedure, had it been enforced in a general fashion, would have distributed wartime costs among all the taxpayers in England. Far from representing a localist outlook, it indicates a deep sense that war yielded no special benefits to any locality, but only extraordinary burdens which ought to be borne in common by all.[96]

The Bristol magistrates' concern for the 'liberties of the subject', then, carries with it some important implications about their idea of the state. These men saw themselves in a co-ordinated relationship with the central government, together with which they were to preserve order and protect the subjects; they were willing to accept state power so long as it helped perform these vital functions. When they anxiously defended their role as local governors, it was not as a buffer against royal government, but because they saw themselves as an essential part of royal government. Order to them meant the union of authority with property, as expressed in their own leadership of their community, and they feared any use of state power that

---

96. *Statutes of the Realm*, iv, pt. 2, p. 1262 (21 Jac. I c. 33 cl. xliv); Robert Ruigh, *The Parliament of 1624; Politics and Foreign Policy* (Cambridge, Mass., 1971), pp. 253–4 and 253–4 n. 182; Russell, *Parliaments and English Politics*, pp. 223–4. Russell views this measure in the context of tax reduction or tax avoidance. But as the debate between Bristol and its neighbouring counties indicates, there is a good deal more significance to it. In the normal course of events military expenditures in England were paid for by a form of 'special assessment' for ships and soldiers that fell most heavily on the places most directly involved in the war. One possible justification for such charges is that such places received the greatest benefits from the war effort. If the war threatened England directly, it threatened the ports and the coastal counties more than the interior. Moreover, a port like Bristol enjoyed the opportunity to engage in privateering, from which a rural county could not directly benefit. The idea behind 'special assessment' for the war, then, was pre-eminently a localist idea. What Phelips and his colleagues in Somerset argued, however, was that the burdens were national burdens which ought to be paid for out of general taxation; and by 1628 the Bristolians agreed. Put another way, the duty of defence was not divisible; a threat to one Englishman was a threat to all, and defence against it should be paid for by all. By 1628 the gentry of Gloucestershire also seem to have come to a similar conclusion: see Willcox, *Gloucestershire*, p. 74.

threatened this union. In resisting the encroachments of the king's officers upon the city's body politic, no Bristol magistrate was anticipating an all-out breach with the monarch in defence of community, much less a Civil War. Many of them, however, were concerned about the best way to distribute power between the local and central authorities for the preservation of order and property, and in the later 1620s they feared that the unrestrained exercise of royal power might result in social chaos. It was also this that troubled them in the plague of commissions in the 1630s; for the commissioners in acting 'as lords and judges over them, as if all law and justice lay in their hands', threatened the networks of co-operation and deference in the city. They forced merchants to tell 'what they know of others their friends and partners . . . [w]hereby some were constrained (for discharging of their consciences) to accuse one another'; even worse they 'tempted' the merchants' factors, servants and seamen 'to accuse the Marchants and owners by whome they liue and are maintayned'.[97] The Bristol magistrates, then, faced the question of political choice not by opposing local loyalties to national, but by concentrating on what would best promote the maintenance of the national polity as they understood it. For most of them, this was a polity in which men rooted in the community, not strangers with few local ties and no comprehension of local conditions, properly exercised authority for the king. In other words, the Bristol magistrates envisioned a political world in which community and state were related to one another as parts are to the whole, not as opponents.[98]

In Bristol, however, relations between the town authorities and the crown had long worked at cross purposes. They not only linked the local community to the English state, but they also drove a wedge between the increasingly dominant faction in that leadership and the larger community over which it ruled. For the role of mayor, alderman and Common Councillor served to separate the office holders from the body politic at large and to give them advantages in dealing with the state on matters vital to their private interests.

For members of this merchant élite, the later 1620s and the 1630s had been a period of conflict with the crown that had ended in accommodation. Other groups in the city were not so fortunate, since

---

97. Adams, *Adams' Chronicle*, pp. 256, 258; P.R.O., S.P. 16/273/1. See also P.R.O., S.P. 16/373/84.

98. In other words the Bristol magistrates appear to have been tending toward a form of 'country ideology': see J. G. A. Pocock, 'Machiavelli, Harrington and English Political Ideologies in the Eighteenth Century', in his *Politics, Language and Time: Essays on Political Thought and History* (New York, 1973), pp. 104–47, esp. pp. 123–4; Lawrence Stone, *The Causes of the English Revolution, 1529–1642* (London, 1972), pp. 105–8; Lawrence Stone, 'Results of the English Revolutions of the Seventeenth Century', in J. G. A. Pocock (ed.), *Three British Revolutions: 1641, 1688, 1776* (Princeton, 1980), pp. 32–7.

they lacked the political resources of the Merchant Venturers. After 1634, for example, the city's soapmakers had no one of their Company among the Bristol corporation. But their difficulties with the crown were just as great as those of the merchants. First the royal patent granted to the Society of Soapmakers of Westminster resulted in a sharp cut-back in legal soap production in Bristol; then the king's impost on soap practically destroyed the industry in the city. By the late 1630s only four of eleven soap-houses survived in Bristol and a full dozen of the soapmakers were lodged in Fleet Street prison for non-payment of the impost. Nevertheless, no one from the Bristol corporation came to the aid of the soapmakers. As a result, several prominent members struck private bargains with the Westminster company and the crown, leaving their fellows to struggle to find a livelihood, a task made all the more difficult by the Merchant Venturers' new charter which deprived them of the right to trade overseas free from Merchant Venturer control. Such were the disadvantages of exclusion from civic office.[99]

The various Bristol responses to the summoning of the Long Parliament also show the existence of a divided community in pre-Civil War Bristol. When parliament was summoned, the freeholders of the borough, namely the corporation members and a few others of similar social rank, selected two Merchant Venturers – Alderman Hooke and Alderman Longe – to sit for the city. In January 1641 these men were presented with the grievances Bristol's Common Council wished redressed in parliament. There were two: the violation of Bristol's rights as a staple town for trade in wool and the actions of those persons who had given unjust information to the king about the merchants, causing them 'to be Pursuvanted up and unjustly handled and ill dealt with'.[100] In other words, the grievances are the complaints of the narrow merchant group that dominated the town. But the excluded members of Bristol's community did not go unheard at this time. In October 1640 – as the Long Parliament was about to be elected – 'a great number of free burgesses of the Citie' petitioned the Common Council for the right to vote in the parliamentary elections. This renewed a request made in 1625 which the Council had denied. The result was the same again in 1640. The corporation preserved to itself its hold over elections.[101]

99. *Proceedings of the Company of Soapmakers, 1562–1642*, ed. H. E. Mathews (Bristol Rec. Soc., x, Bristol, 1939), introduction, pp. 6–8, 194 ff.; P.R.O., S.P. 16/288/49; S.P. 16/289/94; S.P. 16/308/14, 15; S.P. 16/328/33, 33i; S.P. 16/356/101; S.P. 16/377/46; Adams, *Adams' Chronicle*, pp. 256–7; Latimer, *Annals of Bristol*, pp. 121–2.
100. B.A.O., *C.C.P.*, iii, fo. 110[r]
101. B.A.O., *C.C.P.*, ii, fo. 134[r]; *C.C.P.*, iii, fo. 198[r]. Derek Hirst argues that the freemen won a victory in 1640: Hirst, *Representative of the People?*, p. 195. But he misinterprets the evidence. The 'allies' mentioned in the return for this election were the other freeholders, not the freemen.

In the absence of evidence naming the petitioners, or of information about whom they wished to elect, it would be a mistake to over-interpret this petition. But knowing what we do of the social and political structure of Bristol in the early seventeenth century, we can be reasonably certain that among the main beneficiaries of the requested change would have been precisely that excluded group of retailers and manufacturers whom the Merchant Venturers had sought to oust from foreign trade. The petition calls upon the same principles of freemen's rights and community values that this group saw violated by the Society's privileges. In 1571 their predecessors had responded to the Merchant Venturers' monopoly with a similar demand for the right to vote in the forthcoming parliamentary elections.[102] But despite their differences with Bristol's merchant leadership the petitioners did share with them some common understanding of the political process. The redress they wanted involved gaining access to one of the national institutions the Merchant Venturers had long sought to use for their own purposes. Thus the ordinary freeman's political horizons appear to have been almost as wide as those of the mere merchants. Local conflict had not led them to localism.

All politics, it is sometimes said, is local politics, since ultimately power and authority must be exercised in the context of our daily lives. Grand ideological debates and large public questions have little immediacy until they become reduced to such human dimensions. But local politics can be of various types. It can draw in upon itself and make of the connections and rivalries of local inhabitants the fabric of local rule. Or it can reach beyond its own boundaries to participate in a larger world of governmental institutions and political movements. It can be a closed arena or an open gate. Seventeenth-century Bristol gives us an example of the second type of politics. Its little businesses were not the consequences of petty parochialism, but the concrete expression of the great matters that stirred the state. They reveal an underlying structure of politics in which Bristolians participated in both substance and form in the manoeuvring of the courtiers and the affairs of parliaments. In ordinary times the focus of political action was the exploitation of the state for local advantage, but when a national crisis developed, as it did in the later 1620s and would again in the early 1640s, it engaged them immediately because they were a politically integrated part of the realm. In general they moved in their relations with the state to the courtly rhythms of a pavane, but if necessary they could also step lively to a countryman's gavotte. When divisiveness halted

102. B.A.O., 04026(9), fo. 105^r; Vanes, 'Overseas Trade of Bristol', p. 167.

this dance of politics, however, it did not send the dancers home, but turned the music to a quick march; and, as some Bristolians said in 1643, they could not escape 'the surly noise of drums' beating in their ears.[103]

Editorial suggestions for further reading

R. Ashton, *The City and the Court 1603–43* (Cambridge, 1979).
D. Hirst, *The Representative of the People?* (Cambridge, 1975).
C. Russell, 'Parliamentary history in perspective, 1604–1629', *History*, 61 (1976), pp. 1–27.
R. Tittler, 'The emergence of urban policy 1536–58', in J. Loach and R. Tittler (eds), *The Mid-Tudor Polity* (1980), pp. 74–93.

---

103. *The Humble Petition of the Citie of Bristoll, for an Accommodation of Peace between His Majestie, and the Honorable the High Court of Parliament* (Oxford, 1643), p. 5.

INDEX

Adams, W., 306
agriculture, 3, 5, 10, 12, 16, 23, 52–3, 55,
    61, 70, 75, 123, 211, 216, 247, 250
Alldridge, N., 21
almshouses, 256, 268
American colonies, 13, 54, 135, 271, 305
Amsterdam, 40 n11
Antwerp, 61
apprenticeship, 12–14, 24, 74, 105–9, 112,
    114, 116, 122 n4, 123, 125–34,
    137–8, 144, 151, 158, 162, 171–2,
    185, 211, 231, 233, 246–7, 285, 314
    records of, 8–9, 23, 185, 246–7
archaeology, 22–3
Austria, 115–17
Aveling, J., 220

Barnstaple, 267, 272, 307
Bath, 4, 58
Baxter, R., 268–9
Beier, A., 13, 18–19, 121–38
Berkner, L., 115–17
Besant, W., 139–40
Birmingham, 3, 46–7, 51, 58, 67–8, 72, 273
Blackburn, 68
Bolton, 68
books and newspapers, 144, 210, 240–1,
    243, 254, 266–7, 289
boroughs, 2, 27–30, 38, 48 n28, 49, 53
    n38, 164, 272, 277, 302–4
Borsay, P., 33
Boston, 61 n53, 71
Boulton, J., 20, 26
Braudel, F., 71
Bridgewater, 267
Bridgnorth, 53 n38
Bristol, 5, 13, 28, 49–50, 53, 56, 58, 61,
    64–5, 71, 79, 112, 125, 246, 248,
    251, 253, 256, 267–8, 297–8, 300,
    304–33
Browne, J., 264
buildings, 3, 9, 33, 53 n38, 64, 67, 191,
    197, 224–6, 291–2, 295
    castles, 179–81, 221–2, 252
    churches, 33, 181, 214–15
    gates, 33, 214–15, 223
    halls, 179, 181, 192, 224, 226
    prisons, 220, 222–3
    towers, 179, 188, 194–9, 223
    walls, 33, 181–2
    see also housing, topography
Bury St Edmunds, 51–3, 80
Butlin, R., 177

Cambridge, 13, 14, 19, 50–1, 65, 70,
    74–120
Cambridge Group for the History of
    Population and Social Structure,
    12, 75
Canterbury, 51, 254, 272
Cardington, 105
charity, 13, 16–18, 88, 142, 158, 233,
    236–9, 256, 304
charters, 27, 29, 48 n28, 49, 259–60, 263,
    278, 284–5, 287, 289–91, 293–4,
    296, 306–8, 310–11, 314, 319–20,
    327, 331
Chatham, 51, 57–8, 71, 80
Chester, 5, 21, 50–1, 54, 56, 61, 64–5, 72,
    87, 94, 223, 230, 272
Chichester, 272
children, 16–18, 66, 102–5, 112, 115, 118,
    131, 152, 228–33
    orphans, 18, 112, 115, 142, 161, 229

Civil War, 19, 27–8, 31, 143–4, 158, 161,
    203 n78, 244–5, 271–3, 279, 281–7
    297–300, 326, 330–3
Clark, P., 1, 5–6, 19, 24–5, 28, 30,
    244–73, 297
Clayworth, 96
coffee houses, 144
Coghan, T., 217
Colchester, 43–4, 50–1, 56, 64–9, 71–2,
    80, 110, 118, 272
Collinson, P., 30
Colyton, 105
Comenius, J., 144
Constantinople, 40
Corbet, J., 271, 326–7
Corfield, P., 1–2, 9, 11, 35–62, 71
Cornwall, 5
Council of the Marches, 252, 263
Council of the North, 57, 223, 229, 280
    n19, 282
Coventry, 1, 26, 42–3, 49, 51, 53, 63–5,
    67, 70, 76, 110 n137, 213–15, 243,
    272
Coverdale, M., 240
crime, 122, 127–8, 137, 142–3, 156, 221–3,
    255
culture, 32–4, 42–3, 137, 139, 206, 268, 299
Cumbria, 5, 58, 117

Dalton, J., 303–4
Davenant, C., 36
Davis, N. Z., 233
De Vries, J., 6
Defoe, D., 53, 55, 67–9
Dekker, T., 137
Derby, 58
Devon, 79
dialect, 227–8
Dickens, A. G., 240
Drake, F., 227
Dublin, 6, 177–82
Durham, 223
Dyer, A., 6–7, 243

Earles Colne, 76
East Anglia, 124
Eastland Company, 184
economy, 8–11, 27, 35–8, 63–73, 87–8, 304
    see also industry, markets,
        occupations, trade
Edinburgh, 6
education, 142, 144, 206, 229–33, 252,
    265–6, 268, 270–1
Engels, F., 169, 172, 191
environment, 22, 156, 161, 164, 223–4, 242

Essex, 69, 164, 206
Everitt, A., 1, 10, 299–300, 324
Exeter, 2, 49–50, 56, 58, 61, 64, 69, 71–2,
    94–5, 166, 177–82, 225, 234, 241,
    243

fairs, 3, 11, 85, 179
    Stourbridge, 70, 80, 85
festivals and holidays, 12, 30, 33, 159–61,
    208–15, 232, 236, 239–40, 261, 279
fires, 78, 222, 226
Fisher, F. J., 35, 37–8, 88
Fletcher, A., 36–7
Florence, 109, 160
food, 19, 23, 36 n4, 62, 64–5, 71, 119, 131,
    161–2, 211, 215–18, 241–2, 250,
    253, 256, 261, 263, 269, 314
    prices, 16, 19, 161–2, 253
Foster, F., 26
France, 248, 305, 321–2, 325
freemen, 8, 19, 26, 28, 82, 139, 141,
    148–52, 155, 170, 185, 216, 226,
    229, 257, 260, 268, 277, 280–1, 283,
    291, 305, 310, 314, 319–20, 331–2
    records of, 8–9, 23, 39 n9, 66–7, 82–3,
        149–51, 183–7, 202, 214, 219,
        226, 228, 250 nl6, 321 n70

games, 232, 241–2
gardening, 218
Genoa, 88, 109
gentry, 3, 4, 27, 33, 42–3, 52–3, 89, 91,
    99, 100–1, 103–4, 108, 130, 132,
    144, 213, 220, 230, 233, 247, 249,
    252–4, 260, 262–3, 266–7, 269, 305,
    316–17, 329 n96
Geoffrey of Monmouth, 208
George, M. D., 127, 142, 175
Glass, D., 106, 177
Gloucester, 2, 19, 28, 50–2, 53 n38, 80,
    94, 244–73, 327
Gloucestershire, 246–7, 267, 328–9
Goodman, G., 245, 266, 270
Goose, N., 9, 13, 14, 19, 63–120
government
    national, 4, 26–32, 36 n4, 57, 77–8, 82,
        85, 89, 126–7, 131–2, 151, 157
        n40, 208–10, 215, 221, 229,
        244–5, 261–4, 269–71, 274–96,
        297–333
    local, 14, 17, 24–33, 49, 52, 188–91,
        192 n67, 209, 211–14, 219,
        221–3, 225, 234–5, 239, 241–2,
        244–6, 250, 254, 256–62,
        269–333

London, 135–7, 140–65, 303–5
oligarchy in, 24–8, 30–2, 141, 152, 164,
    188–91, 200, 244, 259–62, 269,
    276–9, 284, 287–8, 314–16
    see also boroughs, charters, freemen,
        law, parishes, Parliament,
        precincts, wards
Graunt, J., 158
Greene, R., 137
Grindal, E., 231
guilds and companies, 8, 14, 26–7, 30,
    107, 125, 129 n20, 132, 139, 142,
    147–52, 155, 161–2, 165, 169–75,
    177, 183–94, 201–2, 204, 212, 214,
    225–6, 233, 239, 241, 259, 278–9,
    285, 306–8, 314, 318–24, 331–2

Halifax, 56
Hanham, A., 209–10
Harrison, W., 212
health and illness, 16, 18, 22–4, 126–7,
    206, 215–23, 255
    see also plague, population, sanitation
Hereford, 52
Herefordshire, 246
Hertfordshire, 79
Holman, J., 112
Hoskins, W. G., 1, 18, 63–4, 66, 69, 72,
    80, 177
hospitals, 85, 220, 256–7, 259, 268, 270–1
    Bridewell, 121–2, 127–8, 132, 134–8
    Christ's, 135, 161
households, 12–26, 31, 33, 50 n3l, 74–118,
    133–4, 139, 141, 152–8, 163, 177,
    187 n58, 203, 236–40, 314
houses of correction, 85–6, 122, 135, 256
housing, 17, 20–3, 36 n4, 53, 74, 77–8, 82,
    126–7, 141–2, 146–7, 156, 161, 163,
    166–203, 206, 218, 224–7, 254–5
    see also buildings, topography
Howell, C., 117
Howell, J., 158–9
Howell, R., 11, 28, 274–97, 300
Howes, J., 134–5
Hull, 3, 51, 58, 61 n53, 64–5, 217, 272
Hyde, E., 244

industry, 3, 9, 42, 52, 54, 56, 58, 63–73,
    128–32, 185, 199, 248–50, 269
    cloth, 3, 44, 54, 55–8, 64–72, 80, 85–6,
        99, 128–32, 195–6, 248–50, 253,
        316–17
    clothing, 64–7, 105, 195–6
    coal, 11, 56, 58 n49, 184, 200, 274,
        276, 278

fishing, 11, 55, 57, 211, 213, 253
food and drink, 3, 42, 64–5, 67, 70, 99,
    128–9, 191, 196, 204–5, 217–18,
    317
    leather, 3, 64–72, 128–9, 195–6, 250,
        317
    metal, 58, 64, 67–8, 191, 195, 248–50,
        317
    shipbuilding and shipping, 10, 56,
        128–9, 185–91, 194–7, 204–5,
        325
    wood, 191, 195–6
    see also occupations
inns, alehouses and taverns, 11, 113, 177,
    181 n47, 241–2, 252, 255, 257
Ipswich, 43–4, 50–1, 54 n39, 55, 57
Ireland, 5, 11, 13, 54, 56, 125, 251
Italy, 13, 59 n50, 75, 109, 153

Jones, G. S., 169
Jordan, W. K., 304–5
journeymen, 106–7, 133, 150 n24, 152
    n31, 158, 171–2, 211, 233

Kent, 164
Killingworth, 117
King, G., 47
King's Lynn, 50–1, 61, 64–5, 70
kinship, 109–10, 115–17, 237–40
Knaggs, T., 295–6

Lancaster, 52, 109, 110 n133
Langton, J., 20–1, 166–205
Laslett, P., 74–5, 96, 101, 103, 106–8,
    110–18, 232, 237
Laud, W., 30, 244, 265, 268, 270–1
law, 4, 29–32, 147–8, 156–7, 161, 193–4
    n67, 221–3, 252, 297, 302–6, 308–9,
    314, 327–8, 330
    quarter sessions, 3, 252, 260, 263
    see also charters, government, religion
Layton, 235
Le Goff, J., 215
Lee, E., 230, 240
Leeds, 50–1, 56, 58, 72
Leicester, 51–2, 63–5, 69, 72, 272
Leicestershire, 216
Leland, J., 67, 209, 246
Levellers, 152, 161
Lichfield, 94
Lincoln, 53, 55, 14J
Lindley, K., 26
Lipton, 117
Liverpool, 3, 46–7, 51, 53 n38, 54, 58
localism, 28–9, 274–333

lodgers, 74, 86–7, 93, 112–13, 115, 155, 158, 163
London, 2–6, 10–11, 13, 15, 19–20, 23–4, 26–33, 35–47, 50–2, 55–6, 59–62, 69, 79, 85–6, 88, 94–5, 106, 110, 121–65, 175–7, 182, 200, 223, 232, 245, 250–1, 256, 268, 277, 303, 305–6, 309, 311–12, 327 n88
Ludlow, 53 n38

MacCaffrey, W., 243
Macfarlane, A., 76–7, 117, 206
Maitland, F. W., 313
Maldon, 83 n52
Manchester, 46–7, 51, 58, 68, 72, 241, 273
March, J., 289, 293–4, 296
markets, 3, 9, 10, 11, 52, 56, 70–2, 79, 128, 179–80, 192 n67, 199, 248, 250–2, 297
    see also fairs, shops, towns, trade
Mayhew, G., 8, 10
Mediterranean, 248, 251, 318, 321–3
Metcalfe, P., 293
Middlesex, 122, 124, 127, 135, 140, 163–4
migration, 1, 4–5, 12–19, 23–4, 35–7, 54, 59–62, 77–8, 82–3, 86–7, 93–4, 96, 101, 105, 111, 114, 116, 118, 123–6, 128, 132, 134, 137–40, 142, 144, 161, 246–7
    aliens, 150 n24, 155, 161
    emigration, 13, 23, 136, 271
    see also lodgers, population, vagrants
Moryson, F., 109
Mush, J., 211, 236
music, 211, 214–15, 241, 265 n60, 333
muster records, 39, 46 n22, 159, 208, 250 n16

Naples, 40 n11
Netherlands, 42, 59 n50
Newcastle, 11, 46, 50, 54 n39, 56, 58, 61, 166, 177–205, 223, 272, 274–97, 300
Northampton, 50, 52 53 n38, 64, 69, 272
Northumberland, Earl of, 236
Norwich, 2, 22, 44–5, 49–51, 53, 54 n39, 56–8, 64–7, 71, 79, 94–5, 133, 150, 229, 256, 272
Nottingham, 51, 53 n38, 58
Nottinghamshire, 216
Nuremberg, 242

occupations, 3, 8–9, 13, 21, 49 n30, 61, 63–73, 91–2, 99–105, 113, 114, 118, 128–32, 169–74, 183–205, 250, 266, 316–18
    classification of, 91, 100, 104, 108,

119–20, 130, 190, 203–5, 249, 266, 317
crafts, 31, 103, 108, 144, 147–8, 247, 254–5, 319, 323; bell-founders, 250; bricklayers, 195; cappers, 248–50; cardmakers, 317; carpenters, 150 n24, 162 n59, 239; clothiers and clothworkers, 66, 69, 72, 99, 128–9, 149, 156, 249–50, 254, 256, 316; coopers, 150 n24, 152 n31; cordwainers, 150 n24, 189 n60, 233, 239; feltmakers, 191; fullers, 189 n60, 191; girdlers, 150 n24; glaziers, 226; glovers, 233; hardwaremen, 317; knitters, 67, 128; leathersellers, 150 n24; leatherworkers, 196; masons 224; pewterers, 148 n21; pin-makers, 250; pointmakers, 317; saddlers, 189 n60; shoemakers, 65, 68; silk-throwers, 128; skinners, 189 n60, 191; slaters, 195; smiths, 68, 189 n60, 195; spinners, 67, 69, 86; tailors, 64–5, 68, 72, 149, 189, n60, 212; tanners, 69, 169, 189 n60, 216, 250; threadmakers, 67; tuckers, 320 n66; upholsterers, 156; weavers, 64, 66, 69, 85, 149, 249–50; wiredrawers, 317
labourers, 61, 91–2, 100–5, 107–8, 114, 169, 221, 230, 241–2, 247, 255, 266
merchants, 3, 11, 27, 70, 92, 99, 172, 183–90, 192–3, 197–200, 204–5, 225–6, 232, 239, 248, 250–4, 259, 267, 276, 278–9, 285, 293, 305–8, 310, 312, 316–25, 330–2
professions, 3, 9, 27, 91, 99, 103, 219–20, 252; apothecaries, 219–20, 317; barber-surgeons, 191, 194, 219; clergy, 91, 208, 212, 216–17, 220, 222, 230–1, 233, 238–9, 241, 306; lawyers, 220–1, 241, 252; officials, 91, 99, 103, 233, 309–10; physicians, 219–20, 232, 252; public notaries, 91, 238–9; schoolmasters, 230–1, 252, 271; scriveners, 91, 231, 252; surgeons, 220, 227, 252, 267
retailers, 3, 23, 92, 99, 144, 250–1, 254, 316, 319, 321–3, 332;

Index

brewers, 64–5, 99, 128, 161, 218, 257, 306, 310, 317, 322; distillers, 321; drapers, 149 n24, 152 n31, 184, 189 n60, 212, 231, 267, 322; goldsmiths, 150 n24; grocers, 150 n24, 220, 316–18, 322; haberdashers, 149, 251 317; ironmongers, 150 n24; maltsters, 238; mercers, 72, 150 n24, 184, 189 n60, 250–1, 259 n42, 267, 276, 278–9, 317, 322; soapmakers, 128, 306, 330; stationers, 150 n24, 229, 267; sugar refiners, 321, 323 n71; vintners, 317–18
services, 8–9, 23, 42–3, 61, 91, 108, 185–7, 194, 196–7, 252; alehousekeepers, 218; bakers, 65, 72, 162, 189 n60, 191, 195, 217, 217, 239–40; bellmen, 230; boothmen, 184, 189 n60; butchers, 64–5, 69, 169, 189 n60, 194–5, 241; cooks, 191; costermongers, 218; fishmongers, 150 n24, 317; fruitsellers, 156, 218; innkeepers, 99, 230, 238, 317; market-gardeners, 128; ostlers, 99, 101, 113; prostitutes, 122 n4, 134, 163, 234; street sellers, 156; tapsters, 91, 101, 113; water-carriers, 215, 218, 224; wet-nurses, 16
transport, 91, 108, 128; carriers, 11, 191, 251; coachmen, 156; colliers, 161, 191, 280; keelmen, 191, 194, 280; mariners, 70, 188, 191, 194–5, 280, 330; porters, 91, 99, 101, 149, 191; shipbuilders, 129, 191, 194–5; water-men, 280
see also apprenticeship, industry, journeymen, servants
Oldham, 68
Oxford, 27, 50–1, 81–2, 87, 89, 218, 223

Palliser, D., 6, 22, 33, 64, 206–43
Paris, 40 n11, 143
parishes, 15, 21, 29–31, 142, 145–6, 153–9, 164–6, 212, 214–15, 231, 233, 239, 256–7; 265, 270, 306
registers, 8, 16, 76, 82–3, 129, 145, 208, 214, 228 n40, 246
vestries, 153–5, 159

Parliament, 27–9, 31, 36 n4, 54 n38, 62, 126, 162, 244–5, 253, 262, 264, 271–6, 282–3, 286–7, 291, 298–9, 307, 315, 319, 324, 326–9, 331–2
elections to, 8, 28, 32, 48 n28, 149 n23, 245, 259–60, 262–4, 279, 281–2, 289, 294, 315, 319, 331–2
Patten, J., 1, 63–4, 66–7, 72
Pearl, V., 19, 26, 121, 139–65
Petty, W., 36
Phythian-Adams, C., 6, 14, 18, 26, 64–5, 67, 213
Pilgrim, J., 68
plague, 12, 16–17, 21, 42 n18, 54, 74, 77–8, 84–7, 95–6, 101, 111, 114–15, 118, 144, 203 n78, 216, 219, 223, 227, 246, 255–6, 262, 269
plays, 208, 212, 237, 241–2, 265
Plymouth, 44–5, 51, 57–8, 71
Poole, 61 n53, 94
population, 2, 6–7, 12–17, 35–62, 74–119, 121, 123, 126, 145–6, 164, 207, 216, 227, 246–8
density, 22
fertility, 12, 54, 83, 124, 138, 218, 234–5, 248
marriage, 14, 18, 24, 133, 151, 234–9
mobility, 15, 21, 77, 87, 121, 252
mortality, 12, 14–18, 22–4, 36 n4, 42, 62, 82–4, 101–2, 105, 111–12, 124, 126, 129 n20, 131, 138, 145, 208–9, 216, 218–23, 227, 229, 239, 248, 255–6
returns, 7, 14, 18, 39, 43 n18, 44 n19, 47 n23, 50 n31, 75–8, 81, 88–9, 94–5, 115–18, 145–6, 151, 176
see also health, households, kinship, migration, plague
Portsmouth, 51, 57–8, 71, 80
Pound, J., 64, 66
poverty, 5, 6, 17–20, 25, 28, 52, 66, 74, 77–8, 80–1, 84–8, 101–2, 110, 121–38, 140–1, 157, 161–2, 172, 179–82, 191, 196–200, 217–19, 227, 239, 247, 254–7, 268–9, 297
poor relief, 18–19, 85–7, 141–2, 145, 162, 215, 219, 239, 255–8
records, 66, 87, 177
see also almshouses, charity, hospitals, houses of correction, vagrants
Power, M., 20, 26
precincts, 145, 153–9, 164–5
Preston, 68
probate
inventories, 8–9, 22, 76 n5, 77 n11, 87,

89 n96, 91, 106, 241, 254
wills, 66–7, 76 n5, 89 n96, 91, 106,
    109–10, 117–18, 237–40, 241

Queenborough, 53 n38

Rappaport, S., 19, 26
Rawdon, M., 232–3
Reading, 52, 64–5, 67–72, 80, 106 n121,
    110, 118
religion, 30–2, 144, 208, 210–14, 228–9,
    230–1, 239–41, 244–5, 257, 262,
    264–73, 281, 288–9, 292–7
  anti-catholicism, 32, 244, 265, 289,
    292–5
  cathedrals, 30, 48 n28, 217, 248, 252,
    262, 265–8, 270–1
  catholics, 30, 163, 220, 229, 270, 292–4
  church courts, 125, 234–6, 239, 248,
    252, 270
  Church of England, 27, 30–2, 232–3,
    243, 292–6
  ecclesiastical censuses, 39, 40 n14, 50
    n31, 81, 119
  effects of Reformation, 5, 30, 32–3,
    206, 210–12, 214, 225, 228, 233,
    241–3, 264
  lectureships, 30, 257, 265, 267, 270
  nonconformity, 30–2, 163, 265, 271,
    288–9, 294–5
  presbyterians, 31, 156, 284
  religious houses, 20, 218, 222, 225,
    235, 248, 315
Richardson, M. A., 290
riots, 36 n4, 128, 137, 142–3, 222,
    279–80
Robinson, H., 158
Russell, C., 298, 301–2, 324, 329 n96
Rye, 8, 10
Ryther, J., 210–11, 216

Sacks, D., 11, 28, 297–333
Salford, 68
Salisbury, 2, 49, 51, 89, 256
Sandwich, 86
Sandys, E., 236
sanitation, 17, 22, 223–4
Schofield, R., 84
Scotland, 5, 271, 282, 285
servants, 14, 18, 24, 74, 92, 105–9, 112,
    114, 116, 122 n4, 123, 127,
    129–134, 137, 152, 158, 171, 217,
    221, 247, 266, 330
Sharlin, A., 16
Sheffield, 58, 67

shops, 11, 251
  see also fairs, markets, occupations
Shrewsbury, 50–1, 53 n38, 84, 94–5, 110,
    225, 256
Siraut, M., 82, 94
Sjoberg, G., 166–9, 174–7, 181–2, 192,
    200–3
Slack, P., 1, 5–6, 21, 24–5, 87
societies, 144, 160
  see also guilds
Somerset, 328–9
Southampton, 43, 55, 61 n53, 71, 79, 94,
    110, 201 n73
Southwark, 121, 124, 126–7
Spain, 305, 318, 321–3, 325
Stafford, 94
Stone, L., 116
Stout, W., 109, 110 n133
Stow, J., 127, 161, 303–4, 324
Stroudwater, 250
suburbs, 15, 17, 20–1, 26, 39, 74, 81,
    86–92, 101–2, 111, 113, 121–4,
    126–7, 133–4, 139–41, 145–8, 151,
    166–203, 234
  see also topography
Suffolk, 53, 57
Sunderland, 51
Surrey, 122, 135, 140, 164
Syme, R., 327

Taunton, 50, 69, 272
taxation, 4, 29, 141, 153, 158–9, 163, 229,
    241, 262–4, 270, 281, 302–3, 306–7,
    326, 328–9
  hearth tax, 20–1, 45 n19, 76 n5, 77
    n11, 81, 88, 119, 166, 176–200,
    254
  records, 6–8, 14, 18, 21, 25, 39, 46
    n21, 50 n31, 72, 76, 81, 92, 106,
    118–19, 146, 176, 254, 259
Tewkesbury, 251
Thirsk, J., 10, 52
time, 207–15
  see also festivals
Tiverton, 51, 69, 94
topography, 20–1, 81–2, 90, 146–7,
    166–203, 255
  see also buildings, housing, suburbs
towns
  classification and definition, 2–5, 32–4,
    47–51, 59, 71–3, 79–80, 166–76,
    200–3
  county towns, 2–4, 49–51, 52, 79, 245
  dockyard towns, 9, 44–5, 57–8, 71, 80,
    128–9

European towns, 2, 6, 40, 49 n30, 59
n50
fortunes of, generally, 6–7, 10, 11,
38–62, 70–1
leisure and social centres, 4, 42–3,
52–3, 55, 58, 252–3
manufacturing centres, 2–3, 42–3, 58,
63–73, 247–9
market towns, 2–3, 6–7, 10, 47–8, 52,
53 n38, 59, 71–2, 79, 246–7, 251
ports, 2–3, 5, 23, 38, 44–5, 51, 54–8,
61, 70–1, 79–80, 200–1, 247, 307
regional or provincial centres, 2, 4,
49–51, 59, 79
small towns, 9–10, 27, 42, 47, 53 n38,
59
trade
coastal, 11, 54–7, 61, 70–1, 131, 184
n56, 253–4, 267
internal, 3, 4, 10–11, 42, 55–6, 61, 70,
72, 87, 251, 254, 318
international, 4, 10–11, 42, 54–7, 61,
70–2, 79, 128, 184, 216–17, 248,
251, 305–7, 316–24, 331–2
see also industry, markets,
occcupations
Tranter, N., 105
Trevor-Roper, H., 300

vagrants and beggars, 18, 61 n54, 86–7,
121–38, 158, 212, 239, 247, 255–7
Vance, J. E., 167, 170–7, 182, 192, 200–3
Venice, 158

Wakefield, 50
Waldviertel, 116

Wales, 5, 40–1, 244–5, 251
Wall, R., 105
wards, 29, 145, 153, 166, 177–200
wars, 11, 57, 123 n5, 131, 135, 253, 264,
295, 305–6, 325–6, 328–9
watch, 164
Webb, S. and B., 159, 161
Welford, R., 177, 185, 188
Welwood, J., 295
Westminster, 122, 126, 140, 145, 331
Weymouth, 61 n53
Whately, W., 109
Whitehaven, 58, 94
Whitelocke, B., 287
widowers, 100–2, 111–12, 115
widows, 18, 24, 100, 102–3, 111–12, 115,
117, 187 n58, 240
Wilkinson, E., 165
William of Malmesbury, 227
Wilson, J., 211
Wilson, T., 302–4, 324
Winchester, 55, 86, 272
women, 8–9, 12–15, 23–5, 63, 66–7,
106–7, 127, 129, 133–4, 152, 156,
158, 223, 228, 230, 234–40
see also households, occupations,
widows
Worcester, 43–4, 49, 51, 56, 64–5, 67, 71,
79, 86–7, 241, 243, 250 n18, 269
Worcestershire, 247
Workman, J., 270–1
Wrigley, E.A., 6, 15, 175

Yarmouth, 50–1, 56–7, 61, 71
York, 2, 22, 27, 43–4, 49–50, 53, 57, 64–5,
70–1, 84, 86, 89, 110, 150, 206–43
Yorkshire, 57, 124, 210, 217, 285